The World Beat Series

WILLIAM H. BEEZLEY, University of Arizona
DAVID E. LOREY, The Hewlett Foundation
Series Editors

The World Beat Series consists of books designed for use in undergraduate courses in the social sciences. The general focus is social issues and social change, with many selections highlighting the stories of individuals and communities. All volumes include readings drawn from around the world, presenting a global offering of perspectives and information. Each book provides a mix of previously published articles, unpublished pieces (some of them commissioned specifically for the volume), and primary documents on a particular topic. An introduction by the volume editor places the general topic and the individual selections in their broader contexts. Texts in this series are an easy way for professors to "globalize" their courses in one stroke. World Beat books easily replace outdated course readers and old supplementary texts for undergraduate classes at both the introductory and advanced levels.

Volumes Published

David E. Lorey and William H. Beezley, editors. *Genocide, Collective Violence, and Popular Memory: The Politics of Remembrance in the Twentieth Century* (2002). Cloth ISBN 0-8420-2981-8 Paper ISBN 0-8420-2982-6

Genocide, Collective Violence, and Popular Memory

Genocide, Collective Violence, and Popular Memory

The Politics of Remembrance in the Twentieth Century

THE
WORLD
BEAT
SERIES

No. 1

David E. Lorey

William H. Beezley

Editors

A Scholarly Resources Inc. Imprint
Wilmington, Delaware

Scholarly Resources Inc.
104 Greenhill Avenue
Wilmington, DE 19805-1897
www.scholarly.com

Library of Congress Cataloging-in-Publication Data

Genocide, collective violence, and popular memory
    p. cm.
  ISBN 0-8420-2981-8 (alk. paper) – ISBN 0-8420-2982-6 (pbk : alk. paper)
    1. Genocide—Psychological aspects. 2. Genocide—History—20th
century. 3. Memory—Social aspects. 4. World politics—20th century.

HV6322.7 .G454 2001
304.6'63—dc21

                                      2001049474

This book is dedicated to Steve Toben—
for his encouragement, support,
and companionship

About the Editors

David E. Lorey received his B.A. in history from Wesleyan University and his M.A. and Ph.D. in Latin American social and economic history from U.C.L.A. From 1989 to 1997, he directed the Program on Mexico and was Visiting Professor of History at U.C.L.A. Since 1997, Lorey has served as Program Officer for the U.S.-Latin American Relations Program at the Hewlett Foundation. At Hewlett, Lorey has developed several new grants programs, one of which is an initiative in rule-of-law, human-rights, and public-security issues in Mexico, Chile, Argentina, and Brazil. His publications include *The U.S.-Mexican Border Region in the Twentieth Century* (Scholarly Resources, 1999).

William H. Beezley is one of the pioneers of the cultural history of Mexico. He wrote essays in the early 1980s that examined Mexican popular culture and political humor and in 1987 published *Judas at the Jockey Club*, one of the first monographs to consider the efforts at modernization during the regime of Porfirio Díaz (1876–1911) by investigating topics such as sport, public hygiene, fashion, and consumerism. In the same volume, he offered perhaps the first examination of nineteenth-century material culture and the nature of poverty, and in the conclusion he explored the use of public celebrations as opportunities for political resistance and satire. With Colin MacLachlan, he has written *El Gran Pueblo: A History of Greater Mexico* (1994) and *Latin America: The Peoples and Their History* (2000). He and Michael C. Meyer recently completed *The Oxford History of Mexico* (2000).

Contents

Introduction

David E. Lorey and William H. Beezley

The treatment of the past through remembering and forgetting crucially shapes the present and future for individuals and entire societies.
—Martha Minow, *Between Vengeance and Forgiveness: Facing History after Genocide and Mass Violence,* 119

Repeated episodes of genocide, collective violence, and state-sponsored terror scarred the twentieth century.[1] In a tragic twist of fate, great advances in the sciences, in industry, in mass media, and in government organization—generally celebrated for their contributions to progress—were all employed in the service of the violent potential of human nature. Science and technology made killing more efficient; relentless media coverage seemed to make individuals and entire societies less sensitive to the horrors of the carnage. As the number of episodes of mass killing increased, evil also became banal, to employ the famous formulation of Hannah Arendt: acts of torture and murder became routine to those who ordered them and those who carried them out. They became routine too for those who watched from afar.

Ten million Africans were killed in the Congo Free State of King Leopold II of Belgium between 1880 and 1910. The first half of the new century also witnessed the Turkish massacre of the Armenians in 1915, the purges ordered by Joseph Stalin,[2] and two European world wars, as well as widespread incidents of smaller-scale, localized killing. The world wars, themselves vast episodes of collective violence spanning whole regions and continents, included the systematic extermination of six million Jews and localized atrocities such as the Rape of Nanjing.[3] In the period after World War II the number of episodes of collective violence and new repressive regimes seemed to increase: from the killing fields of Cambodia to Argentina's "Dirty War"; from South Africa's apartheid to the military regimes in Eastern Europe, Greece, Chile, and Brazil; from the Ugandan massacres to the massacre of Igbos in Nigeria to the Ethiopian killings of the Mengistu era. In China, the Anti-Rightist Campaign and the Great Leap Forward of the late 1950s were followed by the Cultural Revolution of the 1960s and 1970s. Some countries were torn apart by almost inexplicable internecine violence; Colombia and Rwanda are perhaps the best examples.

In the postwar period strategic affairs were dominated by the Cold War between the United States and the Soviet Union. While the Cold War had the effect of suppressing conflict between the United States and the Soviet Union, it exacerbated conflict in the developing world, including all the regions treated in this volume. The most brutal conflicts were fought between and within client states aligned with one or the other of the superpowers. Many of the affected countries were home to the poorest people on earth. In general, conflict during the Cold War was aggravated by the development of a global arms trade that sent increasingly sophisticated and deadly weapons from north to south. Many conflicts were protracted affairs, continuing for two decades or more.[4]

After the Cold War, ethnicity and religion came to be more important causes of conflict than ideology. Additionally, most post-Cold War conflicts were intrastate affairs involving issues of autonomy for certain regions or groups. In a period of changing conceptions of national identity, many people involved in violent conflict began to identify with something closer to their daily experience than the nation, such as clan, ethnicity, or region, leading to a breakdown of centralized authority. Collective violence was characterized by factionalization and the diffusion of power. Conflicts in this period did not in general lend themselves to mediation by existing formal and government mechanisms, including international law or precedent (based as it was in the state system).[5]

At the same time that it witnessed terrible human tragedy due to collective violence, the twentieth century also saw the development of a growing commitment on the part of the international community to protecting human rights. Efforts to expose King Leopold's Congolese crimes sparked the first great human-rights movement of the century.[6] The League of Nations, established in the aftermath of World War I, made some reparations to Armenians. Particularly after World War II, laws were drafted by nations around the world outlawing the systematic abuse of human rights.

Building upon the legacy of the Nuremberg and Tokyo Trials conducted after World War II, international laws were developed to permit prosecution for genocide, war crimes, and crimes against humanity, all of which came to have well-established definitions. The Hague and Geneva Conventions of 1948 and 1949, the UN protocols of 1977, and the conventions against torture (1984) and forced disappearances (1992) were gradually put into practice.[7] The permanent International Criminal Court (ICC) established in 1998 (which will become operational when sixty nations have ratified the documents creating it) leaves primary responsibility for trying perpetrators to national courts and seems to have encouraged them to do so. After 2005, when it is expected to by fully operational, the ICC will be able to try criminals not brought to justice in their own countries.[8]

A new impetus for national and international human-rights law came at the century's end, as countries in several regions of the world moved from dictatorship to democracy and began to address the social and cultural legacies of past regimes of violence. Part of this process was a social and political accounting for periods of state repression, human-rights abuses, and collective violence. In the 1970s the process centered in southern Europe; in the 1980s democracy swept through Latin America; and in the 1980s and 1990s African nations moved away from authoritarian and totalitarian regimes.[9] Several prominent court cases strengthened international law regarding human rights at the turn of the twenty-first century. The international tribunals for the former Yugoslavia and for Rwanda in the early 1990s followed the precedent of the postwar tribunals.[10] The detention of the Chilean dictator Augusto Pinochet in London in 1998 affirmed that the European Union was bound by international convention to extradite suspected torturers, contributed to the doctrine of indirect chain-of-command responsibility for human-rights violations, and clarified the potential culpability of former heads of state for human-rights abuses.[11]

The challenge of coming to terms with past reigns of terror and episodes of collective violence yielded many different social responses built upon both international law and developments at the national level. They included establishing truth commissions, opening state files, removing officials from office, publicizing the names of offenders and the names of victims, providing reparations and apologies, providing public services to treat trauma, creating memorials to commemorate victims, and promoting public educational programs to incorporate the experience into the official historical record.[12] These responses gradually created an understanding of the processes of remembering and reconciliation; they also yielded a coterie of academic experts and experienced practitioners.

Truth commissions were important in cutting through myths, rumors, and false pictures about the past, confirming what some had suspected and what others had refused to believe.[13] Thus they functioned on three levels: personal catharsis, moral reconstruction, and political action to bring trauma to an end.[14] The South African Truth and Reconciliation Commission, modeled on a Chilean precedent, stands as the most complete effort to date. It initiated investigative research, provided an arena for victims' stories, published a compendium of terror, developed a structure for providing reparations, and created a mechanism for granting amnesty to perpetrators who came forward with the truth.[15] Ten major efforts at using truth commissions to foster national reconciliation were undertaken between 1974 and 2000: in Uganda, Argentina, Chile, Chad, South Africa, Germany, El Salvador, Sri Lanka, Haiti, and Guatemala.[16]

Other post-violence governments relied on trials of perpetrators to strike a balance between justice and forgiveness and thus achieve lasting peace. Tina Rosenberg, in her study of Eastern Europe after communism, suggests that there are several beneficial results of such trials: preventing private acts of revenge, establishing a general deterrent, deterring specific individuals, demonstrating to polarized nations alternative mechanisms for conflict resolution, and showing that democratic governments do differ from dictatorships.[17] Almost all reconciliation processes have at their center the question of whether justice or truth should take precedence.[18] Almost all processes of national reconciliation attempted also to avoid new violence and to resolve lingering resentments by transferring the responsibility for apportioning blame and punishment from victims to public bodies acting in accordance with the rule of law.[19]

Martha Minow, in her comparative study of reconciliation processes, identifies a dozen goals of efforts to respond to collective violence. Minow's goals include overcoming the official and social denial; establishing facts; creating a foundation for democracies that respect human rights; reconstructing social systems torn apart by violence; fostering healing for individuals, groups, victims, and bystanders, as well as offenders; acknowledging victims; punishing offenders; and expressing the aspiration that never again shall such collective violence occur.[20] This list of goals provides a framework for the present volume, allowing us to compare and contrast the experiences treated in the chapters that follow.[21]

At the very center of all of these issues of recovery, reconciliation, and looking forward is *history*—here in particular, the social processing of memories of genocide and collective violence. All the faces of history are present in this connection: history as imagined; history as practiced by historians, policymakers, and others; history as a battleground of ideas, ideals, and ideologies; history as therapy; history as taught in the schools; and history as the patrimony of a society or nation.

In the aftermath of incidents of genocide and state-sponsored violence, officials, individuals, and a broad array of social groups have attempted to shape the historical consciousness of societies. Such efforts can last for decades. Major conflicts have arisen as social groups battled for the preeminence of a certain interpretation of what happened, who is to blame, and who should be punished. One of the most troubling realities of the aftermath of genocide and collective violence was the attempt to use history in the service of forgetting; historical memory was sometimes abused in order to provide perpetrators with impunity for their earlier actions. Thus, the past became key to interpreting the present and to shaping the future.

This volume grapples with the intersection of these various themes by highlighting the importance of history and debates over history in resolving the wounds left by collective political violence and in allowing individuals and societies to look forward. Societies do not easily forget collective violence: in the twentieth century, old wounds remained open for decades, sometimes not healing until one generation was replaced by the next. Even after the passing of decades, failure to resolve lingering resentments fueled new crises and new episodes of collective violence.

In this volume we present a collection of scholarly ruminations on the processes by which societies come to terms with difficult and violent histories. Without claiming to be comprehensive or exhaustive, we have sought to offer examples of the best recent work on social responses to genocide, collective violence, and state-sponsored terror. Our choices were based principally on the quality of available analyses rather than on any judgment about the importance of the underlying episodes of collective violence or on some other ranking. We looked for authors who treated the aftermath—social, cultural, and political—of collective violence rather than those who were experts on the original episodes of violence. The variety of the pieces demonstrates the global nature of the phenomenon and allows for comparisons among societies.

Our focus is as much on the reconstruction of history and debate over that reconstruction as it is on specific historical moments. In contrast to what Peter Burke calls a social history of remembering, we provide in this volume a selection of readings in what we call the *cultural* history of remembering.[22] By coining the phrase "cultural history of remembering," we mean to emphasize the importance of symbols, ritual, language, and the use of public spaces in coming to terms with episodes of collective violence and achieving national reconciliation. Our focus, then, is not the marketplace of goods and services, not relations among social groups, but rather the marketplace of symbols and ideas.

In this Introduction we use the terms *genocide, Holocaust, political violence,* and *collective violence.* Our authors use their own terms, and we have respected their choices and definitions. One could argue endlessly about whether a certain episode of killing or a particular civil war constituted or contained elements of genocide or holocaust. For example, the killing of two hundred thousand Guatemalans, primarily indigenous peoples of the Central Highlands, during the country's civil war has been referred to as the "Guatemalan Holocaust."[23] We use *collective violence* as a general term to describe intracommunity violence, that is, violence within communities ranging from villages to communities of nations, such as European nations during World War II. We use *genocide* to mean the purposeful murder of a group of people by another group that takes them to be somehow distinct ethnically or culturally. When we say *political violence,* we generally are implying state-sponsored political violence, that is, repression and persecution of social groups by a state in order to establish and retain political control. Finally, we use the term *Holocaust* only to refer to the extermination of Jews during

World War II. In the case of *holocaust* it is perhaps most clear that general-
izing the use of a term can devalue its descriptive or classificatory power.[24]

The memory of recent violent repression is a more volatile political, social,
and cultural issue in Chile than in many other countries with recent violent
pasts. In Chile the 1973–90 dictatorship of General Augusto Pinochet remains
a subtext for both daily life and national politics. Bullet holes from the day of
the coup in 1973 still mark the buildings surrounding La Moneda, which houses
the seat of government. The Chilean military's monument of an eternal flame
has been doused by protesters on numerous occasions; it is now under permanent military guard. One of the regime's most infamous clandestine detention centers—the Villa Grimaldi—has been refurbished as a monument to
memory, decorated with pieces of the original mansion where torture occurred
to emphasize the horror of what transpired there. A law establishing that elementary and secondary school history courses cannot treat the most recent
twenty-five years of Chile's evolution has not been able to suppress discussion
of the dictatorship and its violent beginning. In 1998 the first convention of
former political prisoners was held; along with committees put together to
advance the legal actions of the families of disappeared persons, a committee was formed on memory and history. In 2000 the third post-dictatorship
government erected a statue of Salvador Allende, the democratically elected
president deposed in the coup, in front of the government building in which
he had committed suicide twenty-seven years earlier as troops closed in.

Alexander Wilde, in the chapter on Chile (see Chapter 1), develops the
notion of irruptions of memory, periodic symbolic reminders of the coup of
1973 and the repressive regime that followed.[25] The discovery of mass graves
and clandestine torture centers as well as the decision after the return of
democracy in 1990 to rebury Salvador Allende with a ceremony in the national
stadium (where thousands were held prisoner in the days following the
takeover) forced Chileans to reconsider the past over and over again. Wilde
focuses on the period since 1990, during which two democratically elected
governments have attempted to foster social reconciliation among a populace
still deeply divided over its past. He examines the expressive dimensions of
politics, that is, the uses of, and struggle over the uses of, symbols, memories, and history.

The most recent major irruption in the Chilean case has been the attempt
to bring Pinochet to trial for human-rights abuses during his seventeen-year
dictatorship. In 1998 Pinochet was detained in London at the request of a
Spanish judge on charges of human-rights violations. In March 1999 the
British Law Lords ruled that Pinochet could be tried only for crimes carried
out after 1988, the year Britain signed the international convention against
torture. The Spanish courts immediately added thirty-three charges covering the post-1988 period. Pinochet languished under house arrest in Eng-

land, while lawyers, human-rights activists, and politicians on two continents argued over his fate.

The detention of the general sparked protests by his supporters and celebrations by his opponents and reawakened the debate over Chile's past.[26] In Chile, judicial reforms and individual jurors sought a way around the 1978 amnesty granted military actors. In 1999 five military figures, exonerated under the 1978 law, were indicted to stand trial for what came to be known as the Caravan of Death operation, the execution of seventy-five persons in 1973. Because nineteen of those executed had never been found and their bodies returned to their families, their cases could be considered aggravated kidnappings by the judicial authorities. Aggravated kidnapping is not covered by the amnesty of 1978 and thus the decision opened the door to the prosecution of more than two hundred cases that had been lying dormant in both military and civilian courts.[27]

In an unprecedented development in September 1999 the Chilean Armed Forces sent representatives to a human-rights roundtable convened by the defense minister in an attempt to reconcile human-rights cases during the dictatorship, tacitly admitting for the first time that the military held information about approximately twelve hundred persons detained and disappeared between 1973 and 1990. Also in September 1999, Chileans celebrated a day of national unity, a new holiday created by congressional decree to replace the dictatorship-era celebration of the 1973 military coup. Despite official calls for the nation to further efforts toward a political and social reconciliation, however, the first National Unity Day only highlighted the profound schisms that continued to plague the country. Wilde's chapter provides a foundation for consideration of the ongoing impact of the Pinochet detention and other current issues in Chile.

In Argentina between 1976 and 1983, in what became known as the "Dirty War," at least nine thousand persons were "disappeared"—detained, tortured, and killed by the Argentine military—according to official government reports. Unofficial estimates of deaths during this period range as high as thirty thousand. In 1985, after the disastrous experience of the Falkland Islands war of 1983, five hundred military leaders active during the Argentine "Dirty War," including presidents and members of the military high command, were tried, convicted, and sentenced to life in prison. The National Commission on Disappeared Persons was established as the official truth commission; it produced the now-famous report *¡Nunca Mas!* (Never again!) detailing the atrocities committed against so-called subversives. Conservative political forces, however, eventually slowed the wheels of justice. Under President Raul Alfonsín, in the "full stop" and "due-obedience" laws of 1986 and 1987, officers who acted under superior orders were explicitly exempted from responsibility. After various military challenges to government attempts to diminish the political weight and institutional prestige of the armed forces in the early

1980s (including three military rebellions during the Alfonsín presidency), lower-ranking leaders were granted amnesty in 1990 by incoming president Carlos Menem, a decision made in the name of national reconciliation.[28]

Debate over responsibility for the "Dirty War" and the challenge of bringing still-powerful perpetrators to justice has been characterized in Argentina by continuous irruptions of memories like those described by Wilde for Chile. Other factors have also helped to keep the memory of war atrocities alive. The best-known example is the Mothers of the Plaza de Mayo, who, since 1977, have marched in the central public space of Buenos Aires with their famous white kerchiefs, demanding to know what became of their children at the hands of military leaders. In 1999 the Mothers opened a literary café in central Buenos Aires to keep the memory alive among future generations.[29]

In contrast to the experience of many other countries, Argentine military leaders have stepped forward to make confessions and give details about their roles in the killings. And, in Argentina, military officials continue to be tried for their abuses during the "Dirty War." Officials of the period have been detained and tried for the practice of adopting babies born to mothers who were killed as "leftists." More than two hundred cases of disappeared babies have come out and Argentine courts have established that previous amnesties do not cover abuses against these minor victims of the violence. In 1999 a federal judge indicted seventy-four military officers for their roles in the stealing of babies from detainees who were later murdered.

The selection in this volume on Argentina (see Chapter 2) focuses, like Wilde's piece on Chile, on what can be termed irruptions of memory. In the Argentine case, the sites of torture and detention centers, the Mothers of the Plaza de Mayo, and the babies of victims have provided a focus for coming to terms with the "Dirty War" and its legacy. The authors—Elizabeth Jelin and Susana G. Kaufman—show how the human-rights movement began in Argentina under the dictatorship and how important the notion of universal human rights was to the Argentine process of recovery during the 1980s. Striking in the Argentine case is the extent to which the processes of recovery and reconciliation are conveyed in the language of psychological healing and how widely shared the process has been. The most dramatic example is the army's official recognition that its own members committed crimes.[30]

The epic conflict that devoured Guatemala between 1960 and 1996 stands as one of the longest civil conflicts in the twentieth century in which state-sponsored violence played a major role. Four hundred villages were razed and at least two hundred thousand people died, forty thousand disappeared, and roughly one hundred thousand fled north to Mexico. The struggle pitted the Guatemalan Armed Forces against several groups of insurgents, the most important of which were the EGP, the Guerrilla Army of the Poor, and ORPA, the Revolutionary Organization of the People in Arms. These groups and others united in 1982 as the Guatemalan National Revolutionary Unity or URNG.

The violence reached its peak between 1978 and 1982, when two consecutive administrations, that of General Lucas García (1978–82) and that of General Ríos Montt (1982–83), adopted policies to depopulate the indigenous areas that had become home to the guerrillas. Perhaps half of the civilians killed in the thirty-year conflict were killed in this five-year period.

A succession of military campaigns left the country highly militarized and politically polarized. Many of the worst violations were carried out by people from within the communities organized by the army into civil patrols to spy on their neighbors. Most Indian villagers probably found themselves caught between the military and the guerrilla forces, although debate about this point continues to rage and constitutes a subtext in our selection on Guatemala.

Peace came to Guatemala gradually over a long and difficult decade. Beginning in the mid-1980s with a process of formal political opening, the peace process involved the drafting of a new constitution and the creation of new courts and the appointment of a human-rights ombudsman. A full peace agreement was signed in 1996 between the government and URNG, providing a general amnesty for all who had committed crimes after 1982 and mandating radical changes in the Guatemalan military, including a thorough restructuring of the military and a redefinition of its mission. The accords called for the military to abandon its customary role in internal security and restrict itself to national defense.[31] The military command, however, remained largely intact.

In March 1999 the UN-sponsored Truth Commission issued its report on rights violations during the conflict in Guatemala. The report established the now largely accepted figure of two hundred thousand deaths and laid most of the blame at the door of the military, establishing that between 80 percent and 90 percent of the killing had been carried out by the military. Independent confirmation of these murders came with a report released by the U.S. National Security Archive, a private, nonprofit organization, of military documents recording the detention, torture, and killing of civilians.[32]

The roots of the Guatemalan conflict, addressed at some length by Hal Cohen in Chapter 3, are many and complex, but ethnic and class differences played a major role in creating the tensions that led to war. Land distribution is extremely skewed and the indigenous peoples of the country are viewed as being culturally very different by the mixed-ethnicity elites of Guatemala City. Ethnic difference was magnified by a lopsided national vote in May 1999 that failed to win approval for constitutional changes that would have recognized for the first time the rights of the country's indigenous majority.[33] Polarization continues because thousands of perpetrators remain active all across the country.[34] Although the civil war has ended, many commentators note that the underlying inequalities and prejudices of Guatemalan society remain. The great challenge facing Guatemala is to restructure society so as to make the resurgence of collective violence impossible.

Our selection on Guatemala focuses on the debate over Nobel laureate Rigoberta Menchú. The publication of Menchú's book *I, Rigoberta Menchú*, led to her being awarded the Nobel Peace Prize. But her account of her childhood and the causes of violence in her hometown were challenged in the 1990s. Cohen chronicles the debate over Menchú's history, examining the charges and countercharges of Menchú, her critics, and her defenders. While Menchú's responses to criticism have not directly addressed specific points of fact, they have addressed the question of memory and history. In justifying the presentation of what she now says is a composite of the lives of Indians who suffered during the Guatemalan civil war, Menchú stated during a Mexico City press conference, "I have a right to historical memory, a right to my memory as a woman and as a Guatemalan."[35] A follow-up book entitled *Crossing Borders* has only added to the controversy over Rigoberta Menchú's constructions of history.[36]

Historical construction and reconstruction cast long shadows in Latin America. An interesting example grows out of Nobel laureate García Márquez's *One Hundred Years of Solitude*. In this widely read novel, García Márquez recreates a 1928 massacre of workers on a banana plantation in the town of Macondo, Colombia, and gives the number of deaths as three thousand. While this figure has become accepted in the Colombian historiography and is widely accepted by commentators and historians, García Márquez has said that he purposely exaggerated what he understood to be a handful of deaths to give a sense of the symbolic impact that the violence had on him when he heard of it as a young child growing up in Aracataca, where the killing took place. Recent efforts to investigate the massacre on the banana plantation have established the probable deaths as between fifty and one hundred.[37] The irony here is that the numbers of people killed in many other massacres have been *underestimated;* both underestimation and exaggeration distort history.

Events after 1996 in Guatemala brought the future of the peace process into doubt and raised troubling questions about democratic governance there. When, for example, President Alvaro Arzu appointed General Espinoza in April 1996 to head the defense ministry, he dismissed suggestions that Espinoza had been involved in the murder of Bishop Juan Gerardi, the Catholic Church official responsible for the Church's report on human-rights abuses during the civil war.[38] Two days before Espinoza took over as defense minister, a former judge filed charges with government prosecutors against him and two other officers for plotting the Gerardi killing.[39] Such episodes in the ongoing struggle to establish a lasting peace in Guatemala continue to receive attention by concerned scholars and policy makers throughout the hemisphere.[40]

Africa's episodes with explosions of collective violence began before the turn of the twentieth century with the Belgian genocide under King Leopold and continued to the very end of the century. The violence was systemic and systematic in South Africa, and more episodic and explosive in Rwanda and Uganda. In Rwanda in the late 1990s, hundreds of thousands of people died in a bewildering conflict between the Hutus and the Tutsi, two closely related ethnic groups. When Hutus seized power in 1959, many Tutsis were killed. During the rule of Hutus from 1960 to 1994, Tutsis experienced both discrimination and episodic violence at the hands of Hutus. In 1994 Hutus undertook a program of genocide against the Tutsi, calling all Tutsis enemies of the state. Reprisals against the Hutu, including massacres of Hutu refugees in the Democratic Republic of Congo in 1996 and 1997, began after the Tutsis regained power. Since 1997, however, the Rwandan government has worked to rebuild its justice system, training new police investigators, prosecutors, and judges to process the one hundred thousand people arrested and sent to prisons to await trial on human-rights charges. And in May 1998 the former prime minister of Rwanda pleaded guilty to genocide charges before the UN tribunal.[41]

As Catharine Newbury points out (see Chapter 4), competing views of Rwandan history hardened over time into potentially catastrophic ethnic distrust. Newbury uses a comparison of the late 1950s and early 1990s in Rwanda to suggest a new and more constructive view of the history of the region and of the relationships among its ethnicities. Her new history de-emphasizes the role of the colonial state, which had previously been blamed for the violence in Rwandan society.[42]

Democratic South Africa currently faces the multiple legacies of roughly fifty years of apartheid—a social hierarchy and the associated political structure that systematically privileged white South Africans of European descent over Africans from indigenous social groups. Black South Africans were denied political power and kept in poverty through the use of institutionalized repression and the threat of violence. They suffered arbitrary arrests, beatings, assassination, and torture, as well as the quotidian violence of poverty, malnutrition, inferior education, urban overcrowding, and social strife in the townships.

With avenues for political dissent closed, organizations such as the African National Congress took up arms to fight for liberation. The result was a cycle of increasing violence met by increasing repression, with civilian targets on both sides. Violence was seen as a means of maintaining power and of achieving change. This acceptance of violence as a legitimate route to the resolution of social and political conflict became ingrained in South African society.[43]

In the 1980s South Africa became increasingly ungovernable as organizations took action against the state through strikes, boycotts, protest marches—frequently organized around funerals of murdered activists—and other mobilizations. Challenges to the state were followed by the imposition of states of emergency in 1985 and 1986, which were renewed annually until 1990. Foes of apartheid died as the result of direct actions of the security forces and covert operations of the state to counter unrest. The violence peaked in the early 1990s.

Ironically, the end of apartheid in South Africa was accompanied by an increase in assaults and other common crimes, as well as politically motivated violence.[44] In particular, self-defense units organized by township youth perpetrated revenge and intimidation attacks, community leaders were assassinated, and violent infighting disrupted the transportation sector. Some observers wondered whether political reconciliation adequately engaged the roots of violence in South Africa; one could blame the social inequality created by apartheid or a few pathological individuals within the security apparatus, but neither approach sufficiently explained the violence in South African society.[45]

Overt political violence decreased markedly, however, after the election of 1994, which brought Nelson Mandela to power. The election signaled the end of the apartheid regime and the beginning of South Africa's painful transition to democracy. In 1995 the South African Parliament created the Truth and Reconciliation Commission, with separate subcommittees on human-rights violations, amnesty, and reparations. The South African process highlighted the importance of giving power to victims and providing them an opportunity to tell their stories without interruption or expressions of skepticism.[46] The commission had two years to fulfill its mandate and submitted its final report in spring 1998.

Brandon Hamber's chapter on South Africa (see Chapter 5) is the most technical piece in the volume. It focuses on a crucial, underappreciated aspect of the process of social recovery from collective violence: psychological support services for victims, victimizers, and innocent bystanders affected by regimes of violence. Hamber demonstrates that the recovery process involves more than cultural and intellectual issues. It has very practical aspects related to the personal histories of affected individuals whose needs require major changes in government policy and considerable expenditure in the public health arena. In fact, Hamber uses the South African case to show that successful recovery is not possible without significant investment by post-violence governments in the nuts and bolts of individual recovery. Reconciliation, in other words, is not possible without attention to individual trauma.[47] It may be for this reason that the language of psychological recovery (for example, "healing," "recovery") has featured so prominently in debates over responses to collective violence.[48]

We begin our section on Asia with Cambodia. The brief but catastrophic Cambodian civil war of 1975–79 claimed the lives of as many as two million people, or as much as 20 percent of the entire Cambodian population. This astounding statistic places the Cambodian violence on a different scale from the other cases addressed in this volume. Robert D. Kaplan, in his book

The Ends of the Earth, writes: "In the picture gallery of twentieth-century horrors, Cambodia is a consummate icon."[49]

In the late 1970s, the Khmer Rouge regime adopted a radical communism that attempted to remake Cambodia by emptying the cities, abolishing religion, and closing schools.[50] Drawing on a warrior tradition and their isolation in the tropical forest among ancient temples, the soldiers of the Khmer Rouge, many of them children between the ages of twelve and fifteen, committed acts of unimaginable barbarity. The cities were forcibly evacuated and anyone with an urban or intellectual background was suspect; 90 percent of the country's medical doctors were murdered in four years. After the Khmer Rouge was forced out by the Vietnamese in 1979, famine lashed Cambodia. With continuing conflict, the country became so full of land mines that there was one for every person in the country, and Cambodia achieved one of the highest per capita rates of amputees in the world.

The history of Cambodia's "Democratic Kampuchea" regime was buried for more than twenty years after it ended. Only in 1997 did an alignment of international attention and domestic political changes make possible a reconsideration of the Cambodian terror. Leading efforts to deal with the past was the Cambodian Genocide Program at Yale University, which, with a major grant from the office of Cambodian Genocide Investigations of the U.S. Department of State, worked to document mass killings by collecting and disseminating information and supporting work by historians on Cambodia in the 1970s.

In 1998 the Khmer Rouge finally collapsed as a fighting force, its leader Pol Pot died, and other leaders began reappearing.[51] In the same year two top-level leaders of the Khmer Rouge defected and were welcomed back by the Cambodian government. They received a symbolic embrace from Cambodia's prime minister, who sent them to one of the country's beach resorts, with accommodations at a luxury hotel. One of the two leaders was the architect of the brutal evacuation of cities in 1975 and was later responsible for a wave of purges in which many thousands of people died.[52] Public outrage over such an easy reintegration of the Khmer Rouge into Cambodian society, however, forced the prime minister (who himself had once been a low-level Khmer Rouge commander) to reverse himself the following day, saying that he would support the trial of the two by an international tribunal (as he had told the United Nations in 1997 and 1998).[53] As of this writing, no one has yet been brought to trial for the deaths perpetrated by the Khmer Rouge between 1975 and 1979.

Judy Ledgerwood's chapter on Cambodia (see Chapter 6) brings the perspectives of art history and anthropology to bear on the question of social responses to genocide. Ledgerwood focuses on the Tluol Seng, a secondary school building the Khmer Rouge converted into a detention and torture center that is now a museum documenting the conflict. The museum confronts the past by presenting a photographic maze of thousands of the victims of the Khmer Rouge violence and a map of Cambodia constructed entirely from human skulls and bones. The museum replays both the violence and the human face of those who suffered, standing at the same time as a memorial and a symbolic deterrent to future violence.

Ledgerwood sees the Tluol Seng prison as one of the central sites for the construction of memories of the Khmer Rouge period. She describes the museum as a physical place, discusses what happened there when it was a prison, and examines the process of its subsequent establishment as a museum. She goes on to show how the museum relates to two distinct patterns of narrative in Cambodian history: the story of a glorious revolution stolen and perverted by the Khmer Rouge, and an opposing story that views the entire experience with communist rule as a giant blunder.[54] Ledgerwood refers to the first story as the master narrative of the state and attempts to understand its relationship to the second view, which has roots in more popular visions of Cambodian history.

In Indonesia, in the bloody aftermath of the coup attempt of September 30, 1965, several hundred thousand Indonesians were killed by the military and by paramilitary forces in an effort to stamp out the Communist Party. Most of the killings were over by mid-1966, although occasional episodes continued into late 1969. In the wake of the 1965–66 collective violence, General Soeharto rose to political prominence. Known supporters of the 1965 coup attempt, and hundreds of thousands of suspected supporters, were rounded up and held without trial under the Soeharto regime. Many political prisoners were killed. Government regulations made it impossible for those suspected of being Communist supporters to get jobs, to travel, or to hold public office. Soeharto stayed in power for more than thirty years and was ousted only after weeks of mass demonstrations in summer 1998.

In contrast to the story in many of the other countries included in this volume, in Indonesia the 1965–66 killings were not taken as a point of departure for social reflection on the Indonesian past until relatively recently. Few Indonesians kept records of the massacres, and for years even speaking of them could be dangerous in Indonesia and other parts of Asia. The massacres were also a dispersed affair, with the vast majority of killings carried out by small groups only loosely following commands from on high. Little international pressure was placed on demanding an accounting of the violence. Even the Left, the target of the massacres, avoided retrospection.[55]

Chapter 7 considers the role of art, literature, and performance as forms of resistance in Indonesia in the 1990s. Rob Goodfellow and Dwi Marianto contrast the styles and audiences of protest art under Soeharto and in the period after his fall. Their chapter makes extensive use of representative works of art, specifically paintings and exhibitions of paintings. Painters introduced into their work a very wide array of symbolic references, many with roots in

Indonesia's diverse indigenous cultures. The symbols employed in paintings often established, below the radar of the censors, direct communication between artist and audience. The exegesis of the authors, which is subtle and nuanced, indicates a very rich vein of source materials for future work in the cultural history of remembering.

In China, the tumultuous Cultural Revolution of Mao Zedong, an attempt to reorganize the Communist Party and restructure government, shook society, culture, and the economy to their roots between 1966 and 1976. During the three years from 1966 to 1969, China was thrown into chaos: institutions were dismantled, young people were mobilized into the murderous Red Guard squads, and the army operated as an independent force to repress individuals and organized groups. With the explicit support of Mao, young students attacked their teachers, children denounced their parents, and communities humiliated their local leaders.

The intellectual justification for the Cultural Revolution—that, in order to renew the regime, it was necessary to battle and destroy the "four olds" (old thought, old culture, old customs, and old habits)—quickly gave way to political battles between factions within the central government and among various powerful institutional actors in Chinese society. Attempts to restructure the cultural establishment, particularly universities, had the result of drastically limiting intellectual freedom and research. Hundreds of thousands died, victims of abuse and torture or of armed battles.

The battles of the Cultural Revolution set radicals against conservatives in a confusing reform effort that, by the late 1970s, the government itself recognized as the most severe reversal of the country's socialist cause to date. Both Mao and the Chinese Communist Party lost credibility and legitimacy. In 1981 the party resolved that Mao's methods of perpetuating class struggle and his championing of the persecution of intellectuals were not suitable for socialist construction; Mao's achievements were deemed to have been 70 percent good, 30 percent bad.[56]

Eight years later, on June 4, 1989, the massacre in Tiananmen Square made it clear that the Chinese leadership was not prepared for greater political opening. Just as in the Cultural Revolution, intellectual leaders and student followers were perceived to be enemies of the state. Although the roughly one thousand young people who died in 1989 seems a small number in comparison with the deaths during the Cultural Revolution, the strong response to Tiananmen Square by the international community focused attention both inside and outside China on the long history in China of collective violence. Many observers saw the massacre in Tiananmen Square as the beginning of the end of China's communist history.[57]

Our two brief selections on China focus on the central role that intellectuals and students have played and continue to play in the history of Chinese resistance. Vera Schwarcz (see Chapter 8) paints a rich picture of the historical context of the Cultural Revolution and the student protests of 1989. Intellectuals of both periods drew on a long tradition of symbols and rituals of resistance. Joseph W. Esherick and Jeffrey N. Wasserstrom (see Chapter 9) present the events leading up to Tiananmen Square as political theater, describing how students used both traditional elements of Chinese culture and symbols of the modern telecommunications culture to make their case to national and international publics.

While many foreign commentators and historians have examined China's rituals of resistance, few Chinese have been able to confront the past openly. Not only students but the Chinese population in general took Tiananmen Square to be a warning that, even after a decade of rapid economic opening to global markets, novel and critical interpretations of the past would still not be tolerated by the government. The warning was felt for an entire decade, leading Orville Schell to comment in 1999 that "few countries are in a state of more awkward denial about their histories than China."[58]

We have included two selections on the long shadow cast by World War II, the single greatest example of collective violence in the twentieth century. From a vast European literature, we sought an essay that would address the confusing legacy of the war from the perspective of intracommunity conflict. The same European countries that united in the mid-1990s into the European Union turned murderously inward upon themselves between 1937 and 1942. Untold millions—Jews, Russians, Germans, French, Britons, Italians, and Americans—lost their lives. This watershed conflict, including the Holocaust, shapes and informs the debates examined in almost every other piece collected in our volume.

Robert G. Moeller (see Chapter 10) describes the very difficult process by which Germans have come to terms with the multiple and contradictory legacies of the German experience in World War II. He shows how Germans used the plight of the twelve million Germans expelled by the Soviet Union after the war, and the analogy between German and Jewish victims, to deal with issues of victimization at the same time that they came to grips with the reality of having perpetrated the Holocaust. Reunification in 1995 caused Germans to look back to the division into East and West after World War II and the painful separation of German lives it entailed. An additional attraction of this study of Germany from the end of the war to 1995 is that it spans the Cold War era. Like World War II, the Cold War is a backdrop for the other contributions to this collection.

Julia A. Thomas closes the volume with an analysis of Japan's postwar history as it is revealed and interpreted through a photographic exhibition at Yokohama's principal art museum (see Chapter 11). She examines the issue of the social processing of memories of collective violence, addressing such troubling events in which Japan was involved as the Rape of Nanjing and the systematic abuse of Korean comfort women during World War II. Tying this chapter to the previous one is the issue of how, for many Japanese, the World War was a violence inflicted upon them by other Japanese. Striking in Thomas's treatment is the extent to which various episodes in Japanese postwar history are intertwined. Conceptions about the Japanese nation, about the West, about the war, all are invoked and invoke one another. At the same time, these troubling issues now have to be reconsidered in the light of a series of more recent crises, including the end of the Japanese economic boom, the death of the last dynastic emperor, and evidence of extensive political corruption.

Visitors to the Yokohama exhibition were confronted with remembering the 1940s in the context of the 1990s. An interesting aspect of the exhibit, as Thomas points out, is the central role World War II plays without the inclusion of any photographs showing Japanese military involvement or the destruction caused by the war. While the exhibit was limited to photographs available in the Yokohama museum's collection and by self-censorship imposed to avoid controversy, particularly among the far Right, the selected images nonetheless allowed for a multilayered processing of painful wartime memories by visitors to the exhibit. To Thomas the exhibit was not just a group of discrete photographs but also a historical text.

The essays in this volume are tied together by a common interest in the tension between individual and collective memory in the process of social recovery from genocide and other forms of collective violence. For example, many processes of recovery have raised the question of whether there is such a thing as collective responsibility for episodes of collective violence, or whether only individual responsibility is relevant in cases of systematic human-rights abuses. The great challenge for both individuals and nations appears to be that of forging links between individual and social remembering. On the personal level, as Martha Minow points out, "coming to know that one's suffering is not solely a private experience, best forgotten, but instead an indictment of the social cataclysm, can permit individuals to move beyond trauma, hopelessness, numbness, and preoccupation with loss and injury."[59] Individuals require acknowledgment and, sometimes, justice in order to be able to move forward. For their part, societies must find ways to commemorate and interpret divisive social experiences if they are to accomplish lasting reconciliation.

Another interest shared by the authors of this volume is the relationship, and frequent tension, between the national contexts for collective violence and international debates over human rights and international laws concerning them. While it is not possible to speak of a consensus among our authors, or among scholars in general, it seems safe to say that national and international observation and internationally sanctioned legal processes, working together, can often be very effective in both ending violence and advancing reconciliation.

Finally, almost all of the authors address the issue of generational shifts in the process of remembering and forgetting. While again there is no consensus, all seem to indicate that when memory is passed from one generation to the next, from the generation intimately involved with violence to one that has not experienced the same degree of violence, an important peace with the past can be the achieved. Complete and lasting reconciliation may not be possible in the generation originally affected. But a younger generation perhaps can help the older generation come to terms with its past.

We do not include a chapter on the United States, though of course the twentieth-century history of United States is replete with incidents of violence against groups of people in the aftermath of slavery and Reconstruction and in the civil rights movement of the 1960s and beyond. The legacy of World War II has inspired rancorous debate, focusing on the internment of Japanese Americans and the decision by the United States to drop atomic bombs on Japan. This debate was reopened recently in the controversy over the proposed *Enola Gay* exhibit at the Smithsonian Institution.[60] The Vietnam War continues to engender divisive discussion of human-rights abuses by the United States.

For many observers, the most problematic aspect of U.S. policy is the long record of U.S. acquiescence in state-sponsored terror around the world. In Guatemala, in Chile, in Argentina, and in many other of the countries examined in this volume, U.S. officials were aware of human-rights abuses and in some cases were directly involved through the CIA or U.S. armed forces, but they did very little to curb those abuses.[61] In the case of Cambodia, the United States under President Richard M. Nixon was responsible in part for the emergence of and radicalization of the Khmer Rouge. The bombing campaigns of 1969 and 1973 sent peasants in droves to the Khmer Rouge and the Khmer Rouge leadership came to hate the West. Robert Kaplan comments that Nixon and Henry Kissinger's apparent ignorance of Cambodia and the Khmer Rouge was a foreign policy disaster with few parallels in modern history.[62] After the fall of the Khmer Rouge, the country was ruled by Vietnamese communists; for this reason, the United States supported the ousted Khmer Rouge, a policy that prolonged the suffering of Cambodians. The views and warnings of courageous individual policy makers who questioned U.S. policy in the twentieth century, such as Gordon Vaky in the case of Guatemala, went unheard.

President Bill Clinton's March 1999 trip to Central America highlighted the theme of U.S. involvement, complicity, and responsibility. Arriving in Guatemala two weeks after the UN-sponsored Truth Commission released its report, which blames the U.S.-backed Guatemalan military for most human-rights violations and notes explicitly that the Guatemalan military perpetrated genocide, Clinton apologized for U.S. government denial of its role in massacres and acts of repression. To a group of government officials, representatives from indigenous groups, and members of the Truth Commission, Clinton said, "For the United States, it is important that I state clearly that support for military forces and intelligence units which engaged in violence and widespread repression was wrong, and the US must not repeat that mistake." Then he proclaimed, "We are determined to remember the past but never repeat it." In the first public statement from the Guatemalan government acknowledging U.S. involvement in its civil war, which was enthusiastically welcomed by the military governments at the time, Guatemala's foreign minister Eduardo Stein commented, "The United States, and we always knew it, but now it is officially recognized, stuck its hands deeply into Central America in an irregular and illegal manner." In an address to the Legislative Assembly in El Salvador on the same trip, Clinton acknowledged U.S. involvement in the abuses committed by the Salvadoran government. Clinton's posture on his Central American tour, a strikingly new one for a U.S. President, was complemented by the release by his administration of classified documents pertaining to U.S. involvement in the wars in Central America and the 1973 coup in Chile.

What does permanent reconciliation after episodes of collective violence— what John Paul Lederach has called sustainable peace—require of societies, their leaders, scholars, students, and policy makers? Lederach suggests that we look first at the process of reconciliation rather than the personalities of the statesman and peacemakers involved in the process. Furthermore, we should start thinking of a longer time horizon than is currently the practice, adopting a nested series of time dimensions when we think about recovery, reconciliation, and peace building. Constructive "immediate" action may require six months to a year to plan and execute, short-range planning may require one to two years, and generational vision at least twenty years. This scheme allows societies to address a series of interrelated objectives productively: crisis intervention, preparation and training, design of social change, and, ultimately, the achievement of the desired future.

The process of peace building involves leadership on at least three distinct levels: at the top are military, political, and religious leaders with high visibility who focus on high-level negotiations, such as cease-fire agreements; at the next level are leaders respected in the ethnic, religious, academic, intellectual, and humanitarian sectors who organize and run workshops and provide training in conflict resolution (this level includes peace commissions); at the third, local, level are leaders of indigenous NGOs and representatives for victims groups who focus on grass-roots training, prejudice reduction, and psychosocial work. The fundamental building blocks of a successful process of reconciliation, according to Lederach, are truth (including acknowledgment, transparency, revelation, and clarity), justice (including equality,

"making things right," and restitution), mercy (including acceptance, forgiveness, support, compassion, and healing), and peace (including harmony,
unity, well-being, security, and respect).

To insure success, Lederach calls for harmony in methods of research,
teaching, and practice in the fields of international relations and conflict resolution. International relations has tended to focus exclusively on strategic
conflict between nation-states and to view conflict in terms of the hard politics of the real world. Conflict resolution, in contrast, has conceived of itself
as integrating the deep-lying emotional and substantive concerns of individuals and communities involved in conflict. Practitioners and theorists of international relations tend to view conflict resolution as a "soft field"; practitioners and theorists of conflict resolution view experts in international
relations as locked into abstract and sometimes outmoded paradigms, unable
to address the roots of problems in ways that might lead to lasting solutions.[63]

It is our hope that this volume will help advance the intellectual culture
and theory of change that Lederach advocates by providing some common
ground for theory in practice in international relations and conflict resolution. Each chapter outlines ways in which past conflicts can be constructively
integrated into historical experience and suggests how future conflict might
be addressed and transformed. Conflict between and within groups is
inevitable; successfully transforming conflict into constructive exchange and
problem solving must be one of the central objectives of societies in this new
century.

The history of reconciliation—successful and unsuccessful—in various
national contexts around the world can enhance and deepen the process of
transforming conflict. Hindsight is rarely 20/20. But, with the aid of focused
study, hindsight can certainly be useful, and, with concerted effort, can be
improved. The process of healing, involving the use of the cultural history of
memory illustrated here, holds out the hope of creating a foundation for constructive management of conflict in the future. The fundamental aim of this
volume, then, is to contribute to overcoming the festering, corrosive intergroup
and intragroup conflicts that made massive collective violence a defining characteristic of the twentieth century.

Notes

1. We define these terms in a later section of this Introduction.
2. See William B. Husband, editor, *The Human Tradition in Modern Russia* (Wilmington: Scholarly Resources, 2000).
3. See Joshua A. Fogel, ed., *The Nanjing Massacre in History and Historiography*
(Berkeley: University of California Press, 2000).
4. John Paul Lederach, *Building Peace: Sustainable Reconciliation in Divided Societies* (Washington, D.C.: United States Institute of Peace Press, 1997), 5–9.
5. Ibid.

6. See Adam Hochschild, *King Leopold's Ghost: A Story of Greed, Terror, and Heroism in Colonial Africa* (Boston: Houghton Mifflin, 1998).

7. Martha Minow, *Between Vengeance and Forgiveness: Facing History after Genocide and Mass Violence* (Boston: Beacon Press, 1998), 34. On human rights generally, see Michael Perry, "Are Human Rights Universal? The Relativist Challenge and Related Matters," *Human-Rights Quarterly* 19 (1997): 461–509.

8. The International Criminal Court itself will not be functioning until 2005 at the earliest. Because the United States is afraid that U.S. nationals might be judged by a body not under U.S. control, the United States remains one of the few governments opposed to the agreement establishing the court. See *Toronto Globe and Mail,* January 8, 1999, A19.

9. An excellent discussion, in comparative perspective, of the Eastern European experience is provided in Tina Rosenberg, *The Haunted Land: Facing Europe's Ghost after Communism* (New York: Random House, 1995).

10. Minow, *Between Vengeance and Forgiveness,* 27.

11. Allison Brysk, "Globalization: The Double-Edged Sword," in *NACLA Report on the Americas* 34:1 (July/August 2000): 30.

12. Minow, *Between Vengeance and Forgiveness,* 23.

13. Ibid., 76

14. Ibid., 79.

15. Ibid., 3.

16. David C. Anderson, "Painful Truth, Healing Truth: Commissions Help Wounded Societies Build a Future by Confronting the Past," *Ford Foundation Report,* Spring 2000, 16–21. See also Priscilla B. Hayner, *Unspeakable Truths: Confronting State Terror and Atrocity* (London: Routledge, 2000).

17. Rosenberg, *The Haunted Land,* 404. See also Lederach, *Building Peace*

18. Minow, *Between Vengeance and Forgiveness,* 9.

19. Ibid., 11–12. See also Gary Jonathan Bass, *Stay the Hand of Vengeance: The Politics of War Crimes Tribunals* (Princeton: Princeton University Press, 2000).

20. Minow, *Between Vengeance and Forgiveness,* 87, 88.

21. See also Elazar Barkan, *The Guilt of Nations: Restitution and Negotiating Historical Injustices* (New York: W. W. Norton, 2000).

22. Peter Burke, "History as Social Memory," in Thomas Butler, ed., *Memory: History, Culture, and the Mind* (London: Basil Blackwell, 1989); see also Rubie S. Watson, ed., *Memory, History, and Opposition under State Socialism* (Santa Fe: School of American Research Press, 1994), 2.

23. Edelberto Torres-Rivas, "La Comisión de la Verdad, el castigo, el olvido," in FLACSO, *Anuario Social y Político de América Latina y el Caribe* (Caracas: Nueva Sociedad/FLACSO, [1999]), 81.

24. See Anthony Minnaar, Sam Pretorius, and Marie Wentzel, "Political Conflict and Other Manifestations of Violence in South Africa," in Elirea Bornman, René van Eeden, and Marie Wentzel, eds., *Violence in South Africa: A Variety of Perspectives* (Pretoria: Human Sciences Research Council, 1998), 14–15. The authors discuss the use of the term "multiple fatality incident" in South Africa.

25. Wilde uses the term "irruptions of memory" to mean public events that break in upon the national consciousness to evoke associations with symbols, figures, causes, and ways of life that to an unusual degree are associated with a political past that is still present in the lived experience of a major part of the population.

26. See Ricardo Lagos and Heraldo Muñoz, "The Pinochet Dilemma," *Foreign Policy,* Spring 1999, 26–39.

27. *Santiago News,* July 21 and 22, 1999.

28. Wendy Hunter, "The Dirty War and Its Aftermath: Recent Contributions on the Military and Politics in Argentina," *Latin American Research Review* 34:2 (1999): 203.

29. *NACLA Report on the Americas* 33:2 (September/October 1999): 2.

30. On Argentina, see Marguerite Feitlowitz, *A Lexicon of Terror: Argentina and the Legacies of Torture* (Oxford: Oxford University Press, 1998); and Patricia Marchack, *God's Assassins: State Terrorism in Argentina in the 1970s* (London: McGill-Queen's University Press, 1999).

31. *Noticen,* July 22, 1999.

32. *San Jose Mercury News,* May 20, 1999, 5A. See also Kate Doyle, "Death Squad Diary: Looking into the Secret Archives of Guatemala's Bureaucracy of Murder," *Harpers Magazine,* June 1999, 50–53.

33. *San Francisco Chronicle,* May 17, 1999, A10.

34. *San Francisco Chronicle,* January 18, 1999, A10, 11.

35. *San Jose Mercury News,* January 21, 1999, A4.

36. Rigoberta Menchu, *Crossing Borders* (New York: Verso, 1999).

37. Eduardo Posada-Carbó, "Fiction as History: The *bananeras* and Gabriel García Márquez's *One Hundred Years of Solitude," Journal of Latin American Studies* 30:2 (May 1998): 395–414. For discussion of related issues, see Philip Gourevitch, "The Memory Thief," *New Yorker,* June 14, 1999, 48–68.

38. *EcoCentral,* April 30, 1998.

39. *Noticen,* July, 22, 1999.

40. On Guatemala's conflict and peace process, see Susanne Jonas, *The Battle for Guatemala: Rebels, Death Squads, and U.S. Power* (Boulder: Westview Press, 1991); Ricardo Falla, *Massacres in the Jungle: Ixcán, Guatemala, 1975–1982* (Boulder: Westview, 1994); V. Perera, *Unfinished Conquest: The Guatemalan Tragedy* (Berkeley: University of California Press, 1993); David Stoll, *Rigoberta Menchú and the Story of All Poor Guatemalas* (Boulder: Westview Press, 1999); Jennifer Schirmer, *A Violence Called Democracy: The Guatemalan Military Project, 1982–1992* (Philadelphia: University of Pennsylvania Press, 1999); Francisco Goldman, "Murder Comes for the Archbishop," *New Yorker,* March 15, 1999, 60–77.

41. Minow, *Between Vengeance and Forgiveness,* 124–25.

42. On Rwanda, see David Newbury, "Understanding Genocide," *African Studies Review* 41:1 (April 1998): 73–97.

43. Brandon Hamber, " 'Dr. Jekyll and Mr. Hyde': Problems of Violence Prevention and Reconciliation in South Africa's Transition to Democracy," in Elirea Bornman, René van Eeden, and Marie Wentzel, eds., *Violence in South Africa: A Variety of Perspectives* (Pretoria: Human Sciences Research Council, 1998), 351–53.

44. Elirea Bornman, René van Eeden, and Marie Wentzel, eds., *Violence in South Africa: A Variety of Perspectives* (Pretoria: Human Sciences Research Council, 1998).

45. Hamber, " 'Dr. Jekyll and Mr. Hyde,' " 349–51.

46. Minow, *Between Vengeance and Forgiveness,* 58.

47. On South Africa, see David Goodman, *Fault Lines: Journeys into the New South Africa* (Berkeley: University of California Press, 1999); Antjie Krog, *Country of My Skull* (New York: Random House, 1998); Alex Boraine, *A Country Unmasked* (Oxford: Oxford University Press, 2000).

48. See Minow, *Between Vengeance and Forgiveness,* 63.

49. Robert D. Kaplan, *The Ends of the Earth: From Togo to Turkmenistan, from Iran to Cambodia—A Journey to the Frontiers of Anarchy* (New York: Vintage Books, 1996).

50. *San Jose Mercury News,* December 31, 1998, 18A.

51. Ibid.

52. Ibid., December 30, 1998, 1, 9A.

53. Ibid., January 2, 1999, 1, 6A.

54. On Cambodia, see also Ben Kiernan, *The Pol Pot Regime: Race, Power, and Genocide in Cambodia under the Khmer Rouge, 1975–79* (New Haven: Yale University Press, 1996); Steve Heder and Judy Ledgerwood, eds., *Propaganda, Politics, and Violence in Cambodia: Democratic Transition under United Nations Peace-Keeping* (Armonk: M. E. Sharpe, 1996); David P. Chandler, *The Tragedy of Cambodian History: Politics, War, and Revolution since 1945* (New Haven: Yale University Press, 1991); Alexander Laban Hinton, "A Head for an Eye: Revenge in the Cambodian Genocide," *american ethologist* 25:3 (1999): 352–77. On Tluol Seng, see David Chandler, *Voices from S-21: Terror and History in Pol Pot's Secret Prison* (Berkeley: University of California Press, 2000).

55. Robert Crib, ed., *The Indonesian Killings of 1965–1966: Studies from Java and Bali* (Clayton, Australia: Monash University Center of Southeast Asian Studies, 1990).

56. Debra E. Soled, ed., *China: A Nation in Transition* (Washington, DC: Congressional Quarterly, 1995), 66–68, 91.

57. On China in the twentieth century, see Nicolas D. Kristof and Sheryl Wudunn, *China Wakes: The Struggle for the Soul of a Rising Power* (New York: Vintage Books, 1994); Jeffrey N. Wasserstrom and Elizabeth J. Perry, *Popular Protest and Political Culture in Modern China* (Boulder: Westview Press, 1994); Jeffrey N. Wasserstrom, *Student Protests in Twentieth-Century China: The View from Shanghai* (Stanford: Stanford University Press, 1991); and Marie-Claire Bergere, "Tiananmen 1989: Background and Consequences," in Marta Dassu and Tony Saich, eds., *The Reform Decade in China: From Hope to Dismay* (London: Kegan Paul International, 1990), 132–50. Two very interesting, comparative treatments are Vera Schwarcz, *Bridge across Broken Time: Chinese and Jewish Cultural Memory* (New Haven: Yale University Press: 1998); and Watson, *Memory, History, and Opposition under State Socialism.* On literature, see Geremie Barmé, "The Chinese Velvet Prison: Culture in the 'New Age,' 1976–89," *Issues and Studies* 25:8 (August 1989): 54–79.

58. Orville Schell, The Jiang Zemin Mystery," *New York Review of Books,* September 23, 1999, 77.

59. Minow, *Between Vengeance and Forgiveness,* 67.

60. See also Richard H. Kohn, "History and the Culture Wars: The Case of the Smithsonian Institution's *Enola Gay* Exhibition," *Journal of American History* 82 (1995): 1036–63.

61. On Chile, see Peter Kornbluh, "Dos agentes de la CIA asignados a México, encargados de alentar el golpe contra Salvador Allende," *Proceso* 1185 (July 18, 1999): 48–50.

62. Kaplan, *Ends of the Earth,* 404.

63. Lederach, *Building Peace,* 66, 77, 39, 30, 25.

Latin America

1

Irruptions of Memory
Expressive Politics in Chile's Transition to Democracy

Alexander Wilde

Even before Augusto Pinochet was arrested in London in October 1998, the past hung heavily over Chile's distinctive transition to democracy. This was apparent during the previous year in the attention given to its conflictive recent history in television and radio talk shows and in newspaper and magazine articles. Since the return to elected rule in 1990, volumes on the dictatorship and the Popular Unity government were staples in Santiago bookstores. With the approach of the 25th anniversary of the 1973 military coup, what had been a steady stream of publication turned into a torrent of personal and political memoirs, extended essays, political journalism, and scholarly studies evoking the country's divided historical memory.[1]

Pinochet's arrest and the events that follow catalyse this national mood. Improbable, unprecedented, astonishing in themselves, they challenge what had appeared to be an immovable element of Chile's 'pacted transition', making vulnerable a figure who bears a heavy symbolic freight from a generation at the centre of national life, reviled or celebrated by different parts of the population, borne with a certain fatalism by perhaps the majority. At the same time, however, the whole episode recalls many others, less astounding in their magnitude. In March 1998, Pinochet had resigned his position as Commander of the Army and assumed a seat in Congress as Senator for Life, exchanging his military base of power for formal induction into the country's political class. This provoked demonstrations in the streets outside the Congress and inside the Senate chamber itself, where government members displayed pictures of prominent figures murdered during the dictatorship and protested

From *Journal of Latin American Studies* 31, no. 2 (October 1999): 473–500. © 1999 by Cambridge University Press. Reprinted with the permission of Cambridge University Press.

at Pinochet's incorporation into the legislature under terms of the 1980 Constitution. In the following months the country witnessed a failed attempt to impeach Pinochet and a volley of programmatic manifestos that subjected the policies and moral authority of the government to sharp public debate.[2]

Such moments have been a feature of Chile's political life through every year since 1990. These 'irruptions of memory' are part of a counterpoint of what might be called the expressive dimension of transitional politics, conditioning its character as they interrupt the flow of normal bargaining over budgets and public policies. Characterised as a 'nation of enemies'[3] at the end of the dictatorship, Chile remains haunted by divided memories of a recent history that includes the dictatorship and the sharp polarisation that preceded it, a period from roughly 1967 to 1990. Sporadically but frequently since that time, symbols of these memories have been given public expression by events—official ceremonies, national holidays, book publications, discovery of the remains of disappeared persons, the trial of an official of the dictatorship—which remind the political class and citizens alike of the unforgotten past.[4]

'Irruptions of memory',[5] as the term is used in this article, are public events that break in upon Chile's national consciousness, unbidden and often suddenly, to evoke associations with symbols, figures, causes, ways of life which to an unusual degree are associated with a political past that is still present in the lived experience of a major part of the population. The events considered here are 'public' in the sense both that they receive extensive coverage in the media and involve the authority of public institutions and of the elites responsible for them. They involve a period of recent national history notably framed by conflicting *political* memories—of the acts of leading figures of the dictatorship; of the blame borne by politicians for the conditions that led to the coup; above all of the massive violation of fundamental human rights under the dictatorship. During 'irruptions', such as that triggered by Pinochet's arrest, Chile becomes an arena of deeply divided public discourse, shot through with contending and mutually exclusive collective representations of the past. These charged events are woven into the very fabric of its politics today—symbolic issues, beyond the institutional arrangements well analysed by political scientists, which continue to constrain it in an arrested state.[6]

When assessed against the diverse transitions to democracy throughout the contemporary world, Chile is widely and correctly considered among the most successful. Its two centre-left *Concertación* governments (Patricio Aylwin, 1990–94; Eduardo Frei Ruiz-Tagle, 1994–2000) have retained political stability within a constitutional framework, sustained economic growth averaging more than six per cent annually since 1990, and wielded public policy to address the serious social deficit accumulated under the military regime. For all their real economic and political successes, however, the allegiance of the citizenry remains tepid, and questioning of the transition process itself appears to be growing. In the congressional elections of December 1997, record numbers of Chileans did not vote, spoiled ballots, or failed even to register. A national campaign earlier that year, which had a target of registering one million younger citizens, reached only 100,000.[7]

Between its periodic irruptions, the country's public life since transition has had a certain muffled quality reflective of what might be called a 'conspiracy of consensus' originating among political elites but permeating the whole society. Within the citizenry there appears to be a widespread aversion to open conflict, related to low levels of social trust.[8] The origins of this element of contemporary culture require more study but seem to be rooted in the habits developed over a generation of dictatorship—and in memories of that time and the painful polarisation preceding the 1973 coup.[9] Among political elites, particularly those making up the *Concertación*, there is also an observable tendency to avoid the cut and thrust of public debate that is normally associated with democratic politics. Politicians appear notably defensive about the partial character of the transition to democracy (particularly abroad) and thin-skinned about criticism of government policies and performance (particularly at home). They practice a cautious politics of elite consensus building—almost a kind of political engineering—with few channels to organised civil society or citizens' discontents.

Part of this style of rule undoubtedly stems from the need for internal negotiation within a diverse governmental coalition composed of three principal parties—the Christian Democrats, the Socialists, and the Party for Democracy. From a longer perspective, the politicians of the *Concertación* have faced a difficult task in re-establishing their national leadership in a country fundamentally changed in many respects by the politics and experience of the long dictatorship.[10] Although political parties historically dominated national politics to a degree with few parallels elsewhere in Latin America, the absence of a whole generation from the arenas and practices of electoral democracy challenged them to re-forge fresh ties with society after transition. The difficulties in doing so are evident in their handling of popular protests in a range of issue areas—health care, education, pensions, the environment—in which the dictatorship diminished the direct role of the state in favour of market solutions.

The tendency to privilege elite negotiation over more direct interaction with the citizenry, however, is particularly apparent in the ways in which *Concertación* has dealt with conflicts which recall the politically divided recent past. These irruptions of memory have inescapably contributed to the country's diffuse *desencanto* with transitional politics—a sense that, after eight years of elected rule, political life is not yet fully worthy of the allegiance that democracy should enjoy from its citizens and from the elites responsible for its political institutions.

In considering various explanations for this phenomenon, this article seeks to throw light on aspects of the expressive dimensions of politics—

those relating to the style of the political elite within itself and toward society—since 1990. It examines the efforts of the two *Concertación* governments to foster social reconciliation among a populace still deeply divided over the past, such as a range of early ceremonial gestures, the Truth and Reconciliation Commission, and the Memorial Wall to victims of the Pinochet dictatorship. It also analyses a pattern of events beyond government control, which have irrupted repeatedly in national life, triggering collective memory. It argues that, after an early period of more expressive politics, these governments gave up the initiative and became essentially reactive to 'irruptions' that broke upon them. However, as they practised a realistic politics of power—privileging institutional reforms and agreements among political elites—they have not adequately addressed the need for broader shared social understanding, rooted in common acceptance of human rights, of the country's conflictive past. I then consider how national leaders may wield moral authority to strengthen democratic institutions, and urge scholars to reexamine the dictatorship and the polarising period of democratic breakdown before it as episodes not yet assimilated into citizen attitudes or elite practice which continue to shape the peculiar qualities of contemporary transitional democracy.

A Possible Democracy

Scholars of democratic transitions have rightly singled out the particular character of 'pacted' transitions from authoritarian rule.[11] In such transitions, leaders of the democratic opposition in effect agree to compete for power within the institutional channels established by a dictatorship, entailing a variety of actual or implicit agreements with its own elites and supporters as well as among themselves. Such transitions are compromised (in the several senses of the term) in order to achieve the principal shared goal among democrats, that of ending the dictatorship and establishing the best democracy possible under existing conditions. At a minimum, this implies achieving free elections and other fundamental democratic procedures of 'polyarchy'.[12]

Chile presents a textbook case of such a transition, drawing on a recoverable tradition of democratic competition.[13] Its existing democratic institutions, overthrown in 1973 by military coup, had deep historical roots. In contrast to most of Latin America after independence, Chile after the mid-nineteenth century successfully institutionalised regular elections in which civilian party politicians competed for power. Despite a civil war in 1891, political institutions were reconstituted in a quasi-parliamentary electoral regime that allowed broadening representation of middle and working class interests in the early twentieth century. After an authoritarian interlude (1924–32), politics was stable for three decades but came under increasing strain in the late 1960s, leading to polarisation, disorder, and breakdown under

Allende (1970–73).[14] The military ruthlessly suppressed opposition in its early years in power, and Pinochet ruled arbitrarily until seeking legitimisation in a tainted referendum in 1978 and an authoritarian constitution, approved in 1980. During this early period the voices of civil society were those of the churches and the human rights movement.[15]

Effective civil opposition appeared for the first time nearly a decade after the military took power, in response to a dramatic economic crisis that threw one-quarter of the labour force out of work in the early 1980s. In 1983–84 massive street demonstrations regularly challenged Pinochet's hold on power and led to a National Accord (1985) among political party leaders, supported by the Catholic Church, demanding a return to democracy. However, in the following years, the possibility of transition through popular mobilisation— in the manner of People Power against the Philippine dictator Ferdinand Marcos—faded away. The only viable peaceful option was competing against the regime in the 1988 Plebiscite provided by the 1980 Constitution.[16] After overcoming widespread doubts about the legitimacy and fairness of the process, the *Concertación* organised massive voter registration and a successful campaign that was rewarded by a clear majority voting 'No' to continuation of the Pinochet regime.

The plebiscite of 5 October 1988 opened an intense period of some 18 months that gave final form to the pacted institutional framework inherited by the Aylwin government in 1990. The *Concertación* negotiated with the dictatorship a range of 54 modifications to the 1980 Constitution which somewhat reduced its authoritarian character. These changes were overwhelmingly approved in a national plebiscite in July 1989. During the same period, however, the Pinochet government implemented measures that further restricted the possibilities of democratic change, severely constraining the successor elected governments. These so-called *amarres*[17] (literally, 'mooring lines') included guarantee of tenure to public sector employees, packing of the Supreme Court and Constitutional Tribunal, consolidation of Pinochet's own power within the different military commands (with direct authority over the army until 1998), incorporation of the 19,000 operatives of the CNI secret police into military intelligence under his line command, and destruction of secret police archives.

In all, Chile returned to elected government with a series of well-protected authoritarian enclaves.[18] At one level these consisted of constitutional and legislative impediments to fuller democracy. In addition to the *amarres* already mentioned, Congress includes nine 'designated senators', and the electoral system over-represents the political Right, ensuring a blocking coalition against most systemic reforms.[19] At other levels, democracy was restricted by authoritarian values and mentalities concretely embodied in influential political actors, organisations, and social sectors with at best limited allegiance to democratic practice. These actors—above all the armed forces and the judiciary, but also much of organised business and the media—have exercised significant *de facto* power to retain the existing conspiracy of consensus.[20]

The many obstacles to democratisation have not prevented all progress toward achieving more responsive institutions. In 1997, after years of effort, the Frei government eventually won approval for major judicial reforms. It has gradually made an impact on the Supreme Court through new nominations, which has encouraged lower courts to reconsider a range of human rights-related cases. Both *Concertación* governments, through their role in annual promotions in the armed forces, have been able to force into retirement some officers implicated in human rights violations. These are important gains toward gradually democratising fundamental institutions, the effects of which will be helpful in the longer run. However, they appear to have had limited impact on the style of transitional politics or the broader conspiracy of consensus that ties the country to its authoritarian past. Both *Concertación* governments—Aylwin's in 1993 and Frei's in 1995–96—suffered frustrating public defeats in attempting to achieve constitutional reform and to resolve pending prosecutions of human rights violations, in spite of having given the highest priority to their policies. In both cases it proved politically impossible simultaneously to overcome the Right's control of the Senate and to maintain internal cohesion within the governmental coalition itself.[21]

The *Concertación*'s characteristic (and understandable) response to such public defeats has been to change the subject. Its stance has been to insist on the success of its economic and social policies and to exhort citizens to look to the future. Implicitly, it has returned to patient elite *Realpolitik* rather than drawing on its democratic legitimacy through direct appeals to the populace. These politicians have understood—perhaps too well—the realities of power binding the country's politics to an authoritarian past. Their style of leadership, however, conveys much less comprehension that the *amarres* are also moral moorings that tie citizen sentiments to their national political institutions.

Ceremonies, Sites and Irruptions

From its inception, the transition government of Patricio Aylwin (1990–94) demonstrated a firm commitment to re-establish the moral legitimacy of democracy[22] after the long Pinochet dictatorship and, indeed, the conflictive period of Allende's elected Popular Unity government (1970–73) that preceded it. This reflected a strong consensus within the *Concertación* itself— a coalition of left and centre parties which had made human rights a central element of its programme—but the measures taken under Aylwin clearly also reflected the character of the President himself. From its earliest days, his government implemented policies to address different elements of the authoritarian legacy of human rights violations.[23] It compensated victims of human rights violations and their families and commuted the sentences of political prisoners for acts against the dictatorship. Perhaps most important, it established an objective accounting and analysis of the human rights violations by the authoritarian regime, through a blue-ribbon Commission for Truth and Reconciliation (the Rettig Commission). Its multi-volume report was an extraordinary achievement, impressive not only for its impeccable documentation but also for its broader historical and institutional analysis of the period—including, significantly, the years preceding the dictatorship. With the resolute support and authority of President Aylwin, the Commission built an unshakable foundation of established facts about what had occurred as a contribution to Chile's national history.[24]

Beyond the content or immediate purposes of particular policies, Aylwin also showed sensitivity to the symbolic dimensions of his historic role. His government carried out a series of expressive ceremonies early in his government self-consciously meant to heal the wounds of the country's traumatic past. These began with televised coverage of his assumption of office in the Chilean Senate and of an extraordinary mass inauguration the following day in the National Stadium, a notorious place of detention at which the military government 'disappeared' hundreds of prisoners in the months following the 1973 coup. Through an imaginative programme of speeches, personal testimony, and public recognition of figures long proscribed from national life, the ceremony attempted to acknowledge a long period of collective suffering and exorcise this sinister site. Many observers were particularly moved by the wives of husbands 'disappeared' by the dictatorship performing—alone—Chile's national dance, the *cueca*.

Later in his first year, the Aylwin government made eloquent use of several of the most historical sites of national memory, Santiago's National Cathedral and General Cemetery. Allende's body was brought back from its private grave on the Pacific coast and a memorial service for the martyred President—a socialist and a Mason—held in the Cathedral, which was powerfully identified with defence of human rights during the dictatorship. Allende's casket was then taken in a funeral cortege through Santiago's streets and reburied in the General Cemetery, with the rest of the country's democratic presidents.[25] In a public ceremony and in the presence of his Cabinet, Aylwin delivered a moving eulogy acknowledging his own sharp political opposition to Allende during his government but placing the Socialist president firmly within Chile's national family and democratic tradition.[26]

A true 'city of the dead', the General Cemetery encapsulates to an extraordinary degree Chile's historical memory. In its most beautiful sections, with stately avenues bordered by towering trees, predominate the tombs of the country's great families and political class, together with those for its major corporate entities, from the four armed forces to its different historic trade unions. Allende's monument, impressive in its simplicity and massiveness, is located here. So, too, are the graves of Eduardo Frei Montalva (president

1964–70 and father of the president in the period 1994–2000), of Orlando Letelier (assassinated in Washington, D.C. in 1976 by the dictatorship's DINA secret police, and reburied after the return to elected government), and of Jaime Guzmán Errázuriz (the leading intellectual influence on the 1980 Constitution, assassinated by left-wing extremists in 1991)—all within a stone's throw of each other. The cemetery also has more modest neighbourhoods as well as poorer areas, with simple crosses in rows across bare and ill-kept fields. In their own way, these sections are also witnesses to Chile's conflictive national memory, above all to the fate of those killed for political reasons by the dictatorship, or 'disappeared' after arrest (the *detenidos-desaparecidos*), such as those buried in the notorious Patio 29.

To cap this early phase of ceremonies of reconciliation, Aylwin recurred to the more contemporary medium of television to express basic ethical commitments toward the country's past. In February 1991 he formally received the historic report of the Commission for Truth and Reconciliation from its president, former Radical Senator Raúl Rettig. A month later, he spoke directly to the whole population to acknowledge the crimes of the dictatorship and, in the name of the nation, ask for the forgiveness of its victims and their families. At the same time, he also called for gestures of regret from those in the armed forces responsible for the suffering caused by their acts—a request that has gone unmet through all the years of the transition.[27]

During its early years, the *Concertación* took the initiative in addressing collective memory through acts that reflected the shared moral principles of its leaders toward the past.[28] Its expressive politics also responded to events evoking past traumas that irrupted on national consciousness, independent of governmental policy. The outstanding example is the discovery, in June 1990, of a shallow unmarked grave in the cemetery of Pisagua, a town on Chile's northern coast. Following a massive demonstration in Santiago against military impunity, six government ministers, headed by Interior Minister Enrique Krauss, attended the public funeral ceremony for the 20 victims. At the end of 1990 the government committed itself, in collaboration with human rights groups, to building monuments to the victims of the dictatorship, notably a Memorial Wall in the General Cemetery to political victims and the *detenidos-desaparecidos*. In December it faced an irruption of a very different kind, sabre rattling by the army (the so-called *ejercicio de enlace*) to protest investigations of officers for human rights violations and financial misdealing (including the 'Pinocheques' case, implicating Pinochet's own son).

After the first years of the transition, the *Concertación* showed a declining disposition for acts expressive of the moral distinction between democracy and dictatorship. It gradually found itself more on the defensive, responding to irruptions it could not control. In September 1991, a little more than a year after the discoveries of Pisagua, 135 bodies of the disappeared were disinterred from unmarked graves in Patio 29 of Santiago's General Cemetery.

This time, hindered by the difficulties of identifying the victims, there was no large ceremony. When 15 of them were eventually reburied, in March 1993, it was a solemn but small event, with no government officials present. Patio 29 remains today without a memorial of any kind, officially unrecognised.[29] The eventual fate of the massive Memorial Wall to human rights victims in that same cemetery—one of the Aylwin government's most significant symbolic initiatives—is another eloquent illustration of the waning will for expressive politics. After lagging in construction through several years, the Wall was not officially inaugurated until February 1994, during the country's summer vacation. In sharp contrast to the 1990 ceremonies for Allende, the highest-ranking member of the government present was a sub-cabinet official, accompanied by leaders of several left parties and the public.[30]

In the latter years of Aylwin and the government of Eduardo Frei (1994), Chile was rocked repeatedly by events evoking the traumas of the dictatorship. These irruptions challenge brave public pronouncements of progress and pull the country back into deeply divided memories of its conflictive past. Such episodes imply something important about how Chile has experienced its transitional democracy, even after the Rettig report and the government's significant measures to address 'the human rights problem'. Their pattern also suggests that Aylwin's admirable early use of his public moral authority has been insufficient to construct a shared social understanding that would reconcile Chileans to their recent past and lend fuller legitimacy to their political institutions.

Irruptions of memory fall, roughly, into two categories. The first consists of haphazard events not linked to official actors but which, nevertheless, receive media coverage and evoke associations with the sinister past.[31] These include the discovery of unknown graves; books and newspaper or magazine articles touching on the dictatorship; and acts of political violence. This group of irruptions greatly influenced public sentiment during the Aylwin government. One major event was the April 1991 assassination of rightist Senator Jaime Guzmán by extreme leftists just weeks after release of the Rettig Commission report. Its effect was to abort a major planned educational campaign on the commission's findings and to shift political opinion from a focus on human rights to a concern with terrorism. That latter concern was reinforced in September of the same year by the kidnapping of the son of media magnate Agustín Edwards. Such irruptions continued during the Frei years, most spectacularly in December 1996 when the leftist kidnappers of Edwards escaped by helicopter from Santiago's maximum-security prison.[32]

A second class of irruptions consists of public events catalysed by state actors beyond the authority of the elected government, above all those in which the armed forces demonstrate significant autonomous initiative.[33] Perhaps the most important of these was the so-called *boinazo* (after the black berets, *boinas,* worn by mobilised troops), in May 1993, while Aylwin was

travelling in Europe. In protest against the investigation and possible prosecution of military officers for human rights violations, the army assembled
troops in battle dress in central Santiago.[34] Aylwin was to spend the better part
of his time in the following months to defuse the crisis through high-level con-
sultations with the armed forces and party leaders.[35] In August he submitted
legislation to Congress (the 'Aylwin Law') proposing appointment of special
judges to accelerate investigations and secret proceedings for pending cases
against officers accused of human rights violations. However, in the face of
protests from human rights organisations and opposition from *Concertación*
legislators, the bill was withdrawn in September.

In all, this prolonged episode threw into stark relief the real constitutional
and political impediments preventing Chile from moving toward fuller democratic rule. At the same time, it graphically illustrated the symbolic weakness
of elected civilian authority in the face of an apparently intractable problem.
During his presidency Aylwin showed great sensitivity to the symbolic importance of asserting his formal democratic authority over Pinochet and the military.[36] In his handling of this crisis, however, he followed the counsels of political realism to engineer a solution among political elites, both democratic and
de facto. There was no broad appeal to the nation, and public opinion data in
the period showed widespread ignorance of government intentions.[37] Given
Pinochet's power and past the course chosen was surely understandable but
it did not enhance the moral authority of democratic rule.

Another major episode catalysing the consequences of the past for Chile's
democracy began soon after President Frei assumed office in March 1994,
when 16 former police agents were convicted for the gruesome *degollados*
murders of three Communist professionals in 1985. At one level this decision
represented a triumph of the *Concertación*'s policy of pursuing justice through
individual prosecutions in the courts. At another, however, it showed just how
nominal was the control exercised by Chile's elected leaders, when *Cara-
binero* chief Rodolfo Stange, charged with obstruction of justice in the case,
resisted Frei's call to resign. Insisting on provisions in the 1980 Constitution
protecting him from removal, Stange played out a cat-and-mouse game with
the government for more than a year, in the bright glare of the national media,
before finally resigning 'voluntarily' in October 1995. Under the provisions
of that same constitution, he became an Institutional Senator in 1998.

In 1995 Frei faced an even more significant irruption when, in May, the
Supreme Court found former DINA director Manual Contreras and Chief
Operations Officer Pedro Espinoza guilty of the 1976 assassination of Orlando
Letelier.[38] Defying the decision, Contreras and Espinoza resisted imprisonment for many months. With military complicity, Contreras fled to a countryside retreat in the Chilean south, followed by escape under protection of
the armed forces to a military hospital, where he malingered for weeks, alleg-
ing illness too serious for prison conditions. Espinoza and Contreras both

eventually became inmates in a special prison under military (rather than civilian) guards at Punto Peuco, in countryside north of Santiago. Juridically, this was a triumph for the Frei government's tenacity and a vindication of the *Concertación*'s strategy of prosecution through the courts. At a symbolic level, however, the episode was more mixed. While the eventual punishment of the feared head of Pinochet's secret police produced a perceptible buzz on the streets of Santiago, the citizenry had largely been passive witnesses through the many preceding months, watching democratic leadership once again encumbered by the terms of the transition. In the face of open military defiance, Frei played out a cautious strategy, making only one circumspect appeal directly to the nation. The subsequent effort of his government to work with the Right toward a legislative solution to pending human rights issues (the 'Figueroa-Otero' proposal) was to founder by April 1996.

The courts were another institutional actor beyond governmental control that catalysed Chile's irruptions of memory. Throughout the 1990s the country witnessed a continuing stream of human rights-related cases dealt with in the courts, martial and civil, within Chile and without. Under existing national legislation, prosecution of such cases fell to the existing courts, even though the *Concertación* accepted the conclusion of the Rettig Commission that they failed to protect fundamental rights during the dictatorship.[39] The large number of these cases, and the multiple stages inherent in judicial proceedings, had the effect of keeping the dictatorial past almost continuously in the public's attention. In addition to the Letelier and *degollados* cases mentioned above, notable national proceedings during the eight years of transition also included the 'Operation Albania' case (12 members of the extreme left Manuel Rodríguez Patriotic Front allegedly murdered by intelligence agents in 1985) and the long running story of the sinister *Colonia Dignidad.*[40]

Furthermore, the international character of the dictatorship's state terrorism meant that for Chileans the violent past was evoked not only by cases in the country's own courts but by prosecutions abroad—in Italy (for the 1974 assassination attempt in Rome against Christian Democratic leader Bernardo Leighton), in Argentina (for the 1974 assassination of Carlos Prats, Pinochet's predecessor as Army Commander), and Spain (for the 1976 disappearance and murder of diplomat Carmelo Soria).[41] It was, of course, international courts that, in October 1998, detonated the most evocative of all the irruptions of memory during the Chilean transition.

It is too early to reach more than a preliminary assessment of the Pinochet case, which remained unresolved as this article was sent to press.[42] Its first three months, as witnessed by Chile and the world, were rich in drama and precedent: on 16 October, the aged dictator, recovering from a back operation in a London clinic, was arrested by order of a British court on charges of torture, murder, and genocide brought by a Spanish court; on 28 October, the London High Court unanimously found that the Senator for Life and former head of state was immune from prosecution for such charges; on 25 November, the Law Lords (on a 3–2 vote) overturned this ruling, upholding the prevalence of emerging principles of international human rights law over traditional doctrines of sovereign immunity; on 9 December (Pinochet's 83rd birthday), the British Home Secretary Jack Straw decided to proceed with extradition to Spain; on 17 December, five other Law Lords unanimously overturned the earlier juridical ruling denying immunity, on the grounds that it lacked the appearance of impartiality; throughout Pinochet remained under house arrest in London, awaiting a putatively definitive legal decision on the question of immunity expected in early 1999.

Such a bare account only hints at the alarms, entrances, and exits of the multitude of actors that crowded the stage and spoke from television screens across the world during these months. In Chile itself the Frei government found itself, as with other irruptions, reacting to events linked to the country's conflictive past that abruptly intruded upon the terms of its transitional democracy. Given the venue abroad, it was even more limited in its resources to resolve the matter directly. It opted for a legal and diplomatic defense of Pinochet's immunity from prosecution in Spanish courts and, implicitly, for a political defence of Chile's institutional stability. At home, Frei acted decisively to address military anxieties by meeting with top officers (the first visit to the armed forces' own building by a democratically-elected head of state since 1973) and, on three occasions convoked the National Security Council, one of Pinochet's institutional legacies to transitional democracy, which offered an arena for discussion of the different stages of the unfolding case with the commanding officers of the four services.[43] His government also drew on its reserves of good will within the business community to assure its leaders that economic policy and the fundamental institutions of governance would be maintained within the understandings established by the transition.

Beyond the basic realities of power, the Pinochet case clearly confronted the government with the challenges of expressive politics characteristic of Chile's irruptions of memory. Demonstrations and protests, magnified by projection through television and the print media, evoked the slogans, images, and symbols of the divided past. As in the previous March, political portraits reappeared within the Senate chamber in October, now on the initiative of the outraged political Right, which then boycotted its sessions during two weeks in protest.[44] Through these months investigations of human rights cases continued in the courts and the media gave extensive coverage to the exhumation and identification of human remains from sites identified with the dictatorship's notorious 'Caravan of Death' in October 1973.[45] The prevalence of expressive politics in Chile, in contrast to the legal doctrines argued in British courts, was abundantly clear in public discourse. Frei himself addressed the nation on several occasions, notably in improvised remarks calling for reconciliation on 30 December, and he led a host of national actors calling for a 'gesture' of regret from Pinochet and the armed forces for the traumas inflicted on the nation during the dictatorship.[46]

Human Rights in a Pacted Transition

Following on Chile's many other irruptions of memory, the Pinochet case again made abundantly clear the ways in which its transitional politics remains captive to symbols of its conflictive past and to the unresolved issues of human rights. Both governments of the *Concertación* strove to address the latter and the Pinochet case gave them another opportunity to do so. Whether they will be able to practice an expressive politics conducive to national reconciliation will be a different challenge.

During the 1990s, both governments clearly moved away from an active policy in this regard. In part, this shift can be understood in terms of the different personalities of presidents Aylwin and Frei. Aylwin comes from an older generation of the country's traditional political class. He was a major protagonist in the events that led to the breakdown of democracy during Allende's Popular Unity, a leader in the Christian Democratic party that was central to the democratic opposition that emerged in the 1980s, and the consensus candidate of the *Concertación* coalition that won the 1989 elections. An instinctive as well as skilled politician, he expressed in his early gestures and policies a strong belief in the need to re-establish the moral authority of democratic rule.

These policies and expressive politics communicated two central tenets, one drawn from recent and one from more distant historical memory. The first was to identify Chile's new democracy with the principles of human rights that had emerged as a unifying thread within opposition to the dictatorship, one surpassing old ideological divisions. Despite fears within the *Concertación* about how the armed forces would respond to a truth commission, Aylwin himself took personal responsibility to initiate and design this central symbolic policy.[47] The second tenet was to renew the best traditions of Chile's historic democracy, lost in the polarisation of the late 1960s and early 1970s and then actively suppressed by the military dictatorship. In this regard the whole *mis-en-scène* posthumously re-incorporating Allende into Chile's body politic was central—an act of imagination and courage, particularly at the very inception of the transition.[48] Allende was (and remains) a divisive symbolic figure, but Aylwin was determined to pay official homage to his place within the country's democratic tradition.

> This is a ceremony of ... re-encounter ... with the history of the nation, because Salvador Allende—beyond the contradictory judgements that he arouses—was through more than three decades one of the most outstanding actors in national events. Deputy, Senator, Cabinet Minister, President of the Senate, four times candidate to the nation's highest office, and finally,

President of the Republic of Chile, he came to be the most representative
leader of the Chilean left. From his socialist and revolutionary perspective,
he embodied the aspirations of vast sectors of our people that longed for profound and drastic changes toward a more just society; he fought for them
with courage and gave his life out of loyalty to his convictions. These are
facts that no one can deny.[49]

In contrast, Eduardo Frei is of a younger generation and took up politics
(as the son of President Eduardo Frei Montalva, 1964–70) only after an earlier career in business. This background appears to have won him important
support in Chile's private sector, which had generally prospered during the
dictatorship and long nurtured doubts toward traditional party politicians.
Given the *Concertación*'s determination to demonstrate that democracy could
be comparable with a market economy, this is no small achievement. The
prosperity of the Frei years (at least until the effects of the Asian crisis slowed
growth in late 1998) gave stakes in Chilean democracy to conservative sectors hitherto sceptical of its virtues. At the same time, however, Frei's style
as President has revealed limited instinct for expressive gesture that might have
appealed to the country more broadly during the irruptions that have punctu-
ated his government, although the Pinochet case may mark the beginning of
a change in this direction.

However, the shift that occurred after the early years of the *Concertación*
clearly responded to forces beyond differences in presidential personalities.
The most important of these was the *Concertación*'s shared beliefs about the
transition itself. It was Aylwin who declared the transition to democracy concluded as early as 7 August 1991 (at a press conference in the *Moneda* presidential palace).[50] He repeated this assertion in his presidential address of
May 1992, and Frei would later attempt to use his government's assumption
of office in 1994 to establish a new agenda based on the premise that Chilean
democracy was consolidated.[51] There were good political reasons to take this
stance that Chile had achieved some democratic normality—to reassure the
country itself as well as foreign investors and other observers—and get on with
the business of governing.[52] However, the irruptions of the past facing both
the late Aylwin government and that of Frei suggest that the moral claims of
Chile's new democracy and its links to the country's past democratic traditions require serious and renewed attention from its leaders.

The retreat from expressive politics appears to reflect the preferred style
of political engineering characteristic of the *Concertación* as well as of the
scholarly literature on democratic transitions. These party politicians saw
themselves as the central protagonists in the gradual coalescence of civil
opposition demanding a return to democratic rule. This had been their historic role in a country with an identity strongly shaped by its political institutions, and by the mid-1980s they had assumed leadership of the massive popular protests initially sparked by the trade unions. When their demand for free

elections failed, they created the broad national coalition of political forces that, as the 'Commando for the No' fought and won the 1988 plebiscite. It was they who had the political skills to forge the *Concertación*'s platform and campaign for the 1989 elections, and they who negotiated the exit strategy with the Pinochet regime to make possible the return of elected government in 1990. Through this process they concentrated increasingly on forging agreements within the political class itself (including those in the outgoing dictatorship) as the key to a successful transition. They have largely sustained this style, as analysed in this article, throughout their rule during the 1990s.

The Chilean case provides a striking illustration of this theme, so predominant in the contemporary scholarly literature on democratic transitions. This was not entirely coincidental, since the politicians of the *Concertación* consciously discussed that same literature, which seems to have reshaped and reinforced their own experience—a subject worthy of further study and contemplation by those inclined to see academic analysis as primarily an act of perception and reaction.[53] It also suggests the need for scholars to consider more fully the ways in which the habits engendered by pacted transitions, in addition to the institutional constraints they entail, may limit democratic deepening in the years after the change of regime.

If building the bridge of transition is considered from the perspective of political engineering, the calculations of structure and stress may well limit concern with its expressive significance. In Chile, however, the foundational costs of initial construction were paid not only in the hard coin of power but also the less tangible ones of legitimacy and national identity. With the benefit of hindsight, it can be perceived that, once the span has been built, it becomes increasingly important for leaders to address *where the society has come from* in order to show where it is going. After the early years of the Aylwin government, 'human rights' became an issue identified exclusively with its most serious victims, rather than a guiding principle on which to found a new national politics.

Human rights are the central moral question facing Chile in the Pinochet case. As with earlier irruptions, the government is presented with the challenge of defining policy to address the dimensions of truth and of justice. For the latter, the government may be aided by recent trends within the Chilean courts. After years of judicial decisions routinely applying the 1978 Amnesty Law to close human rights cases, the newly constituted Criminal Bench of the Supreme Court in September and again in December 1998 and January 1999 ruled that, given Chile's international treaty obligations, human rights violations could not be amnestied and that judicial investigation to determine individual responsibility should continue. While these decisions were juridical in character, it seems fair to speculate that they have some relation to the virtually complete change in the Supreme Court membership during the Frei government—and have not been totally unaffected by the international issues raised by Pinochet's detention. If these precedents were applied generally, they could affect some thousand other unresolved cases of forced disappearance. Furthermore, Judge Juan Guzmán Tapia was investigating a dozen complaints against Pinochet whilst the former dictator was being held in London, although the possibilities that they would go to trial appeared remote.

As with the *boinazo* of 1993 and the Contreras case of 1995, politicians and other public figures are again exploring political initiatives to address the issues of human rights. The Catholic Church has called on the government to adopt legal measures to establish truth about the military regime and to take political steps to promote forgiveness for human rights abuses. The *Concertación* has convened a committee of noted human rights attorneys to recommend possible reforms, and there have been calls for a second Rettig Commission that could offer stronger incentives for truthful testimony about crimes committed during the dictatorship. However, the conflicting perspectives on these issues within the *Concertación,* the vagaries of 1999 election-year politics, and above all, the uncertain future unfolding of the Pinochet case itself all conspire against hope for comprehensive policy to resolve human rights issues and foster national reconciliation.

Nevertheless, as Chile entered the new century, there was new consciousness that the issues of human rights went beyond the survivors of the dictatorship's worst infamies and the families of those it disappeared. It is they who bear the deepest wounds, but the victims of that harsh time are far more numerous than this tragic group. They include the tens of thousands unjustly detained and tortured or relegated to internal exile or terrorised in the sweeps of the slums that continued through the dictatorship's final decade, the more than one hundred thousand exiles, the uncounted citizens that waited for the knock on the door in the night or that still cannot find the means to discuss these years with their children. The issues of human rights—and the country's historical memory—concern the whole nation, and not only the family and left-linked organisations that have remained of the historic human rights movement.[54] What Chile as a whole experienced during the dictatorship—and indeed, during the longer period of deep national divisions before 1973—is the subject of that historical memory. As the Pinochet case and the recurrent irruptions over eight years indicate very clearly, what is unacknowledged is not forgotten.

Memory and the Moral Authority of Democracy

This article is an effort both to illuminate important aspects of one country's transition to democracy and to invite scholars to give greater attention to the expressive dimensions of such transitions more generally. The latter purpose is part of the concern of many scholars working on Latin America with how democracy can be 'deepened', when basic consolidation has been achieved and breakdown is not a significant possibility (as it is not, for example, in Chile). It is complementary to the concerns of what Guillermo O'Donnell terms the 'second transition' from democratic government to democratic regime.[55] However, it focuses less on the institutional constraints that maintain semi-democratic rule—a critical and legitimate subject for analysis in itself—than on the culture nurtured in different ways in the populace and elites by a transition held captive by unreconciled memories of a divided past. It proposes a broad hypothesis for research: that in order to progress beyond polyarchy and establish *democracy* over time, it is necessary to strengthen the moral authority of democratic institutions and of those elites responsible for them.

How should scholars evaluate the claim that Chile's transitional democracy must still more fully face this challenge, and more specifically one related to unresolved issues of historical memory? The *desencanto* of its citizens with politics today surely has many other possible causes. Opinion polls reveal the normal concerns and discontents of many democracies—crime, health care, education—and available soundings indicate firm popular support for democracy, in the abstract, compared to other regime alternatives. Considerable political stability has been achieved, and opinion data do not reveal a populace preoccupied day to day with the issues of human rights and the *amarres* that were prominent among its concerns early in the transition. Perhaps time is already working its magic on the country's divided memories—covering them over, in the evocative phrase of Elizabeth Lira and Brian Loveman's book, with 'the soft ashes of forgetfulness'.[56]

Perhaps—but this seems to me an inadequate explanation on several grounds. One is the fact that existing public opinion data from the 1990s does not capture how much the symbols of national identity, strongly associated in Chile with its political institutions and tradition, condition how citizens experience politics since transition—the immediate and accumulative effects of the recurrent events here called 'irruptions of memory'. The existing conspiracy of consensus undoubtedly reflects the low levels of social trust that have been measured, but we really do not know how much it is also shaped by their broader moral sentiments toward the collectivity of which they are a part—its symbols, its constitution, its fundamental public institutions of governance *as a whole.*

Historical study of other societies suggests that this is a worthy topic for research. Henry Rousso's *The Vichy Syndrome*[57] presents a highly suggestive interpretation of France's recurrent re-readings over half a century of the painful episode of Pétain's regime, with shifting roles in public understanding of the Nazi Occupation, the Resistance, French leaders and the general populace. His analysis encompasses a rich range of influences reshaping its place in contemporary history, from scholarly research to official ceremonies to cultural production to political actors and interests. Jeffrey Herf's *Divided*

Memory[58] examines how German political leaders attempted through public policy to interpret the meaning of the trauma of Nazism and the Holocaust within a national history, contrasting the treatment within East and West Germany in the aftermath of World War II. As with Rousso, Herf examines a broad array of evidence to throw light on the deeper question of how leaders attempted to legitimate the political institutions over which they held authority, in the very different 'democracies' created in the two Germanys.

The relevance of such research to Chile's transitional democracy—and indeed, that of other countries in the Southern Cone—is considerable. There are suggestive parallels to the facts of the Chilean case—for example, the efforts of *Bundespräsident* Theodor Heuss through the first decade of the Federal Republic to enlarge the moral comprehension of a reluctant populace with his insistence that Nazism and the Holocaust were repellent aberrations from Germany's own best political traditions.[59] More generally, Rousso and Herf convincingly demonstrate the importance of the expressive dimensions of politics in establishing the moral authority of democratic institutions after historic ruptures—and both employ a multifaceted methodology capable of encompassing the depth and complexity of the task.

Both books also underline the particular importance and responsibility of democratic leaders in such a process, as this paper has tried to establish, in a modest way, for Chile's contemporary transition. The high responsibility of democratic politicians is a major theme of Max Weber's classic 'Politics as a Vocation',[60] a text which had demonstrable influence in shaping conceptions within Chile's *Concertación*. In particular, these politicians were influenced by Weber's famous distinction between an 'ethic of principled convictions' and an 'ethic of responsibility'—the former guided by purity of intention and the latter by a concern for practical consequences. It was this latter ethic that predominated in Chile, in a political class respectful of legal constraints[61] and anxious about the potential for democratic retrogression.

Although their choice of an ethic of responsibility was morally compelling—and not merely pragmatically attractive—the way they applied it in Chile is still subject to debate. It is worth recalling that Weber's essay appeared in the aftermath of World War I. In making his famous distinction, he had a keen awareness of the dangers of an 'ethic of principled convictions' for the fate of the new Weimar democracy (concerns which proved to be borne out by subsequent events). The analogy to Chile—which at the time of its transition possessed a strong economy, could retrieve a long historical democratic tradition, and enjoyed a world context favourable to liberal democracy—deserves further examination. Furthermore, as indicated by Chile's irruptions of memory since 1990, scholars need to devote more attention to the importance of expressive politics for establishing the moral authority of democracy, beyond the earliest stages of transition, because what is conceived as an ethic of responsibility may become indistinguishable from mere pragmatism.

Finally, as the books by Rousso and Herf suggest, scholars have an important contribution to make to historical understanding of how national traumas affect successor democracies. Both draw on substantial earlier scholarship that contributed to important public debates about the past in France and Germany. Sources are available to permit scholars of Chile to make a similar contribution, so that this society will have the means, in time, to come to terms with what it has lived through. The period of 1967–90 already offers abundant published primary material in first-person accounts and memoirs as well as secondary sources, ranging from studies undertaken during the dictatorship to analyses that appeared just before or after transition. Furthermore, there are important archives of primary materials related to human rights violations in these countries, other bodies of officially-collected materials, such as those of the Rettig Commission and its successor, to which there is yet no public access, and abundant documentary materials now scattered among institutions and individuals which are in danger of being lost, for want of any coherent effort to gather them.[62] Finally, there are the living memories of individuals that go unrecorded but could form a vital part of a fuller understanding of how this period was experienced.

What has not yet quite occurred is the emergence of scholarship treating the 1967–90 period as part of 'the past', as prologue to transitional democracy. The relatively new conception of approaching recent history this way— as *le temps présent,* understood as part of the personal memory of a significant part of the populace—offers encouragement that even periods of deep division may be studied dispassionately.[63] Fortunately, there are now hopeful signs that scholars in Chile and elsewhere can now relate transitions in a fuller way to the legacies of authoritarianism and eventually contribute to greater social reconciliation and stronger democratic institutions.[64]

Notes

1. Titles include Tomás Moulian, *Chile actual: anatomía de un mito* (Santiago, 1997) and *Conversación interrumpida con Allende* (Santiago, 1998); M. A. de la Parra, *La mala memoria* (Santiago, 1997) and *Carta abierta a Pinochet* (Santiago, 1998); E. Carmona (ed.), *Morir es la noticia* (Santiago, 1997); M. González Pino and A. Fontaine Talavera (eds.), *Las mil días de Allende* (Santiago, 1997); M. Rivas and R. Merino (eds.), *¿Qué hacía yo sí 11 de septiembre de 1973?* (Santiago, 1997); F. Zerán, *Desacatos al desencanto* (Santiago, 1997); J. Lavandero Illanes, *El precio de sostener un sueño* (Santiago, 1997); and A. Cavallo, M. Salazar, and O. Sepúlveda, *La historia oculta del régimen militar* (Santiago, third ed. 1997 [originally published 1989]) and A. Cavallo, *La historia oculta de la transición* (Santiago, 1998); A. Jocelyn-Holt Letelier, *El peso de la noche: nuestra frágil fortaleza histórica* (Buenos Aires, 1997) and *El Chile perplejo* (Santiago, 1998); H. Vidal, *Política cultural de la memoria histórica* (Santiago, 1997); E. Tironi, *El régimen autoritario: para una sociología de Pinochet* (Santiago, [1998]); D. Tótoro Taulis, *La cofradía blindada: Chile civil y Chile militar—trauma y conflicto* (Santiago, 1998); M. A. Garretón, *et al., Por la fuerza, sin la razón* (Santiago, 1998); G. Arriagada, *Por la razón o la fuerza: Chile*

bajo Pinochet (Santiago, 1998); P. Aylwin Azócar, *El reencuentro de los demócratas* (Santiago, 1998); E. Subercaseaux, *Gabriel Valdés: señales de historia* (Santiago, 1998); J. A. Viera-Gallo, *11 de septiembre: testimonio, recuerdos y una reflexión actual* (Santiago, 1998); L. Maira, *Los tres Chile de la segunda mitad del siglo XX* (Santiago, 1998); J. T. Merino, *Bitácora de un almirante: memorias* (Santiago, 1998); G. Rojas Sánchez, *Chile escoge la libertad* (Santiago, 1998); M. Orella Benado, *Allende: alma en pena* (Santiago, 1998); A. Uribe, *Carta abierta a Patricio Aylwin* (Santiago, 1998); J. A. Cuevas, *Diario de la ciudad ardiente* (Santiago, 1998); H. Soto (ed.), *Voces de muerte*, 2 vols. (Santiago, 1998); P. Verdugo, *Interferencia secreta: 11 de septiembre de 1973*, with CD (Santiago, 1998); and P. Rojas B., *et al., Tarda pero llega: Pinochet ante la justicia española* (Santiago, 1998).

2. The manifesto of the most critical group within the *Concertación* was published in *El Mercurio* as 'La gente tiene razón: las voces disidentes del oficialismo', D8–10, June 14, 1998.

3. *A Nation of Enemies: Chile under Pinochet* (New York, 1991), by Pamela Constable and Arturo Valenzuela. This evocative and sophisticated analysis of the dictatorship, ending with Aylwin's inauguration, has not been published in Spanish translation in Chile.

4. The 'whitewashing' of the past is a major theme in Moulian's *Chile actual.*

5. 'Irrupt': to break or burst in (*The American Heritage Dictionary* [Boston, 1985]). Although relatively rare in English usage, the term closely matches the Spanish *irrumpir,* conveying a sense of a sudden intrusion. The scholarly literature on historical memory is large and growing. Representative works would include Maurice Halbwachs, *On Collective Memory* (ed.) and trans. by L. A. Coser (Chicago and London, 1992 [1941, 1952]); Pierre Nora (ed.), trans. by Arthur Goldhammer, *Realms of Memory* (New York, 1996 [1992]), three vols.; P. H. Hutton, *History as an Art of Memory* (Hanover, New Hampshire, 1993); D. Lowenthal, *Possessed by the Past* (New York, 1996); and J. S. Pennebaker, *et al.* (eds.), *Collective Memory of Political Events* (Mahwah, New Jersey, 1997).

6. It is striking that the events of March 1998 at the Congress—street protests outside, pictures of the murdered and 'disappeared' within—mirror others exactly eight years earlier, when Patricio Aylwin was invested with the presidential office. See R. Otano, *Crónica de la transición* (Santiago, 1995), p. 108. This is an excellent journalistic account—attentive to the expressive, less tangible aspects of politics—of the Aylwin presidency and the period preceding it. The continuity symbolises the institutional constraints of Chile's negotiated transition but also evokes how this small society has *experienced* its recent political history.

7. Voting is compulsory in Chile, and failure to vote complicates any subsequent involvement with the justice system or other state agencies. The recent elections—defying a long civic tradition of high participation in elections, comparable to western European countries—were widely interpreted as indicating generalised dissatisfaction, in spite of the country's rapid modernisation and impressive economic indicators.

8. According to Marta Lagos, a leading national expert on public opinion, Chileans exhibit surprisingly low levels of interpersonal trust, openness about politics, satisfaction with democracy, and perception of full democracy in Chile—despite political stability and economic growth. She locates these attitudes in broader discussion of regional political culture, in 'Latin America's Smiling Mask', *Journal of Democracy,* vol. 8, no. 3 (July 1997), pp. 123–38. These themes are examined in greater depth in the report of the United Nations Development Programme, *Desarrollo humano en Chile 1998* (Santiago, 1998), which relates 'subjective' social responses to broader processes of modernisation.

9. On this theme, see especially Moulian, *Chile actual,* and both works by De la Parra.

10. See Tironi, *El régimen autoritario,* and M. A. Garretón, 'The Political Opposition and the Party System under the Military Regime', in P. W. Drake and I. Jaksic (eds.), *The Struggle for Democracy in Chile: 1982–1990* (Lincoln, Nebraska, 1991), pp. 211–250.

11. This sub-set of transitions, with its awkward name derived from the Spanish case (*transición pactada*), concerns the establishment of democratic rule within the institutional framework of a previous authoritarian regime. The basic reference is G. O'Donnell, *et al.* (eds.), *Transitions from Authoritarian Rule: Comparative Perspectives* (Baltimore, Maryland, 1986). A helpful recent overview of this literature is J. Hartlyn, 'Political Continuities, Missed Opportunities, and Institutional Rigidities: Another Look at Democratic Transitions in Latin America', in *Politics, Society, and Democracy: Latin America,* (eds.), S. Mainwaring and A. Valenzuela (Boulder, Colorado, 1998), pp. 101–120.

12. Robert Dahl, *Polyarchy: Participation and Opposition* (New Haven, Connecticut, 1971).

13. At least two elements of this characterisation of Chile's transition remain contested: the degree to which democratic elites were actually able to negotiate with those of the dictatorship and the nature of the understandings—specific and implicit—reached during that process. As to the former, the processes of consultation that did occur before Aylwin's inauguration in March 1990 (notably over the constitutional reforms of 1989) deserve more study. Pinochet's arrest in London in October 1998 has made manifest ambiguities about the latter. Within the extensive scholarly literature analysing the transition, Edgardo Boeninger's *Democracia en Chile: Lecciones para la gobernabilidad* (Santiago, 1997) is particularly valuable. Boeninger was a central figure during the formation of democratic opposition to Pinochet in the 1980s and in the elected Aylwin successor government. His book combines careful analysis of the various constitutional and institutional restrictions to democracy with an insider's knowledge of the political perceptions and strategies of Chile's democratic elites. It is usefully read in conjunction with Arriagada, *Chile bajo Pinochet,* by the director of the *Concertación*'s 'No' campaign of 1988 and another key participant the democratic opposition, and the account of Sergio Fernández, *Mi lucha por la democracia* (Santiago, 1994). Fernández, Interior Minister in the last Pinochet Cabinet, was a key 'softliner' of the outgoing authoritarian regime. See also E. Cañas Kirby, *Proceso politico en Chile, 1973–1990* (Santiago, 1997).

14. In the large literature on this process, Arturo Valenzuela's *The Breakdown of Democratic Regimes: Chile* (Baltimore, Maryland, 1978) remains classic. Alan Angell presents an excellent recent synthesis in his chapter in the volume on Chile in the L. Berhell (ed.), *Cambridge History of Latin America,* Vol. VIII 1991.

15. The principal organisations were the Vicariate of Solidarity, linked to the Catholic Church, and the Chilean Commission of Human Rights, linked to the democratic parties. In *Moral Opposition to Authoritarian Rule in Chile, 1973–90* (London, 1996), Pamela Lowden presents a well-researched interpretation of the former and their contribution to democratic transition.

16. Andrés Zaldívar Larraín analyses the 1980 Constitution and its dubious approval by plebiscite during the dictatorship in *La transición inconclusa* (Santiago, 1995). Zaldívar is the current president of the Chilean Senate and the Christian Democratic party's candidate for President.

17. Echoing Franco, Pinochet boasted that he had left a political legacy *atado y bien atado,* well and truly tied up. While it is not surprising that a professional soldier would put such stock in political engineering for his own purposes, it is regrettable that the

democratic politicians of the *Concertación* have not found ways to harness the superior moral authority given them by free elections.

18. M. A. Garretón, *La posibilidad democrática en Chile* (Santiago, 1989) and 'Human Rights in Democratisation Processes', in E. Jelin and E. Hershberg (eds.), *Constructing Democracy: Human Rights, Citizenship, and Society in Latin America* (Boulder, Colorado, 1996), pp. 39–56. Elizabeth Lira and Brian Loveman, *Las suaves cenizas del olvido: La vía chilena de reconciliación, 1814–1932* (Santiago, forthcoming), challenge Garretón's influential conceptualisation. They argue that authoritarian characteristics are a consistent feature of Chile's political institutions historically, integral rather than exceptional as implied by the notion of 'enclaves'.

19. A brief, lucid explanation of Chile's current electoral system is given by J. S. Valenzuela, 'Consolidation in Post-Transitional Settings: Notion, Process, and Facilitating Conditions', an insightful early analysis of the transition in S. Mainwaring, G. O'Donnell and J. S. Valenzuela (eds.), *Issues in Democratic Consolidation* (Notre Dame, Indiana, 1992), p. 98, footnote 24. Upon taking his seat as Senator for Life in March 1998, Pinochet became the tenth member of the upper chamber not chosen by popular suffrage. The fact that the *Concertación* could name democrats to become Institutional Senators diluted the blocking coalition but did not in itself diminish the undemocratic character of Congress.

20. The significant influence of such actors, beyond the bounds of Chile's formal political institutions, is regularly recognised in the press, which has dubbed them *poderes fácticos.* Their influence is recognised within the broader Chilean population; e.g. Lagos, 'Smiling Mask', p. 135.

21. The specific reforms proposed, which were somewhat different for the two governments, illustrate both the practical and ethical difficulties of addressing these issues within the *Concertación's* inherited institutional constraints. These efforts, which involved some of Chile's most distinguished human rights advocates, are worthy of separate study. Initial accounts are given in Cavallo, *Historia oculta de la transición,* pp. 217–22 and 296–304 and Alexandra Barahona de Brito, *Human Rights and Democratisation in Latin America: Uruguay and Chile* (New York, 1997), pp. 181–7.

22. It is worth noting that Robert Dahl conceived the notion of 'polyarchy' to distinguish a set of political norms, institutions, and practices from the inescapably *moral* qualities attached to 'democracy' (*Polyarchy*). The multiple confusions around the concept of democracy, however, do not detract from the real consequences that ignoring its prescriptive content may have for achieving vibrant democratic institutions. This essay is a modest attempt to invite scholars to devote greater study to understanding such consequences in contemporary transitional democracies.

23. De Brito provides a detailed analysis informed by shrewd political judgements in *Human Rights and Democratisation.* Boeninger, *Democracia en Chile,* gives an account of these issues seen from within the Aylwin government.

24. The *Report of the Chilean National Commission on Truth and Reconciliation,* 2 vols., trans. by Ph. E. Berryman (Notre Dame, Indiana, 1993 [in Spanish, 1991]). The report's influence on subsequent political discourse, however, can only be regarded as disappointing. Leaders of the Right retained a language—much in evidence in late 1998, following Pinochet's detention in London—denying that any official recognition had been given to conditions leading to the coup and insisting that, at worst, there had been 'excesses' under military rule. At the same time, however, politicians of the *Concertación* itself seldom made use of the Commission's findings and analysis to challenge the Right's framing of public discourse.

25. Only one former President from Chile's long history of elected government is buried anywhere other than the General Cemetery—Gabriel González Videla (president 1946–52), in his native La Serena.

26. P. Aylwin Azócar, *La transición chilena: discursos escogidos, Marzo 1990–1992* (Santiago, 1992), pp. 85–7.

27. Aylwin's remarks in presenting the Rettig Commission report are found in Aylwin, *La transición chilena,* pp. 126–36. After Pinochet's arrest in October 1998, the heads of the different armed forces were publicly supportive of government policy, but Chile has not witnessed any gesture comparable to that of General Martín Balza in Argentina, expressing regret for military responsibility for massive violations of human rights.

28. Arriagada notes that the theme of human rights became an agglutinating force rather than divisive issue within the democratic opposition as it organised for the 1988 plebiscite (*Chile bajo Pinochet,* pp. 246–7).

29. However, Esteban Larraín, a young journalist at the University of Chile, did receive support from the state Fondo del Desarrollo de las Artes y la Cultura for production of his remarkable documentary video, 'Patio 29: historias de silencio' (1998).

30. *La Nación* and *La Epoca,* February 27, 1994. Although the Memorial Wall received public financial support, it also required substantial private funding. A similar 'privatisation' of Chile's efforts to acknowledge its traumatic past is observable in the project to create a 'Park for Peace' on the site of the Villa Grimaldi, a notorious centre of torture and disappearance razed late in the dictatorship. Finally opened in 1996 after heroic private efforts, the Park is more notable for its existence at all than as yet an evocative memorial to collective memory. See *Villa Grimaldi: un parque por la paz* (Santiago, 1996).

31. The cases mentioned in this paper have been prominently and extensively covered in the media. They have selected on the basis of the author's own estimates rather than any scientific analysis of media content. (P. Aguilar-Fernández, *Memoria y olvida de la Guerra Civil española* [Madrid, 1996], pp. 389–434, utilises a methodology that might be applied in Chile.) One recent source of documentation of these issues, including the period of the dictatorship as well as that since 1990, is provided by the Internet site, http://www.derechoschile.com.

32. The escape is recounted by one of those involved, R. Palma Salamanca, in *El gran rescate* (Santiago, 1997), the publication of which evoked bitterly divided commentary. Palma had also been convicted of the assassination of Senator Guzmán and two military officers.

33. In July 1990 a personal conflict between two politicians of the right, Evelyn Matthei and Sebastián Piñera, broke into public view with the disclosure that private telephone conversations had been taped by military intelligence. Cristián Bofill gives a colourful journalistic treatment of the whole episode in *Los muchachos impacientes* (Santiago, 1992). At this early point in the transition, public opinion was stoutly against the continuation of such practices, inherited from the Pinochet dictatorship. See M. A. Garretón, *et al.,* 'Los Chilenos y la Democracia: La opinión pública, 1991–1994, Informe 1992' (Santiago, 1992), pp. 75–8.

34. The 'Pinocheques' case was again also involved (Otano, pp. 306–20). Thus, on several fronts the government was confronted by a crisis expressing the painful past due to the behaviour of public actors—the courts as well as the military—that it could not control.

35. Public opinion data from March to June 1993 shows a sharp decline in favourable responses to the government's handling of relations with the military (48.0 per cent to 27.4 per cent) and of human rights (46.1 per cent to 38.0 per cent); 'Estudio Social y de Opinión Pública no. 20, July 1993', (Santiago, Agosto 1993), p. 52.

36. De Brito, *Human Rights and Democratisation,* pp. 152–88, *passim.*

37. See Garretón, *et al.,* 'Los Chilenos y la Democracia . . . Informe 1993' (Santiago, 1993), pp. 64–6.

38. With the dictatorship under growing international pressure at the time, this case was explicitly exempted from its self-proclaimed 1978 amnesty law. Chile's negotiated transition to democracy entailed acceptance of the legitimacy of this law, which *Concertación* governments were unable to overturn due to the presence of designated Senators and the over-representation of the Right more generally in Congress.

39. Since 1990 governments have attempted, with some success, to promote judges committed to reform and to have cases transferred from military to civilian jurisdiction. On the failure of Chile's courts to protect human rights during the dictatorship, see *Commission on Truth and Reconciliation* and J. Correa Sutil, ' "No Victorious Army Has Ever Been Prosecuted . . .": the Unsettled Story of Transitional Justice in Chile', in A. J. McAdams (ed.), *Transitional Justice and the Rule of Law in New Democracies* (Notre Dame, Indiana, 1997), pp. 123–54.

40. Legal investigation of the Albania case was recently re-opened and, as of December 1998, the alleged perpetrators (members of military intelligence in the period, CNI) have been indicted for murder. *Colonia Dignidad,* a semi-autonomous German settlement in the Chilean south, was a place of detention, torture, and disappearance during the dictatorship. This sinister site was a recurrent news story throughout the whole period since 1990. (It is revealing that, despite having changed its name legally to 'Villa Baviera', the community is regularly described in the media by its old one, which fixes its place in historical memory.) Persistent efforts by the government and courts, with the active support of the German government, have thus far had only limited results in penetrating its presumed secrets.

41. The proceedings against Pinochet in Spain, including the Soria case, are summarised in P. Rojas B., *Tarda pero llega,* which was published in Chile one month before the General's fateful trip to London.

42. Two early appraisals appear in R. Baño (ed.), *Análisis del año 1998* (Santiago, 1999); R. Baño, "La ropa sucia se lava en . . . la medida de lo posible", pp. 11–23, and C. Fuentes, "Cuando lo anormal se convierte en cotidiano: Los militares y la política en Chile (1998)", pp. 59–70. The latter insightfully situates the Pinochet case within the broader evolution of civil-military relations through the eight years of Chile's transition under *Concertación.*

43. Beyond Pinochet's departure from line command in March 1998, the *Concertación*'s steady screening of annual promotions of the different armed services through the 1990s undoubtedly produced an officer corps more amenable to democratic control. During the same week in November as one of the meetings of the National Security Council, General Ricardo Izurieta, Pinochet's successor as Army Commander, announced a new series of retirements that suggest the consolidation of a new officer corps, with few figures associated with past violations of human rights.

44. The political Right, suddenly feeling itself vulnerable by Pinochet's absence from the national scene, turned to expressive politics with a passion. Among many examples, the mock heroism of Mayor Cristián Labbé, a former officer—who refused for some weeks to collect the garbage at the British and Spanish embassies within his Santiago *communa* of Providencia—perhaps best communicates the Right's feelings of frustration and impotence.

45. Although modified in details by subsequent discoveries, journalist Patricia Verdugo provided the basic account of this episode in *Los zarpazos del puma* (Santiago, 1989), which sold more than 100,000 copies and remains Chile's all-time bestseller.

46. Such figures included former President Aylwin (who had made a similar request upon presenting the Rettig Report in 1991), as well as leaders of the political Right, such as the presidential candidate Joaquín Lavín and Senator Sebastián Piñera, whose stances were more cautious but nevertheless reflective of a longer-term goal to move Chile's politics beyond old polarities.

47. See Boeninger, *Democracia en Chile;* Otano, *Crónica;* and Cavallo, *Historía oculta de la transición.* The second volume of President Aylwin's memoirs, at which he is currently at work, will be interesting on this point.

48. J. S. Valenzuela, referring explicitly to Chile in his fine early article on 'Consolidation in Post-Transitional Settings', argued that successful redemocratisations 'require a deliberate effort on the part of the democratising elites to avoid resurrecting symbols, image, conducts, and political programs associated with the conflicts leading to prior breakdown' (Mainwaring *et al.,* eds., *Issues,* p. 79 and footnote 39). Even at this early point, Aylwin was willing to defy this logic in the name of national reconciliation. Chile's 'irruptions' through eight years of elected government suggest the continuing need for democratic leaders to conceive an active policy toward the society's historical memory.

49. 'Con ocasión de los funerales del ex Presidente de Chile, don Salvador Allende G', Santiago, 4 de septiembre de 1990, in Aylwin, *Transición chilena,* p. 85 (my translation).

50. '... [T]he transition has now been accomplished. In Chile we live in democracy'. This was not a slip of the tongue but a conscious political act on Aylwin's part, previously debated within his government. See Otano, *Crónica,* pp. 185–98.

51. In the course of a lucid analysis of the differing meanings given by political scientists to 'democratic consolidation' and their application to current transitions, Andreas Schedler has made the sensible suggestion that the term refer 'to expectations of regime continuity—and to nothing else' ('What is Democratic Consolidation?' *Journal of Democracy,* vol. 9, no. 2 [April 1998], p. 103). Two other major scholarly studies of the question are Mainwaring *et al.* (eds.), *Issues,* and J. J. Linz and A. Stepan, *Problems of Democratic Transition and Consolidation: Southern Europe, South America, and Post-Communist Europe* (Baltimore, Maryland, 1996).

52. Boeninger defended this thesis while he was in the Aylwin government later in his book, *Democracia en Chile* (see pp. 428–33).

53. See J. M. Puryear, *Thinking Politics: Intellectuals and Democracy in Chile, 1973–1988* (Baltimore, Maryland, 1994), esp. pp. 101–59. Cf. Boeninger—a key actor in 'concerting' intellectuals and politicians—in *Democracia en Chile,* pp. 312–40.

54. These groups included the Families of *Detenidos-Desaparecidos* (AFDD), the Defence Committee for People's Rights (CODEPU), and the Social Aid Foundation of the Christian Churches (FASIC). The principal nongovernmental actors for human rights under the dictatorship—the Vicariate of Solidarity, formally disbanded in 1992, and the Chilean Commission for Human Rights—have not catalysed national concern to address issues of historical memory during transitional democracy. The year 1998 has brought some signs that the Catholic Church may become more active in this realm, after the naming of a new Archbishop of Santiago.

55. 'Transitions, Continuities, and Paradoxes' in Mainwaring *et al.* (eds.), *Issues,* pp. 17–56, esp. pp. 18–19, a profound meditation on the unfortunately classic Latin American problem of the *democradura.*

56. *Las suaves cenizas del olvido,* a pathbreaking interpretation of how Chile's elites knit politics back together after major ruptures historically, establishing a repeated pattern of partial accommodation but shaping a culture of forgetfulness. Seen as part of this longer trajectory, many of the features of the contemporary 'conspiracy of consensus' would stem from this deeper characteristic of Chilean political culture. It is an implicit premise of this paper, however, that the rupture represented by the period 1967–90 is deeper and qualitatively different, and that together with the very different global historical context of the 1990s, that difference is expressed in the country's irruptions of memory. Lira and Loveman will deal with this period in a second volume. The Spanish transition suggests that the long passage of time from the

trauma of the Civil War aided democrats in addressing issues of historical memory. See Aguilar Fernández, *Memoria y olvido.* However, it was also assisted by the broader historical context of the 1970s, above all that of European integration.

57. *The Vichy Syndrome: History and Memory in France since 1944,* trans. A. Goldhammer (Cambridge, Massachusetts, 1991 [1990]).

58. *Divided Memory: The Nazi Past in the Two Germanys* (Cambridge, Massachusetts, 1997).

59. Herf, *Divided Memory,* pp. 334–72, *passim.* Herf's interpretation of the contrasting roles of Heuss and the more conservative and pragmatic Chancellor, Konrad Adenauer, is striking. It suggests that utility of the division of public authority between head of state and head of government, as in complementary roles of the King and Prime Minister during the Spanish transition to democracy. As such, it offers support for the scholarly debate over the potential usefulness of parliamentary—as opposed to presidential—systems in creating stable democracies. On these matters, see J. J. Linz and A. Valenzuela, *The Failure of Presidential Democracy* (Baltimore, Maryland, 1994) and Mainwaring and Valenzuela (eds.), *Politics, Society, and Democracy;* C. Huneeus, 'The Pinochet Regime: A Comparative Analysis with the Franco Regime', pp. 71–99; A. Valenzuela, 'The Crisis of Presidentialism in Latin America', pp. 121–39; and S. Mainwaring and M. S. Shugart, 'Juan Linz, Presidentialism, and Democracy: A Critical Appraisal', pp. 141–69.

60. *From Max Weber: Essays in Sociology,* edited and translated by H. H. Gerth and C. W. Mills (New York, 1946), pp. 77–128.

61. In some form, identification with an ethic of responsibility appears with surprising frequency in public statements by the *Concertación* and is particularly clear in its human rights policy. See, for example, José Zalaquett, 'Introduction to the English Edition', *Commission on Truth and Reconciliation,* pp. xxx. Zalaquett, who began developing the relevance of Weber's analysis in a series of paper from the late 1980s, appears to have been a major influence on *Concertación* policy in this area. Chile's long tradition of legalism has been widely noted, and the politicians of the *Concertación* were particularly aware of how badly it had been damaged not only by the Pinochet dictatorship but also by Allende's Popular Unity government, through its notorious use of dubious legal stratagems (*resquicios*) to overcome a Congress in the hands of the opposition.

62. See an initial survey by Louis Bickford, 'Human Rights Archives and Research on Historical Memory: Argentina, Chile, and Uruguay', consultant report, Ford Foundation, Santiago, Chile, 1998.

63. Although not without its expressive aspects, it is noteworthy that the students of the History Institute of Chile's Catholic University organised a daylong conference in March 1998 on 'The History of the Dictatorship'. The History Department of the University of Santiago, in conjunction with an NGO experienced in oral history, has a current project on Chile's historical memory. *El gesto y la palabra,* by A. Joignant (Santiago, 1998), which was received too late for inclusion in this article, is the first sustained study of the expressive dimensions of Chile's return to democracy, concluding in 1990.

64. The International Program of the University of Wisconsin–Madison and the Institute for Latin American and Iberian Studies of Columbia University are currently carrying out multi-year research projects on 'legacies of authoritarianism' in Latin America and other societies. The Social Science Research Council has initiated a three-year research and training project on 'Historical Memory of Repression in the Southern Cone', building on a successful earlier effort to illuminate the 'culture of fear' in this region (J. E. Corradi, *et al.* (eds.), *Fear at the Edge* [Berkeley, California,

1992]). In December 1998 the University of California–San Diego held a large multi-disciplinary conference bringing together scholars from Chile, the USA, and the UK to assess the real achievements of Chile's 'model' transition since 1990 (*Cf.* Drake and Jaksic (eds.), *Struggle for Democracy in Chile: 1982–1990*). University of Wisconsin historian Steve Stern is currently writing a book on Chile's divided historical memories based on in-depth interviews. These complementary efforts all hold promise of catalysing a scholarly field of study relevant to issues raised in this article.

2

Layers of Memories
Twenty Years After in Argentina

Elizabeth Jelin and Susana G. Kaufman

In the midst of deep political conflict and widespread political violence, a military coup took place in Argentina in March 1976. The military government, defining itself as leading a 'Process of National Reorganization', implemented a systematic policy of clandestine repression, including *disappearances* on a massive scale, as the basic policy to handle the political conflict and to wipe out the existing armed political groups. Estimates of disappearances vary, with figures of up to 30,000. Although the military dictatorship lasted from March 1976 until December 1983, repression was harshest during the initial years of the regime.

The purpose of this chapter is to analyse how Argentine society incorporates (or excludes) the memories of its conflicted and painful recent past. It deals not with memories of a war, but with the memories of a period of extreme political violence and of state terrorism. In truth, political and ideological conflict in the early 1970s was extreme in Argentina. There were armed groups on various sides, including a guerrilla movement and paramilitary death-squads. This widespread armed conflict and the military take-over was defined by some as a war, though a 'Dirty War', in which both sides, the leftist guerrilla and the military and paramilitary forces, shared responsibilities. The issue of responsibilities, however, is crucial in alternative interpretations of the period. To talk, as we do, of State Terrorism, i.e. a state apparatus that resorted systematically to terror and repression of citizens and civil institutions without any respect for existing national and international juridical norms, implies a different interpretation of responsibilities and of power relations from the one the military embrace.

Our enquiry is about how memory is produced and constructed. Our goal is to analytically scrutinize processes of reconstructing and rendering meaning

From T. G. Ashplant, Graham Dawson, and Michael Roper, ed., *The Politics of War Memory and Commemoration* (New York: Routledge, 2000), p. 89–110.

to the (diverse, multiple) pasts. It is not an interpretation of what happened in the past, nor the collection of elements (documents, testimonies, 'data') that might help in the societal process of constructing historical memories. Rather than rendering a narrative of the past, we analyse the process of societal remembering (and forgetting), looking at the various *levels* and *layers* in which this takes place. To do this, we first analyse the public/political context in which memory/oblivion of the military dictatorship unfolded, and then present some personal narratives, in which the traces and marks of that past emerge in the development of the life course and in the everyday experiences of people from three generations. Insofar as reality is complex, multiple and contradictory, and that subjective inscriptions of experiences are never a direct mirror-like reflection of public events, one should not expect an 'integration' or 'gelling' of individual and public memories, or the presence of a single memory. There are contradictions, tensions, silences, conflicts, gaps, disjunctions, as well as 'integration'. Social reality is contradictory, full of tensions and conflicts. Memory is not an exception.

For many societal actors in Argentina, the motto *Remember! so as not to repeat!* is a 'given', an unquestionable premise of their lives. In that climate, to carry out critical research is not easy. In the tradition of C. Wright Mills, we attempt to unveil some of the enigmas that emerge at the point of convergence between our personal feelings as involved participants and the public questions and issues that permeate Argentine society. We attempt to do it with analytical depth and rigour, and this leads us to revisit critically our own beliefs and sense of belonging, and at times distance ourselves from those who more forcefully push for memory. Besides the deadening effect of *total memory*—so vividly conveyed in Borges' story of *Funes, el memorioso*[1]—some of the reasons will become clear as we go along.

Argentina: Between Truth, Remembrance and *Nunca Más*

Under the circumstances of the political violence in Argentina in the mid-1970s, a local human rights movement gradually emerged.[2] At first almost in hiding and unseen, then becoming steadily more visible, gaining step by step in political relevance and centrality, the human rights movement and the issues it raised gradually occupied the centre of the political arena. Under the military dictatorship (1976–83) the movement developed a range of activities: supporting victims and their relatives, spreading information to break the imposed silence about the nature and scope of the violations, launching open protests, organizing and promoting international solidarity. The most urgent and immediate task was to stop kidnappings, torture and disappearances, and to free those who had been detained. There was a suspicion that key figures in the government were directly involved in what was going on, but the essence of terror is to create confusion, fear, uncertainty and ambiguity. The systematic and planned nature of repression was not immediately apparent to anybody outside the top decision-making apparatus.

A disappearance is a very special type of wound. What disappears is a human being, a body, but also knowledge and information. Those close to the victim and the human rights movement could only say that something has happened, but could not say clearly what. The first demands on the part of the movement were an insistent claim to know, with some certainty, what had happened in each case. There was a clear recognition of the significance of truth in the process of redress of human rights violations. In this process of searching for the truth, the human rights organizations and their international support network were able to shift the interpretation of what was going on from the military definition as an 'anti-subversive war', to a framework of 'human rights violations', a shift that later allowed the introduction of a juridical dimension into political life.

During the last stage of the military regime (1982–83), information became more public, as testimonial reports of victims were published or otherwise made available. As fear receded and popular moral indignation rose, collective actions geared to denounce and demand became widespread, with street rallies that gathered tens of thousands of people. At that time, the reclamation of the public space came hand in hand with first-hand personal narratives, with claims for life, for justice and for memory (also, with an effervescence of artistic activities devoted to the recent past: theatre, fiction, graphics, paintings). Journalism, including a sensationalist 'horror show' in magazines and on TV, devoted itself to disclosing, to telling, to digging up and excavating the pain of those who could not find a grave or a body.

Within this context of generalized visibility, during the electoral campaign and the inauguration of the democratically elected government in 1983, actions of the human rights movements were geared to secure some form of 'justice' for those who were responsible for repression. Human rights activists and organizations felt the urgency of learning about and publicizing the nature of the massive and systematic violations of human rights during the military dictatorship—the demand for 'truth'—and of seeing that the guilty were punished—the demand for 'justice'. The movement was torn between its political and institutional role, expressed in the demand for justice, and its symbolic role in the construction of a historical memory, which implied actively promoting the need not to forget and developing in different ways and in a variety of settings the symbols and events that would foster the preservation of the vivid memory of the lived traumatic experience.

In 1983, there was no clarity as to what kind of punishment *should* or could be applied. Coupled with the fear that political parties or unions would be ready to compromise and accept amnesties for the military, there were some doubts as to whether any wrongdoing could be established in court—in the event that the new democratic government had the political will to prosecute the military. At that time, there was no clear meaning attached to the demand for justice. On the one hand, the issue involved how to act vis-à-vis the victims, whose rights had to be restored and injuries redressed. This included those directly affected and their relatives, including the abducted children of the disappeared. On the other hand, transition to democracy implies the construction of a new institutional order, one that fully protects the human rights of citizens. How to assure these in the future? What kinds of institutional transformations were needed? On the moral and ideological level, what was the content of the rights to be protected and guaranteed?

One of the key issues of the electoral campaign during 1983 and of the initial governmental decisions was the institutional handling of human rights abuses. The problem of how to 'settle accounts with the past' turned into a critical element in establishing the legitimate rule of law. The elected president, Raúl Alfonsín, took office in December 1983 with an explicit commitment to give an answer to the demands for justice. In his view, however, the political cost of taking the military elite to civilian courts was too great and implied too high a risk for the fragile democratic system. Yet to condone and not to provide any forum for trials was impossible, given the cultural and political climate of the country. The human rights policy of the new government was based on the electoral campaign promise to hold some kind of trials, but also on a desire to limit their scope, as part of the governmental policy towards the military. The proposal was to keep the trials of the military within the realm of military justice.

Human rights activists opposed the decision to prosecute in military courts. The movement wanted civilian courts and a parliamentary commission to investigate repression. The reasoning was that, as elected representatives of the people, legislators would have access to the information in the hands of the military, which would be obliged to provide surviving documents. Such a commission, it was thought, would be able to formulate a political condemnation, a type of punishment that, in spite of it not being in accordance with the juridical procedure, was not irregular. The search was for some sort of legitimate and legal conviction that would serve to reaffirm the basic ethical values of democracy.

The executive acted differently. Instead of a Parliamentary Commission, the investigation was to be conducted by an independent Commission of 'notables' the CONADEP (*Comisión Nacional sobre la Desaparición de Personas*), established immediately after Alfonsín took office, in December 1983. The CONADEP was to receive testimony from relatives of the disappeared and from survivors of the clandestine camps. The Commission set up special offices to collect evidence in several cities. Exiles returned from abroad to testify, and evidence was also taken in embassies abroad. Police and military facilities, as well as clandestine detention centres and cemeteries, were inspected.

The aim of the Commission was not to pass judgement, but to gather detailed information about the fate of the disappeared. At the beginning, there were still some hopes of finding some of the disappeared alive. As it went about its work, the CONADEP became the site of a powerful symbolic indictment of the military dictatorship. Based on the experience and accumulated data of the human rights organizations that had taken it upon themselves to build a data bank on individual cases of abuses and violations, the Commission collected what would become a year later the crucial evidence in the trials of the members of the military juntas.

Its action produced strategic information about repressive techniques and methods. Argentine society learned what had happened. The violations started to become real. Thus, the Commission was an important step towards the moral condemnation of those who were responsible for repression and in the symbolic legitimization of the claims of the victims. Its role was to establish some 'truth'; it was also where the truth could be formally *acknowledged.*

The 50,000 pages of evidence included in the report were presented to the President in September 1984. A special TV programme based on the report, with testimonies of survivors and relatives, was aired at the same time, and the book *Nunca más* (Never Again), with the official report and an annex listing the names of almost 9,000 disappeared, was first published in November 1984. The book soon became a bestseller, and is still being reprinted and distributed widely. As will be seen below when some personal memories are presented, the launching of the book is a benchmark for most people. The book has become part of one's own personal life and recollection.

As could have been expected, it was hard for the general population to realize and believe that these unbelievable stories were part of a very recent and, for most people, silenced past. Many people were 'discovering' what had happened. 'How could I not know what was going on?' was a repeated question. For the victims and their relatives, it was a first step in legitimizing their voice and in having their testimony acknowledged as true. For those who supported the military's 'peace and order', it was a step on their way to perhaps recognizing and condemning the 'excesses'.

The title of the CONADEP report, *Nunca más,* provides a clue to the cultural climate of the country, as well as to the meanings attached to remembrance. That the experience should not be repeated (*Nunca más*) became associated with documenting the 'truth', with collecting a full record of the atrocities the country experienced. In order 'not to repeat', then, one has to keep memory alive: *Remember! so as not to repeat! (Recordar para no repetir)* emerged as the message and the cultural imperative.

The Trial and the Role of Testimony

Is 'moral condemnation' enough? If democracy is about functioning institutions, about rules and about participation, how can moral condemnation be transformed into the foundation of democratic rule? The next stage had to be in a different institutional setting. CONADEP was a way to discover what had happened, to find out and acknowledge the *truth*. Now it was the time to ask for *justice*. The trial of the ex-commanders of the military juntas was a moment of utmost impact (both national and international) of the struggle for human rights in Argentina. The nine junta members who ruled Argentina from 1976 to 1982 were brought to trial in the Federal Court of Appeals in Buenos Aires in 1985.[3] The trial was going to show whether the rule of law could impose itself upon the rule of force. It implied a juridical procedure, with all the rituals and formalities that put the judiciary at the centre of the institutional scene: victims were turned into 'witnesses', repressors became the 'accused', and political actors had to remain 'observers' of the action of judges who presented themselves as 'neutral' authorities, defining the situation according to pre-established legitimate rules.

From a juridical vantage point, the task was almost impossible, not least because it had to use penal legislation geared to homicides to try something more akin to genocide. It had to try persons who had not themselves committed murders, who had not given the orders to commit specific acts of violation of rights of specific persons, but who had organized and ordered massive kidnappings, torture and killings of anonymous individuals. The junta members might not have killed any single person; they might not have given the order to kill individual victims; and yet they were responsible for crimes which they had organized. The strategy of the prosecution was to present evidence (there were more than 800 witnesses) that there was a systematic plan, carried out in all parts of the country following the same method of illegal detentions, torture and disappearances. In spite of the difficulties, after five months of moving testimonies, testimonies of persons who had overcome fears of revenge and the reluctance to reveal publicly shameful and humiliating personal experiences, five of the nine commanders were found guilty.[4]

The construction of juridical proof was based on the testimony of the victims, since military records had mostly been destroyed. This implied the juridical recognition of their voices and their right to talk. In that institutional setting, the harm they had suffered had to be presented according to the legal rules of acceptable evidence. Allowing testimony as proof followed the logic that what cannot be shown (the act of aggression) has to be told, but under precise and controlled conditions, so that what is denounced could be verified. In fact, what is acceptable as juridical proof is bodily injury. Feelings and sufferings cannot be measured and included. During testimony, they had to be suspended. When emotion overtook the witnesses, the judges halted testimony until calm and sanity returned. This intermittent pattern had a very special effect: the hidden message was that, in its full details, in its entirety, the experience could not be told; even less could it be heard.

Testimony in court is still the personal narrative of lived experience, but the juridical framework breaks it into components and pieces: the requirement of personal identification, the pledge to tell the truth, the description of circumstances and relationship with the case. The discourse of the witness had to be detached from experience and transformed into evidence. If disappearance is an experience where there is no law and no rule, where the victim ceases to exist as a subject of rights, the testimony in court (of the victims themselves and of those who had been searching for them) was an insistence on recognition. As one witness (who was himself a victim of disappearance and then jail) expresses it, 'The trial eliminated the spectral nature of the testimonies that were moving around in society. . . . It presented the victims *as human beings,* giving them equal standing with the rest of humanity.'[5]

The outcome of the trial was not only the verdict (in December 1985) condemning the members of the juntas. It was a proof of the systematic nature of repression carried out by the military government, and it implied the collection of a body of information that could become evidence in new indictments of others responsible for repression. Rather than providing a closure to the demand for 'settling accounts with the past' as President Alfonsín had hoped, the verdict of the court actually opened the door for further indictments and trials.[6]

The political temperature rose and, in December 1986, the executive, under mounting pressure from the military, tried to stop further indictments through a Law of *Punto final* (full stop), which placed a 60-day limit on new criminal summonses. Soon after, the government had to take extreme measures to stop further prosecutions. The *Ley de obediencia debida* (Due Obedience Law, in mid-1987) was the final answer for those cases that had not yet reached a verdict. It was in effect an amnesty for most members of the armed forces. The only offences excepted were rape, theft and falsification of civil status (i.e. irregular adoptions). A few years later, in 1989 and 1990, President Menem used his presidential prerogative to grant pardons to free the members of the military juntas who were in jail, as well as other military and some civilians (prosecuted for their participation in armed guerrillas) under prosecution or sentenced and in jail.

The story did not stop there, however. The human rights movement continued to denounce and demand justice (including presentations in international courts), the Mothers of Plaza de Mayo[7] still carry out their weekly rally in the main plaza of Buenos Aires, cases of illegal adoption and the search of the *Abuelas*[8] still keep the judiciary busy. In this connection, the key military

commanders of the Argentine juntas, Videla and Massera, as well as other high
military officers, were arrested in 1998, and charged with responsibility for
the abduction of children born in clandestine detention centres, in several
court cases that the *Abuelas de Plaza de Mayo* have been pushing consistently
over the years.

During the whole period, but with much greater force during the 1990s,
international and diplomatic pressures have been very active. French and
Spanish courts have been investigating the responsibilities of Argentine military in the disappearance of French and Spanish citizens. Other European
countries followed. This led to French courts sentencing (March 1990) to life
imprisonment (in absentia) ex-Captain Astiz, a famous repressor responsible for the disappearances of two French nuns, who could not be convicted
in Argentina because of the indemnity legislation. The Spanish courts have
been receiving testimony from numerous witnesses in their investigations of
violations of human rights in Argentina. The Spanish courts became the centre of international attention with the Pinochet case,[9] a case that has brought
to light the so-called *Operativo Cóndor,* which linked in coordinated joint
actions the repressive military apparatus of the six countries in the Southern
Cone.[10]

Societal Memory, Public Commemorations

In 1995, the year of the tenth anniversary of the trial, the political and cultural scene of Argentina was shaken by a navy officer telling the story of how
repression and disappearances were handled in the navy: aeroplane flights over
the ocean, to throw out prisoners who were still alive but injected with tran-
quilizers. The book that presents his testimony is called *El vuelo* (The Flight).
It was the first time that someone who directly participated in repression confessed what was done and how. There was no tone of repentance or remorse—
just a story to 'set the record straight'. The confession hit the media: newspapers, radio, television shows and magazines carried his story. Relatives of
the disappeared appeared in the media, in the hope that the repressors who
had confessed could give them some clues as to the fate of their disappeared
children. Others denounced government policies that prevented the prosecution of confessed killers. In fact, bits and pieces of information, confessed by
those who were in charge of repression, became part of everyday news in the
country. There was also an institutional response to these confessions. The
army Commander-in-Chief recognized (again, for the first time in the history
of the previous ten years) that the army had committed crimes, and asked the
population for pardon and understanding. His statement was praised in the
international community and in the press, while the navy kept silent, not
admitting anything.

During 1995, the tenth anniversary of the trial was also honoured in Parliament, and societal memory was revived by the publication of many books, films and videos. It is significant also that during that year a new human rights group came to life: HIJOS, the organization of children of the disappeared, now in their early 20s.

The year 1996 marked the twentieth anniversary of the military coup in Argentina. Throughout the year, and particularly during the month of March, the public sphere was occupied by commemorations. It was an opportunity to talk and to tell what had been silenced or forgotten, an occasion where society felt the emotional impact of the testimonies and personalized narratives, the astonishment of listening to stories unknown before, of recognizing what had been denied or moved away from consciousness. People were faced with the 'reality' of re-enacting fears and disturbing feelings, asking themselves how all that happened was possible, while everyday life seemed to go on, maintaining an appearance of normality.

During such moments, the labours of memory become more inclusive and shared, invading everyday life. It is hard work for everybody, on all sides of the controversies, for all people, of different ages and experiences. Facts are reorganized, existing perspectives and schemes of interpretation are shaken, voices of new and old generations ask questions, tell stories, create spaces for interaction, share clues about what they experienced, what they heard, what they silenced before.

Among the events directly connected with collective memory were the initiatives geared to *mark* the physical sites of torture, death and disappearances, mostly clandestine detention camps. Actually, these were attempts to mark the material and 'real' sites where the real and material bodies of people entered the phantom world of fantasy, disappearing. . . . Commemorations of this sort—as well as attempts to establish memorials, museums and monuments—are part of the political struggles in the country. They are political in at least two senses: first, because their installation is always the result of political conflicts and, second, because their existence is a physical reminder of a conflictual past. Those who call for commemoration often find themselves pitted against those who act 'as if nothing has happened here', and against those who may even demand recognition of the 'heroism' and 'patriotism' displayed by the agents of state terrorism. There are also those who 'did not know', who did not see—the bystanders of horror.

Let us look at one such case. In 1995, a project was introduced in the City Council of Buenos Aires, calling for the creation of a 'Museum of Memory', to be housed in the building that during dictatorship was the clandestine detention centre known as *El Olimpo*. This centre operated during 1978–79, in a block (and building) that now houses an automobile registration office of the Federal Police. In March 1996, the councillors who introduced the project reactivated their proposal, calling for the symbolic inauguration of the museum on 22 March (two days before the twentieth anniversary of the military coup). Human rights organizations included this activity in their commemorations, calling for a gathering on 22 March on that site, to collectively paint a mural on the walls of the building, thus marking the symbolic inauguration of the *Museo de la Memoria NUNCA MÁS* (Museum of Memory NEVER AGAIN).

Action, however, does not follow smoothly according to plans. Negotiations among representatives of different political parties and persuasions in City Council dragged on. As one councillor commented, 'If we do not vote on this project this week, when the coup is commemorated, we will never be able to take it out of the drawer.' Boycotting the project, some council members only agreed to vote on a resolution that would *recommend,* rather than *command,* it to the Mayor. Conflict touched also the high ranks of the Federal Police. The response of the head of the Federal Police to the request made by the human rights organizations was: 'If you paint the Olimpo, I have to resign.'

On 22 March, a barrier of a hundred policemen circling the block of the Olimpo was the 'welcome reception' the marchers got when they approached the area. Nearby, the anti-riot armoured trucks were waiting. Police presence in the area indicated that painting the walls of the building would not be possible. The press reported that 'faced with such a display, the 300 people who had gathered in the neighbourhood of Floresta marched around the block once and, on the wet pavement, they managed to paint *"Museo de la memoria NUNCA MÁS"*'.[11] Next day, newspapers included photographs of the police barrier and of a Mother of Plaza de Mayo, breaking the fence and reaching to the wall to place a bouquet of flowers.

In another attempt to mark a site, in August 1997, human rights organizations called for a *Jornada de la memoria,* on the site where the *Club Atlético,* a clandestine detention centre in the centre of the city, once functioned. In fact, this was the second time such a call had taken place. A year earlier, in July 1996, close to 500 people participated in a gathering that included the construction of a papier maché structure of a tree and a public reminder with the faces of victims of repression. On that first occasion, a firebomb placed at night destroyed the tree and the memorial. On the second *Jornada de la memoria,* a plaque remembering the disappeared was set up, the names of the repressors were engraved, and during the commemoration a monument, a 'totem', was collectively constructed on one of the pillars of the highway. During the following night, the plaque was destroyed, the totem was torn down and the engraved names of the repressors were covered with paint.

The struggle for monuments and reminders is currently unfolding in the Argentine political scene. These are initiatives spearheaded by the human rights organizations, with the support of a wide array of social organizations

(labour unions, professional organizations, student and parent school organizations, some churches, some political party groups). There are all kinds of
activities: relatives and friends publish remembrance ads in newspapers, dates
are commemorated, books are published, and names are proposed for streets
and parks. Only rarely are they accepted without controversy or conflict. Societal organizations push, promote and demand. But when these initiatives reach
the governmental level, the lack of political will, the lack of an active 'policy for memory', becomes evident.[12] In fact, very few initiatives to commemorate or remember repression and suffering were approved by the government. Yet, societal actors keep insisting.

What happens when the proposals to locate the act of remembering physically, in a memorial or a monument, fail? When the aim is opposed and
blocked by other social forces, the subjectivity and the will of those women
and men who are struggling for the monument or memorial come out into the
public view, renewing their strength to continue struggling. There is no pause,
no rest, because it has not been 'deposited' anywhere—it has to remain in the
minds and hearts of the people. In a way, the need to turn the unique, personal and nontransferable feelings into public and collective meanings is left
open and active. The unsettling question, one that calls for further comparative and interdisciplinary research, is whether it is possible to 'destroy' that
which people attempt to remember or perpetuate. Doesn't the oblivion that
the opposition/police repression attempt to impose have the paradoxical effect
of multiplying memory and making more real the questions and the debate
about what the society went through in its recent past?[13]

In sum, in the current socio-cultural Argentine context—and we would
claim, in any socio-cultural context—it is impossible to find *one* memory.
There is an active political struggle about meaning, about the meaning of
what went on and also about the meaning of memory itself.[14] Yet the political arena of memory struggles is not simply a confrontation between memory and oblivion. The 'memory camp' is not a unified and homogeneous front.
There are struggles that emerge from the confrontation among different actors
within it: struggles over appropriate means and forms of commemoration,
about the content of what should be remembered publicly, and also about the
legitimacy of different actors to embody memory (the issue of the 'ownership' of memory).[15] Controversies and political conflict about monuments,
museums and memorials are plentiful everywhere, from Bariloche to Berlin.[16]
They are attempts to make statements and affirmations; they are facts and gestures, a materiality with a political, collective, public meaning.[17] They are public and collective, insofar as they convey and affirm a feeling of belonging to
a community, sharing an identity rooted in a tragic and traumatic history.
They may also function as a key to the intergenerational transmission of historical memory, though that transmission and its meaning cannot be guaranteed beforehand.

Layers of Personal Memory

There is no single or easy connecting line between public memory sites and commemorations and personal memory and forgetting. In order to study the way people incorporate in their own lives the experiences of dictatorship in Argentina, we carried out in-depth life-history interviews.[18] Men and women of different social strata and belonging to three birth cohorts were interviewed. There was no claim to statistical representativeness. Rather, the aim was to provide substance, content and meaning to the analytical questions raised. The search for potential interviewees was made through informal networks of colleagues, friends, institutions and NGO activists in working-class neighbourhoods. Within each 'cell' or combination of the three parameters used to define the cases (age, gender and social stratum), the interviewees were selected with a view to increasing as much as possible social diversity (in terms of religion, type of occupational career, family formation patterns, migratory histories and so on). Interviews were recorded, then transcribed and organized so as to allow for multiple readings and approaches.[19]

In the interview narratives, the construction of memory takes on different forms: sometimes a seemingly naive question unleashes anecdotes and remembrances of the times of repression. At other times, memories emerge as major events that were turning points in the life course (experiences of the death of people close to oneself, exile and so on). In some cases the memories of a personal experience with repression are told in such a way that the personal and the historical events of the country are one and the same story. At other times, narratives are much more 'private', with no recognition of the political context.[20]

A first level of personal memory is the 'factual' account of lived experiences:

> J. [a very close relative] was assassinated. He was a political leader; he was kidnapped and then found dead. . . . We had to live for some time away from home, without having been involved in anything . . . just because our names were in his address book. . . . We did everything anyone not involved could do . . . (Horacio)

> They often found bombs at school. . . . The bombs weren't fake, they were real. . . . My mother bought me earplugs the size of a cigarette filter, and I used to take them with me when I went to the park to play with my friends. . . . Every afternoon at three o'clock a siren, like a factory siren but much louder, would blow, and we knew it was time to put our earplugs in because, according to my mother, that was when they would start knocking down walls . . . and with the earplugs, we didn't hear the explosions . . . (Julia)

> One time, in 1975, I had to make an emergency trip to Tucumán because a sister of mine had died. It was a very cold day. I went by plane. She lived in a village . . . so I take a bus, and on the way they stop the bus. . . . With a

kettle, soldiers drinking *mate*. Christ! was it cold! Then a policeman gets on the bus and asks for IDs, 'IDs, IDs'. I take out my ID and show it to him. He asks me what's the matter with me. 'Please don't make me get off the bus . . . I'm a wreck! I'm on my way to bury my sister.' The man ordered everyone back on the bus, and we continued on our way. All this happened to me . . . (Lucía)

When the events happened, Julia was seven years old; Horacio was a young adult of 25; Lucía, around 45. At the time of the interviews (1995–96), Julia, a young woman of middle-class urban background, was engaged in political activism, devoting considerable time to a working-class community centre geared to help women. Horacio was a 44-year-old businessman, married and with two teenage children, devoted to his family's well-being. Lucía was a 65-year-old woman of working-class rural background. She migrated to Buenos Aires in the late 1940s, at the time when the government of Perón developed many welfare policies for the working classes. On her first arrival she became a factory worker, and then worked for many years as an assistant in a physician's private office. She is retired, and never married.

The three of them remember personal experiences, but in a very different fashion. Besides the influence of class membership and gender, age—or rather the moment in their life courses in which these events took place—is a crucial factor that marks the way in which the events were experienced and the meaning they had at the time of their occurrence:

When I was a child, it was *normal* for school to be dismissed because of a bomb alarm. . . . I was 7, and for me, the bad guy was the one who died. . . . During my entire childhood, all this was perfectly normal. I saw the things going on around me through the eyes of a child.

The anecdote I am going to tell you is not funny, *but seen from a child's point of view,* it might seem amusing. . . . I had a schoolmate, a girl who was a friend of mine. I was 8 or 9. This girl lived in a building belonging to the *Prefectura* [Coast Guard]. The building was fifteen stories high, while the one I lived in was ten. . . . One day this girl invited me to her house. 'Come', she said, 'I want to show you what the soldiers keep in a swimming pool inside the barracks.' [Julia lived close to a military post.] Well, I went one afternoon for *la leche* [the children's equivalent of high tea], and inside the pool we saw mannequins which, according to my friend, the soldiers would gather up and take in at night, and then you might see them again the next day, or not see them again for a couple of days. Can you imagine! Of course I told my parents what I'd seen as soon as I got home. My mother's blood pressure went up to 20, and my father forbade me to ever see this girl or go to her house again. Naturally, I couldn't make any sense of what was going on because, as I told you, *things don't seem evil to a child, and neither this girl nor her parents nor anything else seemed evil to me.* (Julia)

During that time, you never knew if the guy next to you was after you or not. . . . You couldn't trust anyone because you never knew what side they were on. . . . I would chat, but never give an opinion. I never said that if someone had been picked up, he must have been guilty of something [*si se lo llevaron, por algo será*]. Nor did I say the opposite ... I was concerned about what was going on ... I tried not to talk much, who knows ... I knew too much or I read between the lines ... I remember in those days reading the newspaper made me sick. I would get dizzy, my blood pressure would drop, and I would start feeling nervous, almost without realizing it ... (Horacio)

after Perón, the military already came. How was that called? De facto governments? They came and went all the time. ... I am a bit forgetful, because after all one's been through, you can't help getting demoralized. (Lucía)

Twenty years have elapsed since these experiences. Subsequent experiences, with temporal distance and more information, allow for reinterpreting and giving new meanings to lived experience. The stage in the life-cycle when the dictatorship took place is crucial in this regard. The key political marker in Lucía's life is Perón's first government (1946–55). In fact, Perón's first presidency is part of her personal life:

[I came to Buenos Aires] in February of '46, the time when Peronism was coming in. It was the frenzy of Peronism. Everybody thought that with Perón things would be great, marvellous. ... I have to recognize that the first Peronist government was truly magnificent. I remember it very clearly, very well. (Lucía)

She repeatedly expresses her strong emotional involvement with that period of Argentine history. What went on after that is part of her 'forgetting' and her 'demoralization'. She confounds dates and places, and has difficulties differentiating violent acts of the military and those committed by the guerrillas. Violence and violations are not strangers to her, but they are incorporated in her life with disbelief and lack of confidence in politics:

We lived through some terrible times between '75, '76, up to 1980. ... One heard so many things ... that a lot of people had been killed, that people disappeared and nobody ever saw them again. ... Did you read that book, *Nunca Más?* I've read some chapters, not all ... I don't take sides. Not in politics, not with governments, not with the military nor anything else for that matter. But there's no doubt that the military did things. You know what politics is like: one person tells you one story, and somebody else tells you another ... (Lucía)

During the dictatorship, Horacio was aware of what was going on. With time, he reinterprets his own feelings and anguish:

I guess it was the sense of powerlessness ... reading things and knowing that much worse things were happening, and somehow one kept on working, living one's life as if it didn't matter. ... Like it was happening somewhere else, not right here to people who could be friends of mine. After a while people I knew began disappearing. And we kept on hearing more and more . . . it was impossible to control the amount of information one took in. Inside me, the information was making me sick. It made me dizzy. While reading the newspaper, my eyes would start to cloud. (Horacio)

For Julia, the search for some meaning in what happened in the country became the leitmotif of her life. She is constantly searching for clues to reinterpret the past, highly aware of her own biography:

Many years later I came to realize. . . . They weren't knocking down walls; they were executing people at that time! And they used the sirens to cover up the gunfire! *But I didn't figure this out until I was much older . . .* I was born during a time when *'No te metás',* 'Mind your own business,' 'Keep your mouth shut,' 'See no evil, hear no evil, speak no evil' were the watchwords . . .

And in another moment of the interview, she locates temporally the stage of 'realizing':

All these things left their mark on me. It showed up not when I was a child, but after I grew up. . . . When I became active in politics. Getting politically involved was like a game for me, like it always is when you're a kid. . . . The book *Nunca Más* had just been launched, and the second edition would come out a year later. I became active in politics, along with some other kids my age. It was very easy to get started, because there was a Radical Party Comité right across the street from school. . . .(Julia)

Actually, most of the interviewees recall the launching of the book *Nunca Más*—whether they read it or not—as a moment when their personal life experience 'touched' the public recognition of human rights violations. The book has become, undoubtedly, a marker for a large part of the population.

When we reach the present, the traces and marks of the experiences that the interviewees went through during the dictatorship are also different. For Lucía, the traces of the military dictatorship of the 1970s seem to fade as one instance in a longer-term perspective, one more case of the political instability and uncertainty that pervaded Argentine history during recent decades. She expresses a sense of living in a threatening environment, insecure and with a lack of protection in relation to her daily life, but also with regard to the political sphere, in sharp contrast with the expectations and hopes that Peronism awakened in her in the 1940s. Horacio suffered the loss of a close relative. The traces are in his fears and in his recurring illnesses. Guilt is a constant mark in his reflective mood, asking himself if he could have done something else or something more. He talks about the fears of the past, of the traces in the present, of the link to his children:

Times were difficult. There was lots of fear. I remember I used to feel afraid when leaving home. Although one appeared calm and composed, one had the feeling that even though one had no involvement. . . . We were marked. I'll be a marked man for the rest of my life. For example, when walking on Libertador, I can't help looking at the ESMA[21] and turning the corner. If I'm on this side of the street, I turn in this direction, and if I'm on the other sidewalk, I turn in the other direction. I can't take my eyes off that building. And these are the things that make me stop and think: Why? Why? Why do I always look? I can't help it; I have no choice. When I'm with my children, I tell them, 'This is where they used to be . . . here's where they killed and made people disappear.' I tell them a little so they'll know what went on. Mainly so they'll know what their parents went through. (Horacio)

Julia is younger. The traces of fear are embodied in her parents:

The words *guerrilla, montonero, revolución* were never spoken at home, they were unnameable; not out of rejection of the people, but out of fear. . . . The years go by, and my dad still hasn't lost that fear. Yesterday there was a student demonstration in the Plaza de Mayo, and my husband was one of the security monitors. . . . And his face appeared in the TV news. Well, my father had a fit! He called, and since we were not at home he left a message on the answering machine: 'How can you do these things? You have to be more careful! It won't be long before you find yourself involved.' It's as if he extracts this image and transports it into the past. Or something like that, right? In other words, the fear is still there.

She saw her childhood experiences as 'normal'. She only began to untangle what had happened later on. And at that time, fear invaded her:

I only began putting together all those stories I told you about what it was like living under the dictatorship in that context [later on], and *when I realized all the horrible things that had gone on, I was invaded by fear!* I even became afraid of being active in the Radical Party. What would happen to me if the military should come and I belonged to a political party? I would be just another disappeared person! I linked those times with what my parents had conveyed to me, the fear, and that is what paralysed so many people for so many years. But then I began to realize that with Alfonsín in power, the military would not come back.

Julia interprets her present and her future in relation to her fears. Her hopes and her energy are put to many diverse activities, all of them related to political and social activism. Her fears are regarding the future:

There are times when I am afraid. But you know what I'm afraid of? Not disappearing. I'm afraid of two things: one is exile, because it could happen, and it would be terrible for me because I'm very nationalistic and love my country and my land very much. To have to leave my friends, my people, my customs, just thinking about it makes me sick. That's one fear. And the other is to disappear without having left anything to show I'd ever been alive. I don't mean a monument or plaque. On the contrary, what I'm talking about are concrete deeds.

For Horacio, personal reflection is centred in his relationships to others, on what one does, or doesn't, and on what one could do for others:

There are many questions one asks about one's life. . . . There are so many things one only realizes later on, and asks, 'How come?' Sometimes I wonder if it is worth looking back. Those times, yes, it was fearful . . . what's left is that sense of fear. . . . I get this feeling of powerlessness, caught between not having done anything and not knowing what I could have done. It's something like what I felt when my dad died and I was left with a feeling of guilt. . . . One tries to say, OK, I have my family, I'm going to protect them. I'm going to do everything I can so nothing goes wrong. At any rate, I have the peace of mind that comes from knowing that I didn't get my neighbour in trouble in order to protect my family. But who knows? I didn't do anything to help my neighbour either. I think I probably belong to the silent majority of the *'No te metás'* [mind your own business]. Nothing ever happened to me. But I still question myself, and above all I want to be honest with myself: I don't think I would have done much if I had known what was going on next door. And I'm not so sure I wouldn't have said *'por algo será'* ('he or she must be guilty of something') like so many other people did when someone was taken away. That's what I ask myself. It's a dilemma that doesn't go away and will never get resolved, I don't know . . . I could look for the right answer, I can say, 'No, I wouldn't have . . .' and rest satisfied. But that's not true. I can't be sure that I wouldn't have . . . I'm not ready to fool myself . . .

These are themes that are not talked about in everyday life. The opportunity to talk and reflect upon offered by the interview situation is recognized by Horacio and Julia:

[The interview] shook everything up inside of me, regarding memories and the past. But it's good to shake things up from time to time because while you reminisce, you remember details you usually forget. The other day I was talking about the interview I had with you with a friend, and in connection with your interview, a lot of memories turned up that you have tucked away without even knowing it . . . (Julia)

What happens is that when I talk to you, it's as if I'm talking to myself. (Horacio)

Actually, it is in these registers of reminiscence and in the way the past is included in the subjectivity of the present, that the 'labours of memory' display their various layers:

- as narratives of facts and remembrances;
- as feelings that are remembered now, and as feelings generated in the act of remembrance during the interview: feelings about people, personal and group silences, and withdrawals;
- as ways in which memory is conveyed intergenerationally: who tells, who listens, who keeps silent;
- as thoughts and reflection about what one has experienced, considering the moment in the life course when this happened, and one's current thoughts about that past;
- as reflections about one's place in the world, about one's own social responsibility.

Some Concluding Remarks: Levels, Layers, Strata of Memory

Memory is an intersubjective relationship, based on the act of transmission and reinterpretation. Even personal memory requires others to remember: it is group support that makes waking life and memory cohesive and structured. *We are never alone.*[22] When given the opportunity to reminisce, people talk as if their memories were there, waiting to be given the opportunity to be expressed in words. The interview, as an intersubjective occasion, takes advantage of this readiness.

But what is forgetting and reminiscing? Reminiscence implies that there was a previous process of engraving, of fixing something in memory. To reminisce involves the forging of a 'new pact' between past and present, taking the remnants of a memory and incorporating them into the way we deal with the present.[23] To forget, on the other hand, does not imply a void or a vacuum. It is the 'presence of the absence', the representation of what was once there and no longer is, the representation of something that has been erased, silenced or denied. In both cases, we are talking about intersubjective experiences. In the words of Luisa Passerini, we are actually dealing with:

> a memory of a memory, a memory that is possible because it evokes another memory. We can remember only thanks to the fact that somebody has remembered before us, that other people in the past have challenged death and terror on the basis of their memory. Remembering has to be conceived as a highly inter-subjective relationship.[24]

Societal forgetting is also a collective intersubjective affair. It implies a societal cleft, a rupture between individual memory and public and/or collective practices (that may become ritualized and repetitious), or a faulty line in the intergenerational process of transmission. The difference between remembering or forgetting events one has experienced in one's own life, and societal memory, then becomes important. Interpretations and explanations of the past cannot be automatically conveyed from one generation to the next, from one period to another, from those who experienced the events to others who did not. As Yerushalmi notes, the past has to be actively transmitted to the next generation, and that generation has to accept that past as meaningful.[25] Good transmitters, but also open receptors, ready to incorporate what is told to them, are needed in order to make sure that understanding of the past will not die with those who experienced it. An active transmission of memory requires fostering a process of identification that can produce a broadening of the 'we', the active subjects of reminiscing. Yet it requires leaving open the door for the processes of reinterpretation, both on the part of the young and of those who were alive at the time but 'did not know what was happening'. Insofar as rendering meaning is an active subjective task, there is no a priori guarantee that a given meaning will result. There is no way to close off new readings of old stories, because the 'same' story and the 'same' truth gain diverse meanings in different contexts and circumstances. And the succession of generations involves, unavoidably, the creation of new contexts. Memory is, in fact, part of the symbolic and political struggle of each time, of each 'present'.

In this chapter, we have dealt with political confrontations over interpretations of the past and about commemorations, and with the various layers of the most personal and even private memories. In them and in between, a variety of confrontations are being played out. Who is the authority to decide what the 'proper' ways to remember are? Who has the right (and the duty) to embody *true* memory? Insofar as official institutionalized channels to recognize the recent past experience of violence and repression in Argentina are very weak, the struggle over the 'truth' of memories, and what are 'proper' memories, is played out in the societal arena. In this arena, there are competing claims. Personal suffering (especially when suffered in one's own body or among close kin) is for many the most significant criterion, indicating a process of essentializing in 'biology' and in the 'body' the legitimacy of the claim to *truth*. Yet, if only those who had a personal experience of suffering are the legitimate voices to express collective memory, the symbolic authority and power they hold can lead to their 'monopolizing' meanings and contents of memory and truth.[26] This power, in turn, may obstruct the mechanisms of societal involvement (the enlargement of the 'us') and of intergenerational transmission of memory, by not allowing for the reinterpretation—in one's own terms—of the meaning of the passed-on experiences. Thus, there is a double historical danger: oblivion and an institutional void on the one hand; ritualized repetition of the horror and tragic history, with no possibility of the creation of new meanings on the other.

When analysing memory, we are dealing with multiple intersubjectivities, multiple transmissions and receptions of partial memories. Fragmented and contradictory, made up of pieces, shreds and patches, of one layer on top of another, of traces and monuments, slips of the tongue and amnesias. When seen in a collective light, as historical memory or tradition, as the process of searching for the roots of identity, the space of memory becomes a space of political struggle. It alludes to the capacity of preserving the past, a capacity that inevitably implies the participation in the struggle for meaning and for power. Collective remembrances become then politically relevant, as an instrument for legitimizing discourses, as tools for drawing boundaries or for enlarging communities of belonging, and as justifications for the action of social movements.

Notes

1. Published in English as 'Funes the Memorious', in J. L. Borges, *Labyrinths* (Harmondsworth: Penguin, 1970), 87–95.

2. A concise analysis of the political process during the military dictatorship and the transition to democracy is to be found in C. Acuña and C. Smulovitz, 'Militares en la transición argentina: del gobierno a la subordinación constitucional', in *Juicio, castigos y memorias: derechos humanos y justicia en la política argentina* (Buenos Aires: Nueva Visión, 1995), 19–99. For the development and strategies of the human rights movement, see E. Jelin, 'La política de la memoria: el movimiento de derechos humanos y la construcción democrática en Argentina', in *Juicio, castigos y memorias,* 101–46. Initially, the human rights movement was a heterogeneous and loosely connected network of relatives of victims, concerned intellectuals and politicians, church-related activists and a variety of other progressive social actors.

3. The civilian Court of Appeals took over jurisdiction from military tribunals when the latter decided that there was not enough evidence to proceed with military trials. This civilian appeal mechanism was part of the reformed Military Code law adopted by Congress soon after the democratic government took office.

4. General Jorge Rafael Videla and Admiral Emilio Massera were given life sentences; General Viola was sentenced to seventeen years in prison; Admiral Lambruschini was given eight years and Brigadier Agosti was sentenced to three years and nine months. The members of the junta that governed between 1979 and 1982 were acquitted because the court found the evidence against them inconclusive.

5. Norberto Liwski, interview at Centro de Estudios de Estado y Sociedad, Oct. 1990.

6. For an analysis of the effects of the verdict, especially its 'Point 30' on further mandatory indictments, see Acuña and Smulovitz, 'Militares en la transición argentina'.

7. The *Madres de Plaza de Mayo* is one of the best-known organizations of relatives of disappeared people. It is composed of mothers of the disappeared, and it has had (and still has) a highly visible role in the demands for justice and redress.

8. The *Abuelas de Plaza de Mayo* is the organization of women who struggle to denounce the disappearance of, search for, identify and recover their grandchildren, namely children who were born in detention camps or who were abducted with their parents. Many of these children have been appropriated by the repressors or given up for illegal adoption. The abduction and falsification of identity are crimes that are not covered by a statute of limitations. Over the years, the *Abuelas* have participated in the recovery of the identity of more than fifty children. Many cases are still under court investigation, and new cases emerge continuously.

9. The request to extradite Pinochet from the United Kingdom to Spain was front-page news after his arrest in October 1998. This case has raised a major debate about the international handling of 'crimes against humanity'.

10. A. Boccia-Paz, '"Operativo Cóndor": un ancestro vergonzoso?', *Cuadernos para el Debate* No. 7, Programa de Investigaciones Socioculturales en el Mercosur (Buenos Aires: Instituto de Desarrollo Economico y Social, 1999), 5–21.

11. *Página/12* (Buenos Aires), 23 March 1996, 5.

12. In 1998, however, the legislature of the City of Buenos Aires approved the creation of a Park of Memory (Parque de la Memoria). During 1998 and 1999, several provincial and city governments were discussing creating museums and documentation centres.

13. Claudia Koonz, 'Between memory and oblivion: concentration camps in German memory', in J. R. Gillis (ed.) *Commemorations: The Politics of National Identity* (Princeton, NJ: Princeton University Press, 1994), 258–80, deals with the debates about memorials in concentration camps in Germany and Eastern Europe, showing that the struggle is intensified, rather than diminished, as time passes and political change takes place in the region. One of the controversies about memorials is whether the construction of traditional monuments and memory sites actually discourages engagement, and how to design new ways (not necessarily sites) that would encourage it.

14. Just to give one clue as to the intensity of the struggle, in August 1997, a new book showed up in news-stands all over the country. *La otra campana del 'Nunca más'*, written by a convicted torturer, Miguel O. Etchecolatz, presents and justifies the repressive measures of the military regime. The book generated a heated public debate that showed the extent of the political conflict, the unreality of 'reconciliation' and the depth of historical wounds.

15. Jelin, 'La política de la memoria'.

16. For instance N. Howe, 'Berlin: monuments and memory', *Dissent* (winter 1998), 71–81.

17. That there are historical (and intercultural) transformations in the ways societies deal with history, memory and commemorations, has been amply documented and researched: Y. Yerushalmi, *Zakhor: Jewish History and Jewish Memory* (Seattle: University of Washington Press, 1989); P. Nora (ed.) *Les Lieux de mémoire* (7 vols, Paris: Gallimard, 1984–92); J. R. Gillis, 'Memory and identity: the history of a relationship', in J. R. Gillis (ed.) *Commemorations*, 3–24. Very little of this tradition of research has reached Latin America.

18. The interviews were collected during 1994–96 as part of the project on 'Rights and Responsibilities: life experiences of citizenship in an emerging democracy', carried out with the support of a Research and Writing Fellowship of the John C. MacArthur and Catherine T. MacArthur Foundation (granted to Elizabeth Jelin in 1994). Marina Elberger participated in the selection of testimonies to be included in this chapter and in their interpretation. As a member of the age-cohort that lived through dictatorship in childhood, the questions she asked and the images she retrieved turned the research process into an intergenerational dialogue. A first interview was designed to elicit a life story, in which each interviewee set the narrative in her/his own parameters and terms. The aim was to get the subject's narrative of her/his family history, including significant links during childhood and adolescence, family involvement in religion, politics and ideology, world-views, educational and political ideals, group belongings. Work experience, and vocational and career issues, were also pursued. A second interview dealt with a more specific set of themes. The guidelines included instances of social participation and views about them (a history of voting behaviour, of encounters with the police and the courts, participation in political and social movements, experiences of social solidarity and so on), and themes of 'historical memory', i.e. experiences and memory of important events in recent Argentine history (including the transition to democracy in 1983, the military coup of 1976, and earlier events).

19. In this chapter, we deal with issues of historical memory of repression. Other published results of the project are to be found in S. Galperin, E. Jelin and S. Kaufman, 'Jóvenes y mundo público', *Investigaciones en psicología: revista del Instituto de Investigaciones de la Facultad de Psicología* (Buenos Aires) 3.1 (1998), 41–53; and in E. Jelin et al., *Vida cotidiana y control institucional en la Argentina de los '90* (Buenos Aires: Nuevo Hacer, 1996).

20. We present here testimonies of a very few interviewees. It was not easy to select the cases to present, since in all interviews there is information that would allow us to show how complex remembering and forgetting is. In subsequent quotations from interviews, all italics are the authors'; the interviewees have been given pseudonyms.

21. ESMA (*Escuela Superior de Mecánica de la Armada*), a large complex of buildings in a very important part of the city of Buenos Aires, was turned into the most important detention camp operated by the navy. It has become the clearest symbol of repression in Argentina. At the beginning of 1998, President Menem proposed tearing down the buildings and constructing a 'Monument for Argentine Unity and Reconciliation' on the site. His suggestion was greeted with the utmost criticism and opposition by almost everybody. There is also an initiative to turn the buildings into a Museum of the Memory of Repression.

22. M. Halbwachs, *On Collective Memory* (1941, 1952; Chicago and London: University of Chicago Press, 1992).

23. 'Reminiscence is the result of a psychic process that consists of working with the remnants of a memory, of a dream or a ghost, so as to build a new compromise between what the past that was lived and experienced by the subject and his/her current way of handling that past, what s/he can tolerate ignoring or knowing about it.' M. Enriquez, 'La envoltura de memoria y sus huecos', in D. Anzier (ed.) *Las envolturas psíquicas* (Buenos Aires: Amorrortu, 1990), 121; our translation.

24. L. Passerini, 'Introduction', in L. Passerini (ed.) *Memory and Totalitarianism* (Oxford: Oxford University Press, 1992), 2.

25. Yerushalmi, *Zakhor.*

26. Symbols of personal pain tend to be embodied in women—the Mothers and Grandmothers in the case of Argentina—while institutional mechanisms seem to 'belong' more often to males. The significance of this gender-related dimension of the issues involved, and the difficulties of breaking the gender-typing of roles and power resources require further attention. Further research should also delve into the significance, in the human rights movement and in society at large, of claims for truth based on suffering, and of the imagery of the family and family relations (J. Filc, *Entre el parentesco y la política: familia y dictadura, 1976–1983* [Buenos Aires: Editorial Biblos, 1997]), in the process of construction of a culture of citizenship and equality.

3

The Unmaking of
Rigoberta Menchú

Hal Cohen

When neoconservative pundit David Horowitz saw the book, he leaped into action. In his *Salon* magazine column, Horowitz touted Middlebury College anthropologist David Stoll's *Rigoberta Menchú and the Story of All Poor Guatemalans* (Westview, 1998) as a ground-breaking assault on multiculturalism, political correctness, and the academic and political left. "The story of Rigoberta Menchú, a Quiché Mayan from Guatemala whose autobiography catapulted her to international fame, won her the Nobel Peace Prize and made her an international emblem of the dispossessed indigenous peoples of the Western Hemisphere and their attempt to rebel against the oppression of European conquerors, has now been exposed as a political fabrication, a tissue of lies," he wrote in January. "The fictional story of Rigoberta Menchú is a piece of communist propaganda designed to incite hatred of Europeans and Westerners and the societies they have built, and to build support for communist and terrorist organizations at war with the democracies of the West."

The right-wing press, from the serious (*The Wall Street Journal*) to the not-so-serious (*The New York Post*), was quick to adopt Horowitz's opinions as its own. With the assistance of a front-page *New York Times* investigation, Stoll's book had apparently established that the story of Rigoberta's political awakening, her transformation from illiterate peasant girl to brutalized and outraged leftist, as recorded in her widely taught autobiographical narrative, *I, Rigoberta Menchú* (Verso, 1983), failed to meet basic journalistic standards of truth. Thus was the credibility of Guatemala's most famous oppressed person—as well as the credibility of the left-wing academics who enthusiastically promoted her *testimonio* in their classes—thoroughly undermined.

From *Lingua Franca* (July/August 1999): 48–55. © 1999 by *Lingua Franca*. Reprinted with the permission of *Lingua Franca*: The Review of Academic Life, published in New York. www.linguafranca.com

Since the publication of Stoll's book in November 1998, the Menchú affair has become a complex jumble of disputed facts and alleged motives. This much, however, is clear: Many of Stoll's admirers appear not to have read his book. If they had, they would have noticed that the anthropologist offers a considerably more nuanced picture of Rigoberta than his champions in the conservative media allow. For Stoll, "There is no doubt about the most important points: that a dictatorship massacred thousands of indigenous peasants, that the victims included half of Rigoberta's immediate family ... and that she joined a revolutionary movement to liberate her country."

Stoll has reason to be exasperated by the right's appropriation of his work. "Menchú is unquestionably the victim of political violence," he insists. "To call her a liar is simply inappropriate." But even as he labors to disassociate himself from his right-wing admirers—with letters to editors, explications of his argument, endless defenses to colleagues—Latin Americanist scholars and human-rights activists accuse him of hidden agendas, factual errors, and even complicity with the Guatemalan military.

Stoll says he set out to honor a venerable anthropological imperative: to grant ordinary Maya voices of their own and to correct the distorted images of indigenous peoples promulgated by ideologues of both left and right. And yet, in writing *Rigoberta Menchú and the Story of All Poor Guatemalans,* Stoll has ended up bringing nearly as much suspicion on himself as he has on Rigoberta and her guerrilla allies.

David Stoll's current notoriety marks a dramatic change for a man whose career has been spent largely pursuing subjects of interest to a select group of Latin Americanists. After graduating from the University of Michigan in 1974, he took a job with a now defunct weekly, the *Ann Arbor Sun.* After about a year, he left and traveled around Latin America gathering information on the then all-but-untouched subject of Protestantism in the region, which would become the focus of his first two books. (Stoll himself is a "lapsed Catholic.") These books, *Fishers of Men or Founders of Empire?* (1982) and *Is Latin America Turning Protestant?* (1990), established two Stoll trademarks: his contrarian streak—he looked critically but sympathetically at the Latin American evangelicals whom most had written off as CIA dupes—and his markedly journalistic tone and methodology. In his second book, Stoll laid the groundwork for his later thinking, arguing that Indians saw Protestantism as an alternative to both the brutality of the military government and the Roman Catholic liberation theology espoused by guerrilla supporters. In 1985, Stoll enrolled in the anthropology department at Stanford University; after completing his dissertation, in the early 1990s, he received various fellowships before becoming an assistant professor at Middlebury College in 1997.

Stoll's dissertation assessed the difficult predicament of the Mayan Indians during the Guatemalan civil war. The war, which had been smoldering in

Guatemalan cities since a CIA-sponsored coup toppled a moderate left government in 1954, ripped through the rural highlands in the late 1970s and early 1980s. Guided by counterinsurgency advisers from the United States and other countries, the army subverted the Marxist-Leninist guerrillas by undermining their potential support: the rural Maya. Through a policy euphemistically termed rural pacification, the army neutralized these Indians. Towns and cropland were destroyed and the peasants relocated to "model villages" reminiscent of Vietnam's "strategic hamlets." Indians were recruited into army-organized civil patrols, and those suspected of ties to the guerrillas were severely punished. In the process of "pacifying" the Maya, the army adopted a policy of crushing and often indiscriminate terror, while the guerrillas—hopelessly overextended and outgunned—could offer little protection. By the time a peace accord was signed in 1996, some 200,000 people had been killed. The vast majority of them, according to several recent human-rights reports conducted by the Roman Catholic Church, U.S. monitors, and the UN's Commission for Historical Clarification, were Maya Indians, noncombatants killed by the army.

In 1988 and 1989 Stoll did fieldwork in Guatemala's Ixil Triangle, a remote area that had suffered frequent and particularly bloody conflict between the guerrillas and the army in the early 1980s. Stoll found that the Indians were hardly committed. The Maya—who account for about half of Guatemala's ten million people—were indeed poor, oppressed, and almost completely excluded from the urban ladino (white or mixed-blood) class that held power. But the Indians also possessed complex societies of their own: They were more attached to their local and linguistic communities than to any externally-assigned "Maya" identity, they were modernizing and attempting to create political space for themselves, and they had many tiers of status, wealth, and property ownership within their communities.

Stoll's dissertation, revised and published as *Between Two Armies in the Ixil Towns of Guatemala* (Columbia, 1993), contended that while many Maya had indeed supported the guerrillas, they had either been coerced to do so or simply determined that, compared with the homicidal army, the leftists were the lesser of two evils. When armed outsiders appeared in the highlands in the late 1970s, Stoll suggested, existing divisions in Ixil society—family conflicts, status disputes, intervillage tensions—exploded into violence. Both the guerrillas and the army exploited these rifts, and both used brutality and intimidation to do so: The guerrillas hoped to increase their numbers and materiel support, while the army tried to impose neutrality on the Indians. But it was the Maya—caught between two armies—who really lost.

In June 1989, while conducting his dissertation research, Stoll stumbled on a revelation that would eventually inspire his book on Rigoberta. In her *testimonio,* Rigoberta relates the powerful story of her brother's brutal death. She describes how her brother, who had been abducted weeks earlier by the

army, was taken with other prisoners to the central square of a town called
Chajul. There, while Rigoberta watched, army officers doused the prisoners
with gasoline and burned them alive. While researching in Chajul, Stoll asked
several villagers about the event. No one, they insisted, had ever been burned
alive in the town square.

At the time, Stoll put this information aside. "I did what any sensible graduate student would do," he writes, "I dropped the subject and scuttled back to
my dissertation." But Stoll had become suspicious, and he decided to look further into the matter. "It was only later, back in the United States, that I realized I would have to face the authority of Rigoberta's story. An unimportant
discrepancy, over how her brother died in Chajul, was the first sign of a more
significant one: the considerable gap between the voices of revolutionary commitment incarnated by Rigoberta and the peasant voices I was listening to."

On the rare occasion when Stoll did talk about what he had found, he did
so off the record. But at the 1991 Latin American Studies Association conference in Washington, D.C., a literary critic and friend of Rigoberta's made his
findings public. "Reactions were horrified," Stoll says. The field of Latin American studies is, by and large, deeply sympathetic to Latin American guerrilla
movements and indigenous peoples, and it was certainly sympathetic to Rigoberta. Everyone understood that *I, Rigoberta Menchú* was a highly politicized
account, but at the same time it was treated with kid gloves by those reluctant
to deny Rigoberta a voice. She had become such a powerful and persuasive
symbol of indigenous resistance and integrity to many of these scholars that a
challenge to her credibility, however small, was inconceivable.

From Stoll's perspective, this brook-no-criticism reverence was perni-
cious: "Her version of events has been so attractive for well-intentioned foreigners that it has overshadowed other peasant, Maya perspectives," he says.
Stoll was concerned that Rigoberta's account—in which the Indians find their
land appropriated by ladinos and are forced into seasonal wage labor, thus
making them natural allies of the guerrillas—served the political interests of
the left while ignoring those of the Maya, whose own political organizations
remained at arm's length from the guerrillas. Certainly Rigoberta's story flatly
contradicted Stoll's belief that the Maya were caught between two armies.
Now that Stoll knew that at least part of it was patently untrue, he set out to
put the record straight. Although colleagues told him that continuing his investigation would be professional suicide, Stoll decided that a reckoning was necessary: Rigoberta had to be brought down to earth.

Over the next several years, he spent considerable stretches of time in the
area where Rigoberta grew up. He interviewed more than 120 people, either
in Spanish or—with the help of Barbara Bocek, a Stanford-trained anthropologist who was doing rural development work as well as researching peasant reactions to the war—in the local language, K'iche'. What he learned contradicted in sometimes dramatic ways many of the details of *I, Rigoberta*

Menchú. In 1997 Stoll completed his manuscript and sent it to Rigoberta. He got no response.

At the same time, Rigoberta, perhaps out of concern over Stoll's investigation, began to distance herself from the book that ostensibly contained her life story. She had not actually authored *I, Rigoberta Menchú,* she pointed out. She had dictated her story to an anthropologist, who had subsequently edited the transcripts (and quarreled with Rigoberta over the profits). As published, Rigoberta declared in 1997, the finished product "does not belong to me morally, politically, or economically." Then, in *Crossing Borders* (Verso, 1998), Rigoberta took further pains to modify some of her biographical details already in print.

At this point, Stoll could not find anyone who wanted to publish his book. He says that one editor informed him that the topic was not worthy of an academic press and that he "should try *Vogue* magazine." Columbia and California (which had published earlier books by Stoll) and Stanford (his alma mater) turned him down, despite his previous books' relatively strong sales and the virtual guarantee of an even better performance by the controversial new work. Finally, Westview, a Boulder, Colorado–based academic imprint, agreed to take the book on. It was the thirty-first publisher Stoll had approached.

So what had Stoll said? His central argument (which no one refutes) was that *I, Rigoberta Menchú* is an intensely political document designed with ideological objectives in mind—specifically, bringing international attention to widespread human-rights abuses in Guatemala and generating support for the leftist opposition there. To do this, Rigoberta presented herself as an Every-Maya, incorporating the experiences of others into her own story. She witnessed events she could not have seen and suffered injustices she could not have known firsthand. Rigoberta presented her family as the impoverished victims of ruthless, government-backed ladino landowners. Stoll found out that Rigoberta's father was not a poor peasant who was radicalized by his quarrels with rich ladinos but a relatively well-off farmer who cultivated his land with help from Peace Corps advisers. Nor was Rigoberta completely uneducated, as she claimed: Stoll discovered that she had attended a Catholic school in Guatemala City. Furthermore, her schooling, according to Stoll's figuring, would have made it highly unlikely for her to have worked on the coastal farms, as she had recounted.

More generally, Stoll charged that Rigoberta's distortions served the purposes of a Marxist-Leninist guerrilla movement that did not necessarily take the interests of rural indigenous people to heart. By "making armed struggle sound like an inevitable reaction to oppression, at a time when Mayas were desperate to escape the violence," Stoll alleged, "*I, Rigoberta Menchú* became a way to mobilize foreign support for a wounded, retreating insurgency." In the mid-80s, the leftists refused to stop fighting a war that they had already lost, callously knowing that the Maya were the ones suffering the property destruction and casualties. Just as pointedly, Stoll insisted that the left bore considerable responsibility for starting the rural violence in the late 1970s and that the army was essentially reacting—albeit with brutal excess—to the guerrillas.

These stances did little to endear Stoll to solidarity and human-rights activists who saw the guerrillas, for all their brutality, as the only plausible counterweight to a national security–obsessed terrorist state. Rigoberta, for all her shortcomings, was seen as almost single-handedly responsible for bringing international attention to Guatemala's human-rights record and thus for the pressure that eventually brought about the UN-brokered peace accord. Stoll had taken a bold risk: He wished to challenge the assumptions and worldviews of human-rights activists and guerrilla sympathizers without challenging their belief that the army was responsible for most of the actual killing. Of course, the left's case against the government was largely made in terms of "structural violence"—militarization of power, refusal to grant the opposition any political space, institutionalized economic disparity—while Stoll focused on the more specific matter of who fired the first shots in the rural highlands. In the polarized world of Latin American academics and politics, it was perhaps inevitable that the details and subtleties of Stoll's arguments would be drowned out by louder voices (his own included).

Last fall, in an effort to assuage Stoll's early concerns about "giving ammunition to the enemy," Westview sent out review copies of *Rigoberta Menchú and the Story of All Poor Guatemalans* to a selective audience that did not include the right-wing press. At the same time, Stoll authored a provocative, anti-P.C. polemic for the book's dust jacket that was virtually tailormade for conservative writers. And in the book's splashy and excerpt-friendly preface and final chapter, Stoll departed significantly from his stated purpose of reexamining *I, Rigoberta Menchú*. He waxed at some length about his categorical opposition to armed guerrilla movements and his extreme distaste for their romantic leftist allies abroad.

The only response to Westview's publicity campaign was from Larry Rohter, the Latin American bureau chief of *The New York Times*. Rohter did his own independent investigation using Stoll's sources and others. His research confirmed Stoll's claims about Rigoberta. Faced with the threat of a publicity nightmare, Rigoberta—in statements peppered with denunciations of the racist campaign to "make liars of all the victims" and protestations that concentrating on the "little details" of her life was undignified—conceded that some of the charges leveled at her story were indeed true, offered alternate explanations for others, and ignored the rest.

In the academic world and the human rights community, Stoll's enemies are numerous and highly vocal. Arturo Arias, a Guatemalan novelist who teaches cultural studies at San Francisco State University, has led the charge. "Stoll did a reductive analysis," says Arias, who is editing a collection on the subject titled *The Properties of Words: Rigoberta Menchú, David Stoll, and Identity Politics in Latin America* that is tentatively scheduled for publication by the University of Minnesota Press in early 2000. "And now everything Rigoberta's *testimonio* defends becomes tainted, and it becomes the basis for undermining the credibility of what happened—genocide, massacres, personal losses for many people. It became a whitewashing of history that is similar to discourses that deny the Holocaust." (Ironically, Stoll's rebuttal to his right-wing "allies" at *The New York Post* took the same tack, suggesting that the paper's downplaying of the Guatemalan military's crimes verged on "the Central American equivalent of Holocaust denial.")

In the monthly column he writes for *El Periódico de Guatemala*, Arias is especially unforgiving. "Only the stupid gringos of the right or left—Puritans all—could really believe that what they were seeing [in *I, Rigoberta Menchú*] was absolute truth," he fumed in January 1999. "The defense is not to analyze the nature of the text itself to confirm supposed 'truths' or 'lies' as if this were a courtroom TV drama, but rather, to question why [we] grant more credibility to the prejudiced Protestant opinion of a third-person anthropologist who is male, white, tall, and gringo, than to a Nobel laureate with a proven record of dedication in defense of the oppressed, whose only sin is to be female, short, of color, and Guatemalan."

Arias fulminates that "for Stoll the Mayas are essentially objects, not human beings. Stoll would not care a whit if all the Mayas died of hunger, or if they disappeared off the map. For him what matters is (1) to figure as a 'public intellectual' despite his mediocre academic credentials, (2) to guarantee the defeat of Marxism and socialism in general, and the [Guatemalan guerrillas] in particular, and (3) to advance his Protestant crusade." But Arias's most far-flung accusation is that Stoll "interrogated—excuse me, 'interviewed'—informants in the presence of armed soldiers." (Stoll vehemently denies this, and Barbara Bocek—Stoll's traveling companion—says categorically, "There was no involvement, authorization, assistance, or oversight at any time by anyone from the armed forces.") However spurious, such charges have found some purchase on the Guatemalan left because of the widespread perception that the military and its defenders feel vindicated by Stoll's book.

Many North American scholars are no less critical of Stoll. His work on both the Maya and Rigoberta depends heavily on interviews conducted as an outsider, a strategy that reminds academics of his journalistic background and raises the suspicions of anthropologists who prefer to rely on observation and immersion in a culture. But even granting the validity of the interviews, many scholars are concerned about how much time Stoll spent with his subjects, how he presented himself, and how well he understood the way Maya speak—or do not speak—about the violence. Paul Yamauchi, a sociology Ph.D. candidate at Cornell and the founder and former director of the

International Center for Human Rights Research, spent ten years studying human-rights abuses and has conducted thousands of interviews with both Maya and ladinos. "I am horrified to see what Stoll did," he says. His practice of conducting interviews in a *pensión* that he himself describes as a "ladino and gringo-controlled environment," his admitted lack of familiarity with "the intimate details of [village] life," and his failure to work "in the native tongue of most of the population" all conspire, Yamauchi argues, to undermine Stoll's supposedly objective results. Furthermore, Yamauchi contends that Stoll's lack of familiarity with Maya social conduct led him to do his interviews in public spaces, a fatal error in his research. "No one will give you accurate information about how they feel unless you meet in secrecy," Yamauchi says. "In my experience, anyone who is interviewed in a public space will say they were not for the guerrillas or the army—exactly Stoll's thesis."

Carlota McAllister, a Johns Hopkins graduate student who has recently completed two years of fieldwork in Guatemala, seconds this claim. "It is impossible to ask a more loaded question in the Guatemalan highlands than 'To what degree did you willingly support the guerrillas?' Not least because it's the question soldiers would ask prior to beginning a massacre or a torture session," she says. "In my community, the same people can easily give me ten radically different answers to that question, depending on how I ask them and how well they know me. Stoll's big thing is 'just the facts,' but he confuses people's subsequent interpretations of their experience with strictly referential statements." On points of interpretation such as these, Stoll acknowledges that there is only so much any outsider can know—a problem compounded by the fact that anyone who was available to talk to him had reached some sort of accommodation with the army. "I did the best I could do," he says.

There are other problems with Stoll's argument, problems that do not require any specialized knowledge to spot. For example, Stoll notes with regret that there is little documentation for many of the statements he sought to confirm, then goes on to cite that very lack of evidence as a symptom of a falsehood. Stoll allows that in guerrilla warfare, inevitably, "the main source of knowledge is rumor." But to contend that Rigoberta's father was not the peasant leader and activist that Rigoberta claims, Stoll writes, "If there is a single publication that claims [her father] as a member, I have yet to find it."

Furthermore, the broad claims in Stoll's conclusion rely on some sleight of hand. He is eager to make sweeping statements about the nature of rural insurgencies ("at bottom rural guerrilla strategies are an urban romance, a myth propounded by middle-class radicals who dream of finding true solidarity in the countryside"), the international left ("it is time to face the fact that guerrilla strategies are far more likely to kill off the left than build it"), and Guatemalan society ("Guatemalans are also less likely [than Menchú's foreign admirers] to feel the need to vindicate the left's tradition of armed struggle, just as few of them wish to justify the Guatemalan right's history of repression"). But evidence for these speculative claims eludes him: His book, after all, is a study of a particular region.

If Stoll's book has prompted an avalanche of criticism from Latin Americanists, it has earned the cautious support of other scholars. Most notable among them is Dartmouth College's John Watanabe, a cultural anthropologist who has shuttled back and forth between the United States and Guatemala for twenty years and whose research and analysis are respectfully cited by everyone from Arturo Arias to Stoll himself.

Watanabe basically agrees with Stoll's between-two-armies thesis, and has few doubts as to why Stoll has taken so much heat: "The left denounces Stoll's book and Stoll personally, because he has gored their sacred cow of a heroic revolutionary guerrilla-fighter-cum-martyr." The critics, he says, discount the possibility that in the late 1970s armed insurgency was not the only option and that it was the violence itself that closed off whatever nonviolent alternatives were available. Watanabe also takes issue with the sanctimonious tone of much of the criticism, saying, "I find it ironic that some who would stand by Ms. Menchú's narrative, right or wrong, in the name of multiculturalism would be the first to suspect such an authoritative, homogeneous voice in the work of a colleague."

More substantively, Watanabe believes that there is a basic misunderstanding at work. He thinks that Stoll's critics are mistakenly applying their knowledge of Guatemala's urban guerrilla conflicts to a rural context. "The injustices and repression against organizing, let alone mobilizing, the urban poor and the powerless go back a long way," he explains, "and the guerrilla movements arising in the early 1960s most certainly did not start the killing, much less provoke the repression. For urban leftists who have this history in mind, to hear anyone say that the guerrillas 'started' the violence anywhere in Guatemala amounts to blasphemy. Indeed, this viewpoint is what made Rigoberta's *testimonio* so powerful and persuasive to the left and its supporters: It related a parallel rural experience of inequality, injustice, violence, and political radicalization that mirrors their own largely urban experience."

Robert Carlsen of the University of Colorado at Denver sees a significance to Stoll's book that has been lost on both its friends and foes: "Had his critics really read the book, they could realize that Stoll actually casts Menchú in a sympathetic light." Carlsen, whose fieldwork also essentially concurs with the between-two-armies thesis, is further frustrated by leftist attacks and rightist celebrations because "lost in all the critiques of Stoll's new book is the fact that it is the most damning tome to date on the Guatemalan army." As Stoll explains, "What I heard [in Guatemala] was almost more awful than what so many have read in [*I, Rigoberta Menchú*], where at least campesinos die for a cause that is their own. What I heard about was a preemptive slaughter of peasants who had little or nothing to do with the guerrillas."

Even those sympathetic to Stoll take occasional issue with him, often noting his confrontational and journalistic tone. Watanabe wonders at Stoll's "readiness to bait the left," while Carlsen says, with a politic smirk, Stoll "might have been advised to frame his arguments in less polemical ways." And to a person, everyone feels that the timing of Stoll's book—intentional or not—was awful. At the moment when the February 1999 UN report was about to hold the Guatemalan military accountable for its genocidal policies, why encourage the media to give Rigoberta's personal deceptions equal billing?

Unlikely as it may seem, Holocaust studies may provide a useful counterpoint to the Guatemalan case. An entire subfield of academic criticism has emerged in the last decade or so that focuses on the construction of memory in Holocaust testimonies. Discussing Holocaust survivors, Primo Levi wrote in *The Drowned and the Saved:* "The greater part of the witnesses . . . have ever more blurred and stylized memories, often, unbeknownst to them, influenced by information gained from later readings or the stories of others." Few, if any, mainstream Holocaust scholars find such arguments threatening, because none of these critics questions the basic facts of the Holocaust (just as Stoll does not question the basic facts of the Guatemalan violence). If, however, someone were to devote years of research to finding factual lapses in the iconic Holocaust survival narrative of, say, an Elie Wiesel, the controversy would be considerable.

Guatemalan studies is clearly a different case. The country's nightmare is not yet a generation in the past, and its perpetrators still exert a good deal of power. But the parallel is instructive: Is Stoll offering objective context to subjective memory to understand better what took place, or is he gratuitously smearing an essential symbol of terrible crimes? "I don't like Rigoberta; I never have," says Jorge Castañeda, a leading Mexican intellectual and the author of *Utopia Unarmed,* a landmark history of Latin America's revolutionary left. "But she's a symbol for some things—for the right and the wrong reasons—and those things are important, and they don't have a hell of a lot of symbols. Peasants. Indians. Women. Peasant Indian women. And I just don't see the need to do a hatchet job on all of that."

Then again, does an icon of Rigoberta's celebrity and influence perhaps require our scrutiny all the more? "That a valuable symbol can be misleading is the paradox that obliged me to write this book," Stoll contends. "In Guatemala, much of what needs to be debated about the last half century of revolution and counterrevolution, bloodshed and peace-making, is still wrapped up in symbols that prevent frank discussion." Moreover, he says, "The air of sacrilege about questioning the reliability of *I, Rigoberta Menchú* gives us reasons to do so."

Watanabe agrees. "I ceased teaching [*I, Rigoberta Menchú*] a number of years ago," he says, "precisely because I found that it rang true for students for all the wrong reasons, by playing on their romanticized stereotypes. Her story had the power to erase an entire term's discussion of the more complex ways in which [Indian] communities could be both cooperative and divisive. Stoll's book serves not simply to expose untruths told, but to ask why we find her truths so compelling."

While his detractors contend that by debunking Rigoberta, Stoll is denying the Maya a voice, his defenders claim the opposite: "It seems to me," says Barbara Bocek, "that he is the one arguing that all indigenous people, not just famous ones, have agency and authenticity." As Stoll himself says, "Obviously, Rigoberta is a legitimate Maya voice. So are all the young Maya who want to move to Los Angeles or Houston. So is the man with a large family who owns three worn-out acres and wants me to buy him a chain saw so he can cut down the last forest more quickly."

Stoll contends that Rigoberta embodies a neoromantic notion of an Indian: a subaltern noble savage. In the academic left's eagerness to amplify her voice, it—and she—has refashioned her identity to fit its needs. Those needs, in Stoll's view, primarily involve bolstering the misguided cause of Ché Guevara–style revolutionary violence. Says Stoll, *I, Rigoberta Menchú* "enshrined a rationale for guerrilla warfare that continues to enchant the latte left long after it lost its appeal in rural Guatemala." Stoll goes so far as to offer his work as a political corrective: "Facing the limitations of *I, Rigoberta Menchú* will, I hope, help the Latin American left and its foreign supporters escape from the captivity of Guevarismo."

Ultimately, Stoll's most powerful thesis—and his most troubling one—is that the Indians were trapped between two armies. In many respects, it's an attractive idea, one grounded in empirical detachment and offered in profound sympathy with war's innocent victims. The Vietnamese soldiers of the 1950s who yearn to go back to their farms and raise rice in Graham Greene's novel *The Quiet American,* the Central American peasants who suffer at the hands of guerrillas and army alike in John Sayles's film *Men With Guns,* and the dispossessed West Bank Palestinians in David Grossman's reportage *The Yellow Wind* are all caught between two armies. It is Stoll's allegiance to this thesis that underpins everything in *Rigoberta Menchú and the Story of All Poor Guatemalans,* and it is what makes his book more than an exposé of Rigoberta's inaccuracies. To the contrary: His certainty that the Maya were tragically manipulated encourages him to extrapolate his case studies—whether in the Ixil Triangle or of Rigoberta's life—into a universal parable of political error.

But if the between-two-armies thesis can reveal crucial and neglected facts, it can also be used to obscure injustice and brutality. A Guatemalan army officer once said of the violence, "The poor Indians, they didn't get involved

in anything. They were between two armies." Stoll never acknowledges that
the government helped to create the Mayas' unhappy predicament, and his failure in this regard is easy to read as a tacit endorsement of the status quo. Castañeda—himself a vocal critic of both Rigoberta and the revolutionary left—
puts it this way: "Stoll might be right. The Indians might have been caught
between two armies." But this political stance, he says, "comes from the right.
You had thirty—not to say five hundred—years of the rulers beating the shit
out of the Indians. And the left tried to help the Indians, and the right fought
back very intelligently and made it clear to the Indians that the cost would be
horrible. What is missing from Stoll is the realization that in a guerrilla war,
counterinsurgency strategy is precisely to place noncombatants between two
armies. It's exactly what you're after."

It is Stoll's refusal—however noble his intentions—to consider the political context of his words that has most frustrated his enemies and even some
of his potential allies. Most academics aspire to a level of detachment; they
wish to critique left and right and, in so doing, rise above politics. But Stoll's
efforts to convince others of his detachment have so far proven largely futile.
Faced with activists and colleagues who see no neutral intellectual ground in
Guatemala, it is no wonder that Stoll has become a cause célèbre for the right,
a whipping boy for the left, and an albatross for many of those who navigate
in between.

Africa

4

Ethnicity and the Politics of History in Rwanda

Catharine Newbury

Hundreds of thousands of people have died in the Great Lakes region of Africa over the past four years. Most of them were innocent civilians massacred by armies or militias or decimated by disease or starvation as they fled from danger. These horrors can be traced to intense struggles over power carried out by leaders—struggles involving the politicization of ethnicity and a perverse dynamic of violence and fear. The conflicts have been based in part on intellectual foundations, on mental maps of history.

It is these competing visions of the past—the politics of history—that I explore here. Such inquiry is of more than academic interest in contemporary Rwanda. The debate about the nature of the country's history is central to the process of political reconstruction; the postgenocide government in Kigali has not only to deal with the trauma of a whole people and society, but it also has to consider how its policies will be interpreted within the context of various conceptions of Rwanda's past.

A key element in politicizing ethnic cleavages in the recent history of Rwanda has been the development and propagation of a corporate view of ethnicity.[1] The generalization of blame was dramatically evident in the genocide against Tutsi in Rwanda in 1994, when hardliners in the Hutu-dominated government labeled all Tutsi in the country as enemies of the state. The genocide was calculated to exterminate them; the hateful vitriol used against the Tutsi in the press and on radio broadcasts illustrated this thought process.[2] A corporate perception of ethnicity was also evident in the recent massacres of Hutu refugees in the Democratic Republic of Congo (formerly Zaire) in 1996 and 1997. During and after the genocide in Rwanda in 1994, hundreds of thousands of people (mostly Hutu) fled to neighboring countries—primarily Tanzania and Zaire[3]—but some also fled to Burundi and Uganda. For the

From *Africa Today* 45, no. 1 (March 1998): 7–24. © 1998 by Lynne Rienner Publishers. Reprinted with permission of *Africa Today*.

Tutsi-led government of Rwanda that assumed power in July 1994 after the genocide, the refugee camps in Zaire came to be a particularly irritating problem. Fearing reprisals, most of the refugees refused to return home; meanwhile these camps were being used as bases for guerrilla attacks from Zaire against western Rwanda. Among the refugees in the crowded camps along Zaire's eastern border with Rwanda and Burundi were persons who were certainly guilty of genocide, including former soldiers and officers of the Rwanda armed forces (the Rwandan army of the pre-1994 government) and members of militias such as the *Interahamwe*. They posed a serious threat then, and they still do today. But such individuals constituted perhaps 30,000 to 50,000 people in the camps—5 percent of the total refugee populations. To be sure, others in the camps were indirectly implicated in the genocide, but many were not. Moreover, the majority of refugees in the camps were women and children who were neither major perpetrators of the genocide nor a military threat. In the Goma area, for example, 80 percent of the people in the camps were women and children.

Beginning in October 1996, the camps in Zaire were attacked by troops of the Rwandan Patriotic Army (RPA), the army of Rwanda's postgenocide government, with help from soldiers of Laurent Kabila's Alliance of Democratic Forces for the Liberation of Congo/Zaire (ADFL). After the camps were destroyed, many of the Rwandan refugees returned to Rwanda. The remaining refugees who also survived attacks against the camps, probably several hundred thousand people, fled west into the mountains and forests of eastern Zaire. During the war in Congo (which was fought not so much against Mobutu's army as against Rwandan refugees), soldiers from the RPA and the ADFL pursued the refugees for months, attacking their small encampments and massacring men, women, and children at will.[4]

An example will illustrate how Hutu were collectively held responsible for the genocide and tracked down, even on foreign soil. In March 1997, more than 100,000 of these refugees found themselves blocked at Ubundu, on the banks of the Congo River. To Immaculée Mukarugwizwa, a widowed former schoolteacher, their prospects seemed grim:

> We are hungry and we are sick but above all we have lost all morale. Our elders are shrivelled and dying and our children already look old. Are all of us guilty of genocide, even these little children? We have been chased through the bush like animals. And in three days, Kabila's men will be upon us again, leaving 100,000 of us with a choice of death under their bombs or in the jaws of crocodiles.[5]

A corporate view of ethnicity, which targeted all Tutsi during the genocide, was also used in this case to label all Hutu refugees as *génocidaires* (persons who helped perpetrate genocide), and this view seemed to be part of a political program of vengeance directed against Hutu. In deploring the tendency to globalize blame for the genocide in Rwanda to all Hutu, the former schoolteacher Mukarugwizwa's plea highlights a more general perception of ethnicity; such a perception of ethnicity brought with it tragic consequences in the past—and those continue into the present.

In these situations, explaining how and why the uses and abuses of power led to violence in the past could serve as an important lesson to leaders who wish to build a different society in the future. Yet, not surprisingly, in such a polarized atmosphere, historical reconstruction is itself highly contested. Here, with an intensity that surpasses the normal clichés, there is no single history: rather there are competing "histories."

Contested Histories

Vigorous debates have resonated before now over Rwanda's history. There were, for example, divergent interpretations of the Rwandan Revolution of 1959 as well as different views regarding the importance of ethnicity in Rwanda's precolonial (and colonial) past. Consider the following two interpretations of the Rwandan Revolution:

One view holds that the changes from 1959 to 1962 in Rwanda were engineered by Belgian colonial authorities and the Catholic Church. Although previously these powerful external actors had supported the monarchy and its political structures dominated by Tutsi chiefs, in the 1950s they switched support to the Hutu majority.[6] From this perspective, manipulation by external forces was the main reason for political violence in Rwanda during the terminal colonial period, as well as the cause of the collapse of royal power, the reversal of power relations, and the subsequent exodus of many Tutsi into exile.

A contrasting view claims that while some Belgians and leaders in the Catholic Church supported change, it was Hutu leaders and the rural majority in Rwanda who effected the revolution, by reacting to the double colonialism of rule by Tutsi and Belgian authorities.[7] In this view, a Hutu counterelite demanded an end to the privileging of Tutsi in employment, education, access to political power, and economic advancement and thereby an end to discrimination against Hutu. Rather than emphasizing external actors, this view of the Rwandan Revolution highlights rural impoverishment, grievances over exactions by chiefs, and insecurity of land tenure as central factors in the conflicts that accompanied decolonization and the victory of Hutu candidates in the elections of 1960 and 1961.

There are also contrasting views of the history of relations between the three main ethnic groups in Rwanda. One view holds that in the precolonial past, Tutsi lived in symbiosis and harmony with Hutu and Twa. European colonialism created cleavages and divisions between Hutu, Tutsi, and Twa and also put an end to the social mobility that had been possible in the past.[8]

Therefore, some who use this line of reasoning assert, in order to overcome the divisions that have led to violence, the ethnic categories should simply be abolished and the terminology of ethnic groups forbidden.

A different version of these relationships asserts that Hutu were conquered in the distant past by clever and wily Tutsi, who imposed an oppressive, exploitative rule on Hutu and made them the servants of Tutsi.[9] Colonial rule under Germany and then Belgium exacerbated and intensified (but did not cause) divisions that were already there. From this perspective, abolishing the terms "Hutu," "Tutsi," and "Twa" is portrayed as a ploy promoted by a historically dominant minority trying to maintain power. Given the history of discrimination in Rwandan society, some proponents of this view have argued, it is only by retaining the categories that one can measure progress in redressing inequalities from the past.

As will be evident, the first versions in both debates noted above tend to be advanced by those wishing to rationalize rule by Tutsi; the second versions are more characteristic of powerholders in the Hutu-dominated governments that ruled Rwanda from 1961 until 1994. But there is a noteworthy convergence as well: at various times, hardliners in both groups have accepted the myth introduced early in the colonial period by Europeans about ethnic pasts. Tutsi were from different racial stock; they came to Rwanda from the northeast; and they were superior to Hutu in both intelligence and political abilities.[10]

None of these positions, however, provides an adequate explanation of either the Rwandan Revolution or the historical dynamics of ethnic relations in Rwanda; rather, they reflect political positions more than valid historical reconstruction. Each tends to use a monocausal and static explanation for complex interacting processes that have varied over time; in fact, synergy, not singularity, is the bedrock of Rwandan history.

Colonial State Building, Ethnic Polarization, and the 1959 Revolution

The arguments over historical visions advanced today are remarkably similar to debates at the time of decolonization forty years ago. It is, therefore, worthwhile to review some aspects of Rwanda's recent history that have tended to be ignored in these debates—then and now.[11]

By the end of the nineteenth century, Rwanda was already a centralized, hierarchical kingdom with important class distinctions. In many parts of what is today Rwanda, however, local populations had not been fully incorporated into the Rwandan state, and the distinctions of Hutu and Tutsi were not significant. Clan, lineage, and family ties were more important for political interaction. Even within the Rwandan kingdom, relationships between Tutsi and Hutu varied. In some areas, significant numbers of Tutsi and Hutu lived similar lifestyles, keeping cattle and cultivating their fields—many Hutu (but not all) in precolonial Rwanda owned cattle, and many Tutsi (but not all) practiced agriculture.

Colonial rule did, of course, have important effects on Rwandan politics and society. Although German and later Belgian colonial rulers did not create state domination and Hutu/Tutsi inequality—for these already existed—colonialism did significantly alter the reach of the state, the forms of domination, and the nature of political competition.[12] Particularly onerous demands of the colonial state and its chiefs fell most heavily—and in some cases exclusively—on rural cultivators classified as Hutu. This situation accentuated ethnic distinctions and gave them a cultural meaning different from earlier periods.

Moreover, Rwanda's European colonial rulers were intent upon preserving what they saw as "traditional" structures of power, in which Tutsi aristocrats ruled over Hutu peasants. This model, based on colonialist interpretations of monarchical structures in the center of the country, was not accurate even for central Rwanda, much less for regions on the periphery. Nevertheless, the Belgian administration in Rwanda, even more than in most colonial systems, sought to structure social order, to rationalize and standardize heterogeneous social relations, and to reinforce the powers of the "natural rulers." In the 1930s, they issued identity cards that indicated a person's ethnic category. These cards then became a tool of the state used to determine an individual's life chances. Again such measures did not create ethnicity; instead they served to mold its social salience.

Thus, in colonial Rwanda, Hutu came to be classified as second-class citizens. This was starkly illustrated in the allocation of new colonial social and economic resources. For example, Hutu had dramatically fewer opportunities to attend school and achieve postprimary education than Tutsi, and they came to be excluded almost entirely from high-level administrative positions. Twa were discriminated against even more intensely, and few had opportunities to attend school.

Colonial rule, then, provided the resources, imposed the structures, and asserted the pressures that helped shape the state-building process in a particular way. A major effect of this process was the propagation of a corporate vision of ethnic groups. Tutsi, Hutu, and Twa came to be viewed as internally homogeneous groups, and their members came to be treated in distinctive ways by the state. This made groups that had previously shown more internal flexibility appear more like biological groups.

The ideology constructed to rationalize this process portrayed the groups corporately—as racially, culturally, and historically different—and the three characteristics were often seen as virtually synonymous. Such an intellectual framework was premised on (and in turn advanced) the view that the Tutsi were superior both in intelligence and in political acumen, as reiterated in virtually all colonial documentation on Rwandan social organization. But this ideology was constructed not just by Europeans; it emerged as a joint undertaking between Tutsi powerholders and the colonial authority. The point is made forcefully in a recent analysis by Alison Des Forges. As she explains, the creation of a myth that glorified and exaggerated the role of Tutsi in founding Rwandan state structures and exerting control over Hutu was a "collaborative enterprise," involving European administrators, missionaries, and scholars as well as Rwandan chiefs, poets, and historians at the royal court.[13]

Thus, the vision that colonialism disrupted a perfectly harmonious system does not concur with the record: precolonial Rwanda was a state with serious social inequalities, and some powerful political actors used their power arbitrarily and abusively. There were Hutu who were dispossessed of their cattle by Tutsi, for example. But there were also Tutsi who were despoiled of their cattle. Positions of great power and prestige were held mostly by Tutsi, but there are also examples of influential Hutu sought as allies by the royal court. And while assassination of individuals was part of the political process (though perhaps exaggerated in the drama of court poetry), mass murders of people on the grounds of ethnic category did not occur in precolonial Rwanda.

These precolonial state structures were reshaped by the changes wrought during colonial rule and the emergence of a "dual colonialism" that benefited both European and Rwandan powerholders. In the long run, these transformations helped to create the conditions for widespread rural discontent at the end of the colonial period. In the 1950s, as the prospect of independence from Belgium loomed on the horizon, a Hutu counterelite began to pressure for democratization. Calling for an end to the monopoly of political life by a few powerholders, a group of activists issued a "Hutu Manifesto" in 1957. Though its demands were moderate—equality of opportunity and improved access to education, employment, and social services for all Rwandans regardless of ethnic background or social rank—the Hutu Manifesto used racialist terminology, mirroring the ideologies of the time.[14]

Such calls for change provoked a backlash among prominent members of the Rwandan power structure; their intransigent attitudes served to polarize further the political factions. In May 1958, a group of conservatives at the royal court responded to the Hutu Manifesto in arrogant, dismissive language. In a public statement, these notables wrote that there was no basis for brotherhood and cooperation between Hutu and Tutsi, since many years ago Tutsi had subjugated Hutu by force. Their racialist language foreshadowed the language that would be used more than three decades later by Hutu extremists.[15]

This intemperate response by court conservatives contributed to fears and anxieties that were already escalating. For in response to multiple pressures for change, the High Council of the Country was preparing to carry out a program of redistributing land—even though the High Council had not even one Hutu among its members. Then, in an open letter to the king and the High Council, a group describing themselves as "fifteen elderly Tutsi, grand clients of the court" warned that if the land distribution were to proceed, "there will be revolts in the whole country and you are going to provoke the death of those who have land and those who do not, such that those who have the possibility to do so will be obliged to emigrate towards the British territories."[16] *Mutatis mutandis,* such concerns proved prescient of later events, both in the 1960s and in the 1990s.

Within this highly charged political landscape, people in power feared losing their privileged position and being mistreated by former subjects. Hutu activists experienced harassment, and some feared they would be targeted for liquidation.[17] Late in 1959, recently recognized political parties began to organize publicly; tensions grew as Rwandans awaited a report by the Belgian government about the program for elections in preparation for decolonization.

On 1 November, a Hutu subchief (one of only ten in the country) was assaulted by a gang of Tutsi youths. Rumors spread that he had been killed, and this almost instantaneously sparked rural uprisings in several parts of the country: gangs of Hutu roamed the countryside, chasing out Tutsi inhabitants and burning houses. Tutsi generally felt threatened. But in these early conflicts, much of the violence was aimed against those who held administrative posts (such as chiefs or subchiefs) and members of the Tutsi aristocracy, rather than directed indiscriminately at all Tutsi. That came later, when political action caught up with the rhetoric of corporate views of ethnicity.

The Belgian administration declared a state of emergency and brought in troops from the then Belgian Congo in attempts to keep order, separate the warring parties, and protect leaders who were threatened. Political violence had escalated dramatically: many observers of the time note that the royal armies of the past had been remobilized and Hutu leaders and officials in the Belgian administration feared that the royal court was preparing to eliminate its Hutu opponents.[18]

In these circumstances the pervasive political discourse increasingly projected corporate views of ethnicity. But it is noteworthy that political action diverged significantly from this verbal contestation. In the conflicts associated with the Rwandan Revolution of 1959–1961, rural dwellers often distinguished powerful and wealthy Tutsi from Tutsi commoners. The primary targets of attack were those who were in a position of power.

Similarly, in the political conflicts of the 1950s and electoral battles of 1960 and 1961, moderates on both sides emphasized the importance of addressing the needs of all disadvantaged groups in Rwanda—the poor and powerless were not just Hutu but Tutsi and Twa as well. In fact, the leaders of two of the most moderate parties, Association pour la Promotion Sociale de la Masse (APROSOMA) and Rassemblement Démocratique Ruandais (RADER)—the first primarily Hutu, the latter primarily Tutsi—tried to downplay ethnicity and make an appeal to the "common people"—whether Hutu or Tutsi. Moderates were also present during the early 1990s; but then, intense

cleavages that echoed earlier political divisions led several of the new political parties to split between the "moderate" and "power" factions. This was
to be a critical factor in the subsequent political realignment preceding
the genocide.

All the same, in the late 1950s as in the early 1990s, an ethnic appeal
still resonated strongly in certain areas of the country and among certain
social strata. One important reason for this was that almost all of the high political positions in the national government were monopolized by one group;
most of those who were powerful and wealthy in the 1950s were Tutsi. Then,
as in 1962 under a postindependence, Hutu-dominated government, only a
small proportion of the group said to be in control benefited directly from positions of power. Nonetheless, one principal strategy for mobilizing a political
following was to consolidate the mental image of a corporate view of ethnicity.
The political extremists sought to tag all members of the opposing social category with the responsibility of the actions of a few. Thus, in 1996 when all
Hutu became portrayed as *génocidaires,* so too in 1959 all Tutsi came to be
portrayed as *monarchistes;* and in 1994, all Tutsi were labeled as agents of
an "evil" Rwandan Patriotic Front (RPF).

Contests Over Power and the Dynamics of Fear

As I have argued elsewhere,[19] the Rwandan Revolution of 1959 occurred in
large part because of widespread rural grievances. This strong disaffection
from the regime was articulated by a Hutu counterelite (at times supported by
Tutsi moderates linked with the RADER party), who were pushed into more
radical action by the intransigence of the monarchists. Powerful external institutions (the Belgian administration, the Catholic Church, and at certain points
the United Nations) were also involved, to be sure. Although their support
helped the revolution succeed, the events in Rwanda were not engineered from
outside; this was an "assisted revolution,"[20] not an "imposed revolution." The
difference is significant, for the concept of an assisted revolution reflects certain realities of the years immediately following independence in 1962. Many
rural people had a stake in this new political order, and they shared a strong
commitment not to return to the "old order" in later years.

To interpret the events of the 1990s in Rwanda, one must take account
of the rural population's disaffection (and in some areas outright anger among
many Hutu) toward the behavior of many Tutsi authorities under colonial
rule, as well as the intense struggles over land that accompanied the decolonization process. Moreover, one tragic result of the conflicts during 1959 and
after (continuing through 1964) was the exodus of large numbers of Rwandans, mostly Tutsi, who took refuge in neighboring countries. It was these
exiles, and their children, who organized the Rwandan Patriotic Front in
Uganda in the late 1980s. In October 1990, the RPF led a military attack

against Rwanda; they sought to win the right for Rwandans in exile to return and, the RPF asserted, they wanted to push for democratization of the authoritarian Rwandan government.

At the time of the RPF attacks, official rhetoric claimed that the Habyarimana government represented all rural segments in the country, and that this government was a continuation of the ideals of the 1959 Revolution. In reality, the government was dominated by a wealthy, powerful clique (the "Akazu"). By the end of the 1980s, widespread popular disaffection had weakened the regime, particularly in the southern and central areas of the country; intense struggles (mainly among Hutu) based on class and regional differences threatened the continued hegemony of those in power.[21] To be sure, Tutsi were discriminated against in education and access to government jobs; but before October 1990, systematic harassment of Tutsi was not characteristic of the Habyarimana regime. At that time, Tutsi did not face exclusion from private sector employment or local-level positions in the teaching, agriculture, or medical fields.

In the wake of the attacks of 1990, Habyarimana accused the RPF of seeking to overthrow the Hutu government and reestablish monarchical rule and Tutsi hegemony—in other words, he accused them of seeking to reverse the results of the 1959 Revolution. The RPF vigorously denied that this was their goal. Nonetheless, the invasion resuscitated conflicts and fears from the recent past. Even if many rural Rwandans of any social category chafed under the authoritarian rule of Habyarimana and his clique, they were not necessarily eager to embrace rule by the RPF. In intellectual terms, then, the ethnic polarization that occurred in Rwanda during the 1990s, culminating in the genocide of 1994, was in many respects a continuation of the evolving tensions of late colonial rule.[22] Therefore, in efforts to seek pathways to a more peaceful future for Rwanda, it is necessary to understand the complexity of these contested histories of ethnic relationships and their connections to the Revolution of 1959.

But it is also necessary to move beyond such dichotomized debates. Exploring parallels between the violent conflicts of the early 1990s and the events of decolonization in Rwanda would appear to be particularly fruitful. Three such parallels will be discussed briefly below. One concerns the marginalization of moderates in the recent history of Rwanda. A second parallel is seen in the dynamic of fear associated with political competition in these struggles. A third (and related) focus highlights the political patterns that accompany major crises of governance in Rwanda's recent politics.

Marginalization of Moderates

A major characteristic of the 1950s conflicts, as in the 1990s, was the destruction of the political middle ground. In both crises, there were courageous voices of moderation that called for inclusiveness, the restructuring of power relations, and the necessity to attend to the needs of all Rwandans, regardless of ethnic background. But in both cases, hardliners on both sides who made an ethnic appeal gained the upper hand in the debates, effectively marginalizing the more moderate voices in the 1950s and physically destroying such individuals in the 1990s.

Such polarization was already evident following the elections of 1960 and 1961 in Rwanda. The elections had brought to power a republican government dominated by Hutu, with inclusion of a small number of Tutsi in the parliament and cabinet. But in 1964, Tutsi guerrillas invaded the country, attempting to overthrow the fragile government of Grégoire Kayibanda. The invasion collapsed; in its wake the Tutsi members of the government were executed, and the Hutu authorities allowed (or encouraged) massacres of several thousand rural Tutsi residents. These victims were targeted not because they had done anything wrong; rather, they were punished as scapegoats because their ethnic "brothers" (note again the corporate view of ethnicity) had attacked the country.[23]

A similar dynamic was evident in 1990, in the wake of the RPF attack on Rwanda. Within four days of the October invasion, the Habyarimana government had arrested more than 9,000 people, mostly Tutsi, but also Hutu seen as critics of the government. After several months, most of these people were freed, thanks to the efforts of a nascent human rights movement within Rwanda and the pressures of Western donors. But some died, and many suffered serious aftereffects from the ill treatment and poor conditions of incarceration. This was the beginning of a series of minipogroms against Tutsi in different parts of the country carried out by the Habyarimana government—what later would be seen as rehearsals for the conflagration of 1994. Here one can see a recurrent pattern: the tendency for a regime threatened by external attack to target an internal scapegoat and to rationalize its behavior by propagating a corporate view of ethnicity.

Since July 1994, when the RPF ended the genocide and took control of the country, the new Rwandan government has been led by Tutsi in conjunction with the Rwandan Patriotic Army (the military wing of the RPF). Critics of this government assert that the pattern of scapegoating continues. But now, those threatening the regime are Hutu associated with the former Rwandan army (the FAR) and the *Interahamwe* militias. This time, the power of the Rwandan military has expanded; the scapegoats are not only those within the country but potentially all those living in areas where the FAR or *Interahamwe* are known or believed to be operating (including, apparently, refugees in Zaire). The rationale has been well rehearsed in recent Rwandan history: if it is impossible to capture the *Interahamwe,* it is acceptable to liquidate civilians assumed to be associated with them. While this approach may be effective in terrorizing the citizenry, it does little to enhance the legitimacy of the current regime or give it strong roots in the rural population.

Dynamic of Fear

A second parallel between the 1950s and the early 1990s in Rwanda is the tendency for political struggle to be associated with a pervasive dynamic of fear and rural discontent.[24] In both cases, those in power feared losing their position of privilege, with attendant economic consequences and the political risks of being punished for past misdeeds. And those demanding change feared their dissent might bring personal harm. Meanwhile, ordinary citizens feared the consequences of political struggles they knew could have important implications for their tenuous hold on jobs or land they needed for family survival.

Political Patterns

A third parallel places these struggles in broader historical context. Before the mid-twentieth century, crises of governance in Rwanda often had violent consequences, but the violence was limited to a relatively small group of key participants in the competition, often members of the same ethnic group. The losers—usually highly placed political actors—often faced death or exile.[25] Political violence was more often intraethnic than interethnic.

Although this was not unique to Rwandan succession struggles, key aspects of such earlier crises of governance were a winner-take-all pattern for the victors and death or flight for the losers. But in light of recent tendencies to see all conflict in Rwanda as tribal warfare, it is important to note that these were not ethnic conflicts; rather, they were conflicts among competing Tutsi lineages for control of the state.[26] Patterns found in these earlier goverance crises—nonethnic, but involving winner-take-all outcomes and violent exclusion of the losers—reappeared in political conflicts of the terminal colonial period in Rwanda.

These later conflicts, however, occurred in a different context: colonial state building and policies of ethnic favoritism had broadened the stakes and deepened ethnic polarization. The struggle for power had widened, such that in the 1959 Revolution political contestation was perceived as (at least in part) an ethnic struggle. Changes in the state and the new corporate view of ethnicity contributed to implicating whole "ethnic" groups in political competition, and also making them targets of political violence. Whereas rival politicians at the court had in the past been the main protagonists in crises of governance, now ethnic groups came to be seen as collective actors in the political game.

In the early 1990s, Rwanda faced yet another crisis of governance, a struggle over who would control the state. The political landscape was more complicated, and the results of this struggle were much more destructive than in the past. But earlier patterns were still discernible. Contenders for power tried to mobilize their constituencies using an appeal to solidarity based this time, as in 1959, on ethnic identity. Aware of past patterns, some of the protagonists feared that if they should lose this struggle, they and their families would face liquidation; the outcome left hundreds of thousands dead. And when the RPF-led government assumed power, they inherited a shattered polity and society.

Often in Rwanda's recent history, appeals to ethnicity have served as a pretext for political actors seeking to gain or obtain power. It is this type of power struggle that Rwandans must try to avoid in the future. Such was the conclusion of a group of Rwandan intellectuals who debated these issues recently. In their view, a central challenge in the postgenocide era is how to find ways to avoid the winner-take-all politics, liquidation of opponents, and (more recently) mobilization of ethnic factions that have proved so destructive in the past.[27]

Conclusion

Parallels between the politics of the early 1990s in Rwanda and earlier political processes of the late 1950s are striking. At the same time, dramatic differences between these episodes of conflict are sobering, most notably in the scale of violence and loss of life, and the extent of destruction of the country's social fabric and its material infrastructure. Understanding these complicated dynamics is an important challenge for those attempting to revisit Rwandan history and move beyond the debates noted at the beginning of this article.

In reassessing Rwandan history, a focus on changes made by Europeans is important but should not be allowed to deflect attention from those aspects in which Rwandans themselves were involved. Years ago, in an analysis of colonial state building in Rwanda, I argued that politics and policies of the state need to be seen as critical elements in shaping ethnic relations and ethnic consciousness.[28] From this perspective there is ample evidence that it is in the reach of those in power to manage and dampen ethnic tensions by the types of policies they pursue. Paradoxically, however, "managing" ethnic tensions requires transcending them and addressing other forms of social inequality as well.

A case in point is found in the efforts of the Habyarimana regime to dampen ethnic tensions over the period from 1973 to the mid-1980s. Ultimately, the regime's controversial policy of ethnic quotas for government jobs and educational opportunities undermined the effort. Attempts to reduce ethnic tensions did not relieve class inequalities and other serious problems with the patrimonial state in Rwanda. Thus, when faced with a political crisis, those in power found it too easy to use the "ethnic card" to divert attention from unresolved contradictions in the country's political economy.

One of the problems in focusing obsessively on ethnicity is that this may lead one to overlook questions of power and class. Surely such issues were important in the contestation of the 1950s, as in the 1990s, but how were they important? Perhaps in revisiting this history, Rwandans will wish to explore more fully the issues and inequalities that underlay these political conflicts—conflicts that were only partly "ethnic."

To do so, historians and others will have to engage with the competing visions of the past discussed in this essay. They may have to go beyond them rather than choose between them, but they cannot avoid them. To judge by past experience, the way in which the powerholders address these issues could have an important bearing on the lives of millions of people over the coming generation.

Notes

1. See David Newbury, "The Invention of Rwanda: The Alchemy of Ethnicity," paper presented at the annual meeting of the African Studies Association, Orlando, Fla., November 1995.

2. Jean-Pierre Chrétien et al., eds., *Rwanda: Les médias du génocide* (Paris: Karthala, 1995).

3. In May 1997, when the rebellion led by Laurent Kabila successfully overthrew Zaire's president, Mobutu Sese Seko, the country was renamed Democratic Republic of Congo. Zaire is used here because that was still the name of the country during the period in which these events took place.

4. See Human Rights Watch/Africa and Fédération Internationale des Ligues des Droits de l'Homme, "Democratic Republic of the Congo: What Kabila Is Hiding: Civilian Killings and Impunity in Congo," 9, no. 5 (A) (October 1997); and Scott Campbell, "What Kabila Is Hiding," *Washington Post* (22 September 1997), p. A19. Additional information is found in *Dialogue: Revue d'Information et de Réflexion* (Brussels), special issue on "Les réfugiés rwandais: Le drame persiste," no. 198 (May–June 1997); Gérard Prunier, "Rwanda: The Social, Political and Economic Situation in June 1997," Writenet-UK (http://www.unhcr.ch/unhcr/ref-world/country/writenet/wrirwa07.htm), July 1997: John Pomfret, "Rwandans Led Revolt in Congo," *Washington Post* (9 July 1997), p. A1.

5. Howard French, "In a Zaire Forest, Hutu Refugees Near End of Line," *New York Times* (13 March 1997), pp. A1, A7.

6. The monarchist interpretation holds that the Belgians agreed to block the move to immediate independence out of unwillingness to let go of power. The Belgians, however, argue that their policy changed to accommodate the rise of new voices from below. One of the participants in these events, Guy Logiest, later explained that he decided to support Hutu counterelites during the revolution to promote democratization: he believed that rapid moves toward decolonization would preserve existing inegalitarian structures of power and would be harmful for the mass of the population. B. E. M. Guy Logiest, "A propos de 'Le Rwanda, son effort de développement,'" *Chronique de Politique Etrangère* (1972), cited in Filip Reyntjens, *Pou oir et droit au*

Rwanda (Tervuren, Belgium: Musée Royal de l'Afrique Centrale), p. 272. See also Jean-Paul Harroy, *Rwanda: De la féodalité à la démocratie* (Brussels: Hayez, 1984); and Catharine Newbury, *The Cohesion of Oppression: Clientship and Ethnicity in Rwanda, 1860–1960* (New York: Columbia University Press, 1988), p. 187ff. In a prescient use of current academic terminology, the Hutu Manifesto of 1957 noted that the vast majority of Rwandans had been relegated to "subaltern roles." This manifesto (described below) was part of a rising movement subversive to the internal structure of late colonial hierarchy. "Manifeste des Bahutu," in Fidèle Nkundabagenzi, ed., *Rwanda politique, 1958–1960* (Brussels: Centre de Recherche et d'Information Socio-Politiques, 1962), pp. 20–29.

7. For an early statement of the notion of dual colonialism, see "Manifeste des Bahutu."

8. For one such statement regarding harmonious relations between Rwanda's groups, see "Les chefs du Rwanda expriment leur loyalisme envers le Mwami," *Le Courrier d'Afrique* (1 October 1956), in Nkundabagenzi, *Rwanda politique,* p. 34. An influential academic version is found in Jacques Jérôme Maquet, *The Premise of Inequality in Ruanda* (London: Oxford University Press, 1961).

9. See selections from the Rwandan newspaper *Kangura,* reproduced in Chrétien, *Les médias du génocide.* For analogous accounts among Rundi refugees articulating extremist versions of Rundi history, see Liisa Malkki, *Purity and Exile: Violence, Memory and National Cosmology Among Hutu Refugees in Tanzania* (Chicago: University of Chicago Press, 1995).

10. Alison Des Forges, "The Ideology of Genocide," *ISSUE: A Journal of Opinion* 23, no. 2 (1995): 44–47. Des Forges traces the creation of a myth that glorified and exaggerated the role of Tutsi in founding Rwandan state structures and exerting control over Hutu. She notes that "even the majority of Hutu swallowed this distorted account of the past, so great was their respect for European-style education. Thus people of both groups learned to think of the Tutsi as winners and the Hutu as losers in every great contest of the Rwandan past" (p. 45).

11. From the end of the nineteenth century, the Rwandan kingdom came under the colonial control of first Germany (until 1916) and then Belgium. Following the Revolution of 1959–1961, the monarchy was abolished and a republican government took power at independence in 1962. Rwanda's president, Grégoire Kayibanda, was overthrown by Maj. Gen. Juvenal Habyarimana in 1973. From 1990, the Habyarimana regime faced a series of challenges: war, economic crisis, an internal democratization movement, increasing political instability, and escalating ethnic violence; the plane crash that killed Habyarimana on 6 April 1994 initiated the genocide in which over half a million people died. For an analysis of the genocide, see Catharine Newbury and David Newbury, "A Catholic Mass in Kigali: Contested Views of the Genocide in Rwanda," *Canadian Journal of African Studies,* forthcoming 1998.

12. For a detailed analysis of alterations in the powers of chiefs and rural class relations in colonial Rwanda, see Newbury, *The Cohesion of Oppression.* See also Jean Rumiya, *Le Rwanda sous le régime du mandat belge, 1916–1931* (Paris: L'Harmattan, 1992).

13. Des Forges, "The Ideology of Genocide," p. 45.

14. "Manifeste des Bahutu," in Nkundabagenzi, *Rwanda politique,* pp. 20–29. The subtitle for this document is "Note on the Social Aspect of the Native Racial Problem in Rwanda," illustrating the language of division of the colonial period: racial categories.

15. "Voici le détail historique du règne des Banyiginya au Rwanda," statement by twelve grand clients of the royal court (*bagaragu b'ibwami bakuru*) (17 May 1958), in Nkundabagenzi, *Rwanda politique,* pp. 35–36.

16. Letter from fifteen elderly Tutsi, grand clients of the court to the king and the High Council of the country of Ruanda (18 May 1958), in Nkundabagenzi, *Rwanda politique,* pp. 36–37.

17. In July 1959, Mwami Mutara Rudahigwa (Rwanda's king who had reigned since 1931) died suddenly while visiting Bujumbura, Burundi. This unexpected event served to polarize the situation further. Various theories have been put forward that blame his death alternately on the Belgians, on Tutsi hardliners at the royal court, and on Hutu activists. None of these theories has been proven, and mystery continues to surround his death—just as we still do not have reliable proof as to who was responsible for shooting down the plane carrying Rwanda's former president Juvenal Habyarimana in April 1994. But in both cases, the drama of an unexpected death left plenty of leeway for several groups to cast blame. Politically, an unresolved tragedy may have been useful for several competing groups; they could interpret the causal factors in ways that justified their antagonism.

18. On these events, see Newbury, *The Cohesion of Oppression,* pp. 195–196; René Lemarchand, *Rwanda and Burundi* (New York: Praeger, 1970), pp. 159–169; Donat Murego, *La révolution rwandaise, 1959–1962* (Louvain: Institut des Sciences Politiques et Sociales, 1975), pp. 915–922; Ian Linden with Jane Linden, *Church and Revolution in Rwanda* (Manchester: Manchester University Press, 1977), p. 267; and Reyntjens, *Pouvoir et droit au Rwanda,* pp. 260–264. The Belgian administration believed that Tutsi partisans would retaliate against Hutu on a massive scale. For example, the governor-general at the time asserts that the Union Nationale Rwandaise (UNAR), the monarchist political party, consciously provoked the Hutu uprising in November. He claims that the court strategists planned to kill "all the Hutu leaders—according to a carefully prepared list—and to carry out in selected regions—Astrida—enough massacres of the peasant population to eliminate the possibility of a Hutu reaction before independence . . . or after." Jean-Paul Harroy, *Rwanda: De la féodalité à la démocratie* (Brussels: Hayez, 1984), pp. 291, 305. The official number of deaths resulting from the November conflicts was fifty, of which thirty-seven were allegedly caused by Tutsi, thirteen by Hutu; in Jean R. Hubert, *La Toussaint rwandaise et sa répression* (Brussels: Académie Royale des Sciences d'Outre-Mer, 1965), p. 40. However, Reyntjens indicates that there were "several hundred deaths, several thousand houses burned, about 10,000 refugees, and about 20 chiefs and some 150 sub-chiefs forced out of their posts"; in Reyntjens, *Pouvoir et droit au Rwanda,* p. 261. During 1960 and 1961, the numbers of victims grew, and many more people fled their land and homes. But the scale of destruction was small compared to what occurred in later episodes of violence, particularly in 1964, but most dramatically in 1994.

19. Newbury, *The Cohesion of Oppression,* esp. chap. 9–10.

20. The term "assisted revolution" derives from Harroy, *Rwanda.* While it is obviously in the Belgian interest to retire to the background, in this case the data seem to support such a concept.

21. See Catharine Newbury, "Rwanda: Recent Debates over Governance and Rural Development," in Goran Hyden and Michael Bratton, *Governance and Politics in Africa* (Boulder and London: Lynne Rienner Publishers, 1992), pp. 193–219; and Timothy Paul Longman, "Christianity and Crisis: Religion, Civil Society, and Democracy in Rwanda" (Ph.D. diss., University of Wisconsin-Madison, 1995).

22. Catharine and David Newbury, "Identity, Genocide and Reconstruction in Rwanda," paper presented at the conference "Les racines de la violence dans la région des Grands Lacs." European Parliament, Brussels, 12 January 1995. Mahmood Mamdani makes a similar argument in "From Conquest to Consent as the Basis of State Formation: Reflections on Rwanda," *New Left Review,* no. 216 (March–April 1996): 3–36.

23. The scenario brings to mind analogous events in 1972 in Burundi. There, an external attack by Hutu exiles led to a massive repression in which anywhere from 100,000 to 200,000 people (mostly Hutu) were killed by the Tutsi-dominated army and militias composed of Tutsi youth. This was about ten times the number of deaths in Rwanda in 1964. See René Lemarchand, *Burundi: Ethnocide as Discourse and Practice* (Cambridge: Cambridge University Press, 1994); Lemarchand, *Selective Genocide in Burundi* (London: Minority Rights Group, 1973); Filip Reyntjens, *L'Afrique des Grands Lacs en crise: Rwanda, Burundi, 1988–1994* (Paris: Karthala, 1994).

24. During the latter part of the 1980s and the early 1990s, economic conditions in Rwanda deteriorated, while class polarization intensified. Land accumulation for people with money incomes (often associated with the state or donor-funded development projects), corruption by highly placed officials, unfavorable prices for peasant production, and inadequate social services placed large numbers of rural dwellers in an increasingly vulnerable position. Meanwhile, the lack of opportunities for youth, in conditions where land, jobs, or even hope for the future were in short supply, sharpened rural and urban tensions.

In 1989, a steep drop in the world price of coffee reduced the incomes of rural smallholders as well as revenues of the state; in the same year, a serious famine (the first since 1943) ravaged parts of southern and western Rwanda. As one analyst observed, the combined effect of government predation, severe land pressures, and "growth without development" in Rwanda had led by the end of the 1980s to an "impoverishment of the peasants [that] . . . exceeded the limits of what was acceptable"; in Fernand Bézy, *Rwanda 1962–1989: Bilan socio-économique d'un régime* (Louvain-la-Neuve: Institut d'Etudes du Développement, 1990). Under pressure from the International Monetary Fund and the World Bank, Rwanda devalued its currency and began implementing a structural adjustment program in November 1990. The cutback in government spending and increased prices of food and other necessities associated with this program had negative effects for most Rwandans, but these fell particularly heavily on the rural and urban poor.

Evidence on Rwanda's intensifying economic crisis and political disaffection associated with it during the years preceding the 1994 genocide is found in a number of sources. Among others, see Bézy, *Rwanda 1962–1989,* and Catharine Newbury, "Background to Genocide in Rwanda," *ISSUE: A Journal of Opinion* 23, no. 2 (1995): 12–17; Newbury and Newbury, "A Catholic Mass in Kigali"; Newbury, "Rwanda: Recent Debates over Governance and Rural Development," esp. pp. 202–216; Longman, "Christianity and Crisis"; Danielle de Lame, "Le Sens des violences," paper presented at the conference "Les racines de la violence dans la région des Grands Lacs," European Parliament, Brussels, 12 January 1995; Jean-Claude Willame, *Aux sources de l'hécatombe rwandaise* (Brussels: Institut Africain-Cédaf; Paris: L'Harmattan, 1995), chap. 5; Michael Chossudovsky, "Economic Genocide in Rwanda," *Economic and Political Weekly* (13 April 1996): 938–941; André Guichaoua, *Destins paysons et politiques agraires en Afrique centrale,* Vol. I (Paris: l'Harmattan, 1989); S. Marysse, T. de Herdt, and E. Ndayambaje, *Rwanda: Appauvrissement et ajustement structurel* (Brussels: Institut Africain-Cédaf, 1994).

25. During a workshop in 1996, a group of Rwandan intellectuals, social activists, and government officials identified such long-standing patterns of conflict as critical in fostering political violence. For a lucid summary of the proceedings of the workshop, see Charles Ntampaka, "Le colloque de Bamako," *Dialogue,* no. 197 (March–April 1997): 23–33.

26. The Coup of Rucunshu, occurring on the eve of colonial rule, is a case in point. Mibambwe Rutarindwa had been enthroned in 1895 on the death of his father, the

renowned Kigeri Rwabugiri: in fact, Rwabugiri had named him coregnant before his death. Several months after taking power, Rutarindwa was attacked and killed along with his ritual supporters and protectors. The conspirators were led by Kanjogera, Mibambwe's adoptive queen mother, and two of her brothers, Kabare and Ruhinankiko, all members of the Abakagara lineage of the Abeega clan.

They placed a young boy on the throne, Kanjogera's biological son, and then proceeded to purge chiefs and other political authorities associated with the royal Abahindiro lineage of the Abanyiginya clan. Many of the paternal brothers, uncles, and cousins of the dead king who were not killed fled into exile or, at the least, were relieved of their positions of command.

De Lacger refers to these events as a "holocaust"; Louis de Lacger, *Le Ruanda,* 2d ed. (Kabgayi, Rwanda: Imprimérie de Kabgayi, 1959), p. 367. He continues (p. 369): "The Banyiginya [the clan identity of the kings] . . . remain today only a shadow of their former selves and owe to the arrival of the whites the fact that they were not exterminated entirely." See also E. Ruhashya, *Rucunshu* (Kigali: Imprimérie Nationale du Rwanda, 1984), an epic poem on what some Rwandans refer to as "the first genocide." For general accounts of the events at Rucunshu and the factions involved, see Newbury, *The Cohesion of Oppression,* pp. 57–59; de Lacger, *Ruanda,* pp. 358–359, 361–369; Marcel d'Hertefelt and André Coupez, *La royauté sacrée de l'ancien Rwanda: Texte, traduction et commentaire de son rituel* (Tervuren; Belgium: Musée Royal de l'Afrique Centrale, 1964); Alison Des Forges, "Defeat Is the Only Bad News: Rwanda Under Musiinga, 1896–1931" (Ph.D. diss., Yale University, 1972), pp. 21–22, 26; Alexis Kagame, *Un abrégé de l'histoire du Rwanda,* vol. 2 (Butare: Éditions Universitaires du Rwanda, 1975), pp. 117–126. For a thoughtful discussion of political violence in Rwanda in historical perspective, see Claudine Vidal, *Sociologie des passions* (Paris: Karthala, 1991).

27. Ntampaka, "Colloque de Bamako," p. 28.

28. Newbury, *Cohesion of Oppression,* esp. chap. 1, 10. The literature on the interplay of ethnicity with political context is extensive. For a thoughtful recent discussion of the contingent character of ethnicity in politics, see John Bowen, "The Myth of Global Ethnic Conflict," *The Journal of Democracy* 7, no. 4 (October 1996): 3–14. For Africa and beyond, see especially Crawford Young, "The Dialectics of Cultural Pluralism: Concept and Reality," in Crawford Young, ed., *The Rising Tide of Cultural Pluralism: The Nation-state at Bay?* (Madison: University of Wisconsin Press, 1993), pp. 3–35; Crawford Young, "Nationalism, Ethnicity, and Class in Africa: A Retrospective," *Cahiers d'Études Africaines* 26, no. 3 (1986): 421–495; Crawford Young, *The Politics of Cultural Pluralism* (Madison: University of Wisconsin Press, 1976); Leroy Vail, ed., *The Creation of Tribalism in Southern Africa* (London: James Curry, 1989).

5

The Burdens of Truth
An Evaluation of the Psychological Support Services and Initiatives Undertaken by the South African Truth and Reconciliation Commission

Brandon Hamber

Introduction

Apartheid South Africa was characterised by extreme levels of brutality and state initiated violence. To attempt to deal with the aftermath of this violence and break the silence associated with decades of human rights violations— the South African Truth and Reconciliation Commission (TRC) was established. The purpose of this Commission was to facilitate a "truth recovery process" aimed at reconciling South Africans with the past. However, like all truth commissions, the South African TRC was essentially created for political reasons. Broadly speaking, it was created to assist in smoothing the political transition from authoritarian to democratic rule. It has also been used by the new government to demonstrate their willingness to break with the past and usher in a new political and social order based on the protection, rather than violation, of human rights.

A further justification for the entire endeavour has been psychological in nature. Namely, that to deal with the thousands of traumas the apartheid system has inflicted on South Africans, the nation as a whole and its individual citizens both have to re-live the past so as to come to terms with it. It has been argued that survivors of traumatic events, and more broadly governments in transformation from past political conflict like South Africa, are often urged *to let sleeping dogs lie* or to *let bygones be bygones.* However, psychologically

From *American Imago* 55, no. 1 (Spring 1998): 9–28. © 1998 by The Johns Hopkins University Press. Reprinted with permission of the Johns Hopkins University Press.

sleeping dogs do not lie; past traumas do not simply pass or disappear with the passage of time (Hamber 1995). Psychologically the past can never be ignored and past traumas can always be expected to have emotional consequences for an individual and the society at large. For individuals repressed pain can stunt emotional life and manifest itself in a range of psychological and physical symptoms. Psychological restoration and healing can only occur through providing the space for survivors of violence to feel heard and for every detail of the traumatic event to be re-experienced in a safe environment.

The paper will focus exclusively on the degree to which the limited psychological services that have been set up by the TRC have aided this sort of individual psychological restoration. A limited degree of emphasis will be given to the national or collective psychological impact of the TRC. The paper will begin by summarising the work and mandate of the TRC. The limitations on the TRC's ability to offer services to those who testified before it and exactly how the TRC has psychologically affected these individuals will be briefly discussed. Thereafter, the different psychological and support services that have been set up, or failed to be initiated, will be outlined and critically scrutinised.

Summary of the Mandate of the TRC

The Truth and Reconciliation Commission was the first independent body established in South Africa to deal with the issue of past political violence and the prevention of future human rights abuses. The TRC was brought into existence through an act of Parliament known as the National Unity and Reconciliation Act. The TRC began operating in December 1995. Since its inception it has aimed to give voice to the experiences of victims, witnesses and perpetrators of apartheid-era violence so as to uncover as complete a picture as possible of the causes, nature and extent of past abuses that occurred between the period 1 March 1960 to 10 May 1994.

The TRC has the express purpose of facilitating a truth recovery process through taking statements from survivors and families of victims of gross violations of human rights (i.e. murder, attempted murder, abduction and torture or severe ill-treatment). So-called representative and demonstrative cases are chosen from among the statements and these individuals are given public hearings. At these hearings, survivors and families of victims relate how they were victimised. At other hearings, perpetrators' confessions and amnesty applications are heard. At the end of its term of office in July 1998 the TRC is obligated to write a policy which will ensure that survivors and families of victims are granted reparation. The government is responsible for implementing this policy.

As part of its reconciliatory function, the TRC is also responsible for the granting of amnesty.[1] This means that perpetrators of gross violations of human rights, who apply and meet the TRC criteria for amnesty, are freed from prosecution and all criminal and civil liability. To receive amnesty, perpetrators must have committed politically-motivated crimes and fully disclose all the information concerning their deeds.[2] In effect, this means that amnesty is not automatic in South Africa, but if the criteria for amnesty are met the TRC will substitute or trade retributive justice for the full truth. It is intended that the information made available through this process will assist in leaving an undisputed account of history and document how violations occurred. This theoretically opens up the possibility to learn from the past and in so doing ensure that future violence does not occur. At the end of its full term of office the TRC will have to submit its findings to Parliament in a comprehensive report, hand over its reparations policy to government and make recommendations aimed at preventing such large scale abuse from ever occurring again.

The TRC has taken some 20,000 statements from survivors or families of victims of political violence. A number of representative cases have been selected for public hearings based on these statements. Over fifty public hearings were held spanning a total 244 days at which victims told their stories to the nation.[3] The TRC also received approximately 7,050 amnesty applications. Although toward the end of the TRC, only a relatively limited number of these had been processed either through public hearings or in Chambers.[4]

The Psychological Impact of the TRC on Individuals

The individual psychological impact of the TRC has been extensive in South Africa. Any South African will hotly debate the merits, and faults, of the process. Their views are generally informed by their own personal emotional reactions toward the TRC and South Africa's conflict-ridden past. Feelings range broadly and are often dependent on a person's individual relationship to past violations. Different reactions have been witnessed depending on whether one was directly victimised, a victimiser or complicit with the entire apartheid system and responsible for violations by omission rather than commission. However, what is clear is that uniform reactions, and the personalised impact of the TRC, are difficult to ascertain and measure.

Some feelings that have been prominent are extreme feelings of anger from the victimised and victimisers because of the violations of the past being revealed by the TRC, feelings of denial and avoidance by all sectors of the population, remorsefulness on behalf of some perpetrators and those complicit in violations, indifference from others and enormous feelings of guilt, pain, sadness and hurt for many South Africans.

In terms of those who actually testified before the TRC—who are the main focus of this paper—a range of psychological difficulties and symptoms have been identified. A plethora of psychological symptoms and signs have been observed including typical symptom profiles denoting post-traumatic stress disorder (PTSD), crippling self-blame, enormous anger (sometimes heightened by the work of the TRC with regard to amnesty granting), social and interpersonal problems and abundant cases of complicated and unresolved bereavement. These symptoms are largely the result of the traumas, which have often been continuous in nature, that many South Africans—and particularly those actively opposed to apartheid—endured over the years.

On the whole, most individuals have presented with a mixture of issues related to social, psychological and medical problems. Uncomplicated post-traumatic stress has not been a common feature mainly because, in most cases, individual past traumas (e.g., being tortured, abuses by the police, etc.) have been overshadowed by present psychological and social problems.[5] Furthermore, the ability to draw direct causative links between the initial trauma (i.e., the situation or violation presented to the TRC in a statement or through a hearing) and the present difficulties experienced by most survivors has generally been complicated by the protracted time that has passed since most violations occurred. In some cases, survivors and families have testified about violations that took place in the 1960s.

Dire social circumstances have made it difficult for individuals to deal with or prioritise past psychological traumas. At times, so-called present difficulties (i.e., occupational problems, substance abuse, relationship breakdowns, etc.) are symptoms of long-term traumatisation which has been compounded by impoverished living conditions. However, at other times, the impoverished living conditions (e.g., over-crowding, hunger, being forced to work away from home, etc.) have heightened the primary trauma and have also in themselves caused a range of new psychological difficulties and problems.

Evaluation of the Support Services Set up by the TRC

The psychological impact of the TRC outlined above clearly indicates that there is a need for a range of psychological support mechanisms for those interacting with the TRC. The need for additional support services was recognised by a range of key stake-holders and organisations prior to the establishment of the Commission. Several submissions were made to the TRC with regard to this.[6] Other suggestions concerning the need for psychological services during the process of the TRC were also made in seminars and discussions at the beginning of the TRC and during the process.[7]

A core argument implicit in all the submissions was that, although the TRC may have been necessary to deal with the past, in terms of the psychological well-being of those testifying and interacting with it, it was not sufficient. To this end the submissions made several useful recommendations and suggestions. These included, amongst others, the need for ongoing counselling services for survivors and families of victims of political violence; briefing and de-briefing before and after testifying for those giving evidence to the TRC;

the training of TRC staff to deal with people in a psychologically sensitive way; the setting-up of psychological support networks (including traditional services, i.e. support from churches and traditional healers) to ensure support services were available and accessible for survivors and families of victims; the need for survivor-offender mediation services and for support groups for the TRC staff in order to combat the dangers of vicarious traumatisation.

Despite these useful suggestions, the position of the TRC with regard to actually providing psychological support has, from the start, been an ambivalent one. It has already been stated that there was strong opinion that the TRC was a necessary step to address some of the psychological needs of those victimised in the past but that it was not sufficient. However, the Act that defined the operations of the TRC made no reference to the TRC supplying any form of psychological support. As a result it has been a point of debate within the TRC as to whether it is responsible for supplying any form of psychological support to those testifying.

This is indicative of the TRC's largely legal interpretation of its mandate which has dominated some of the TRC's operations, particularly during the early stages of the Commission. It also points to the enormity of the workload of the TRC and hence its reluctance to undertake additional work. A legal framework remains the TRC's primary point of reference and it is doubtful as to whether there has been a change in the mindset, particularly of those Commissioners from legal and political backgrounds, with regard to the importance of dealing with the psychological impact of the past on individuals (de Ridder 1997). In many ways mental health issues and a psychological approach to dealing with the past remains marginalised in the TRC.

As a result of this narrow interpretation of the Act—even despite the best intentions of some Commissioners and staff to ensure additional services— exactly how support services should be provided, and from where the funds should come, has remained an ongoing source of tension within the TRC. Nonetheless, the TRC did employ a mental health care specialist and several other staff members who were assigned to take care of the psychological needs of the staff and those testifying.

The following sections review the successes and failures with regard to the TRC's ability to supply or support initiatives aimed at ensuring that survivors and families of victims receive adequate psychological support.

The four areas that will be discussed are:

Building Networks and Supplying Services: This section focuses on the TRC's ability to build networks of service providers and for its staff to make appropriate referrals to social and psychological support organisations.

The Implications of Giving Testimony: This section analyses the psychological benefits of the story-telling process facilitated by the TRC.

Briefing and Debriefing Services and Statement-Taking: The complexities and limitations of these services and undertakings—the mainstay of the TRC's direct psychological interventions—are discussed.

Support for the TRC Staff: The levels of vicarious traumatisation amongst the Commission staff are briefly discussed and some of the TRC's initiatives to deal with this are examined.

Building Networks and Supplying Services

Any discussion about mental health and social support services in South Africa has to be understood within the context of the extremely limited mental health care services in the country. For example, in the Northern Province, where the TRC in fact had hearings, there are approximately 5.3 million people. State health, at present, does not have a clinical psychologist employed in their service and only three private practitioners work in this largely rural province. Successful referral from the TRC, or from any other source for that matter, to formal psychological services remains highly contingent upon such factors.

This situation makes it clear that networks of support organisations, the utilisation of traditional and community support and an efficient referral strategy are needed in order to set up any psychological support system in South Africa. The TRC—being aware of the need for networking—did make various attempts to establish such a network and referral strategy to deal with the multiple needs of survivors. This has worked with varying degrees of success and in some cases poorly, although marked regional differences have been observed in terms of successful networks.

In some areas, for example the Western Cape, many referrals have been made to support organisations through the TRC. In contrast, in Gauteng fewer referrals have been made and a limited number of individuals have received counselling services. Many other individuals have presented at clinics and service providers during the life of the Commission, although they have not always been referred by the TRC itself. Others who have had past memories and difficulties evoked by the TRC have chosen to seek support, when it is available, before going to the TRC. Furthermore, in South Africa, often due to extreme levels of poverty and social problems, many people do not prioritise mental health needs over dire social circumstances. A lack of awareness about the benefits of using psychological support services and their traditional unavailability has meant that, even where services are accessible, they have been under-utilised by those who have been to the TRC.

Importantly, it should also be noted, that in the South African context much of the social and psychological support occurs through church and community structures due to the inaccessible and underdeveloped mental health services. It is likely that many churches have had to provide psychological and social support to those interacting with the Commission. Similarly, informal victim support groups have played a major role in supporting survivors and families of victims of violence.[8]

However, at this stage it is apparent that inadequate follow-up, limited referral and sporadic support of individuals who have testified or made a statement to the TRC has occurred across the board. This is certainly the opinion of all the organisations that made submissions to the TRC regarding the need for psychological support services. The fragmented and limited services set up or supplied by the TRC have, in part, been due to the restricted quantity of support services in South Africa. However, it is fair criticism that the TRC has also not always utilised all avenues for support and built extensive networks of service providers during its first eighteen months of operation. The TRC, possibly due to resource difficulties and the mandate questions raised earlier, has not always participated as actively as possible in ensuring ongoing support despite the willingness of many organisations to provide free services to the TRC.

The Psychological Implications of Giving Testimony

One of the main consequences of political violence and turmoil in South Africa has been the development of what can be termed a "culture of silence." This has been marked by misinformation, a reluctance to speak out about abuses due to the fear of repercussions and the enforced silences of the so-called "official story." This silence has been individually destructive and resulted in individuals being excluded from social, emotional and political life. This has left most survivors feeling misunderstood and that nobody is willing to hear their story. A process of truth recovery—at least in theory—can be instrumental in contributing to psychological rehabilitation by breaking this culture of silence and allowing individuals to re-experience or "live through" the traumas of the past, and in so doing come to terms with them. Structured and facilitated story-telling can serve the cognitive function of re-shaping the event for the survivor and allowing for the essentially abnormal event to be integrated into the cognitive and emotional matrix of his or her life.

The South African TRC—coupled with a whole new democratic dispensation—has, on a societal level, begun the process of breaking the silences of the past. On an individual level the TRC has also aided psychological restoration, albeit in a limited way, through the testimony giving functions of the Commission. Providing space for victims to tell their stories, particularly in public forums, has been of use to many. It is indisputable that many survivors and relatives of victims have found the public hearing process psychologically beneficial. The process has been described as relieving and cathartic by many. Furthermore, many of those who testified in a public hearing did receive additional support in the form of briefing/debriefing which was unquestionably of use for most survivors, regardless of its inherent limitations (which are discussed in detail in the next section).

In addition, for the first time, many South Africans have been able to tell their stories to sympathetic ears. In the past, often due to police complicity, most people were turned away from police stations, particularly when their cases were of a political nature. Cases were never investigated and through the TRC all cases have now been referred for investigation to the sixty-odd national investigators of the TRC Investigation Unit.[9]

Despite these successes of the hearings, the actual psychological impact of giving public voice to trauma and interacting with the TRC has, on an individual level, had varying and highly personalised consequences for survivors and families of victims. These consequences have not always received adequate attention by the TRC and others. The cathartic nature of the public hearing process has, at times, been overemphasised by the media and others, including the Commissioners, during the process. Perhaps a more cynical view would be that there has been a popular misperception that as long as individuals have been crying at the hearings some healing has been occurring. This may be true in some cases where testifying before the TRC was the final step for an individual on their personal healing journey. However, for most survivors the testifying process is more than likely their first step on their road to psychological restoration. For many, although public acknowledgement of their suffering may have restored their dignity and taken away personal feelings of guilt, psychological healing remains far off. Such healing usually requires ongoing support from professionals, community groups, relatives and other support structures like religious bodies.

It is the long-term processes of healing that the TRC has not addressed as adequately as it has the task of providing a forum for public expressions of emotion. Extensive networks of service providers and adequate referral has not always followed the hearings and statement-taking process, as has been discussed above. Without this follow-up, many victims have described feelings of initial relief following the hearings and then, weeks or months later, feelings of despondency and a re-emergence of the trauma.

A further weakness of the entire process is that perpetrators have been largely neglected from a psychological perspective. Some perpetrators have presented at various institutes for counselling and support, but a large scale focus on them and their families has been limited. Support for the families of amnesty applicants, who undoubtedly must be confronting a range of psychological issues and ambivalences, has remained sorely neglected. Perhaps this is due to the moral complexity of treating perpetrators in a country that has so recently emerged from violent conflict. The limited focus on perpetrators may also be due to the fact that many organisations have only recently started to work with perpetrators and remain inexperienced with such work. During the turbulent times of apartheid the plight of victims was always prioritised by most orga-nisations. The operations of the amnesty committee and its quasi-judicial process has also made access to perpetrators and their families difficult.

Furthermore, insufficient psychological attention has been paid to the thousands of individuals, from all sides of the political spectrum, who are both victims and perpetrators. A good example are the youth who were involved in intra-community conflict in the early 1990s. This group has had limited interactions with the TRC, often due to individuals' dual roles as survivors and perpetrators of violence in the past. An assumption implicit in the TRC has been that, at least to some degree, there have been two sides to the con-flict and that there have been two main categories of protagonists, i.e. victims and perpetrators. The reality is that as the TRC has unfolded, a complex set of relationships and roles has surfaced. Often organisations that have seen peo-ple for counselling have been challenged by having to deal with the dual roles of many clients.

Briefing/Debriefing Services and Statement-Taking

At the start of the process it was acknowledged by the TRC that there was a need for briefing/debriefing services for those who were to testify before the TRC at public hearings. The TRC hired staff members known as "briefers" to carry-out this function. In many senses, briefing/debriefing became the major direct psychological intervention that the TRC undertook.

The intentions of the briefing sessions were to ensure that the witness had sufficient information about the legal implications of their public testimony (e.g., the naming of perpetrators) and that they were psychologically ready to testify. The briefers also accompanied the witness during the hearing and pro-vided ongoing support. As a result the briefers have colloquially become known as "Cry People" as they have regularly been seen comforting wit-nesses during harrowing emotional testimonies.

The briefers were not clinical psychologists or social workers, although most had some basic psychological training or counselling skills. They were given some additional training by the TRC and other support organisations. This training included some elementary information on post-traumatic stress disorder (PTSD), gender awareness skills and basic counselling skills. This training was not uniform in each region and differed in content and intensity. There were differences in the competencies of the briefers and their level of experience dealing with traumatised individuals. This resulted in differential levels of effectiveness in terms of their abilities to deal with the psychologi-cal problems of the witnesses and those interacting with the TRC. Never-theless, it appears as if the briefing/debriefing process of those at public hearings was of great assistance to the witnesses. It did provide some form of psychological holding and containment for those testifying and was generally appreciated by survivors and family members of victims.

The briefers were also responsible for referring those who needed ongoing support to psychological support service providers. As a result, some referrals to support services occurred through this process—although this was not extensive.[10] Perhaps many other witnesses are receiving ongoing support from community structures, churches and victim support groups (as they may have been doing for years prior to the event), but this remains to be confirmed. Long-term follow-up of individuals has not been extensive, and very few witnesses have been consulted about their present mental health status, or other details about their case and progress with regard to investigation for that matter, since their hearing. There are a large number of survivors and families of victims who accuse the TRC of opening old wounds and then failing to support them in dealing with their pain.

The causes of this situation are many. In part it may be due to the enormity of the task of following-up all the witnesses personally. A further reason may be that directly after the hearings—and the debriefing sessions—most of the witnesses appeared to be psychologically intact. The adrenaline-filled and cathartic experience of testifying publicly, although traumatic in itself, often initially masked the long-term or deeper psychological issues that were at play. As a result, at the Trauma Centre for Victims of Violence and Torture in Cape Town, it is only after some time that the real impact of the hearings has started to be seen. Only months after their testimony are survivors and families of victims beginning to present with a range of psychological problems at the Centre (de Ridder 1997).

A further limitation was that briefing services were largely only supplied to those who had public hearings. The majority of survivors and families of victims only gave a statement to the TRC and it was seldom that these individuals were seen by briefers. The statement-takers generally had a much lower degree of psychological knowledge and experience than the briefers, thus making their interactions with the survivors less beneficial psychologically. To compensate for this they were trained by the TRC and Non-Government Organisation (NGO) specialists about the psychological importance of the story-telling process and with some basic knowledge about PTSD. The statement-takers were also responsible for identifying those who needed psychological support and then making the appropriate referrals—in some regions they were trained with referral making skills.

Internal to the TRC, particularly in the early stages of the Commission, there was also disagreement on how the statements should be taken, and this impacted on the potential psychological value of the statement-taking process. The investigators often demanded a police style, fact-driven statement whereas other workers from psychological backgrounds wished to focus more on the psychological importance of story-telling. These tensions compromised the ability of the statement-taking process to be used in the most beneficial psychological manner.

Having said this, these limitations should not be used to undermine the statement-taking process as a whole, as it was an essential component of the work of the TRC. Furthermore, statement-takers were extremely limited in their available time with each individual, thus decreasing the possibility of a substantial psychological intervention. There were also regional and individual differences as to how the statement-takers interacted with the survivors and families of victims. The inexperience, limited psychological knowledge and inadequate psychological skills-training of the statement-takers left some of the witnesses' feelings exposed and not dealt with after giving their statement. Some statement-takers did not always make appropriate referrals or perceive the psychological problems of the witnesses and take the appropriate action. However, in some regions people who gave a statement were given a list of potential support organisations in their communities, but this was not always the case. Furthermore, this did not always result in the person contacting these groupings. This was probably due to limited knowledge on behalf of the witnesses of the role of psychological support services in South Africa, but also because, in some regions, statement-takers were not adequately trained to make appropriate referrals.

Despite these difficulties, some referrals did occur and the statement-takers and briefers were responsible for several ad hoc referrals to support services. Some statement-takers' abilities and basic interpersonal skills were also of a high quality and this helped ensure that some witnesses were given adequate psychological support during the statement-taking process. Furthermore, as was mentioned in the previous section, there are a number of intrinsic psychological benefits of story-telling in a closed and structured environment—even if this is a one-off occurrence—from which many of the witnesses benefited.

In retrospect, despite the criticisms raised, the briefing/debriefing added a valuable component to the work of the TRC. However, given the complicated psychological difficulties experienced by many survivors and families of victims outlined earlier, it is unlikely that the briefing/debriefing would have been sufficient to deal with these problems. This was never the intention of the briefing/debriefing and reinforces the need for appropriate referral and networking. Similarly, trauma counselling targeted at an isolated past trauma was not sufficient in many cases. The nature of the compounded psychological and social difficulties experienced by most witnesses requires a sophisticated and consistent intervention. There clearly has been a need for most witnesses to try and resolve their traumas personally. Those who have been afforded the opportunity of counselling through a support organisation have engaged with the therapeutic process, attended sessions regularly and undoubtedly benefited (de Ridder 1997).

Support for the TRC Staff

All of the TRC staff, throughout the period of the Commission, have been constantly confronted with the painful traumas of those interacting with the TRC. As a result, the risk of vicarious and secondary traumatisation has been high and, in fact, high levels of traumatisation have been observed in all regions where the TRC has operated. Some of these symptoms and signs of vicarious traumatisation which many of the staff working for the TRC have presented with are nightmares, paranoia, emotional bluntness, physical problems (e.g. headaches, ulcers, exhaustion, etc.), high levels of anxiety, irritability and aggression, relationship difficulties and substance abuse related problems. Interestingly, the data-processors and others who have had to work with cases on paper or computer have manifested more symptoms than those working directly with traumatised individuals (Grenville-Grey 1997).

This situation probably arose because those working with individuals directly have had more space to integrate the information received into their own cognitive schemata based on a full understanding of the difficulties faced by the traumatised individual. For example, the traumatised individual may show signs of coping, resilience or having support systems. Thus making the traumatised individual's problem seem less drastic and consequently affecting the interviewer or TRC worker to a lesser degree. For those working with statements or computer data there is less chance for this cognitive integration to take place, and on top of this, the quantities of traumatic information processed are much greater.

In response to these levels of traumatisation the TRC did set up some internal support structures that appear to have worked relatively successfully within the constrained environment of the TRC. The groups were not initially envisaged as therapy groups but rather as general support structures to which all the staff were invited. The groups appear to have served this function and more. The groups provided a forum for the staff to raise their grievances with management and their difficulties experienced with the monolithic structure (e.g., over 300 staff members) that the TRC created to fulfil its mandate. The groups also served as a debriefing forum. At this point, the groups are undertaking so-called closure programmes. These focus on issues such as the long-term personal effects of working for the TRC, future personal and professional roles, coping skills after the TRC ends and feelings about expectations with regard to the original motivations of staff for working for the TRC.

Conclusion

Psychological support services initiated and undertaken by the South African TRC have been limited. Nevertheless, through the TRC process a number of individuals have received some psychological support that probably would have been denied to them without the TRC. Ironically, the TRC through its quest for truth and the uncovering of past pain, has generated a need for extensive mental health care services in the country. If one accepts the position that these needs, generated by the devastation of apartheid, required addressing with or without the TRC, then the pressure created by the TRC can only be seen as a useful force to ensuring services are set up. The danger, of course, is that if these services are not forthcoming then an enormous amount of trauma will remain exposed and unresolved. This can have a number of consequences, including the development of revenge cycles and the general undermining of the human potential available in South Africa.

Clearly, the road to reconciliation and personal healing in South Africa remains a thorny one. Undoubtedly, the TRC has helped smooth the path. The value of publicly revisiting the sad and brutal days of apartheid is that it has opened the eyes of many and has contributed to developing a collective history for South Africans. It has also allowed some survivors to evolve new meanings for their suffering and it has created some legitimate space for them to voice their feelings. However, individual processes of forgiveness, psychological restoration and reconciliation have not always intersected with the collective process offered by the TRC. Ongoing psychological support and follow-up by the TRC has been limited and, as a result, a heavy mantel has been placed at the door of the limited mental health care workers and services in the country. Much psychological debris remains to be mopped-up and contained, pointing to the need for the continued development of more extensive mental health care services in South Africa.

At present, the TRC is still operating, and two processes hold some hope for further psychological support and referral. The first is that post-hearing follow-ups are occurring in some communities. These entail returning to communities to discuss the needs and problems that may have arisen consequent to the hearing. Second, each case has to be reviewed to make a finding if the person should be classified as a victim according to the TRC criteria—thus ensuring their eligibility for reparation. As a result, through this process many witnesses may be identified as needing referral or ongoing support and referred to a service provider.

In conclusion, South Africa's collective story-telling process facilitated through the TRC has had its psychological benefits and has helped break the silences of the past. However, it is a mistake to assume that story telling and giving testimony, either in public or private spaces, equates with healing. Truth alone will not lead to reconciliation or guarantee that a human rights culture will permeate the society and that those who suffered in the past will be able to deal with their traumas. A great deal of work remains to be done to engage actively with the offending institutions (like the security forces), to secure lasting change and to ensure that those violated in South Africa's abusive past receive adequate social and psychological support. Furthermore, this is complicated by the ongoing disparities of wealth and the inequities in South Africa. At this stage, real economic change remains the greatest threat to lasting reconciliation because without changes in basic living conditions all the truth and psychological support mechanisms in the world will not address the multiple effects, psychological damage and miseries created by ongoing poverty in South Africa.

Notes

1. The granting of amnesty has a complicated and long history in South Africa. It has been argued that amnesty needs to be understood as a necessary and unavoidable precondition to the negotiated peace settlement; *see* Asmal, Asmal, & Roberts 1996; Simpson & van Zyl 1995.
2. The decision to grant amnesty also has to be considered in light of the motive of the person who committed the act, the context in which the act was committed, the legal and factual nature of the act (including the gravity of the offence), the object and objective of the act, and whether the act was carried out by order or approval of a political body, institution or individual. The relationship of the act to a political objective and the proportionality of the act also needs to be considered.
3. It is estimated that ten to twenty percent of those who gave statements received a public hearing.
4. If amnesty is being sought for a gross violation of human rights then a public hearing has to take place.
5. This has been confirmed by the Centre for the Study of Violence and Reconciliation's work with the Khulumani Support Group. In a personal interview, Trudy de Ridder of the Trauma Centre for Victims of Violence and Torture in Cape Town has also noted similar patterns with her support work with survivors of violence who have testified before the TRC.
6. *see* Centre for the Study of Violence and Reconciliation. 1995; Coalition of Kwazulu-Natal Mental Health and Human Rights Organisations. 1995; Kwazulu-Natal Programme for Survivors of Violence. 1995; Mental Health Response. 1996.
7. *cf.* Bosset 1995; Hamber 1996a, 1996b; Stauffer & Hamber 1996.
8. One such group is the *Khulumani or Speak-Out Support Group,* who are a Gauteng based group. They have offered survivors and families of victims some support, albeit limited due to resource problems. This structure—and there are examples of smaller groups elsewhere in the country—has in some cases introduced the truth commission to the victims, found indigenous ways to reconcile with the past and lobbied the TRC concerning the rights and concerns of survivors and families of victims. For more information on the group see *http://www.wits.ac.za/csvr.*
9. It is important to note that the investigators of the TRC are hopelessly overloaded with the enormous numbers of violations that have been presented to them to be investigated. Many survivors and families of victims complain they have heard very little regarding their cases at this point and are voicing frustrations with the TRC in this regard.
10. A creative initiative to use Community Trained Briefers was also undertaken. In communities, people were identified who could be trained and used in the briefing process and support the witnesses after the hearing. Individuals recognisable to the community, such as leaders and clergy, were chosen to be trained. These individuals played a critical role in the hearings process.

References

Asmal, K. L. Asmal and R. S. Roberts. 1996. *Reconciliation Through Truth: A Reckoning of Apartheid's Criminal Governance.* Cape Town: David Philip Publishers.

Bosset, M. 1995. "Co-existence and Community." In *The Healing of a Nation?* Edited by A. Boraine and J. Levy. Cape Town: Justice in Transition.

Centre for the Study of Violence and Reconciliation. 1995. "Psychological and Social Support for the Truth and Reconciliation Commission." Submission made to the Truth and Reconciliation Commission, Johannesburg, South Africa.

Coalition of Kwazulu-Natal Mental Health and Human Rights Organisations. 1995. "The Implementation of the Truth and Reconciliation Commission in Kwazulu-Natal." Submission made to the Minister of Justice on the Truth and Reconciliation Commission, Kwazulu-Natal, South Africa.

de Ridder, T. 1997. Telephonic Interview by author. June 1997. Johannesburg, South Africa.

Grenville-Grey, T. 1997. Telephonic Interview by author. June 1997. Johannesburg, South Africa.

Hamber, B. E. 1995. "Dealing with the Past and the Psychology of Reconciliation: A Psychological Perspective of the Truth and Reconciliation Commission." Public address at the *4th International Conference on Psychology and Peace.* June 1995. University of Cape Town: Cape Town.

———. 1996a. "The Need for a Survivor-Centered Approach to the Truth and Reconciliation Commission." *Community Mediation Update,* Issue 9. Johannesburg: Community Dispute Resolution Trust.

———. 1996b. "Sleeping Dogs Do Not Lie." *Recovery (Research & Co-operation on Violence and Rehabilitation of Young People),* Volume 1, Number 3. Kwazulu-Natal: Children's Inquiry Trust.

Kwazulu-Natal Programme for Survivors of Violence. 1995. "Preparing Survivors of Violence for the Truth Commission." Submission to the Truth and Reconciliation Commission, Kwazulu-Natal, South Africa.

Mental Health Response. 1996. "Preliminary Perspectives from the Western Cape." Submission to the Truth and Reconciliation Commission, Cape Town.

Simpson, G. and P. van Zyl. 1995. "South Africa's Truth and Reconciliation Commission." *Centre for the Study of Violence and Reconciliation.* Johannesburg: South Africa.

Stauffer, C. and B. Hamber. 1996. "Putting a Face on the Past: Survivor-Offender Mediation and the Truth and Reconciliation Commission." Paper presented the *Centre for the Study of Violence and Reconciliation Seminar No. 1 for 1996.* 20 February. The Centre for the Study of Violence and Reconciliation, Johannesburg, South Africa.

Asia

6

The Cambodian Tuol Sleng
Museum of Genocidal Crimes
National Narrative

Judy Ledgerwood

At the end of Benedict Anderson's *Imagined Communities,* he writes about biographies of nations—narratives of national identity. Unlike individuals, nations cannot write their biographies as a string of natural "begettings." Rather than births, the fashioning of narrative "is marked by deaths, which, in a curious inversion of conventional genealogy, start from an originary present. World War II begets World War I, . . . the ancestor of the Warsaw uprising is the state of Israel" (1991:205). These deaths are not ordinary deaths; the nation's biography takes the suicides, martyrdoms, assassinations, executions, wars, and holocausts to serve the national purpose and these "must be remembered/forgotten as 'our own'" (ibid.:205–206).

The Tuol Sleng Museum of Genocidal Crimes in Phnom Penh, Cambodia, is discussed here as the central site for construction of memories of Democratic Kampuchea, better known as the "Khmer Rouge period." Between April 1975 and January 1979, "hundreds of thousands"—"up to a million"—"more than a million"—"more than three million" Cambodians died—the numbers placing authors who used them in the contested fields of national memory.

This paper describes Tuol Sleng as a physical place, discusses what happened there when it served as a prison, and its subsequent establishment as a museum. It then posits two parallel patterns of narrative. The master narrative of the successor state, the People's Republic of Kampuchea, tells of a glorious revolution stolen and perverted by a handful of sadistic, genocidal traitors who deliberately exterminated three million of their countrymen. The true heirs to the revolutionary movement overthrew this murderous tyranny three

From *Museum Anthropology* 21, no. 1 (Spring/Summer 1997): 82–98. © 1997 American Anthropological Association. Reproduced with the permission of American Anthropological Association.

years, eight months, and twenty days later, just in time to save the Khmer people from genocide.

A second, parallel narrative corresponds closely to what Michael Vickery (1984) has disparagingly referred to as the "Standard Total View." In this all-encompassing narrative the worst individual experiences during the Democratic Kampuchea (DK) period are imagined to have been the result of deliberate policy decisions and the common experience throughout the country during the entire period. Vickery's view is that such characterizations of the Khmer Rouge period are "false," that is, historically inaccurate.

This paper analyzes the correspondence between the master narrative of the state—the story told in the museum of "genocidal crimes"—and the popular narrative of the "Standard Total View." The correspondence between the two, and the ways in which they reinforce and invigorate each other, run counter to some previous analyses of the relationship between history and memory in the context of state socialism. I argue that rather than being asked to remember events that did not happen, or to recall the unfamiliar, Cambodians generally accept the story of the museum as true to their experiences.

This paper, therefore, accepts Vickery's notion that the Standard Total View (STV) is a widespread common method of describing the DK period, but rejects the notion that the STV is a creation only of refugees, in justification of their decision to flee, and of Western anti-communist governments and media. The state narrative presented at the museum and the standardized remembrances of the DK times, like the movie *The Killing Fields,* present a prepackaged, summarized, public version of events for view both by Khmer and by foreigners. It precisely collapses space and time in ways that Vickery labels distortions. In doing so, the museum provides an explanation for the inexplicable, and creates from death a reestablished sense of national identity.

The Museum Compound

Before the wars of the last twenty-five years, the compound now called Tuol Sleng was a high school called Tuol Svay Prey (the hillock of the wild mango). On a quiet, sunny afternoon looking out across the grounds, one can still imagine it as such. Inside, the presentation of the horrors of Democratic Kampuchea are so vivid and ghastly that visitors find it deeply disturbing. The name of the museum, Tuol Sleng, the hillock of the Sleng tree (the fruit of which is poisonous), was previously the name of a nearby primary school. During DK times the site was called "S-21," but it was a secret facility known only to the prisoners, those who worked there, and a handful of high-ranking officials. David Chandler writes that when people were arrested they were not told they were going to S-21, only that they were "called to study," or "called for consultation." "To industrial workers quartered nearby, the prison was known only as a place where 'people went in but never came out'" (Chandler 1995).

The central compound consists of four three-story concrete buildings, two in a row facing east, one each on the north and south ends, and a wooden building in the middle (see map). The visitor enters the front gate and proceeds to the left as one would circumambulate a temple. A guide normally accompanies visitors, though they are permitted to walk through on their own if they so desire. First, the visitor approaches a set of graves of the final fourteen prisoners whose bodies were present when the Vietnamese troops discovered the facility on January 14, 1979. They were killed and left in the torture rooms of building one as the Khmer Rouge fled. In each room is a metal bed with a photo on the wall of the room as it was discovered, that is, with the body of the victim present. The torture instruments are still there, and the floors are still stained faintly with blood sixteen years later.

Building two contains primarily photographs; three walls of the first room are covered with photos of the people who died at Tuol Sleng. Displayed prominently opposite the doorway are the photos of a dozen or so foreigners who died there. From this room you enter a second room of photos, and then a third. From a distance, across the room the images are squares of black on white, six squares by six squares, thirty-six people per block, ten blocks per section, three hundred and sixty squares. As you walk closer, they become distinguishable as individual people, with expressions: a frown, a smirk, bewilderment, anger, shock, withdrawal, fear, most often fear. Most of these photos were taken in a standardized form as a bureaucratic act of record; others are of people taken as they were undergoing torture, or in death.[1] The third room also has a wall-size photo of the "killing field" at Cheung Ek, where the prisoners from S-21 were taken to be killed and their bodies disposed. In front of this photo are shackles used for the prisoners, a bust of Pol Pot, and the mold from which it was made.[2]

The second floor of this building contains the archive of "confessions," approximately 200,000 pages of documents, including more than 4000 "confessions" of individuals and some 6000 photographic negatives. Incomplete arrest logs suggest that more than 14,000 entered: approximately 200 in 1975, 2000 in 1976, 6000 in 1977, and 5000 in 1978 (Chandler 1995:20).[3] Some 1000 to 1500 prisoners were present at a given time. Execution schedules list activities completed: 15 October 1977, 418 killed; 18 October, 179 killed; 27 May 1978, 582 killed (Hawk 1989:210). The archive, however, is not on the standard tour; the trip through the museum is almost entirely visual, with limited written text.[4]

Building three contains old classrooms that were bricked in to create small individual cells. A photo on one cell notes that it was occupied by the famous revolutionary figure Hou Nim.[5] More important prisoners were kept in individual cells, less important ones were held in the classrooms, shackled together and to the floor in long rows.

Building four provides some written text of interpretation, including the figure of three million dead. The first room contains a map with the patterns of population movements after the evacuation of the cities. In this room is the chair where prisoners sat to have their pictures taken. Photos on the walls in this room are the perpetrators: the administrators, interrogators, cooks, and their families. The next two rooms contain pictures and paintings of the destruction of people and property during this era, as well as sample torture devices with large garishly colored paintings of the devices in use. These paintings are the work of one of the seven known survivors of S-21.

The last room has a large map of Cambodia made of skulls with the rivers and the great lake in the center of the country painted blood-red. The map is shocking and disturbing, the emotional climax of the tour.

Outside the last building is a monument to the souls of those who died there. Like a stupa, the monument symbolically contains the remains of those who died at S-21. One walks past this monument back to the central building, completing the circuit. Until 1992 or so, visitors were then ushered into a room containing a book in which they could write their impressions. A contribution box stands near the front gate.

Visitors are invited to visualize what the place was like when it was a prison and torture center. Though doing so is impossible, even a glimpse of the scene through one's imagination is overwhelming. I worked at Tuol Sleng for five months in 1990–91, helping to conserve documents and microfilm the archive.[6] Over time, one begins to see the details. On stairway landings, for example, holes have been knocked in the wall so the stairs could be cleaned by sloshing water down the staircases. Below each of these openings on the building exteriors one can still see stains of the blood that ran down the sides, as though the buildings themselves had bled.

As we worked in the archive, tour groups would wind through the complex every day, taking pictures, speaking in muffled tones. Khmer from overseas would visit, looking through the pictures for relatives missing then for nearly twenty years. On a few occasions people would come to the archive, hoping to find any word on the fate of a loved one, even the knowledge that they had been tortured into producing one of the extant confessions. In July 1995, I went back to the museum and spent several days reading the comments in the visitors' books, trying to understand the reactions of those who came to see the Tuol Sleng museum.[7]

S-21—The Prison

S-21 was only one of many prison facilities around the country, but it was the most important. The majority of the people murdered there were cadre who were accused of betraying the revolution. The files of some prisoners contain only a one- or two-page summary biography, often without any mention of the crimes they are suspected of committing. Other files contain many versions of "confessions," written and rewritten after sessions of torture.

A basic pattern is apparent across these documents. The first version is as straightforward an account of a life as could be imagined under the circumstances:[8] I was born here, my parents are named such and such, I was educated here, I joined the revolution in this year, sometimes ending with the assertion that they have always been faithful to the revolution. After intervals of torture, the prisoner writes successive versions of the account. In the margins of some of the documents are notes written by the prison authorities, in red ink, giving instructions to the interrogators: "Ask him more about this person"; "Ask more about that event"; "He is lying here!" One chilling comment reads simply, "This despicable one is too hardheaded, just beat him 'til he dies." In the final version, the prisoner generally "confesses" to being part of a conspiracy to destroy the revolutionary movement. Many were accused of being CIA, which, David Chandler points out, came to mean more generally "joining the enemy."[9]

The purpose was not only to force the prisoners to confess their guilt, but to name their co-conspirators. The files of high-ranking cadres are thick with lists of names and complex organizational charts of "strings" (*ksae*) of traitors within their military units, collectives, factories, and families. To be named in such listings meant likely arrest and, eventually, entry to S-21. Prisoners were sometimes brought in with their entire families, all of whom were also executed.

Since the leadership saw the revolution as perfect, any problems in Democratic Kampuchea, from the theft of food to the failure of the harvest in an area, had to be explained as sabotage. Each had to be a deliberate act of a traitor, and all such traitors had to be found and destroyed. In the parlance of the S-21 archive, they had to be "smashed to bits." Traitors were often accused of being in league with foreign powers, most commonly the CIA and/or the Vietnamese. While a few hundred foreigners died in S-21, most were Khmer. But the Khmer labeled as traitors were pushed beyond the boundaries of the new nation; in a speech in 1977, Pol Pot said, "These counterrevolutionary elements which betray and try to sabotage the revolution are *not to be regarded as being our people*. They are to be regarded as enemies of Democratic Cambodia, of the Cambodian revolution, and of the Cambodian people" (cited in Jackson 1989:56, emphasis added by Jackson).

The more that the confessions in S-21 produced "evidence" of secret networks of traitors everywhere within the "organization" (*angka*), the more the paranoid and fanatical Khmer Rouge leadership sought to purge the movement. Over the course of the regime, Tuol Sleng grew in importance. With up to 1500 prisoners at one time, it must have been a crowded and extremely busy place. The revolution was devouring itself.[10]

The Establishment of the Museum

The end of Democratic Kampuchea as a regime came in January 1979 with the invasion of Cambodia by the army of the Socialist Republic of Vietnam.

The People's Republic of Kampuchea (PRK), the successor government, was installed by Vietnam, whose military forces eventually withdrew ten years later, in September 1989. Providing evidence to the outside world that the invasion by the Vietnamese army was indeed a liberation was the primary concern of those who designed Tuol Sleng as a museum.

The museum did not formally open to the public until July 1980, but already by March 1979 tours of the site were being given to foreigners, mostly members of fraternal socialist parties abroad, to convince them of the extent of Khmer Rouge atrocities. A 1980 report from the Ministry of Culture, Information, and Propaganda says that the museum was "used to show the international guests the cruel torture committed by the traitors to the Khmer people . . . the center was not open to the public, but for the international guests and participants [sic] only" (1980:4).[11]

The museum opened to the public July 13, 1980, and in the first week had 32,000 guests, 1930 of them foreigners. From January to October 1980, when the report was issued, the museum had 320,241 visitors: 11,000 foreigners and 309,000 Khmer (Ministry of Culture, Information, and Propaganda 1980:23). The Ministry report notes that the museum was open to the public every Sunday, as it was an "important element in educating the masses." Organized visits by foreign and local groups took place on weekdays. The numbers are remarkable if one considers that most of those 320,000 people went through on Sundays, the days when it was open to the public, over just a four-month period (July to October).

Unfortunately, we do not know the internal discussions that went into the design of Tuol Sleng as a museum. The kind of behind-the-scenes view offered in Edward Linenthal's discussion (1995) of the creation of America's Holocaust museum is impossible to reconstruct. But one of the designers of the museum, a Vietnamese specialist on researching battles and war crimes, Mr. Mai Lam, gave an interview on the subject last year.[12]

Mai Lam, now seventy-four years old, began his career in the army as a member of the "war researching committee." When a battle was over, he would arrive to "research, to film, take pictures, take proof of every battle." After the war, he helped create the Museum of American War Crimes in Ho Chi Minh City as well as Tuol Sleng. He worked in Cambodia from February or March 1979 until 1988. Mr. Mai talks about himself as a researcher, as someone whose job it was to document the Khmer Rouge genocide.

His goal, or his "duty" as he calls it, was to research what happened, to provide the proof of DK crimes, and therefore an understanding of what happened to average Cambodians. Mr. Lam said:

> For seven years I studied this to build the museum, held many classes, provided many speakers, for the Cambodian people to help them study the war and many aspects of the war crimes . . . for the regular people who cannot understand, the museum can help them. Even though they suffered from the

regime, as a researcher I want them to go [to the museum]. Even though it makes them cry. . . . The Cambodian people who suffered the war could not understand the war—and the new generation also cannot understand (Sara Colm, personal communication 1995)

But there is also evidence that the museum was designed primarily for foreign consumption, including the fact that it opened first to "international guests." The Ministry of Culture, Information, and Propaganda report (1980:3) notes the need for bright lights in the rooms so that the foreigners can take pictures easily. Requests are made for more workers who speak French and English in order to help with research and preparation of documents for publication.

More controversial is the issue of whether the site was remolded into a "holocaust" site. Serge Thion has argued that parallels to Nazi camps were deliberately constructed when the museum was "refurbished" by Vietnamese experts, "in an effort to attract part of the sinister charisma of Auschwitz" (1993:182).[13] When asked by the interviewer if Tuol Sleng was modeled after any other museums, Mai Lam said that he had traveled to Germany, Russia, France, and Czechoslovakia to research other museums. The report of the Ministry of Culture, Information, and Propaganda (1980) also confirms help from East German specialists, where, the Holocaust literature notes, death camps were memorialized as monuments to socialism and Soviet liberation.

At issue, I think, is not whether the museum Tuol Sleng is the site of S-21, or whether S-21 was in fact a prison where people were tortured and executed, but rather, whether crafting Tuol Sleng as a "genocide" museum superseded and distorted preserving S-21 as it existed in DK times.[14] Entwined in this dilemma is whether or not the presentation of the artifacts in the museum is "authentically" Khmer or not. The very fact that Vietnamese advisors working with Khmer staff designed and set up the museum raises questions of authenticity for many Khmer.

At the center of this controversy is the map of skulls. Mai Lam admitted in the interview, after some hesitation, that the map of skulls was his idea, as was the monument of skulls at the "killing field" at Cheung Ek. He said that preserving the skulls was "very important for the Cambodian people—it's the proof" (Sara Colm, personal communication 1995). Displaying the skulls in this manner became a public issue again in 1993, when the newly re-crowned King Sihanouk proposed cremating the remains in accord with Khmer Buddhist custom, a topic to which we will return in the conclusion of this paper.

Constructions of Meaning by the State—
The People's Republic of Kampuchea

As Mai Lam emphasized in his interview, Tuol Sleng was intended to be in a very literal sense "evidence" of the crimes of the Khmer Rouge. James

Young says that memorials at Majdanek and Auschwitz, are "devastating in their impact: for they compel the visitor to accept the horrible fact that what they show is real" (1993:120). Young writes: "In contrast to memorials located away from the sites of destruction, the remnants here tend to collapse the distinction between themselves and what they evoke. In the rhetoric of their ruins, these memorial sites seem not merely to gesture toward past events but to suggest themselves as fragments of events, inviting us to mistake the debris of history for history itself (1993:121).

The power of the museum as proof of crimes against humanity, or "genocidal" crimes, is clear in the writings of foreigners in the Tuol Sleng visitors' books from the early 1980s. Foreign delegations, including journalists and members of communist or socialist parties from abroad, often penned that while they had been skeptical about stories of atrocities, they were now convinced. Nayan Chanda writes that such reporting had real political consequences:

> Since 1980, the Vietnamese had flung open Cambodia's door to Western media. Reporters and television crews were allowed to freely travel around the country, observe the mass graves, talk to countless survivors, and visit the notorious Tuol Sleng Prison in Phnom Penh, where thousands of pages of confessions were exacted under torture and where gruesome photographs of victims stood in silent testimony to the "efficiency" of Democratic Kampuchea's murder machine. The reports and television films that resulted from those visits caused worldwide revulsion and led Britain and Australia to withdraw their recognition of Democratic Kampuchea. (1986:382)

The theme of foreigners promising to return to their countries to tell people what "really" happened in Cambodia remains a dominant one throughout the years that visitors were signing the Tuol Sleng books.

While foreigners saw evidence of atrocities, many Khmer, particularly in the first two years of the museum's operation, were coming to view the photos to search for missing relatives. They were also, of course, searching for meaning, for some explanation of what had happened. A visit would not have been an easy task; people who went through the museum in the first year said that the stench of the place was overpowering. But still they came, standing in line for hours to file through, carefully checking each photo.

For the local Khmer audience, the goal of the state was to provide a "monologic historical explanation" to events[15]—and evoke specific responses. As Rubie Watson points out, "Under state socialism, Marxism-Leninism was not one ideology or political economy among many, but rather was the inevitable and glorious outcome of a discernible historical process" (1994:1). Reconciling the horrors of one failed communist regime with the logic of an inevitable march of progress is the underlying text of the museum.

According to the state explanation, it was the (newly renamed in 1979) Kampuchea People's Revolutionary Party who had gained a glorious victory over the imperialist Americans in April 1975. The victory, however, was then stolen by a small number of murderous criminals who killed true revolutionaries, many in this facility. The code phrase for this gang of criminals was the "Pol Pot–Ieng Sary genocidal clique," often shortened simply to "Pol Pot," narrowing and personalizing the responsibility for events. Now the true victors, the former DK cadre and remnants of the old pro-Vietnamese wing of the Cambodian Communist Party who formed the new PRK government, had regained their rightful status as leaders of a glorious revolutionary movement.

The PRK government and the Vietnamese army faced armed resistance from the remnants of the Khmer Rouge and their allies, two non-communist resistance groups. A formal resistance coalition was formed in 1982, called the Coalition Government of Democratic Kampuchea (CGDK), which received support from China, the United States, and the Association of Southeast Asian Nations (ASEAN). When Khiev Samphan became the vice-president of the CGDK, the key phrase for the traitor group expanded to the "Pol Pot–Ieng Sary–Khiev Samphan genocidal clique." An economic blockade choked an already devastated Cambodia and drastically slowed recovery. In the propaganda war to win the hearts and minds of the Khmer people from the resistance to the Vietnamese-backed government, Tuol Sleng played a central role.

Tour groups, often from education and information organs, were brought in from different areas of the country to visit the museum.[16] To foster a sense of identification with the message of the museum for citizens from all parts of the nation, the Ministry of Culture, Information and Propaganda report (1980:22) notes that skulls used in the making of the map were collected from "killing fields" in every province of Cambodia, and that the map notes the percentage of persons killed in each region.

The museum figured prominently in state publications for internal and external consumption, and the message of the museum was very quickly standardized. Some of the earliest visitors to the museum just wrote that they had visited and signed their names; but soon the writings echoed almost precisely the rhetoric of the state publications. Standardized phrases emerged. The message was first, that Cambodians *want to remember* the criminal acts of the Pol Pot–Ieng Sary–Khiev Samphan clique [*pracheachun kampuchea deang mul chang cham chea nic ukriddhakamm nai robab pol potieng sari-khiev samphan*];[17] and second, that the purpose of this remembering is to *prevent the return of the Khmer Rouge to power* [*dac khat min qaoy qatatakal da khmav ngongit nuh vil tralap mok ving ban loey*].[18]

The third, and perhaps most important message, was powerful in its simplicity. The phrase most often written by Khmer in the visitors' books at Tuol Sleng is *chheu chap*—*chheu* means pain or suffering, agony, or torment—*chap* means to grab, to hold, to seize—*chheu chap* is an aching or agony that seizes you physically and spiritually. Khmer say that linked to this notion is a sense of betrayal, as when a lover betrays you, and frustration because there is nothing that can be done to resolve the pain.

Therefore, partly contained within this notion is anger born of betrayal and frustration. It is the anger that the state propaganda machine focused on in its presentation of Tuol Sleng and of the DK period more generally. The phrase *chheu chap* in state publications becomes a compound: *kamheng chheu chap, kamheng* meaning anger or rage. From an irresolvable grief is born a pain that results in rage. Take, for example, a quotation from a 1984 PRK publication in Khmer, which reads, "*kiev phneak po penh dov daoy kamheng chheu chap* [the pupils of our eyes are full of rage born of agony]" (Ministry of Information and Culture 1984:24).[19]

Kamheng chheu chap was not necessarily a "natural" or "logical" reaction to DK atrocities; arguably the case could be made that for many Buddhist Khmer such a response was not forthcoming,[20] but it was the state message designed to rally an exhausted and stricken population to the new government. It was designed to inspire young men to join the army and people to "give" rice tax donations for the war effort. Each year, May 20 was set aside as "the day of hatred." On one such day, I saw school children taking turns to strike an effigy of Pol Pot with a large stick; the effigy was then set aflame.[21]

The central message of the government was, and remains to this day: you must support us because to fail to do so will result in the return to power of the Khmer Rouge.[22] The message is the phrase on a state propaganda poster—distributed in 1990 at, among other places, Tuol Sleng—which reads, "In the past, as in the present, as in the future, Pol Pot still remains genocidal."

The "Standard Total View"

Michael Vickery in his book *Cambodia 1975–1982* (1984) puts forward the argument that the history of the DK period has been distorted into a narrative that is, in its totality, untrue. The Standard Total View, or STV, is a description of life under the DK that is standardized across time and geographical space. At all places throughout the DK period, for example, children were taken from their parents, there were no hospitals or schools, and people were routinely executed in front of others. Vickery spends much of the text meticulously documenting how the circumstances of DK life varied in different regions and over time; from his interviews, he notes here the mention of a hospital, there of a school. He refutes some of the most commonly told stories of the period, that everyone with eyeglasses was killed, for example, or that all of those who returned from overseas were executed.

Vickery's meticulous research is important in that he documents, with regional and temporal variation, the details of life under DK. He acknowledges that over the course of the regime, conditions worsened. Vickery writes,

"There could hardly any longer be serious doubt that the DK regime, however it started out, had become something very much like that depicted in the STV" (1984:48). But Vickery's stance on the period is read by many as an attempt to downplay the seriousness of DK atrocities. His estimate of the number of dead is significantly lower than other estimates (from 400,000 to 740,000) (1984:186–188). Although I agree with Vickery that taken as a whole the STV includes inaccuracies in fact, this paper critiques the origins and meanings that Vickery ascribes to the STV.

Vickery attributes the origins of the STV "distortions" to refugees in the border camps in Thailand. He asserts that these refugees were almost exclusively urbanites trying to go to "one of those Western paradises about which [they] had always dreamed" (Vickery 1987:297). That the city people found the work intolerable under DK, he argues, reflected their inexperience with rice production. According to Vickery, much of the media treatment of DK "was not inaccurate just because some of the refugees were incapable of accuracy or were liars, but because the journalists responsible for publicizing the STV selected the information most suitable for sensational publicity and ignored the rest" (1984:56). Such sensationalism dovetailed with anti-communist rhetoric in the West, causing "the truth," that is, history, to be ignored.

There are several problems with focusing on the source of the STV in refugee tales and the sensationalizing of their stories by the Western press. Contrary to Vickery's arguments, it was not only urbanites who suffered and died in massive numbers under the Khmer Rouge, as Ebihara's recent work (1993) has clearly demonstrated (see also Uimonen 1994; Davenport, Healy, and Malone 1995). Life-long peasants also died of disease and malnutrition under the back-breaking labor. Poor peasants and fishermen fled to the border as refugees.

More importantly, it is not only diaspora Khmer who tell the story of DK times in terms of an STV-type standardized narrative. Farmers tell of state-arranged marriages, restrictions on movements, separation from their children, collective dining, and a host of other despised DK innovations, regardless of precisely when these changes were initiated in their home regions. They do speak in general terms about atrocities experienced throughout the country. Khmer in Cambodia, like their former countrymen abroad, extend their own individual indignities and sufferings and project them across space and time to include their fellow *Khmae yoeng,* "we Khmer."[23]

Individual oral stories of DK times often include "tellings" of a type Vickery refers to as an "extreme" STV: that the ultimate goal of the DK was literally genocide, that they intended to kill everyone in the country— presumably excluding the cadre themselves. Stories abound of preparations being made in the final days of the regime to poison or "smash" whole villages en masse. Khmer say people were being ordered to dig trenches that would be the final mass graves for the remaining population. Banquets, which would be laced with poison, were being prepared (see also Ebihara 1993, Uimonen 1994). People are saying, "If it had not ended when it did, we would *all* be dead."

This notion of the regime killing for the sake of genocide (*bralay pouch-sah*), literally exterminating the Khmer *pouch* (race, line or species),[24] is the state narrative of the PRK, the narrative of Tuol Sleng.[25] The museum confirms for Khmer that their experiences were "national" experiences shared across the geographical area of Cambodia, the most ghastly and powerful memorializing of this notion being the map of skulls. A new kind of national boundary is imagined between those who suffered the agony of DK and those who did not.[26]

In Watson's work (1994:6) on memory and history under state socialism, she writes that in the former Soviet Union, eastern Europe, and China, people had to come to terms with the fact that their memories were different from historical orthodoxy. People were asked to "remember" events that did not occur, or that were described in terms alien to their own experiences. People had to hide shadow memories that conflicted with official histories. In contrast, I argue that in Cambodia the STV presents a shared perception of facts as remembered now by Khmer who experienced it.

Tuol Sleng presented Khmer with an interpretive framework that did ring true to the horrendous experiences of the DK years. The brutality and violence portrayed so vividly, the faces of all the dead staring at them from the four walls of the rooms, did evoke and reinforce their memories—if not their memories of the entire period in every place, then certainly the crucial, central memories of the worst individual moments of that era.[27]

Thion has argued that PRK propaganda, because it was perceived as propaganda, "obliterated the survivors' ability to build up their own retrospective understanding" (1993:183). I would argue that the opposite is true, that Khmer relied upon and responded to the PRK state narrative in creating their own understandings of the recent past. Watson writes of the Cultural Revolution that for ten years the killings, torture, forced migrations, and internecine warfare seemed independent, unrelated events: "without a vocabulary to name, classify, and so analyze their experiences, victims and victimizers alike remained confused and fundamentally isolated in the aftermath of their ordeal" (Watson 1994:67). The Chinese state failed to offer a plausible framework of explanation. On the contrary in the Khmer case, the meta-narrative of the PRK state, of criminals committing genocide ousted by patriotic revolutionaries, framed and provided an explanation for seemingly incomprehensible events.

But such propaganda is not accepted or rejected totally and blindly. Acts and evocations of national memory making can have multiple and simultaneous meanings, as Nina Tumarkin proposes in discussing of the "cult" of the great patriotic war in Russia. She writes that the Victory Day celebrations in

Russia, include: "... managers seeking to manipulate popular emotion inspired by a genuinely traumatic past experience in order to mobilize public energies in support of the Party and state, a time for the inescapable barrage of self-serving hype—and a day for families to lay flowers on the graves of their loved ones or to leave bouquets at their local war memorial" (1995:37).

The PRK state narrative of genocide is one of multiple and overlapping explanations, but it is one of the most powerful and encompassing "tellings."[28] Tuol Sleng condenses and explains to Khmer, as per Mai Lam's comments above, and to foreigners, what the DK horrors were like. Most Khmer I talked with want foreigners to go to the museum so that they can understand what happened, in much the same way as Khmer-Americans want their American friends to see the movie *The Killing Fields.*

Conclusion

In December 1994, King Norodom Sihanouk offered to pay the cost of official cremation ceremonies for the skulls and other bones that were left as memorials at Tuol Sleng and the famous "killing field" at Cheung Ek. Sihanouk, who had long argued for national reconciliation, made the case that Khmer Buddhist tradition demanded that proper respect be shown to the souls of the departed. On December 7 international newspapers carried the story that the government had decided to cremate the remains. The Cambodian Peoples' Party (CPP)—the former PRK period communist party, and the most powerful component of the newly formed coalition government—strongly objected, and the idea was dropped.

The king was trying to lay to rest not just the souls of the dead, but the deep divisions between the coalition partners in the new royal government— those placed in power by Vietnamese "liberators" and those who fought a war of "liberation" against Vietnamese "occupation." The former non-communist allies of the Khmer Rouge are now part of the government. The role of Tuol Sleng as evidence of Khmer Rouge atrocities, of horrid brutality and attempted genocide, is acceptable across this political spectrum. But the Tuol Sleng narrative that treats the PRK leadership as the saviors of the nation, thus recognizing them as the singular heirs to legitimate power, has been complicated by the 1993 elections.

Who were the "traitors" that the DK torturers spent so much energy trying to find? Who wanted to sabotage the revolution? In the Tuol Sleng Museum version, the traitors are the Pol Pot–Ieng Sary–Khiev Samphan genocidal clique, those who ran S-21 and other facilities like it. In an ironic twist, the Khmer Rouge become enshrined as what it is that they set out to destroy. But the process of a search for "traitors" that is preserved in the archives still continues.

The Khmer Rouge refused to demobilize their forces or participate in the UN-organized elections in 1993, and remain a resistance force along the

Thai-Cambodian border.[29] In 1994, the Khmer Rouge response to the king's suggestion was to deny that the victims at Tuol Sleng had died under their rule: "The communist Vietnamese collected skulls and bones from graveyards all over north and south Vietnam, brought them by trucks to Cambodia, and displayed them in an exhibition at Tuol Sleng as part of a psychological campaign to legalize their aggression against and occupation of Cambodia" (UPI, 16 December 1994, citing DK radio, The Voice of the Great National Union Front). The DK thus not only question the authenticity of Tuol Sleng by suggesting that the story of genocide was made up by Vietnamese, they also challenge the "Khmerness" of the dead. Pushing the victims beyond the Cambodian nation, paralleling the way the victims were made "foreign" in their confessions, removes the museum from the realm of evidence of DK atrocities.

The CPP's desire to keep the Tuol Sleng Museum intact constitutes political resistance to a legitimization of the returned resistance fighters, and a corresponding labeling of themselves as Vietnamese puppets and sympathizers. The CPP co-Prime Minister has made a series of speeches in which he lashes out at "terrorists" and "traitors" within the country who, like worms, must be found and destroyed.[30]

In the early months of 1996, controversy erupted again over whether to celebrate January 7, the day of the Vietnamese "liberation"/"invasion" as a national holiday. For the members of the coalition government who returned from the resistance, celebrating this day is an affront. There is little middle ground on which to base a compromise; at stake is the fundamental notion of whether or not a coalition is possible.

While the rhetoric of Khmer politics proceeds in this chillingly familiar fashion, at Tuol Sleng itself another kind of change is steadily taking place. The government provides no funds for its maintenance. Contributions from the box are used to supplement the meager salaries of the administration and staff. Over the years they have sold parts of the front walls, and the rolled barbed wire is gone. The housing across the south end of the complex has been fenced off, privatized, repaired, and, in some cases, sold. The wall has been knocked down right up to the corner where the name of the museum is displayed. No funds are available for electricity so the complex is usually dark, and the air-conditioner provided to help preserve the documents sits idle. The bloodstains have faded, and some of the skulls are dangling from the edge of the map. The memorial stupa needs a coat of paint. Tuol Sleng is quite literally fading away.[31] The only new addition is a souvenir and drink shop that first appeared as a small stand by the front entrance, but which by July 1996 occupied the front section of the central building. Museum workers sell refreshments, Khmer crafts, and video movies about the DK years.

Genocide and death, as displayed at Tuol Sleng, have become the national narrative, the biography of Cambodia as a nation. Democratic Kampuchea, in Anderson's terms, is the ancestor to Angkor Wat, the other ultimate symbol of Khmerness. Jayavarman VII, the great twelfth-century king, becomes an ancient Pol Pot, or Pol Pot imagines himself as a modern Jayavarman.

The national narrative as constructed by the PRK and the Vietnamese, and told through Tuol Sleng, corresponds closely with and reinforces the various individual tellings of the Standard Total View. While many enforced and false tellings of historical occurrences are being reevaluated in former socialist countries, the STV in contrast does seem to correspond to people's memories, certainly their worst memories of the worst times.

Cambodians remember Khmer Rouge times as "their own," accepting the metanarrative of death and destruction as standardized across the motherland—skulls from every province—with Tuol Sleng as a central site for constructing this new national identity. But Tuol Sleng, like S-21 before it, also serves as a place to designate heroes and traitors. Letting the museum fade away may demonstrate an unwillingness to face these issues directly, and less willingness on the part of most Khmer to smash effigies, or their fellow Khmer, in yet another day of hate.

Acknowledgments

I would like to express my gratitude to Geoffrey White, David Chandler, and the two anonymous reviewers for *Museum Anthropology* for their comments on this paper.

Notes

1. A special issue of the journal *Photographers International* (No. 19, April 1995) presents a collection of these photos.

2. The bust of Pol Pot, as well as some painted portraits of "brother number one" as he was known, was the work of prisoners at Tuol Sleng. On the issue of whether a "cult of personality" was being developed around Pol Pot, see Chandler 1992:157–161.

3. Chandler's figures (1995) are based on extensive work with the documents microfilmed by Cornell University. The figure given by the People's Republic of Kampuchea of 20,000 persons is calculated, according to Ung Pech (Tuol Sleng Museum ex-prisoner and staff member in the early 1980s), on the assumption that an additional 2000 children perished who were not forced to "confess," and that the files for the intake in the second half of 1978 have not survived (Barnett, Kiernan, and Boua 1980:671). For discussions of Tuol Sleng documents, see: Barnett, Kiernan, and Boua 1980; Becker 1986; Chandler 1991, 1992, 1995; Hawk 1989; Heder 1990; and Kiernan 1996.

4. The languages of the museum are Khmer, French, and English, though not all text appears in all three languages. Some signs appear only in Khmer and French, others in Khmer and English.

5. This photo had disappeared when I went through the museum in July 1995.

6. I was project director of the Cornell University Document Conservation Project in Cambodia for over two years. The goal was both to preserve the originals and to

make microfilm copies of documents at the National Library, National Museum, and Tuol Sleng Museum. Project funding was provided by the Henry Luce Foundation and the Christopher Reynolds Foundation. The archive currently exists on microfilm at Cornell University Library, as well as at the Tuol Sleng Museum.

7. Unfortunately, I could read only the comments in Khmer, English, and some of the French. It would be fascinating to undertake the task of translating the comments from other languages: Russian, Vietnamese, Japanese, Chinese, and so on.

8. For a discussion of the difficulties of using the documents for historical research, see Heder (1990). He writes, "You have to assume that every word may either be a falsehood forced upon a terrorized writer by his torturing interrogators, or an equal falsehood concocted by the same terrorized writer in some desperate attempt to save his or her life by denying what is true or parroting some lie that he or she hopes against hope might mollify the organization. And yet long before one is through the first thousand pages, it becomes obvious to the reader that some things are undoubtedly true" (Heder 1990:2; see also Chandler 1992:130–132, Kiernan 1996:464).

9. David Chandler, personal communication.

10. This period has been written about in some detail: See Chandler 1991, 1992; Chandler and Kiernan 1983; Kiernan 1993, 1996; Picq 1984.

11. I am grateful to Steve Heder for providing me with a copy of this report, as well as copies of his interviews conducted along the Thai-Cambodian border in 1980, including an interview with Ong Thong Hoeung, an archivist at Tuol Sleng from August to October 1980. Kiernan reports that Tuol Sleng was "unveiled" as a museum in May 1979 (1996:465). David Chandler notes that the word *participants* here may refer to the foreigners who attended the genocide trials in August 1979 (personal communication).

12. The interview of Mai Lam was conducted by Sara Colm in Ho Chi Minh City, 1 March 1995. The discussion that follows is based on a text of this interview provided to the author by Sara Colm. I am most grateful to her for sharing this unpublished research.

13. Serge Thion then attacks legitimizing "memory" over "history." He writes, "Jews and Khmers do not mourn and bury their dead in the same way and there is a risk that our Western concept of memory could be entirely irrelevant to the Khmers who obviously have their own. I wish we may not succumb to the temptation to force our views on them, as we do already in so many other fields" (1993:182). This paper is intended to discuss patterns of narrative associated with a particular Khmer place, not merely echo memories of Jewish Holocaust sites. The extent to which Tuol Sleng may have been made to be "like" Auschwitz will have to be addressed elsewhere.

14. On the issue of the authenticity of the documents at Tuol Sleng, I would agree with Steve Heder's assessment: "The answer is that there is absolutely no doubt that they are authentic in the sense that the documents are certainly the genuine files of S-21. This is the conclusion intuitively apparent to anyone who reads seriously through the documents. The files are so massive and so detailed that it is inconceivable that anyone, no matter how highly motivated by whatever political purpose, would or could possibly have ever succeeded in concocting them" (1990:2).

15. This phrase is from Kligman's (1990) "Reclaiming the Public: a Reflection on Creating Civil Society in Romania," cited in Rubie Watson (1994:2).

16. The current director of the museum said that in the early years it was representatives of these organized groups, not individuals, who signed the visitors' books (interview July 1995).

17. Here literally, "the entire Cambodian people want to remember always the criminal acts of Pol Pot–Ieng Sary–Kiev Samphan" (Ministry of Information and Culture 1984:3).

18. Here literally, "We must absolutely prevent the return of that former black darkness" (Ministry of Information and Culture 1984:3).

19. In anthropological literature, perhaps the closest expression of this notion is Renato Rosaldo's discussion (1984) of the logic of Ilongot headhunting.

20. See Welaratna (1993) on the notion of Buddhism and forgiveness.

21. Serge Thion (1993:182) points out, however, that for many, perhaps most, Cambodians, the day of hate was performed without enthusiasm.

22. For this theme as central to Cambodian People's Party (CPP) propaganda before the 1993 elections, see Heder and Ledgerwood (1996).

23. The questions for researchers are incredibly difficult, as the following example demonstrates. With the passage of years more and more Khmer, especially people who were children at the time, tell of *seeing* people murdered, rather than just seeing people taken away, something Vickery and others who did interviews at the border immediately after the collapse of the DK almost never heard. Does this mean that refugees on the border were still too afraid to tell such stories to researchers in the camps? Does it mean that survivors who tell such stories now are not telling the truth? Does it mean that tellings collected at the time are "more pure" than memories of people years later?

24. *pouch* (pronounced puich), "race, species, family (biol.), stock (of animals)" (Headley 1977:659).

25. Serge Thion (1993:176) notes that this is the original meaning of the word genocide, in contrast to how it is used today.

26. This is certainly problematic for overseas Khmer who did not live in Cambodia during DK times. Their "authenticity" as Khmer is in question. Such a notion also leaves Khmer Rouge themselves beyond "Khmerness." For a discussion of this notion see Frank Smith (1989); I believe it is also reflected in the stories that Vickery repeats about the DK being "dark people" from the jungles. These culturally elaborated creations of non-Buddhist, dark-skinned people become in Vickery's text the "real" people. See also Uimonen (1994).

27. In another version of this paper, I discussed the stories of DK experiences in terms of Lawrence Langer's concept (1991) of "deep memory." In deep memory tellings, normal patterns of narrative are disrupted as people literally see these horrific events unfolding again before them.

28. Of course there are many other competing versions of this explanatory narrative, the most important of which rely on Buddhist explanations of what happened under DK (see for example, Smith 1989, Mortland 1994). These explanations are pointedly absent from Tuol Sleng, a communist state construction. The intersection of religious and state explanations of meaning occurs, not surprisingly, in the context of ritual activity. Each year at the festival for the dead, *Pachum Ben,* the Tuol Sleng Museum becomes a site for prayer and offerings to Buddhist monks. Since during this time the spirits of the dead return to the earth to "haunt" their descendants if they have not successfully moved on to a new rebirth, the festival is treated very seriously at Tuol Sleng.

29. As of August 1996, the remaining Khmer Rouge had split into two factions; one faction led by Ieng Sary was negotiating with the Royal government about integrating his forces into the national army.

30. *Phnom Penh Post,* 3–16 November 1995, p. 1; 1–14 December 1995, p. 3. The rhetoric is hauntingly similar to that of DK times.

31. On January 23, 1997 (as this paper was being edited for publication) the Associated Press reported that a South Korean businessman named Seo Seong-ho had proposed a $1 million dollar renovation of Tuol Sleng. Pen Yeth, the secretary of state of the Ministry of Culture and Fine Arts is quoted as saying: "We will not allow the historical image of the museum to be destroyed, but improvements are necessary if we wish to preserve the past. In addition to building new displays and adding a park and

murals, Seo wants to create a 'sound and light' show with slides, music and a historical narrative . . ." (Som Sattana 1997:n.p.). The story notes that "many Cambodians are wary of the plan," particularly if it means turning the museum into a "business venture" (ibid.).

References

Anderson, Benedict
 1991 *Imagined Communities*. Rev. ed. London: Verso.
Barnett, Anthony, Ben Kiernan, and Chanthou Boua
 1980 Bureaucracy of Death. *New Statesman,* 2 May: Pp. 668–676.
Becker, Elizabeth
 1986 *When the War Was Over: Cambodia's Revolution and the Voices of Its People*. New York: Simon and Schuster.
Chanda, Nayan
 1986 *Brother Enemy: The War after the War.* New York: Macmillan.
Chandler, David
 1991 *The Tragedy of Cambodian History.* New Haven: Yale University Press.
 1992 *Brother Number One: A Political Biography of Pol Pot*. Boulder: Westview Press.
Chandler, David, and Ben Kiernan, eds.
 1983 *Revolution and Its Aftermath in Kampuchea*. Monograph No. 25. New Haven: Yale University Southeast Asia Studies.
Davenport, Paul, Sr., Joan Healy, and Kevin Malone
 1995 *Vulnerable in the Village*. Phnom Penh: JSRC.
Ebihara, May M.
 1993 "Beyond Suffering": The Recent History of a Cambodian Village. In *The Challenge of Reform in Indochina*. Borje Ljunggren, ed. Pp. 149–166. Cambridge, MA: Harvard Institute for International Development, Harvard University Press.
Ebihara, May M., Carol A. Mortland and Judy Ledgerwood, eds.
 1994 *Cambodian Culture Since 1975: Homeland and Exile*. Ithaca, NY: Cornell University Press.
Hawk, David
 1989 The Photographic Record. In *Cambodia 1975–1978*. Karl D. Jackson, ed. Pp. 209–214. Princeton: Princeton University Press.
Headley, Robert J.
 1977 *Cambodian-English Dictionary.* Washington, DC: The Catholic University Press.
Heder, Steve
 1990 Khmer Rouge Opposition to Pol Pot: "Pro-Vietnamese" or "Pro-Chinese." Paper presented at Australian National University, August.
Heder, Steve, and Judy Ledgerwood, eds.
 1996 *Propaganda, Politics, and Violence in Cambodia*. Armonk, NY: M. E. Sharpe.

Jackson, Karl D., ed.
  1989 The Ideology of Total Revolution. In *Cambodia 1975–1978.* Karl D.
         Jackson, ed. Pp. 37–78. Princeton: Princeton University Press.
Kiernan, Ben, ed.
  1993 *Genocide and Democracy in Cambodia.* Monograph No. 41. New
         Haven: Yale University Southeast Asia Studies.
  1996 *The Pol Pot Regime.* New Haven: Yale University Press.
Kligman, Gail
  1990 Reclaiming the Public: A Reflection on Creating Civil Society in
         Romania. *Eastern European Politics and Societies* 4:393–439.
Langer, Lawrence
  1991 *Holocaust Testimonies: The Ruins of Memory.* New Haven: Yale Uni-
         versity Press.
Linenthal, Edward
  1995 *Preserving Memory: The Struggle to Create America's Holocaust
         Museum.* New York: Viking Press.
Ministry of Culture, Information, and Propaganda, The People's Republic
of Kampuchea
  1980 *Report: Angkor Conservatory—Museums: National Museum, For-
         mer Royal Palace and Tuol Sleng.* Phnom Penh.
Ministry of Information and Culture, The People's Republic of Kampuchea
  1984 *Dik Dey Angkor Bacchobban.* Phnom Penh: Publications Office.
Mortland, Carol M.
  1994 Khmer Buddhists in the United States: Ultimate Questions. In *Cam-
         bodian Culture Since 1975: Homeland and Exile.* May Ebihara,
         Carol Mortland, and Judy Ledgerwood, eds. Pp. 72–90. Ithaca, NY:
         Cornell University Press.
Phnom Penh Post
  Vol. 4, No. 22. 3–16 November 1995, p. 1.
  Vol. 4, No. 24. 1–14 December 1995, p. 3.
Picq, Laurence
  1984 *Au delà du Ciel: Cinq ans chez les Khmer Rouges.* Paris: Barrault.
Rosaldo, Renato
  1984 Grief and a Headhunter's Rage: On the Cultural Force of Emotions.
         In *Text, Play, and Story: The Construction and Reconstruction of Self
         and Society.* Edward Bruner, ed. Pp. 178–195. Washington, DC: The
         American Ethnological Society.
Som Sattana
  1997 Businessman Proposes Renovation of Infamous Khmer Rouge
         Museum. Associated Press, January 23 [camnews@lists.best.com].
Smith, Frank
  1989 *Interpretive Accounts of the Khmer Rouge Years: Personal Experience
         in a Cambodian Peasant World View.* Occasional Paper No. 18. Madi-
         son: Center for Southeast Asian Studies, University of Wisconsin–
         Madison.
Thion, Serge
  1993 *Watching Cambodia.* Bangkok: White Lotus.

Tumarkin, Nina

1995　*The Living and the Dead: The Rise and Fall of the Cult of World War II in Russia*. New York: Basic Books.

Uimonen, Paula

1994　*Responses to Revolutionary Change: A Study of Social Memory in a Khmer Village*. Master's Thesis, Anthropology, Stockholm University.

Vickery, Michael

1984　*Cambodia 1975–1982*. Boston: South End Press.

1987　Refugee Politics. In *The Cambodian Agony*. David Ablin and Marlowe Hood, eds. Pp. 293–331. Armonk, NY: M. E. Sharpe.

Watson, Rubie, ed.

1994　*Memory, History, and Opposition under State Socialism*. Santa Fe, NM: School of American Research Press.

Welaratna, Usha

1993　*Beyond the Killing Fields*. Stanford: Stanford University Press.

Young, James

1993　*The Texture of Memory: Holocaust Memorials and Meaning*. New Haven: Yale University Press.

7

Buajingan!

Indonesian Art, Literature, and State Violence around the Downfall of President Soeharto

Rob Goodfellow and M. Dwi Marianto

Before the Fall[1]

Over three days from the 1st of August 1997 a remarkable national campaign against violence toward women in Indonesia was launched at the Museum Benteng Vredeburg, Yogyakarta, Java. (Yogyakarta is known internationally as Indonesia's cultural and educational capital.) Powerful and passionate speeches heralded the opening of "Kampanye Anti-Kekerasan Terhadap Perempuan Indonesia," an impressive exhibition of fine art, installation, sculpture, and printmaking, accompanied by music and drama. One speech in particular marked a significant departure from contemporary Indonesia's dominant culture of the suppression of public discussion about "sensitive issues."

Nyi (a form of Mrs.) Mardiyem recounted her experiences as a *jugun yanfu* (Japanese Army slave-prostitute) during World War II. Speaking in reserved but confident tones to a spellbound audience, she described how she was forcibly recruited, together with other "young girls" from her village, into a life of shame and degradation. The campaign organizers offered her comfort and support as she ended her speech with an emotional prayer to Allah for long life so that she could continue to bear testimony to the violence and humiliation committed against her and tens of thousands of other Indonesian and foreign women during the Japanese occupation. Unexpectedly, the event received wide media coverage, especially in the Yogyakartian press. Leading local dailies and popular magazines carried half-page advertisements promoting the exhibition and stating the movement's objectives of exposing the intimidation, discrimination, and abuse of women and children by men.

Watershed

The Nyi Mardiyem case came at a time when few Indonesians expected to hear public discussion of the plight of the former *jugun yanfu*s. Her bold speech and the accompanying exhibition marked a watershed in both the reporting and the artistic representation of contemporary violence in Indonesia. Nyi Mardiyem played an important role in raising public consciousness. Her statement to reporters that rape is "only one level of violence in [Indonesian] society," and that there were other, deeper examples, "below the surface," both "physical and non-physical" had an invigorating effect on the press.[2]

Ashadi Siregar, a reporter for the daily newspaper *Kedaulatan Rakyat,* responded by raising a raft of issues constructed around the life of the well-known Raden Ajeng Kartini, nationalist heroine and champion of women's rights and opportunities in Indonesia (1879–1904). Having provided a non-committal first paragraph to placate the government censor, Siregar goes on to examine discrimination and violence in a broader context, from AIDS to workers' rights and conditions, from labor market segregation to the structural problems and interpretation of the State Ideology—*Pancasila,* or the "Five Principles" of an independent Indonesia: Belief in One Almighty God, Nationalism, Humanitarianism, Social Justice, and Democracy. Finally, the journalist raises the cause célèbre of the murdered factory activist M'bak (Miss) Marsinah, who, according to Siregar, was singled out "first because she was a common worker, second because she was an activist, and third because she was a woman."[3] (Marsinah was a twenty-four-year-old factory worker and labor activist whose mutilated body was discovered in a forest on May 8, 1993. Her killers, widely thought to be soldiers or members of Tentara Nasional Indonesia [TNI], were never brought to justice.)

In the article Siregar constructs a bold comparison between Marsinah and the "structure and ideology" of violence in Indonesia and the case of Ibu (Mrs.) Megawati Sukarnoputri (the daughter of Indonesia's first president, Sukarno), at that time the "deposed" leader of the opposition Indonesian Nationalist Party or PDI. Sukarnoputri's, the author argues, was another case of "ideological violence," in fact a "portrait" of "naked discrimination and intimidation in the public [rather than the private] domain."

Dramatic Representations

Public discrimination and intimidation was the subject of "Carousel atau Komidi Putar," a dramatic production staged on the second night of the exhibition by Sanggar Garasi, a group from the University of Gadjah Mada. Nyi Mardiyem's evocative comments about the depth of violence in society gave Sanggar Garasi an opportunity to condemn brutality, in this case through the prism of communal violence. The producer, Baskoro Budhi Darmawan, very carefully described the play to the press as designed to open up discussion of unresolved contemporary issues. In contrast to these modest comments, however, the performance was a disturbingly graphic representation of violent incidents, using flaming props and giant images on a slide screen backdrop. The play was a clear condemnation of both the genesis and finalé of communal violence, encompassing many issues, including the rape and murder of women. The immediate subject was a hypothetical urban street riot. The enormous screen flashed real-life images of savagery from Jalan Thamrin in Jakarta to police firing rubber bullets at rock-throwing youths in Gaza, from napalmed children during the Vietnam War to caged political prisoners in Chile and Nazi execution squads shooting old men in an open grave. The play's final act, creating a crescendo of pathos, was an unmistakable reference to the July 27, 1996, riots in Jakarta, with echoes of a previous and more brutal "historical problem": the killings, disappearances, detentions without trial, and imprisonment of up to three million Communists, Socialists, *abangan* (nominally Islamic-leftist peasants), and Chinese Indonesians by elements of the Indonesian Army in 1965–66, in particular Kostrad, the army's strategic reserve, under the command of General Soeharto himself.

1965–66

On October 1, 1965, one day following an unsuccessful putsch by a misguided clique of pro-Sukarnoist military personnel, the Indonesian Armed Forces, or ABRI (Ankatan Bersenjata Republik Indonesia), launched their own highly successful countercoup. The main thrust of ABRI's "psych-war" was not against the disorganized plotters but against their old foe, the Indonesian Communist Party, or PKI (then the third largest Communist party in the world after those of Soviet Russia and the People's Republic of China). The strategic thrust of the Kostrad campaign was to implicate the entire organizational structure and mass base of the PKI (and indeed any member of a Communist-affiliated organization) in what ABRI termed a "Communist-inspired attempt to over-throw the Indonesian State."[4]

The response of the Kostrad was swift and brutal. Approximately 1 million Indonesians died in the slaughter that ensued, and 1.5 million "Communist sympathizers" were detained without trial. Since that time politically "unclean" Indonesians have been intimidated and carefully monitored by various manifestations of the government's internal security organization. Anyone who was alleged by the Indonesian military to have been involved in the so-called Communist coup attempt is now permanently identified as an irreconcilable enemy of Soeharto's New Order state. They have the letters *ET,* for ex-*tahanan politik* or ex-*tapol* (former political detainee) on the personal identification papers that they, like all Indonesians and especially all "category A, B, and C" New Order political detainees, must carry at all times.

Approximately ten thousand Category A political prisoners from across the archipelago were transported to the prison island gulag of Buru in Eastern Indonesia. This group, which included the Indonesian novelist Pramoedya Anata Toer, was not released until as late as 1979 and not before intense international pressure was brought to bear on the Indonesian government. However, for most untried 1965–66 political detainees and the fewer number of convicted Communists referred to as "*napol*" (from *naradipana politik*) the Soeharto years were characterized by the pervasive application of collective punishment. Before 1995 when the *ET* label was officially removed from identity cards, both *tapol* and *napol* had no right to compensation for destroyed or confiscated property. They were barred from employment in any government department or in the media, in a strategic industry, or in a state-owned corporation; they could not vote or be elected to public office or belong to a political party; they were for the most part banned from obtaining a passport or from traveling overseas (except under special conditions to take the Haj to Mecca); they could not move freely between cities within Indonesia; and they could not obtain credit from a bank or receive employment entitlements from positions held prior to 1965.

The Politically "Unclean"

Furthermore, under Government Regulation No. 6 of 1976, a screening process was established to ensure that all candidates for official or "sensitive" positions were subject to a background check. According to the government the purpose of this measure was to ensure that candidates came from an environment "free from Communism." The background check, however, was merely one stage in the protean development of New Order anti-Communism. In preparation for the twenty-fifth anniversary of the coup of September 30, 1965, President Soeharto, on April 17, 1990, issued a decree that introduced a new word into the New Order anti-Communist lexicon—"*keterpengaruhan.*" It was defined as "acting, speaking, writing, or showing any attitude in a way that resembled or assisted *PKI* strategy." The effect of the decree was to link the "historical" events of 1965 with present-day political crime—a catchall provision that made all forms of dissent synonymous with Communism and therefore subject to the full weight of the government's significant internal security resources. More than any other factor the selective use of the *keterpengaruhan* facilitated the silencing of any dissenter and especially anyone who was politically "unclean."

Sitor Situmorang

It was against this background that on the evening of the August 11, one week after the launch of the antiviolence campaign at Vredeburg, the liberal-

Catholic magazine *Basis* sponsored a evening of poetry reading in honor of Sitor Situmorang. The site was one of the palace residences of the younger brother of the Sultan of Yogyakarta. Sitor, a prominent literary figure during Sukarno's so-called Old Order era (1945–66), was chairman of the left-wing National Cultural Institute or LKN (Lembaga Kebudayaan Nasional) from 1959 to 1965. (Both Sitor's chairmanship of LKN and his literary career were abruptly terminated when he was arrested in October 1965 for his alleged but unproven involvement in the September 30 coup.) When asked by someone in the audience why he had not published anything between his 1965 work *Sastra Revolusioner* and his 1976 work *Dinding Waktu,* Sitor, setting aside issues of literary merit, explained what he believes does and does not constitute a dark period in a writer's life and whether not publishing work can be considered a sign of unproductivity. He used intimation, double-entendre, and punning to avoid any direct mention of his imprisonment but nonetheless made clear his views about the violent upheaval of 1965 without once having to state them explicitly. His words had a profound effect on the audience, who were at this time unaccustomed to discussing the issue in a public forum.

Petrus: *The Mysterious Gunmen*

Coincidentally, early August 1997 also saw the local publication of the novel *Ojo Dumeh* by Agnes Yani Sardjono. The story is set in Central Java and uses the Petrus (Mysterious Gunmen) Affair as the social canvas for the central character, the freelance journalist Samhudi. The Petrus Affair refers to the 1983–85 killing of thousands of organized criminals, and "others," by specially trained army hit men. The book conjures the rich, dark world of the organized criminal gangs who ruled the streets of most Javanese cities before their eventual extra-judicial annihilation. It is about friendship, trust, and betrayal. But it is also about unresolved historical issues and unexcavated memories. The greatest achievement of Samhudi's novel is that it puts flesh and bones on characters that would otherwise remain anonymous victims of the army gunmen. In a climate of repression and intimidation, Indonesians in summer 1997 were extremely reluctant to express their criticisms of the government through linear narrative. But just as Sardjono's novel probed unresolved memories, Nyi Mardiyem's story transformed the myth surrounding the former *jugun yanfu*s into historical discourse, and Sitor Situmorang's description of the effect of his literary dark period personalized the experience of thousands of formerly imprisoned Indonesian writers, poets, and other artists. Together these examples raised the prospect that in the closing years of Soeharto's rule Indonesians would be able to confront their history openly. The journey, however, was to be a difficult one.

The Art of Bramantyo

Three 1997 paintings, all oil on canvas, by the Indonesian artist Bramantyo further reflect this prospect and the fact that during the Soeharto era art was a safe place from which to raise "delicate" issues. In these works the past and the present, the traditional and the modern, Javanese myth and contemporary Indonesian political reality exist side by side, but the artist blurs the boundaries between them so that his paintings become vehicles for veiled criticism of the government.

The first painting, *Bagong Leaving for the Campaign,* features a *panakawan* named Bagong, one of the mythical personalities who are considered "good." These characters are in fact mythological archetypes without whose support the ruler cannot rule. Bramantyo uses the *panakawans'* association with rulers to make an oblique reference to President Soeharto.

According to the artist, his Bagong is "basically a good guy who has absolutely no ideas of his own."[5] He always comes out on top. He is fearless, but at the same time he represents total faith. And he is a follower who is entirely preoccupied with practical issues, such as food and comfort. Thus, he is the ideal follower of Golkar, the Indonesian state party.

The yellow that dominates this work represents Golkar and is the artist's statement of condemnation against the New Order government. In the last Soeharto-controlled general election, in 1997, entire towns and villages were painted yellow as a sign of the local inhabitants' loyalty to the New Order government. Interestingly, the "yellow" areas of 1997 roughly corresponded to the "red" or Communist districts of the Sukarno period (1945–66). Clearly, ordinary people were prepared literally to paint the town in order to distance themselves from the politics of the past and to insulate themselves from charges of being pro-Communist or antigovernment. During the Soeharto era it was forbidden to discuss any topic related to or in sympathy with "Communism," a term that was and continues to be official code for anyone who opposes the government, including outspoken liberal democrats, organized workers, and simple farmers concerned about forced land acquisition. Any criticism, then, of the government's "development policy" can be interpreted as anti-order and therefore "Communist inspired."

In *Bagong Leaving for the Campaign* Bramantyo safely pokes at the government by including in the painting a light globe and a car, symbols of modernity—the obtainable and the impossible. He uses the light globe not to symbolize inspiration as one might assume but to suggest the unlikely occurrence that electricity has arrived in a Javanese village. Thus, Bramantyo's work is a type of nonverbal, unauthorized history, obliquely encoded in paint and canvas. Its acceptance suggests that during the Soeharto era art had become a safe place from which to raise "delicate" issues carefully.

Bagong Leaving for the Campaign, by Bramantyo.

In *The Temptation of Petruk* we encounter another of the *panakawan,* this time Petruk. Petruk always laughs in his heart, receiving all things without being disturbed because he is unattached. He takes everything in but remains empty. His shape, which is long in every respect, including his penis, symbolizes patience.[6] Bramantyo's Petruk represents Indonesia's contemporary intellectuals. The contrast between him and Bagong is sharp, as is the metaphor for life in an intellectually repressed society that demands that everyone be a Bagong and not a Petruk. Petruk's erection and his rather satisfied expression tell us that Bramantyo believes that Indonesian intellectuals find their own creative space, their own "life energy." This point is very intentional. Historians in Indonesia, for example, must still be very careful about expressing nonofficial discourse. Any deviation from the official story of what is said to have happened is *di gebuki,* "banged on the head." Bramantyo's *Petruk* again

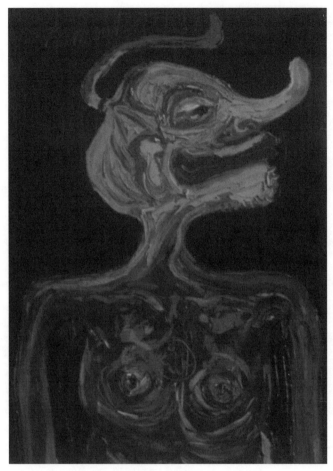

The Temptation of Petruk, by Bramantyo.

reminds us about how Indonesians responded to a politely repressive government—carefully, creatively, and obliquely.

In *The Poet of Maliboro Street,* we are introduced to a new subject, street
children, represented here by Mas (young master) Pendheck, one of the best
known of Yogyakarta's street personalities. Pendheck spent much of his early
life living on the street, sleeping in piles of rotting garbage, cocooned in the
stench from thieves, child molesters, and the police. Pendheck's struggle has
been a desperate attempt to survive in a world that has scant regard for the
sensitivities of a homeless, unwanted street urchin. But like Bramantyo's other
representations *The Poet of Maliboro Street* operates on several levels. Its
purposely obscure message dares to suggest that Pendheck is the lost voice

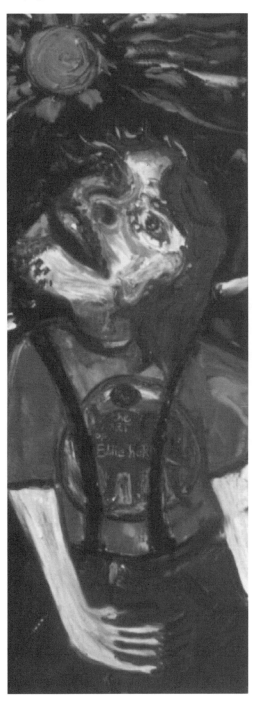

The Poet of Maliboro Street,
by Bramantyo.

Indonesia 1999: Hunting a Wild Boar, by Djoko Pekik.

of thousands of children who were orphaned and cast to the street after their parents "disappeared" in 1965–66.

After the Fall

In the immediate post-Soeharto period a great change occurred in the artistic representation of violence in Indonesia. Two distinct themes illustrate this change. The first is, paradoxically, fear of and desire for revenge, and the second is a new directness and boldness in conveying criticism through art or graphic symbolism. Both of these themes are illustrated in the art of the Indonesian painter Djoko Pekik, in particular his painting *Indonesia 1999: Hunting a Wild Boar* (oil on canvas).

Hunting a Wild Boar

On August 16, 1998, only three months after the forced resignation of Soeharto and on the eve of celebrations of Indonesian Independence Day (August 17, 1945) celebrations, Pekik's solitary work was exhibited in Yogyakarta, where it received national attention through both the broad sheet and the popular press. The painting shows two bare-chested peasants carrying a wild black boar over their shoulders. All four legs of the boar and its snout are tightly bound to a stake. The tusks indicate that the beast is old. The scene is dominated by the animal's small but piercing, savage eyes and is set in the Indonesian capital of Jakarta with the Soeharto family-owned toll road filling the entire background space. In the mid-ground appear masses of people who are witnessing the carriage of the boar. Most are *rakyat* ("common people") celebrating the event by dancing joyously. However, some faces also reflect anxiety and concern.

The painting relates to a well-known folk tale about a husband and wife in the village of Ambarawa, Central Java, who wished to become rich, quickly. Their rapacious plan involved one of them becoming a *babi jadi-jadian* or *babi ngepet,* a magical or evil pig, through a supernatural transformation. According to legend the *babi ngepet* has the ability to suck the material wealth from common people. Even if the boar is trapped and killed it still has the capacity to come back to life should someone find a piece of the creature's hair and attach it to an enchanted amulet. Once the boar is mystically "resurrected" it returns to the village filled with rage and revenge to again steal and plunder from the people. The painting makes a bold reference to the behavior of Soeharto and his family and business cronies, as well as to the fear that "the boar" may return in another form intent on reprisal. This highly charged representation is politically courageous and as such would have been unthinkable prior to May 28 of that same year.

The colloquial expression that inspired *Indonesia 1999: Hunting a Wild Boar* is *Buajingan!* which translates as "You rat!" or "You pig!" For most Indonesians, who did not share in the spoils of Soeharto's misappropriated state wealth, the image of the boar evokes their condemnation of the nepotism, brutality, collusion, and corruption that characterized his rule. In particular it represents the rage of Indonesians like Djoko Pekik who have endured persecution at the hands of the Indonesian Armed Forces and Police. In this situation the problem of aesthetics and refined artistic forms is temporarily inappropriate. What has sprung back in the heat of passion for revenge are expressive colors and new messages, declared with a fresh directness and boldness.

Brutal "Nowhere-ness"[7]

The extraordinary thing about post-Soeharto art is that these new representations of violence have long been prophesied through isolated, yet powerful Indonesian contemporary works that were displayed publicly despite the suffocating and limiting parameters imposed by the New Order. Moreover, the existence of any form of "subversive art" during the Soeharto years is remarkable given that formal cultural representative bodies, which were funded under the Indonesian Constitution to represent the people, exclusively represented the government, specifically a small elite group led by one man— Soeharto. Reacting to this situation, and despite the consequences, a small number of artists dared to form secluded forums and exhibiting spaces in order to circulate fresh, resistant ideas.

The desire to be free from the "iron fist" of authoritarian rule gained momentum in the second half of the 1990s. Almost all artists who currently shape the contemporary art world in Indonesia were raised in this milieu, including Heri Dono, Dadang Christanto, Agung Kurniawan, Hanura Hosea, S. Teddy, Arahmaiani, Nindityo Adipurnomo, and Tisna Sanjaya. The private exhibition spaces created by these artists more or less became "secret" places for society to meet and exchange ideas. The first of four examples is an installation by the artist Semsar Siahaan entitled *Re-Excavation 1993–94*. The work is made from a large dugout. At the bottom of the pit are a number of "human bodies" that remind patrons of the violent acts that have occurred in Indonesia since 1965. The work also recalls the controversy over the discovery of mass graves in North Sumatra, allegedly the result of regional military operations against the Free Ache Movement.

The second example is the work of Agung Kurniawan. His art portrays the everyday experience of irony and paradox. In a piece from 1998 entitled *Souvenir from the Third World* (acrylic on cardboard), Kurniawan depicts one of his subjects in military combat gear. The figure is clearly intoxicated and menacing. There is a robotic inhuman quality to it that reminds observers of the brutal consequences of such acts of militarism as the mass killing of

The Choir That Cannot Say No, by S. Teddy.

1965–66 and the attempted genocide of the East Timorese people in September 1999 by militia gangs backed by the Indonesian Army.

The next example is S. Teddy's *The Choir That Cannot Say No* (oil on canvas). This painting depicts a large number of yellow chickens massed like a choir. As in Kurniawan's work, the irony here is only vaguely concealed. The chickens' identical gestures indicate that they utter the same sound. Produced in 1996, at the height of Soeharto's power, this work challenged viewers to shake off the deep sleep of New Order political hypnotism, which had mesmerized most Indonesians with promises of "order," "stability," "national development" at the expense of basic human rights, the rule of law, and bureaucratic transparency.

Finally there is a work by Pintor Sirait. It shows three ballot boxes, each having a slot joined without a partition to represent the three official political parties that supposedly participated in the 1997 General Election—referred to by the New Order Government as a "festival of democracy." The absence of a divider between the boxes indicates that all ballots end up in same place. Thus, choosing one party or another would have made no difference whatsoever to the outcome of the 1997 election—not surprisingly a resounding victory for the state party Golkar. The work of these four artists reflects the emerging social attitudes of many Indonesians who were and continue to be cynical about New Order rhetoric and weary of Indonesia's spirit of brutal "nowhere-ness."

The Return of Popular Political Expression

What emerged to replace New Order cultural stagnation in Indonesia has been a refreshing, liberating, and exhilarating ability to create parody, to mock and to ridicule the system through art. The elite, the power holders, the authorities, the vested interests, the special lobby groups, the crony capitalists, and the military have since May 1998 been powerless to contain this outpouring of popular political expression—to a great extent the province of the young, the eager, and the impatient. Indonesian contemporary art is adopting new and evolving ways to represent and condemn violence and these forms are shaping the Indonesian art world in a way that could not have been imagined before May 1998. Installation, performance, and happening art are exploding. Dadang Christanto's *For Those Who Have Been Killed,* Heri Dono's *Gamelan of Rumor,* and Arahmaiani's *Nation for Sale* represent the Indonesian people's resistance to repression, oppression, and the collusion of the military with big business. These acts of resistance, which during the early 1990s were at the periphery, are beginning to penetrate the core of the contemporary art world and popular consciousness.

Armed with this new-found confidence, artists began to parody, tease, and even ridicule formal state institutions, as well as the state power holders themselves. There have been performances, for example, parodying the speeches of both Soeharto and the post-Soeharto caretaker president Habibie. There were theatrical performances by Butet Kertarejasa and musical performances by Jaduk Ferianto. Expressed through art are feelings of refreshing ambivalence toward nationalistic and national development slogans used repeatedly by the former regime. These slogans were often wrapped in traditional symbols of the past in order to gain cultural and symbolic legitimacy. But this wrapping has now been peeled back to expose inconsistency, dishonesty, and hypocrisy in the government's rhetoric.

Popular Consciousness

In the immediate post-Suharto period these new artistic representations have not been restricted to the work of professional artists. For example, most Indonesian villages customarily decorate the ubiquitous village gateway to illustrate the struggle for independence from the Dutch. The basic elements of these façade entrances are figurines or drawings, especially of combat fatigue-clad village "freedom fighters." New Order Independence Day festivities were actually a form of rigidly controlled and enforced public political theater, demanding the inclusion of all Indonesians in the "celebrations" but forbidding their participation. During the Soeharto era neither the method of depiction nor the role of the people as passive observers was ever called into question. It was in fact part of a great rewriting of Indonesian history that transformed the very popular and left-wing "Indonesian Revolution" into the politically neutral "Indonesian War of Independence." This scripting of propaganda as history produced only one very narrow narrative—that of New Order political orthodoxy.

In post-New Order Indonesia people are beginning to ask, "Are these violent symbols appropriate?" "Are they in fact overly nationalistic, patriotic, or romantic?" Gapura statues often depict resolute, determined, fierce-faced guerilla fighters carrying weapons, including sharpened bamboo spears, rifles, or pistols. These depictions clearly elevate the subject of violent armed struggle to the highest position within the story of Indonesian nationhood. Conversely, the intellectual, diplomatic, or cultural struggles, which were also an integral part of Indonesian independence, are rarely, if ever, presented.

During the celebrations of August 17, 1998, the decorated military gateway that has characterized the Independence struggle since the late 1960s was nowhere to be seen. In its place were simple, colorful, nonmilitary representations. Even at the grass-roots level of Indonesian society the violent images of the Soeharto era had been neutralized. Significantly, on the same day the commercial television station SCTV, in the noon bulletin, reported that the Independence Day celebrations were the quietest experienced since the beginning of the New Order.

Notes

1. Rob Goodfellow, "A Fresh Wind Is Blowing," *Inside Indonesia* 55 (July–September 1998): 28–29. The inspiration for this general line of thinking arose out of a conversation with Professor Herbert Feith in Yogyakarta, August 1997, and from a series of letters exchanged between the author and Professor Ben Anderson of Cornell University, Ithaca, New York.

2. "Gambaran Murni Perempuan Bila Dianggap Ibu," *Kedaulatan Rakyat* (Minggu, 3 August 1997).

3. Barbara Hatley, "Ratna Accused and Defiant," *Inside Indonesia* 55 (July–September 1998): 7.

4. Rob Goodfellow, *Api Dalam Sekam: The New Order and the Ideology of Anti-Communism* (Working Paper Number 95), (Clayton, Victoria, Australia: Monash University Centre for South East Asian Studies, 1995).

5. Rob Goodfellow, "History Imitating Art, Imitating Life: The Art of Bramantyo," *Art AsiaPacific* 22 (June 1999): 64–67.

6. The work is in fact longer than represented in this photograph. During the exhibition of *The Temptation of Petruk* in Yogyakarta during 1997 a *sarong* was wrapped around the figure's waist to cover the penis. This was in response to possible threats of violence from extremist religious groups. The figure of Petrus in Javanese mythology is charactered by a long nose and very large penis. For a more comprehensive discussion of these characters, see Paul Stang, "Mystical Symbolism in Javanese Wayang Mythology," in *Essays on Mysticism and Java (1977–1993)* (Sydney: Cambridge University Press, 1993).

7. See M. Dwi Marianto, "Surrealist Painting in Yogyakarta" (PhD diss., University of Wollongong, Australia, 1997).

8

Mnemosyne Abroad
Reflections on the Chinese and Jewish Commitment to Remembrance

Vera Schwarcz

"Chinese history should be studied because it can be seen to make sense in the same world of discourse in which we try to make sense of the West. If we make this kind of sense, perhaps we can make this kind of world."

Joseph Levenson, "The Genesis of Confucian China"[1]

Disparate histories, such as those of Chinese and Jewish culture, may be likened to great rivers. They do not cross, do not flow into one another unless individuals create, or become, an interpretative canal. The one proposed here centers on the valorization of memory in two different worlds that touched my own life. A child of Holocaust survivors from Romania, I have been writing about the dilemmas of Chinese intellectuals for nearly two decades. At first, the cross current between Chinese and Jewish history was subterranean, below the surface of texts that detailed the politics of forgetting which had enveloped the lives of my subjects in China. Now, the time has come to construct, to acknowledge explicitly, the connective channel.

The history of Chinese intellectuals victimized by Mao Zedong is not theirs alone. It demands to be made sense of in the same world of discourse in which I try to fathom the experience of Jewish survivors. In spite of vast differences in cultural outlook and sufferings endured, both speak a common language: the language of memory rescued—with great difficulty—from publicly enforced, as well as personally cultivated, amnesia.

I heard this language afresh in Beijing on May 20th, 1989. It was the first morning of martial law. The tragic fate of the democracy movement was

From *Points East* 6, no. 3 (October 1991): 1–14. © 1991 by The Sino-Judaic Institute. Reprinted with the permission of the Sino-Judaic Institute.

now evident, though mass violence was still a couple of weeks away. On this day, forty intellectuals gathered in a cavernous hall on the Qinghua University campus to commemorate the 80th birthday of a well-known philosopher. The contrast between the imminent repression on the streets (which would distort the entire history of the Tiananmen events) and the rituals of remembrance carried out with intense mindfulness inside the university gates was no accident. It mirrored the tension within Chinese intellectuals themselves. They still struggled to retain fidelity to their own history in the face of a political system determined to dictate the parameters of permissable memory.

The large commemoration hall had been set aside many months before May 20th. It was intended to accommodate hundreds. Now, it held a few dozen guests who managed to come by bicycle on a morning when all bus transportation had been cut off in Beijing. Those present experienced themselves as a fragment, a conscious remainder of community fractured once again by repressive politics. They carried out the commemorative ceremony with added intensity. Their collective reanimation of one man's past was a gesture of mutual encouragement, mutual consolation for the difficult months that lay ahead.

Co-memorializing a still living teacher enabled the assembled guests to reaffirm the Confucian tradition long suppressed by Chinese Communism. Zhang Dainian, the guest of honor, had made his mark in the scholarly world on the basis of his scrupulous and imaginative reinterpretation of traditional Chinese philosophy. His students—disciples, in the self chosen appelation of the speakers at the ceremony—now gathered to pay tribute to the master's *weiren,* his inner humanity.

They dwelt on Zhang Dainian's spiritual endurance during repeated waves of persecution, from the 1957 Anti-Rightist campaign through the Cultural Revolution of 1966–69. Each speaker also offered some token of appreciation: a classical poem or an ink brush painting. The unifying theme of theses offerings was the rugged pine, a traditional symbol of steadfast moral purpose in an unjust and corrupt world. While guns were loaded on the streets of Beijing, these intellectuals managed to create an hour of stillness. Their gathering bore witness to Nietzsche's earlier intuition: "The great events, they are not our loudest, but our stillest hours. Not around the inventors of new noises, but around the inventors of new values does the world revolve. It revolves inaudibly."[2]

In isolation, each intellectual faced the noisy eventfulness of martial law and the imminent crackdown with terror. Together, however, for a brief moment, Zhang Dainian's disciples managed to tell history their own way. And that story, on this morning of May 20th, revolved around one guardian of tradition. The commemorative ritual embodied and expressed the importance of remembrance for individual and collective survival.

I was the only foreigner at the May 20th gathering. I knew Zhang Dainian, the guest of honor, well. We had been talking about the dilemmas of intellectuals in modern China for a decade.[3] There was between us something known as Chinese as *zhiyin,* the sound of mutually appreciated music. It wasn't music as such that echoed through our conversations, but rather a shared obsession with the vicissitudes of history. On the day that martial law engulfed the city of Beijing, in the company of practiced survivors—who had learned how to mask personal memories in the garb of public commemoration—I came to understand better my own side of *zhiyin.*

I had gone to China in 1979 to study the politics of amnesia. In the process, however, I became interested in the connection between memory and cultural identity not only in the lives of Chinese intellectuals, but those of my parents as well. Beneath public, Party enforced forgetting (that I had researched in Beijing and witnessed in my native country of Romania), I glimpsed a wide array of personal strategies for consolation through recollection. These were not novel, or even modern survival techniques. Rather they were rooted in memorial practices as ancient and as varied as the Chinese and Jewish traditions.

Memory and Endurance

At the ceremony in honor of Zhang Dainian's 80th birthday, I reflect anew on the Confucian virtue of endurance. In Chinese, the word for endurance, *ren,* echoes the moral ideal of "humaneness" (also prounced *ren*). The first term describes an individuals' capacity to bear up under the burden of prolonged suffering. It holds the key to the second kind of *ren,* to becoming fully human. The ideograph for "endurance" shows a heart beneath the cutting edge of a sword and suggests a difficult, protracted struggle between inner resources and outer violence.

With martial law in the air, with the students' bold hopes for instantaneous democracy dashed, there was nothing left for older Chinese intellectuals but to retreat into—or rather, to reanimate—the Confucian definition of the moral person. As if describing the predicament of Zhang Dainian and his disciples, Confucius remarked fifteen hundred years earlier: "He has taken humanness as his own burden—is that not heavy? Only with death does his course stop—is that not long?"[4]

Confucius left no doubt about the origins of his own capacity for endurance and for humanness. It lay in disciplined, critical remembrance, in what the Analects called "*hao gu*" or "love of the ancients." The same kind of "love" lies at the root of Jewish endurance as well. Remembrance lies at the heart of the covenant between God and the people of Israel. To be fully human as a Jew is to be rooted—as in Confucius' world—in conscious memorial practice. In both Chinese and Jewish tradition, memory is neither abstract, nor simply personal. To remember is to take the collective experience of the past to heart in such a way that one is thoroughly transformed by it.

Zachor, the Hebrew word for remembrance, recurs as a constant theme in the Bible. It is the axis around which Jews have defined both their identity and moral practice. Meaning at once, "memorial sign," "memorial offering," "to record," "to commemorate" and "to take the heart",[5] *zachor* requires constant attention to outer events and inner realities. It is grounded in the idea of a mindful heart—a notion devoid of contradiction in Jewish, as well as Chinese tradition.

Jewish memory words developed out of the root term mind-heart.[6] In Chinese, *xin* means literally both mind and heart. To remember, thus is linked to a willingness to take into one's inner being the object of remembrance. Language, in both Chinese and Jewish culture, functions as a re-minder, as an aid in the transmission of cultural identity. Both Chinese and Jewish tradition have fostered an uninterrupted sense of cultural identity based on ancient texts that remain compelling and intelligible to the moderns. Heirs of a long, nuanced repertoire of memorial rituals, Jews and Chinese have faced historical crisis well armed. Even in the wake of traumas such as the Holocaust and the Cultural Revolution, something essential has endured within individuals, and prevailed in the world at large. As Elie Wiesel put it in his Nobel Peace Prize acceptance speech: "The call of memory, the call to memory comes to us from the origins of our history. No other commandment figures so frequently or so fiercely as in the Bible. It is incumbent upon us to remember the good that we have been graced with, as well as the evil we have endured . . . To forget is to desert memory, to betray it and history itself. To put it another way, to forget is to risk war."[7]

This link between memory and survival, however, is not the discovery of Jews or Chinese alone. The ancient Greeks understood it also when they elevated memory to the status of a divine being. The goddess Mnemosyne was deemed the mother of the nine muses. Out of her union with Zeus, she gave birth to all the various arts that were to endow human life with grace and meaning. Not only dance and music grew out of the power of memory. Mnemosyne birthed Clio, history, as well.

But the modern West has fled from what philosopher Edward Casey's has called the "*dark embrace*" of Mnemosyne.[8] Other gods, other ideals have supplanted memory as the source of artfulness and meaning. Descartes led the flight with his fierce determination to ground identity in the individual cogitator as opposed to communal recollection. The rules of his *Discours de la methode* centered on the elimination, on the suppression of doubt. And memory, as the pioneering psychologist Pierre Janet noted in 1928 "has always preoccupied and annoyed the Cartesians . . . The Cartesian wants nothing to do with memory because memory is filled with doubt, because, since Aristotle, we have had to ask if memory is true."[9]

Post-Cartesian Western thought has had a marked preference for amnesia, purging itself repeatedly of what Confucius called "love for the ancients" in the name of scientific rationality and cultural enlightenment. As a result, we moderns face the world with a much impoverished vocabulary for remembrance—so diminished, in fact, that most the varied use of memory words is now found not in the realm of Mnemosyne's daughter, history, but in computer science. We are in danger of abdicating memorial powers to machines of our own creation.

Forsaken by the modern West, Mnemosyne remains a resourceful presence abroad. In the recesses of ancients-loving traditions, such as the Chinese and the Jewish ones, memory continues to nurture a sense of cultural identity in spite of historical crisis and historical trauma. Even when warring with tradition, even when doubting its viability in the age of critical reason, Chinese and Jewish modernizers maintain a dialogue with the living past. A commitment to remembrance—to anchor plans for the present and visions of the future in an informed appreciation of the communal past—runs like a golden thread through both Chinese and Jewish history. Whether in the memorial rituals created to commemorate the victims of the Holocaust or in the stories told by China's youth wounded by the Cultural Revolution, one cannot but recognize Mnemosyne at work in a new disguise.

Recently, the Chinese film series, *River Elegy* (first aired for a mass television audience in the summer of 1988) catalogued the memory metaphors that weigh most heavily on the modern Chinese imagination. These include the Yellow River, the imperial dragon and the Great Wall.[10] These symbols are very different from those that animate Jewish remembrance: The rivers of Babylon, Masada and the Wailing (Western) Wall, to name but a few of the loci of Jewish remembrance. How then is one to cross the great divide between the Wailing Wall and the Great Wall, between what is more conveniently distinguished in French as *le mur* and *la muraille?* How is one to make sense of the cosmological, historical, and linguistic differences between Chinese and Jewish memorial practice? How is one to meet Joseph Levenson's challenge of bringing China into the same world of discourse in which we try to make sense of the West?

When such questions threaten to overwhelm the possibilities of thought, Franz Kafka can be counted on for help. His story, "The Great Wall of China"—written in 1917, the year of the Russian Revolution and Kafka's own diagnosis with tuberculosis—opens up a world where Chinese and Jewish dilemmas intermingle quite freely. In this work, the most tortured of moderns takes on the voice of an ancient builder of the Great Wall. In that time-worn tongue, the author begins to probe the connections between memory, power and an ongoing sense of cultural identity.

Kafka's Wall builder confesses from the beginning that he is but a small brick in an edifice of what will become the hallmark of China's greatness. Kept

wilfully ignorant of the nature, the extent, the plan of the huge imperial project, each mason works for a limited amount of time on a fragment of the
whole. And yet the urge to know, the urge to create something that will with-
stand the test of time, unlike the Tower of Babel, triumphs over the comforts
and the prohibitions of a memoryless, historyless building plan.

Forbidden to think about the nature of his labors in the native context,
the Kafka's mason turns to comparative history: "During the building of the
wall and ever since to this very day I have occupied myself almost exclusively
with the comparative history of the races—there are certain questions which
one can probe to the marrow, as it were, only by this method—and I have discovered that we Chinese possess certain folk and political institutions that are
unique in their clarity, others again unique in their obscurity. The desire to
trace these phenomena, especially the latter, has always teased me and teases
me still . . .[11]

Like Kafka's builder, I also feel drawn to the obscurities of comparative
history. My studies of Chinese memory and amnesia have brought me closer
to the dilemmas of Jewish survivors. Repression, reservation, distortion pro-
liferate, in the shadowy realm inhabited by both Chinese intellectuals and Jewish survivors. I want to explore the "unique obscurity" of each. But first, certain "clarities" within each tradition must be affirmed. These are nowhere
more apparent than in the cosmologies that inform Chinese historical practice on one hand, and Jewish religious belief on the other.

Differences in Chinese and Jewish Cosmology

In the traditional Chinese world view there is no transcendant being, no God
in the Jewish sense of the world. Confucian memorial practices are rooted in
an organic cosmology that assumes a fundamental unity, an intimate collaboration between Heaven (Nature) and man. Jewish memory, by contrast, is
rooted in a covenant with a supreme force beyond the human universe. The
God of Israel sets the tone and becomes the ultimate model of fidelity through
remembrance. The Jewish community, in turn, emulates this example of mindful memory with varying degrees of success, often falling far short of it.

And yet, out of the disparate cosmologies represented by biblical Judaism
and ancient Confucianism, there emerged a similar emphasis on the sacred-
ness of history and on the individual's obligation to take collective memory
to heart. In ancient China, during the same axial age that witnessed the birth
of Hinduism, Buddhism and Judaism, the Sages taught about the *Dao*. Called
simply "the Way", the *Dao,* unlike the great theological religions, defined the
meaning of existence in distinctly humanistic terms. While Hindus, Buddhists
and Jews puzzled over the origins of the universe, of suffering and of man's
dominion over nature, the Chinese sages taught the message of *tian ren he yi,*
that Heaven and man are one. In this world view, which Tu Weiming has

described as "anthropocosmic," humanity becomes a co-creator of the universe, a guardian of natural processes, a "participant of the creative transformation of Heaven and Earth."[12]

By the time of Mencius (371–289 BC), ancient Chinese had developed an entire rationale, indeed a plan, for the perfectability of human nature through self cultivation. Vague intimations about the unity of Heaven and man developed into a detailed vision of "divine humanity". Anyone could become a Sage by grasping the sacred significance of "learning" (*xue*)—an activity that was not simply, or even primarily cognitive. Rather, it demanded intense psychological concentration in order to realize and manifest one's humanness (*jen*). As Mencius put it: "For a man to give full realization to his heart is for him to understand his own nature and a man who knows his own nature will know Heaven."[13]

In biblical Judaism, by contrast, man and God face each other as creature and Creator. The ontological gulf is crossed not through "learning" in the sense of self cultivation but through a covenant that defines and transforms communal identity. Israel emerges as a people in conscious relationship to the absolute power of God. Jews become witnesses to God's role in history. They become, what poet Allen Grossman recently termed a "God bearing" or theophoric nation.[14] To be "chosen" in this sense is to take on the burden of human events in light of a transcendant purpose.

While the ancient Chinese also experienced themselves as unique in history—and called their realm *Zhong guo,* the Central Kingdom, out of which emanated all civilizing wisdom—human events continued to be interpreted in an organic universe. Jews, by contrast, fastened upon certain events and endowed them with sacred significance. Out of a vast field of historical experience, six "key memories"[15] were chosen to be remembered each day. These events reaffirm through re-collection the essential meaning and obligations of Jewish identity. Out of the six "memories"—the Sabbath, the revelation at Sinai, the Golden Calf, Miriam's sin of speaking ill of her brother Moses, Amalek's ambush of the Jews on their way out of Egypt and the Exodus— it is the last which is most formative for Jewish historical consciousness.

The departure from the house of bondage is a concrete sign of God's direct intervention in human events. Exodus starts the ticking of "real" historical time and marks the beginning of the historical mission of the Jews. This one event, which is the first of the six memories recaptured in the daily devotions of pious Jews, became the model for divine intervention in human affairs. It promised—allowed, really—Jews to endow history with meaning, much the same way as Mencius' self cultivation enables a man to know his own heart and Heaven at the same time.

The intelligibility of history thus is dependent upon a sense of how an individual or a culture fits into the larger pattern of cosmic significance. From very different starting points, Chinese and Jews alike came to see in human

events a critical mirror for communal identity. For Jews, history was meaningful because man is made in the image of God and because the community
of Israel was chosen to understand and bear witness to God's purpose in the
world. For Chinese, history was meaningful because man is part of the very
same organic universe in which various forces play out their cosmic design
and because human beings have the unique capacity—indeed responsibility—to record and interpret the concrete unfolding of the *Dao.*

Underneath both the Chinese and Jewish concerns with meaningful history lies a powerful conviction that time is real, that events in time are crucial for communal identity and welfare. Unlike the Hindu, the Buddhist and
the Christian world views that emphasize the illusory, painful limiting nature
of human time, Chinese and Jewish traditions insist that human destiny is ful-
filled through historical time.

If we can put aside, for the moment, outworn debates about circular ver-
sus linear concepts of time, we may be able to glimpse a similarity between
Chinese and Jewish attempts to historicize time. What matters in both cases
is a collective sense of coming into being through history—what the Jewish
philosopher Amos Funkenstein has analyzed as the distinctive "historical consciousness" of the Jews, and Chinese philosopher Li Zehou described as a
"Chinese disinterest in eternal time in favor of experimental, human centered
temporality."[16]

To experience oneself as rooted in historical time is to forego the consolations offered by world views that dwell on the illusory nature of early life.
Chinese and Jews alike have cultivated the soil of historical remembrance
because they believed it to have the same kind of sacred properties—the same
ability to heal and to guide—that other religions invested in trans-temporal
religious practice. Confucianism, because it had even less room for supernatural forces than theophoric Judaism, considered historical knowing a form
of sacred wisdom.

Confucius himself was the first sage to embrace the sacred calling of history when he assigned himself the task of editing the chronicles of his home
state of Lu. His *Spring and Autumn Annals* became a model for scrupulous
yet morally motivated historiography. Si-Ma Qian, the Grand Historian of the
Han Dynasty (220 BC–200 AD) followed this sacred calling with his own
magnum opus, the *Shiji,* completed after the author chose castration over suicide so as to bring to fruition a task begun before political humiliation. Si-
Ma Guang, the philosopher-official of the Song Dynasty (900–1300 AD) fur-
thered and deepened the Confucian attachment to history in his masterpiece,
Mirror for Government. For all three epitomes of Chinese historical practice,
the calling of the historian was a sacred obligation. Although the urge to
instruct political rulers was never far from their minds, all three sought to use
actual, real events in human history to illuminate the meaning of the *Dao,* of
the way. They became guardians—indeed, architects of collective Chinese

memory—because they believed the historian to be a diviner, a seer who had the responsibility of decoding a cosmic pattern.

This vision of the historian's sacred calling developed directly out of the ancient Chinese office of the *shi,* the scribe in charge of recording the meaning of oracle bones. The interrogation of Heaven and the recording of human events that followed gave Chinese historians their first sense of empowerment. Subsequently, the *shi* became involved in astronomy and the establishment of the imperial calendar. Cosmic and human events remained related in the office of the historian-astronomer. During the long course of Chinese imperial historiography, the accumulated wisdom of the past assumed greater and greater authority. Even when thoroughly politicized as a guide to bureaucratic practice, history did not lose its claim to the repository of ultimate value in Chinese society."[17]

Reference to history was also held in sacred regard in biblical Judaism. God's purpose was known through the actual, eventful experiences of the Jewish people. The unfolding of His vision was synchronous with the unfolding Jewish history. With the destruction of the Second Temple, Jewish life entered a long period of displacement. Away from the sacred sites of Jewish origination, history became a reminder of losses suffered. Jewish historical knowing became wedded to religious memory—a compensation for exile that made it meaningful and bearable. Chinese historiography, by contrast, did not carry this compensatory burden because it never lost contact with the soil of Chinese cultural origination. Firmly grounded in the valley of the Yellow River, Chinese historical practice developed a wide array of conventions ranging from dynastic annals, to local gazeeters and exemplary biographies. Jewish historical consciousness in exile, "by the rivers of Babylon" as it were, paid less attention to local events and was more mindful of the ways in which contemporary events mirrored biblical paradigms.[18]

Although the biblical past was the primary one, a sense of the importance of historical precedent deepened over the course of Jewish history in a way that parallels Chinese attachment to historical references in philosophy, poetry and bureaucratic practice. According to Amos Funkenstein, in the realm of Jewish law, of *Halakha,* distinctions of time and place were scrupulously maintained. Not unlike in Chinese guides to imperial government, in rabbinical debate "every event was worthy of remembering, including the minority opinion."[19]

Chinese and Jewish rememberers treasured the details of human history. They were considerably less interested in the logical connections between cause and effect that so fascinated Greek historians and Hindu cosmologists. What mattered for Chinese and Jews is meaning in history—or to put it more precisely, the conviction that human events are decipherable like texts, are sacred texts in themselves. Attachment to language, and through language to texts is a marked feature of both traditional Chinese and Jewish culture.

In both, what was prized, what was cultivated through arduous study, is the ability to read history with moral discernment.

When Confucius said of himself "I transmit, but do not create, I believe in and love the ancient" (*hao gu*)[20], he both consolidated and revolutionized his own culture. Until then, ancestor worship sufficed to bond individuals, especially of noble lineage, to their particular familial spirits. With Confucius, however, the ancestors became absorbed (not repudiated, Heaven forbid) into the "ancient"—a moral ideal with which one could challenge and judge contemporary times. There was no need to invent new, abstract ethical criteria. For Confucius, it sufficed to insist, over and over again, that the present live *up* to the past, to become worthy of its inheritance.

In Chinese, the ideogram for the past is literally synonymous with "above." Last month, last week is visually, conceptually above today and tomorrow. When Confucius asked his contemporaries to hark back to the ideals of the ancients, he was asking of them no more, and no less, than the Jewish prophets who reminded contemporaries of the fall from the covenant. To be historically minded in this sense is to be reminded of a past that is anything by passe. It is, instead an ethical imperative, a call to action, a call to return—if not to the actual state of affairs in ancient times, then at least to a state of mind less at ease with the corrupt, forgetful ways of the present.

Fu gu, "return to the ancient", has been the rallying call for reform in China, since the time of Confucius. In the Han, Tang, Song, Ming and Qing dynasties, individuals gathered under the *fu gu* banner to quarrel with everything from the literary style to the agricultural policies of the State. Some reformers were treated as crackpots, others persecuted as disloyal subjects of a present oriented imperial government. Most were venerated by posterity because they dared to remember the ancient and had lived by something other than the cannon of contemporary expedience. *Fu gu* thought, in the words of Stephen Owen, was the very incarnation of the Chinese "covenant of remembrance," whereby one cherishes the past and hopes to be worthy of remembrance in turn.[21]

Remembering the rememberer becomes a consummate art in classical Chinese literature. In Jewish tradition, it became the very stuff of life, and death, as experienced in the diaspora. In biblical times, *zachor* was a religious commandment which bound the Jewish people to the God of the Exodus. In exile, the covenant of remembrance bound Jews to one another through the vast reaches of alien space, and time. As the writer of Psalm 137 warns, life itself withers in exile unless watered by consciously cultivated historical memory: "If I forget thee, O Jerusalem, let my right hand forget its cunning. If I do not remember thee, let my tongue cleave to the roof of my mouth."

This fierce attachment to memory does not make sense unless we recall the biblical admonitions against Israel's frequent proclivity to amnesia. In fact, the Jewish commitment to remembrance makes no sense unless we grasp the psychological realism that undergrids it. People, Jews, forget all the time. It is more convenient to forget than to remember. Hence the effort-fullness of memory.

In this matter of psychological realism, as with their historical realism, Chinese and Jews are like. Though spared the anguish of Jews in exile, Confucius, nonetheless, railed against contemporaries who would rather forget than "love" the ancients. An itinerant teacher, he was unrewarded with office in his life time precisely because it was easier for Chinese rulers (and subjects!) to move on in time, to adopt, to adapt morality and historical vision to state—building requirements of the day.

The Jewish psalmist who equates amnesia with powerless and speechlessness finds kindred spirits among Confucius' followers. One ardent proponent of *fu gu* thought was the Tang poet Meng Jiao who wrote:

> Hold with the past, don't lose the past:
> If you lose the past, your will easily breaks;
> If you lose the past, even the sword snaps;
> If you lose the past, the zither too laments.[22]

Crippled hands and mournful zithers came to symbolize Jewish and Chinese ambivalance about historical memory. Neither tradition left any doubt about the importance of remembering the past. Neither, however, assumed remembrance to be an easy, or a natural function of human community. Instead, they both nurtured a commitment to historical memory that took account of the prevalence of amnesia. They both textualized memory and transmitted it from generation to generation with sacred awe.

Expressions of the Commitment to Remembrance

Memory is a natural function of human beings. The commitment to remembrance, however, is a profoundly natural act that varies from culture to culture. Chinese and Jewish tradition share an attachment to the past that is informed by a long standing appreciation of the human proclivity to both remember and to forget. In both cultures, memory is not left to nature, or fate or the foibles of human interest. Rather, it is cultivated through a relationship to fragments of the invisible, vanished past which nonetheless claims the loyalties, the emotions of the present.

Stones, persons, tales, texts—and most concretely, language itself—is used as a reminder in Chinese and Jewish culture. Even when they dwell on forgetfulness, Chinese and Jewish writers are reminding their countrymen about the importance of a commitment to the past. Meng Jiao's "Autumn Meditations," appeal for conscious remembrance by reminding contemporaries that Confucius, the arch memoralist, was also grieved by amnesia: "And the Master's tears for the loss of the past in those days fell in torrents."[23]

Mournful as Meng Jiao was, his was not a lacrimose, nor a passive attitude in the face of the natural erosion of a commitment to remembrance. Rather, the *fugu* poet was a cultural activist. A moody, determined rememberer, he tried to live connected to the soil of former times. Similarly, the Jews exiled in Babylon did more than weep for the loss of the land of Israel. They cried, and wrote and told tales that kept the idea of a return alive in spite of political repression and the natural desire to adjust to the present.

In the 20th century, Chinese and Jewish writers have continued this commitment to remembrance in the face of far more traumatic breaks with the past than experienced by their forerunners in Confucian or Babylonian times. What is striking is not the persistence of cultural memories, but faith (both personal and social) in the possibility of rebirth through recollection.

China's foremost modern writer Lu Xun, expressed this faith in a characteristically gloomy fashion. Having lived through revolutionary times, he knew only too well the dangers of forgetting, of moving in step with the new as if the old was a discardable cloak. But Lu Xun could not, would not take the mantle of the past off so easily. He bore witness to the traditional Chinese value of *nianjiu,* attachment to the past.[24] He likened his stories to unforgettable nightmares. He refused to get over them. Instead, he not only recalled the past, but took it to heart, was willing to let it trouble him:

> I have some memories, but fragmentary in the extreme. They remind me of fish scales scraped off by a knife, some of which stick to the fish while others fall into the water. When the water is stirred a few scales may swirl up, glimmering, but they are streaked with blood, and even to me they seem likely to spoil the enjoyment of connoisseurs.[25]

Lu Xun was a mindful participant in times of revolutionary change, but never joined the Community Party. After his death in 1936, Communist revolutionaries like Mao Zedong deified Lu Xun without troubling themselves with the problem of memory. They never understood why Lu Xun held on to the bloody fragments of the past. They never looked past a melancholic attachment to the long lost glories of Chinese history. But Lu Xun knew that memories, especially bloody ones, like fishscales, are the very stuff of personal and cultural survival.

In very different historical circumstances, Auschwitz survivor Elie Wiesel also affirmed the importance of bloody memories for his own and his people's survival. In his Nobel speech, Wiesel used an old Hassidic tale to illustrate the importance of memory to those who would survive with hope:

> Once, the great Rabbi Israel Baal-Shem-Tov, the Master of the Good Name, undertook an urgent, dangerous mission—to hurry the coming of the Mes-

siah. His punishment for having tried to change the course of history was
exile. In his cast out loneliness, he was followed by a faithful servant. The
servant begged the Master to use his magic powers to cancel the exile. The
Master was powerless. He, in turn, asked the servant to pray. The simple man
knew nothing but the letters of the Hebrew alphabet.

Together the Master of the Good Name and the simple servant recited the
alphabet. Over and over again until suddenly, the Baal-Shem recovered his
powers. He recovered his memory.[26]

Speaking in French, the Translyvanian Jew concluded his Oslo story as
follows: "C'est memoire qui a sauve le Besht, c'est elle qui sauvera l'homme
du desespoir. Disons-le tout de suite: un espoir sans memoir est comme une
memoir san espoir. Ort de meme que l'homme ne peut vivre sans reve.... Si
le reve reflete le passe, l'espoir appele l'avenir ... l'oppose de l'avenir n'est
pas le passe, mais l'oubli de passe."[27]

For Elie Wiesel, as for Lu Xun, there is a deep link between memory,
dreams and the difficult struggle against forgetting. Lu Xun never received a
Nobel prize for keeping his country's dreams and nightmares alive, though
he earned it. Like the Translyvanian survivor of the Holocaust, the Chinese
writer was willing to let the past wash up, wash over him again and again,
especially when his contemporaries appeared most taken by the promise of a
revolutionary future. That is when Lu Xun reminded his countrymen of the
most painful, most difficult parts of their shared past.

To remember, in this sense, is to dare to re-animate the past. To give it a
second chance, yet another life in a way that marks, transforms the present
life of the rememberer. Both Chinese and Jewish tradition offer precedents
for this practice of mindful recollection. Embedded in the Biblical usage of
zachor, for example, is the idea of memorial sign, something that alters not
only stone and parchment but the heart itself.[28] Subjective and objective meanings of memory intermingle freely in this language/thought world which
requires active participation by those who live in keeping with covenant
of remembrance.

The Passover ritual is the most concrete embodiment of this requirement
for personal commitment in commemoration: "In every generation let *each*
person regard himself as though he had emerged from Egypt," tells us the Hag-
gadah. Distance from the time of the Exodus event does not sanction self
abstention from its memorial obligation. The Seder ritual is meant to cement
each year the connection of past and present, to display—bring into play—
what Wiesel termed the "mysterious power of memory, without which existence is neutral, passive and opaque."[29]

Similarly in Chinese tradition, memorial rituals were developed to cement
a living connection with the distant past. Mourning ceremonies strengthened
the bond between ancestors and descendants by fostering among the living a
concrete indebtedness to the dead. Beyond the memories of one's own family

or clan, the Chinese language itself, and Confucian culture more generally, elaborated a nuanced vocabulary for reminders that nourish remembrance.

At the heart of Chinese cultural practice lies the expression and experience of *huaigu*—a meditation upon, a cherishing of the past. Like the Hebrew word *zachor,* the Chinese ideograph *huai* has embedded in it the willingness to take into one's bosom the object of remembrance. Subjective and objective meanings of memory are mingled here as well, and not by accident. To give oneself over to *huaigu,* like participation in the Passover seder, requires the rememberer to inscribe the past into his or her own heart.

Such cherishing meditations upon the past were provoked by, built into Chinese religion, Chinese poetry, even into the architecture of Chinese gardens. Bent upon transforming a place into a site for active, personal reminiscence, the Chinese garden guides the visitor with carefully planned paths, poems inscribed on rocks. All these are meant to allude to, to reanimate the experiences of the rememberer's forerunners.

One place in traditional China well known for its ability to unlock the mysterious powers of memory was the Weeping Stele on Mount Xian. Built in the middle of the third century by Yang Hu—a local governor, this fragment of stone became a sacred place for subsequent generations of rememberers. They reenacted Yang Hu's mountain climb, they gazed out upon the vast expanse he had first glimpsed and wept in ritual commemoration of an individual who had come to this wilderness to think about the nameless dead. Not unlike Jews who continue to meditate and weep at the Wailing Wall— also a fragment from a broken yet re-collected past—the Tang Dynasty poet Meng Haoran (689–790) took the pilgrimage to the Weeping Stele and wrote:

> In human affairs there is succession and loss. Men come and go, forming present and past. Rivers and hills keep traces of their glory, And our generation, too, climbs here for the view ... Yang Hu's stele is still here: Done reading, tears soak our robe.[30]

The Weeping Stele, like the Wailing Wall partakes of the alchemy that is memory. A broken fragment becomes transformed into a potent, cherished reminder. A pilgrim to Mount Xian is renewed through the act of co-commemoration, though communion with a lost past and a community of contemporary and former rememberers.

In the world of the Tang poet, however, unlike the Jewish tradition, the passage of time is experienced as something quite natural. The losses it occasions are no more than what is to be expected through the succession of generations. Rivers and hills maintain traces of the past that forgetful humans overlooked. The world of nature is a guardian of remnants that bring back the full flavor of the past in the eyes of caring beholders such as Meng Haoran.

Jewish remembrance, by contrast, is marked by a profound dislocation from space. Always mindful of the predicament of exile, the rabbis insisted upon a fierce attachment to time and time bound events such as the Sabbath, Exodus and the revelation at Sinai. After the destruction of the Second Temple—and later with repeated expulsions as the one from Spain in 1492— rivers and hills could not be counted on to safeguard remnants of Jewish memory. Human memory had to bear this burden instead.

In the classical Chinese lexicon, memory is a less cumbersome affair. Anchored in a world that is replete with reminders (from ancestor villages to imperial temples) a rememberer has the luxury of drifting in out of several memory worlds at once, of playing with time. This sense of playful, nature-nourished recollection is quite alien to Jewish tradition. Its hallowing of time is a serious undertaking, precisely because it is intended to compensate for losses suffered in the realm of space.

In classical Chinese poetry, one of the most suggestive metaphors for the experience of recollection is *menghen*—"dream traces," especially of spring dreams. *Menghen* connotes a graceful, delicious dalliance with the past in a season marked by constant change. It suggests that what once was cannot be brought back, but it can be dreamt up momentarily, provided one does not grasp it too firmly, or burden it with more meaning than a spring dream might bear. The Song dynasty poet Su Shi (1037–1101), a scholar official like all the intellectuals of his time, embroidered upon the classical usage of *menghen*, when he wrote:

> The east wind cannot yet enter the east gate. But riding horses, we seek out the old place. Men, like wild geese, keep the promise of return. While things vanish like a spring dream without a trace. . . . Since we have agreed to meet here each year. Why bother calling back the spirits of the dead.[31]

In Su Shi's poem, a group of friends has just set out for a reunion at a lake. Spring, with its east winds, finds no admittance to this rural hideaway. The poet and his friends, like wild geese, have kept the promise of return. Their yearly gathering, according to Su Shi, has the power to obstruct the course of natural amnesia, even of death itself. Spring dreams leave no trace but in the poem itself. It memorializes the vanishing moment. It recalls the past momentarily, and lets it go again.

Subsequent generations of Chinese writers elaborated the metaphor of *menghen* to fit disparate memorial experiences. In all of its proliferations, however, the link between remembrance and the traces of a vanishing spring dream was maintained with delicate care. In poetry, as well as in prose, memory is seen as something precious and tenuous all at once. The historian Wang Huizu (1731–1807) articulated this duality most clearly in a preface to his autobiography, *Dream Traces From a Sickbed:* "Having been paralyzed in old age, I think about the past all the time: everything is still very clear in mind, so I started to dictate this history to my two sons.... Su Shi's said that 'things vanish like a spring dream, without a trace.' But I don't care to look at life as though it were a dream. Perhaps dreams are unreal. But traces of recollections are not. Therefore I have tried to record my life as honestly as I can."[32]

The urge to leave a trace, to write an instructive history of his life for posterity, led Wang Huizu to endow recollection with more significance than Su Shi was willing to seven centuries earlier. The cumulative record of Chinese history, the vast corpus of literary musings on *menghen* enabled the Qing historian to give memory more substance than the poet before him. By checking and verifying the evidence in his autobiography, Wang Huizu sought to make remembrance something more than a vanishing dream. He enhanced traces with a lifeweight lacking in the season of pure change.

A rather different intensity animates Jewish reflections on the truth value of remembrance. In the wake of exile and repeated historical trauma, memory had to lament, to console and to commemorate all at once. There was little room even in classical Judaism for doubt about the evidence of recollection and even less for soft spoken analogies to the world of nature. Instead of traces of spring dreams, the poets of Lamentations, for example, forced themselves to recall events that curdled the stomach and singed the eyes. Writing about children expiring from hunger in the streets of a besieged city, one of them confessed:

> My heart is in tumult
> My being melts away.[33]

Meaning literally, "my liver spills on the ground"—(*nishpakh la'arets keyedi*)—this metaphor for recollection colors all of Jewish memorial literature. Its visceral violence mirrors the brutal persecution that is a frequent theme in the literature of penitential poems (*piyutim*) from David Bar Meshullam of Speyer (who memorialized the mass suicide of a Jewish community in 1096, at the height of the First Crusade) to Hayim Nahman Bialik (who bore poetic witness to the Kishinev pogrom of 1908).

The experience of gut splitting anguish was not alien to Chinese poets. They called it *duan chang,* a metaphor for being broken hearted that means, literally, "torn apart inards." Some of the Chinese poets' best work was born out of these wretched depths. But whereas the remorse and agitation of the Jewish authors of penitential prayers, or *piyutim,* was rooted in historical trauma, Chinese writers' inspiration often came from personal loss confronted in the world of nature.

Su Shi, the Song dynasty poet who had likened memory so skillfully to the traces of a spring dream was also the author of one of the most powerful memorial poems in classical Chinese literature. Mourning the death of his wife, the poet longs for her distant grave with the full force of *duan chang:*

> A decade splits off your death
> From my life, a dreary desert
> No mind can cross.
> Your orphaned grave's too far away,
> No place beyond the tall, straight pines.
> To break my heart, to voice my bleak lament.
> Night brings spring dreams,
> I'm home again.
> Outside the window,
> I watch you comb your hair.
> We look, but do not speak,
> A blank page marred by streaks of tears.
> And even if our paths did cross
> You would not know me,
> A man grown ghostly pale.[34]

The double loss of death and distance took this Chinese poet into some of the same thickets as Jewish poets who stretched language to accommodate the demands of the commitment to remembrance. But the Chinese writer's excursion into this ache-filled region is constantly moderated by a cultural injunction against dwelling on the painful past too long. Although memory is to be consciously, artfully cultivated, it must not become an overwhelming obsession. A Daoist classic of third century went as far as to identify memory as the source of all emotional troubles, suggesting that harmony within and beyond the self is best maintained through forgetting: "Emotions (that upset natural harmony) arise out of memory. Where there is no memory, emotions (obsessions) will dissolve as well."[35]

The Daoist preference for unruffled amnesia was qualified in Chinese culture by a Confucian appreciation of the healing power of memorial metaphors. As in Hebrew literature, remembering is a sacred activity that mends the breach between past and present. It regenerates even in the process of mourning. For the Lamentation poets there was little doubt that mournful verses can and did comfort Zion, "like the restored children of a grieving mother."[36]

On the Chinese side, a similar faith in the comforts of recollection lives on through the remorse filled epic, the *Li Sao.* Authored by Qu Yuan, an exiled official who committed suicide in 27 BC, this poem became an inspiration for generations of Chinese intellectuals who found themselves outcasts in times of greed and violence. Qu Yuan's meditations on the grief of wandering away from home are recalled every year during the Dragon Boat Festival. The memory of China's earliest and most famous political dissident literally nourishes his descendants who partake of the ritual of earing *zongze* (rice dumplings wrapped in leaves).[37]

Rituals like the Dragon Boat Festival and Passover cement the bonds between past and present. They make some future possible, conceivable, despite the historical traumas that continue to haunt Chinese and Jewish culture in the 20th century. In the wake of the Holocaust and of the Cultural Revolution, Chinese and Jewish writers could not but reanimate *and* interrogate the language, the values of the past. To write is, literally, to remain in a continuum with Qu Yuan and the poets of Lamentations.

Dan Pagis, born in Bukovina in 1930, expressed this indebtedness to tradition most eloquently in "Sealed Transport" (*Karon hatum*), a cycle of poems about the destruction of European Jewry during the Second World War. In this collection, Pagis bears witness to personally endured trauma in a unique voice that nonetheless maintains a vivid link to the literature of the Psalms and of Lamentations. When he finally comes to the subject of his own survival, the poet shows himself unable to give up the burden of remembrance. With one foot already out of the nightmare, a new passport in hand, he writes:

> Imaginary man, go. Here is your passport.
> You are not allowed to remember . . .
> You have a decent coat now,
> a prepared body, a new name
> ready in your throat.
> Go. You are not allowed to forget.[38]

Similarly, the young Chinese poet Bei Dao, born in 1949 along with Mao's China, has steadfastly refused to forget the ravage of the Mao's revolution. In 1978, when Deng Xiaoping was just beginning to bring the nation out of the shadow of Maoist politics, when young people were being asked to get over the tragedies of the recent past and to dedicate themselves with optimism and renewed faith to the project of reform, Bei Dao penned his refusal in the form of a poem entitled "The Answer." Full of unanswered questions about Mao's past and Deng's present, the poet wrote:

> The Ice Age is over now,
> Why is there still ice everywhere?
> The Cape of Good Hope has been discovered,
> Why do a thousand sails contest the Dead Sea?
> Let me tell you, world,
> I—do—not—believe!
> Even if a thousand challengers face you
> Number me as one thousand and one.
> A new constellation of glimmering stars
> Adorn the unobstructed sky,
> they are five thousand year old pictographs:
> The staring eyes of future generations.[39]

This haltingly crafted Chinese poem expresses the same determination to bear witness as Dan Pagis' tightly woven one. Here too, a young man uses personal memory to interrogate public history. Mindful of the "five thousand year pictographs" that are his inheritance, Bei Dao insists that old answers will not do in the present crisis. The "staring eyes of future generations" demand that he not forget, not "get over" the Cultural Revolution. Like Dan Pagis, Bei Dao refuses to cross the boundary with a new overcoat, as if all was well now.

Nothing was quite well (the "Cape of Good Hope" had been discovered, but. . . .) for these writers who could not forget the historical traumas of the 20th century.

The Holocaust and The Cultural Revolution

How can one speak in the same breath of two such disparate events as the Holocaust and the Cultural Revolution, you ask? If what you are concerned with is the magnitude of suffering, the numbers killed or the kinds of humiliations endured, then the writings of Chinese and Jewish survivors cannot be considered side by side. But if, on the other hand, you are interested in the fertility of memorial traditions in the face of historical trauma, then the Holocaust and the Cultural Revolution, illuminate each other a great deal. If furthermore, you hear—as I did—Chinese intellectuals use the precedent of the Holocaust over and over again to explain their own wanton persecution during the Cultural Revolution, then the boundaries between Chinese and Jewish survivors wear thin indeed. Almost unwittingly, one is cast in a cosmopolitan world of memory metaphors, where, as Joseph Levenson insisted Chinese usage must be allowed to make sense in the same world of discourse in which we try to make sense of the West.

For me, Chinese and Jewish memory metaphors began to cross, to interrogate one another in 1980 in the mining village of Datong. This North China hamlet houses Buddhist cave sculptures from 6th century as well as an abandoned Class Struggle Education Museum. Built during the Cultural Revolution, the museum was intended to commemorate the murder of Chinese miners in the Japanese labor camps of the 1940s. But Mao's political purposes, his penchant for bold, didactic lessons from the past took over. Around a few local remnants, the exhibition hall became a theater for his urge to engrave ever lasting messages about class struggle on the minds of new generations of Chinese proletarians. They forgot the museum soon after Mao's death.

In the cavernous, now deserted Class Struggle Exhibition Hall, I began to think about the *Yad Vashem* museum in Jerusalem, about its initially modest, black and white photographs and now increasingly, lavish contemporary monuments. In Datong, I began to take stock of what happens when remembrance becomes de-gutted, its compelling, troublesome inards cast out in favor of glossy lessons about the past.

In Datong, genuine remembrance appeared sequestered to a few dark corners where the mythifying light of political commemoration failed to penetrate. After Datong, I continued to find such corners, such snippets of the past—some poems, some memoirs in which Chinese and Jewish rememberers took me closer to the real anguish of the Cultural Revolution and of the Holocaust. Their shared understatement, their willingness to strain inherited idioms to accommodate unprecedented nightmares suggested more common ground than I had previously imagined.

Both the Holocaust and the Cultural Revolution assaulted traditional values in the name of an incomprehensible, all powerful demonology—so-called humans (Aryans and Proletarians) against the so-called social vermin (Jews and class enemies). Both in the Holocaust and in the Cultural Revolution it was intellectuals (those most dependent upon, most addicted to traditional culture) who suffered the greatest injuries in mind, body and soul. In both settings, it was intellectuals who emerged with a conscious sense of complicity in the horrors of their time. It is they who continue to nurture the frail but life sustaining bonds of remembrance between the present and the past.

The Cultural Revolution and the Holocaust, however, are also very different events: During the Holocaust, Jews in concentration camps faced a predicament that transcended both precedent and reason. Primo Levi and Jean Amery—barrack mates at Auschwitz—have pointed out that the *lager* was a world apart, a universe with his own "death logic." Prisoners[40] had been thoroughly dehumanized through the foodless, airless transport trains, through the daily spectre of mass murder in the gas chambers, through forced labor and the endless, intentional humiliation of the roll call—day or night, winter and summer. To be a concentration camp inmate was to be a number, not a sentient being. If Germans styled themselves to be humans larger than life, the Jew was less than an animal. As the opening quote of Art Spiegelman's vivid tale *Maus* makes it clear, Hitler consigned his victims beyond the pale: "The Jews are undoubtedly a race, but they are not human."[41]

Demonology prevailed in China during the Cultural Revolution as well. Mao's victims were labeled "snake spirits" and "cow demons" before being incarcerated into "cow pens." This systematic dehumanization of the "enemies of the people" had begun in the 1950s. But during the sixties it became a means for mass persecution.

In spite of the life-denying labels, however, Mao's reign of terror never reached full fledged genocide. Intellectuals (*zhi shi fenzi* the "knowledgeable elements") were targeted for persecution over and over again during the long Mao era from 1942 to 1976. But each campaign against intellectuals, including the 1957 "Anti-Rightist" campaign and the Cultural Revolution assault on "the stinking ninth" (a collective indictment of the intelligentsia deemed by

Mao to be more odious than traitors, Guomindang agents, landlords, capitalists, etc.) was carried out in the name of real, or imagined charges against individuals. No group was singled out for systematic destruction the way that the Jews had been during the Nazi terror.

Hence the breakdown of the inner world of Chinese victims was never as encompassing as that of the inmates in the death camps. Intellectuals in Hitler's concentration universe were stripped of all of their spiritual resources. As Jean Amery writes, "the intellectual person was isolated, thrown back entirely upon himself . . . he no longer believed in the reality of the world of the mind . . . the reality of the camp triumphed effortlessly over death and over the entire complex of so-called ultimate questions."[42] Simply put, Amery argues, the intellectual was defeated, not only annihilated in Auschwitz. The mind had been brought to its limits, and found impotent. In fact, Amery concludes, the intellectual was less fit for survival than other camp inmates because of his lingering attachment to useless philosophical ideas, to fragments of meaningless poetry, to the subtleties of language.

Chinese intellectuals, by contrast, never experienced such extreme spiritual depravation. Although they were the objects of repeated criticism campaigns, they never lost a sense of connectedness to the nation and its cultural past. The survivor literature in China is full of consolations derived from reciting Tang poetry in Mao's prison cells, from reading Mao's anti-Confucian rhetoric with an eye to the lingering values of Confucian humaneness. Almost every intellectual sent down to forced labor "education camps" managed to hide some slim volume of spiritual nourishment beneath the *Quotations from Chairman Mao* that was the only truly safe book during the agonizing years of the Cultural Revolution.

Simply put, the Chinese intellectuals' world was never as hermetically sealed as Jean Amery's in Auschwitz. Even in Dachau, Amery reminds us, some inmates could read Goethe for spiritual relief. In China, such furtive consolations proliferated even more. Philosopher Li Zehou, for example, managed to hide Kant's *Critique of Pure Reason* among his belongings in 1972 as he set off for what he believed to be a life long exile in the countryside. A few years later, Li Zehou emerged with a thorough critique of Kant[43]— a concrete testimony to one survivor's faith in the power of the mind, so unlike the devastating disillusionment experienced by Jean Amery.

Chinese intellectuals seemed to have never lost the certainty that their suffering was part of a larger tragedy visited upon the Chinese nation as a whole. The Cultural Revolution, in spite of its pointed humiliation of the "stinking ninth" was an intra-family affair. What kept this Red Terror somewhat in charge, and what accounts for its distinctive brutality as well, is that it was an internecine struggle. Far from setting the superhuman (Germans) against the inhuman (Jews), Mao's campaign exploited the deepest loyalties within Chinese society.

The Cultural Revolution, young critics agree today, was the outgrowth of old habits of thought, especially of the need to belong to a group and to submit unquestioningly to paternalistic authority. Sun Longji, in a scathing series of essays entitled *The Deep Structure of Chinese Culture,* argues that Chinese culture has been held in thrall for centuries by "sodality"—a network of human relations built on a system of favors and obligations that keeps an individual "infantilized" from birth to death. If we are to understand how and why Mao became the unchallengeable Great Helmsman during the Cultural Revolution, how and why his ardent followers committed unchecked atrocities in the name of loyalty to this Great Red Sun, we cannot but reckon with Sun's claim that:

"Within the network of Chinese Sodality there is a great need for interdependence. . . . And, in typically, infantile fashion, when a man's somatized needs are satisfied over by another person, then he must surrender his Heart-and-Mind. Thus the individual comes to obey authority. In this way the Chinese adult never totally outgrows childhood. Throughout Chinese history, the Chinese common man has been the little child of a paternal, but dictatoral ruler."[44]

The memoir literature after the Cultural Revolution bears ample witness to the cult of loyalty that flourished during the late Mao era. Unlike the recollections of Jewish survivors who catalogue catastrophies endured, Chinese remembrances are filled with details about participation in the Mao cult—even if/when the narrator was a victim of the Red Terror. A deep sense of religious community was fostered in China during the Cultural Revolution (unlike the scrupulous demarcations of the death camps). Daily practices such as the morning bow to the picture of the Chairman, the work place recitation of quotations from the Red Book, the ritualized exchanges of quotations before any purchase in the supermarket, the "loyalty dances" that took the place before calestenics all contributed to a sense of a shared faith in Mao's divine proletarizing mission.

In *Man, Ah Man,* one of the earliest novels to explore survivor memories of the Cultural Revolution, a young woman explores the meanings of *jiaoxin*—that "handing over of heart-mind" which students, teachers, peasants and workers practiced daily during the Cultural Revolution. Giving concrete form to Sun Longji's meditations on sodality, this novel dresses up memory in the garb of a surrealistic dream. As in Kafkaesque world, an entire city is afflicted by a strange illness: people are ripping out their own hearts to offer them up in public places. The one person who will not tear open her chest is deemed mad.[45]

Complicity and acquiescence constitute a powerful undercurrent in Chinese memoir literature. Since the Cultural Revolution was an intra-family affair, few Chinese were able, or willing, to risk the kind of "madness" that would have cut off the nurturing bond to Mao Zedong—and through Mao, to the community as a whole. In retrospect, shame looms large in survivors' minds, even if only as a shadow holding back the details of remembrance.

Not that the weight of guilt is absent among Jewish survivors of the Holocaust. It is very much there, but different from the sense of complicity that animates the most thoughtful of Chinese memoirs. Primo Levi gives voice to this feeling of unworthiness when he writes: "The worst survived, that is, the fittest; the best died. . . . We, the survivors, are not the true witness. . . . We survivors are not only an exiguous but also an anomolous minority: We are those who by their prevarications or abilities or good luck did not touch bottom."[46]

The extreme conditions of depravation and humiliation suffered by Levi and others in the death camps were unmatched in China, even in the so-called "cow pens". And yet, survival during the Cultural Revolution also required "prevarication" and "good luck." Most of all, it depended on real or simulated enthusiasm for Mao's religious campaign. Qian Zhonghu, the noted literary critic, who was deported to a labor camp in 1969, describes the impact of this coping strategy in the preface to his wife's memoir, *A Cadre School Life:* "Our only boldness was a lack of enthusiasm for the endless movements and struggles we participated in. . . . An acute sense of shame can result in selective amnesia. A guilty conscience can make you guarded."[47]

Many intellectuals in China shared Qian Zhongshu's "boldness." Very few, however, have been able to articulate its deforming impact on their remembrance. Yang Jiang, Qian Zhong Shu's wife—an accomplished dramatist and translator in her own right—acknowledged both selective amnesia and an enduring attachment to Chinese memorial tradition in her recollection of the Cultural Revolution. Her intensely understated memoir is modeled on a late eighteenth century work, *Six Chapters from a Floating Life.* Like its precedessor, Yang Jiang's work dwells on the small details of daily survival: a stray dog, a chance meeting with her husband, the jade color of leaves in the countryside after the rain washed off the dust.

Political persecution and physical depravation is alluded to rather than described here. The very indirectness of Yang Jiang's work testifies to what her husband called the burden of shame, the guardedness that follows upon complicity. Such reticence can—and has been—mistaken as simply a preservation tactic in the post-Mao era. Yang Jiang, after all continues to live and write on the Chinese mainland, in the midst of the very community that inflicted suffering upon intellectuals like herself and her husband. But there is more than self-preservation at work here. Precisely because Yang Jiang and Qian Zhongshu are such mindful rememberers, they can draw upon classical Chinese precedents to make sense of their predicament in Communist China.

The historical trauma of the Cultural Revolution did not occur in a memorial vacuum. Much as Mao Zedong tried to eradicate old ideas, old books— and the people who embodied them—traditions of recollection survived his ravage. The very characters used in Chinese writing, bring with them a tradition of acquiescence to *and* interrogation of patriarchal authority. When Yang Jiang uses an intensely personal memoir from the 18th century to frame her labor camp experience, she is, in effect, taking history back from Mao. She not only survived his persecution campaigns, but managed to record them in a way that transcends Mao's memory denying logic.

Similarly, Jewish survivors of the Holocaust reach back in time to find words, metaphors, sanctions for remembering the most mind baffling of experiences. Some, like Elie Wiesel, have dwelt on the virtues of silence, on the impotence of words beyond a certain point of pain and horror. Others, like Primo Levi, Dan Pagis and Paul Celan, have probed more deeply the vertigo of language and memory. They emerged from the darkness of suffering with snatches of remembrance that directly challenge the logic of murder and amnesia. Even when writing about the most incomprehensible aspects of the Holocaust—maybe precisely when nearing these thought-defying realms, they borrow, they rely upon the language of the Hebrew Bible. Primo Levi, for example, in a chapter called "Shame" describes the physical and mental anguish of survivors by recalling the second verse of Genesis where "anguish inscribed in everyone the 'tohu-bohu' of a deserted and empty universe crushed under the spirit of God but from which the spirit of man is absent: not yet born or already extinguished."[48]

Those of us born after these traumatic events must approach the memorial record with care. We have to be mindful of cultural and historical precedents as well as our immeasurable distance from those who survived such sense shaking experiences as the Holocaust and the Cultural Revolution. Otherwise, we risk arrogance, denial, or both. We must be on guard against intellectual constructs that seek to distance us from unanswered questions in the survivors' memoir literature. In both the Chinese and Jewish contexts, barriers have already been erected in the guise of sympathy for victims of "post-traumatic distress syndrome."[49] But survivors are more than victims. They are carriers of dark secrets that affect us all. We do not need new medical categories to encapsulate—and dispose of—their narratives. Rather, we need to expand our notion of historical understanding to make room for their troubling memories.

The Historian as Physician of Memory

The effort to flee from memory is as old as history itself. Whether they followed the model of ancient Chinese diviners who sought to codify the pattern of cosmic events, or, the modern priesthood that holds dominion over empirical facts, professional historians have shied away from Mnemosyne's dark embrace. Memorial evidence is too fragmented, too murky to be "true," if by truth we mean serviceable generalities for the so-called common good.

But the value of remembrance lies precisely in its ability to challenge prevailing notions of the common good. In China, on the eve of martial law in 1989, intellectuals were powerless to question the State's version of recent events. With tanks already on the streets of Beijing, questions could only be posed obliquely. And yet in the very moment when history seemed defeated, the memorial gathering for Zhang Dainian reaffirmed the ability of intellectuals to survive repression with a modicum of integrity. In the company of Chinese intellectuals attending that commemorative occasion, I came to appreciate anew the resiliency of Jewish survivors as well. Both have deep roots in memorial traditions that precede and encompass traumatic events. Both have developed strategies of overcoming publicly enforced as well as personally cultivated amnesia. In spite of such adverse soil, remembrance has continued to flourish, to be a source of renewal in both Chinese and Jewish culture.

This enduring attachment to recollection runs counter to the modern Western commitment to progress through reason. The utility of Descartes, however, is becoming increasingly outworn. Widely disparate thinkers are currently reclaiming the neglected, doubt-ridden terrain inhabited by Mnemosyne. Eugen Rosenstock-Husey is one of the historians who pioneered the study of memory by historians. In 1964, he had the audacity to publish an *Autobiography of Western Man.* Wrestling with the aftermath of the two world wars—two events not unlike the current "revolutions" in Eastern Europe in that they challenge, empty all forms of political discourse—Rosenstock-Husey could not but bid a "farewell to Descartes," the title of his book's epilogue. This farewell was accompanied by willingness to probe the problems of collective and individual remembrance. But how is the historian to venture into the Mnemosyne's uncertain domain? As a "physician of memory" Rosenstock-Husey argued:

> It is his honor to heal the wounds, genuine wounds. As a physician must act, regardless of medical theories, because his patient is ill. So a historian must act under a moral pressure to restore a nation's memory, and that of mankind. Buried instincts, repressed fears, painful scars come for treatment to the historian. The historian regenerates the great moments of history and disentangles them from the mist of particularity.[50]

Two and a half decades after, Rosenstock-Husey wrote these words, the need for "physicians of memory" is even greater to counter the flood of nationalistic mythology cresting in newly "democratized" corners of the world. At the same time, however, we cannot take the heroic image of the "physician" at face value. The medical profession has shown itself to be every bit as immune to the deeper meanings of suffering as the historical one. Doctors have grown used to treating medicable diseases, not the kind of chronic illness Rosenstock-Husey was seeking to heal.[51] It would be a great mistake, if we now traded an earlier, priestly image of the historian for the equally limiting medical one. Rosenstock-Husey himself courted this danger when he sought to life the "great moments of history" out of "the mist of particularity". The old rhetoric of enlightenment colored his voice even as he claimed to be leaving Descartes behind.

"Particularity," misty and messy, is the very stuff that a comparative historian must contend with all the time. To consider the Chinese and the Jewish commitment to remembrance in one project, for example, is to risk injuring the distinctive meanings of each. I took this risk here because the great wall dividing the two traditions that affected my life has begun to crumble. But, this is not simply a personal project. It is a way of bearing witness to a new meaning of historical understanding. Out of the disparate particularities of Mnemosyne abroad it is possible to weave a new tapestry. "Misty details" need not be expunged but may be cherished here.

If memory is to recover her rightful place as Mother-Muse of history, her dark, shadowy weight cannot be wished or analyzed away. In the words of philosopher Edward Casey, Mnemosyne's "thick autonomy" must be recognized as both the repository of past experience and a growing fund for new experience.[52] Without memories, we have no history at all. Memories translated into history allow the future to be born anew.

Notes

1. Joseph Levonson, "The Genesis of Confucian China and Its Modern fate", in Curtis ed., *The Historian's Workshop.* (New York, 1970) p. 287.

2. F. W. Nietszche, *Thus Spake Zarathustra* (New York, 1924) p. 158.

3. From 1979 onward, Zhang Dainian has been an active informant in my research project concerning the life of his older brother, Zhang Shenfu (a founder of the Chinese Communist Party and China's foremost expert on Bertrand Russell). The results of our decade long collaboration will appear in my book *Time for Telling: Dialogues with Zhang Shenfu, Founder of the Chinese Communist Party.* (forthcoming, Yale University Press, 1991).

4. *Analects* 8:7, translated in Wing-tsit Chan, *A Source Book of Chinese Philosophy* (Princeton, 1969), p. 33.

5. For a thoughtful analysis of the etymology of "*zachor*" see, Brevard S. Childs, *Memory and Tradition in Israel* (London, 1962) especially pp. 9–16, 66–74.

6. *Ibid.,* pp. 18–19.

7. Elie Wiesel, *Discours d'Oslo* (Paris, 1987) pp. 28–29.

8. Edward S. Casey, *Remembering—a Phenomenological Study* (Bloomington, 1987) p. 18.

9. Pierre Janet, *L'evolution de la Memoire et de le Notion du Temps* (Paris, 1928) vol. 2, p. 185.

10. For a fuller discussion of the impact of "River Elegy" upon mass audiences in the People's Republic of China, see Geremie Barme. "TV Requiem for the Myths of the Middle Kingdom," *Far Eastern Economic Review* (1 September, 1988) 38–44.

11. Franz Kafka, *The Great Wall of China* (New York, 1946) p. 162.

12. Tu Weiming. "The Way, Learning and Politics in Classical Confucianism" in *Classical Confucianism* (forthcoming, Singapore, 1990) p. 2.

13. *Ibid.*, p. 7.

14. Allen Grossman, "Remarks toward a Jewish Poetry." *Tikkun* (May/June, 1990) pp. 47–48.

15. Arnold Jacob Wolf, "Remember to Remember," *Tradition* (June, 1972). pp. 33–42.

16. Amos Funkenstein, "Collective Memory and Historical Consciousness," *History and Memory* (Spring/Summer 1990) p. 12; Li Zehou, *Huaxia meixue* (Aesthetics in Ancient China) (Beijing, 1989) p. 57.

17. For an excellent overview of the meanings, uses of "history" in Chinese culture see, Yves Chevrier, "La Servante-Maitrese: Condition de la Reference a l'Histoire dans l'Espece Intellectual chinois," *Extreme Orient/Extreme Occident* No. 9 (1986) pp. 117–142.

18. The evolution/distortion of Jewish historical consciousness in the post biblical period is discussed by Yoseph Hayim Yerusahlmi in *Zachor: Jewish History and Jewish Memory* (Seattle, 1982).

19. Funkenstein, *op. cit.*, p. 17.

20. This text and its implications for Chinese culture has been analyzed by Wang Gungwu in "Loving the Ancient in China," *Who Owns the Past,* (Melbourne, 1985) pp. 176–195.

21. Stephen Owen, *Remembrances: The Experience of the Past in Chinese Literature* (Cambridge, 1986) pp. 16–32.

22. *Ibid.*, p. 18.

23. *Ibid.*

24. The concept of *nianjiu,* "attachment to the past" is discussed in Lin Yusheng, *The Crisis of Chinese Consciousness,* (Madison, 1979) pp. 158–64.

25. Lu Xun, "In Memory of Wei Suyuan," *Selected Works* (tr. Yang Xinyi and Gladys Yang) vol. IV (Beijing, 1980) p. 67.

26. Elie Wiesel, *op. cit.*, p. 22.

27. *Ibid.*, p. 23.

28. Childs, *op. cit.*, p. 19.

29. Wiesel, *op cit.*, p. 35.

30. Owen, *op cit.*, p. 24.

31. Su Shi, *Su Shi Xuanji* (Selected Poems by Su Shi) ed. Liu Naichang (Jinan, 1980) pp. 78–79.

32. Wang Huizu, *Bingta menghen lu* (Traces of Dream from a Sickbed). (Imperial edition, 1796), p. 3.

33. Quoted and discussed by Alan Mintz in *Hurban: Response to Catastrophe in Hebrew Literature* (New York, 1984) p. 28.

34. Su Shi *op. cit.*, p. 75.

35. I am indebted to Professor Yu Yingshi of Princeton University for extended conversations about the sources of personal and public memory in traditional China. It was Professor Yu who first drew my attention to the late 3rd century Daoist classic *Jin Shu* in which appears a most concise warning against indulgence in memory. The passage "*Qing you yi sheng, bu yi ze wu qing*" may be translated as follows: "Feelings arise out of memory. If there is no memory, feelings will dissolve as well." This Daoist injunction against memory as the focus of disturbing emotion is also echoed in Confucian admonitions on filial piety that require one to maintain mental well being—if not for one's own sake, at least for one's parents'. In the view of these Confucians, as well as Daoists, to dwell on the painful past is to arouse distressing, dangerous—and, in the long run, unfilial—emotions.

36. Alan Mintz, *op. cit.*, p. 30.

37. *Ibid.,* pp. 262–267.

38. *Ibid.,* pp. 267–68.

39. Bei Dao (Zhao Zhengkai), *"Huida"* (Answer) *Xinshi shiji* vol. 1 (Beijing, 1985) p. 13.

40. Jean Amery's term in *At the Mind's Limits* tr. S. Rosenfeld (Bloomington, 1980) p. 6.

41. Art Spigelman, *Maus: A Survivor's Tale* (New York, 1985).

42. Amery, *op. cit.,* pp. 15–19.

43. Li Zehou "Houji" (Postface) *Pipan zhexue de pipan* (*Critique of Critical Philosophy*) Beijing, 1979.

44. Sun Longji, "The Deep Structure of Chinese Culture" in *Seeds of Fire* (ed. G. Barme) Hong Kong, 1986, p. 32.

45. Dai Houying's novella *Ren, a ren* (Man, Ah, man) has been the subject of extensive analysis in Michael Duke's work, *Blooming and Condescending: Chinese Literature in the Post-Mao Era* (Indiana, 1985) pp. 141–181.

46. Primo Levi, *The Drowned and the Saved* (New York, 1986) p. 82.

47. Qian Zhongshu "Preface" to Yang Jiang, *A Cadre School Life* (Hong Kong, 1982) p. IV.

48. Levi, *op. cit.,* p. 85.

49. Arthur Kleinman, a psychiatrist and China scholar has been long involved in a critique of the medical profession's use of certain categories to immunize itself against the meanings and implications of human suffering. In a recent paper, "Suffering and Its Professional Transformation: Toward an Ethonography of Experience" (presented at the first conference of the Society for Psychological Anthropology, October, 1989) he took direct issue with the uses of "post-traumatic distress syndrome": "The very idea of post traumatic stress as a disorder invalidates the moral and political meaning of suffering. After all in both traditional Chinese and Western culture, the idea of suffering turned on the idea of having to endure or bear great hardship. The idea of suffering carried the moral significance of endurance. Those connotations are lost when suffering is configured as stress with which we cope (either adaptively or ineffectively) or a disease that can be 'cured' ". (p. 30)

50. Eugene Rosenstock-Husey, *Out of Revolution* (New York, 1964) p. 696.

51. See, Arthur Kleinman, *The Illness Narrative,* (New York, 1988).

52. Casey, *op. cit.,* p. 294.

9

Acting Out Democracy
Political Theater in Modern China

Joseph W. Esherick and Jeffrey N. Wasserstrom

For two and a half months in the spring of 1989, China's student actors dominated the world stage of modern telecommunications. Their massive demonstrations, the hunger strike during Gorbachev's visit, and the dramatic appearance of the Goddess of Democracy captured the attention of an audience that spanned the globe. As we write in mid-1990, the movement and its bloody suppression have already produced an enormous body of literature—from eyewitness accounts by journalists (Morrison 1989; Zhaoqiang, Gejing and Siyuan 1989) and special issues of scholarly journals (*Australian Journal of Chinese Affairs* Nos. 23, 24; *The Fletcher Forum of World Affairs* 14.4), to pictorial histories (Turnley and Turnley 1989) and documentary collections (Han 1990; Wu 1989), and, most recently, textbook chapters (Spence 1990) and analytical works (Feigon 1990; Nathan 1990)—tracing the development of China's crisis. Despite a flood of material too massive to review in the present context, we still lack a convincing interpretive framework that places the events within the context of China's modern political evolution, and also provides a way to compare China's experience to that of Eastern Europe. Such an interpretation should help us to understand why massive public demonstrations spurred an evolution toward democratic governance in Eastern Europe, but in China led only to the massacre of June 3–4 and the present era of political repression.

None of the most frequently mentioned characterizations of the movement seem truly adequate. The Chinese leadership, for example, has portrayed both the 1989 movement and its predecessor of 1986–87 as manifestations of "bourgeois liberalism," or acts of *luan* (chaos) reminiscent of the Red Guards in the Cultural Revolution, or some combination of the two (Han 1990:83–103; CQ Chronicle 1989:672; on 1986–7: *China News Analysis*

From *The Journal of Asian Studies* 49, no. 4 (November 1990): 835–43; 856–65.

1328 (1 February 1987):8; *Renmin ribao,* December 25, 1986). But if the 1989 protests were the result of "bourgeois" contamination, why was the most prominent anthem of the student demonstrators "The Internationale," and why did protesters carry pictures of Mao Zedong and Zhou Enlai (Orleans 1989; *San Francisco Chronicle,* May 19, 1989)?

Official characterizations of recent protests as acts of *luan* and Red Guardism are even more deeply flawed. Protesters unquestionably committed disorderly acts in both 1986 and 1989, and there were certainly continuities between the 1960s and the 1980s in student tactics (e.g., the use of wall posters and the insistence upon free train passage to Beijing) in part because some young teachers advising the students were former Red Guards. Yet most foreign observers were impressed by the discipline and orderliness of the students (Forster 1990; Fox 1990; Pieke 1989). The prominent role of march monitors, the security forces that maintained order in Tiananmen Square, the student "arrest" of youths for defacing a portrait of Mao—these activities hardly suggest an atmosphere of *luan.* The complete lack of either anti-Western rhetoric or devotional loyalty to any living CCP leader by the students of the late eighties makes all analogies with the Red Guards extremely tenuous.[1]

The analyses offered by Western social scientists, foreign journalists and Chinese dissidents, though considerably more persuasive than the official CCP line, are also problematic. Many, especially the professional Pekingologists of political science, stress the role that power struggles between Li Peng and Zhao Ziyang played in shaping the 1989 events (Dittmer 1990; Gong 1990; Feigon 1990). There is no doubt that internal divisions paralyzed the party leadership in April and May, preventing an effective response to the demonstrators. But at the start of the movement, one of the protesters' most common abusive rhymes in Beijing and Tianjin was "*Ziyang, Ziyang, xinge buliang*" (Zhao Ziyang, Zhao Ziyang, you are not a good man; Fox 1990:139) and as late as May 19th (long after the Voice of America and BBC broadcasts had been focusing on the Li-Zhao conflict) the protesters' posters and slogans in Xi'an still had two central targets: Deng Xiaoping and Zhao Ziyang. Corruption in Zhao's immediate family made him so unpopular that it is impossible to see him successfully manipulating the movement for his own ends. Indeed, like Hu Yaobang before him, Zhao Ziyang became a hero only after (and to a large degree because) he was ousted from power by the alliance of hard-liners and party elders around Deng.

The Western press and Chinese dissidents abroad usually characterize the events of China's spring as a "democracy movement." There is no question that "*minzhu*" was frequently invoked in the protesters' banners and slogans, but it would be hasty to associate *minzhu* (literally: "rule of the people") with any conventional Western notion of democracy. Consider, for example, Wuer Kaixi's words in the televised dialogue with Li Peng on May 18th. Early in the meeting, Wuer Kaixi explained what it would take to get students to leave

Tiananmen Square: "If one fasting classmate refuses to leave the square, the other thousands of fasting students on the square will not leave." He was explicit about the principle behind this decision: "On the square, it is not a matter of the minority obeying the majority, but of 99.9 percent obeying 0.1 percent" (Zhaoqiang et al. 1989:204). This may have been good politics—and Wuer Kaixi certainly made powerful theater—but it was not democracy.

The hunger-striking students in Tiananmen Square adopted a position designed to preserve their unity and enhance their leverage with the government. But in elevating the principle of unity above that of majority rule, they were acting within the tradition of popular rule (*minzhu*) thinking in modern China. When Sun Yatsen assumed the presidency of the Republic of China in January 1912, his message to the revolutionary paper *Minlibao* was a simple slogan (in English): "'Unity' is our watchword"—not "democracy" or "republicanism," but "unity" (*Sun Zhongshan xiansheng huace* 1986: plate 199). Closer to the present, the dissident magazine *Enlightenment* wrote in 1979 of the miraculous effects that the "fire" of democracy would have on the Chinese people:

> The fire will enable people completely to shake off brutality and hatred, and there will be no quarrel among them. They will share the same views and principles and have identical ideals. In lofty and harmonious unity they will produce, live, think, pioneer, and explore together. With these dynamic forces they will enrich their social life and cultivate their big earth. (Cited in Nathan 1985:6)

While Western democratic notions are normally linked to pluralism and the free competition of divergent ideas, *minzhu* in China is here linked to a vision in which people will "share the same views" and have "identical ideals." It is thus difficult to analyze the events of China's 1989 spring as a "democratic movement" in the pluralist sense of the term.[2]

Nor do the words and deeds of the protesters of either 1986–87 or 1989 fit easily with more radical Western ideas of direct or participatory democracy. In many cases the students seem to have read the *min* in *minzhu* in a limited sense to refer not to the populace at large but mainly or exclusively to the educated elite of which they are part. This elitist reading of *minzhu* was clear in the wall posters that appeared in Shanghai in December 1986, many of which took their lead from the speeches Fang Lizhi gave at the city's Tongji University earlier that year. The main theme in these posters, as in Fang's lectures and writings (Kraus 1989), was not that the CCP should be more responsive to the ideas of China's masses, but rather that it should allow the intelligentsia a greater voice in national affairs. This elitist strain carried over into student tactics in 1986: at one point, when Shanghai workers came out to support their protesting "younger brothers," the students told them just to go home.

The situation in 1989 was somewhat different, since at times the students actively sought (and received) the support of nonintelligentsia groups. Nonetheless, some educated youths continued to see democratic reforms in elitist terms. For example, two foreign observers found Fujian students "horrified at the suggestion that truly popular elections would have to include peasants, who would certainly outvote educated people like themselves" (Erbaugh and Kraus 1990:153). Other reports (e.g., Forster 1990:98) highlight student distrust of the *laobaixing* or untutored masses (a distrust symbolized by groups of students who roped themselves off from bystanders during some marches), and the intelligentsia's lack of concern for the needs of workers and peasants (Chan and Unger 1990). Western critics and Chinese dissidents alike have taken leaders of the movement to task for behaving in nondemocratic and elitist ways, both at the time of the occupation of Tiananmen Square and during the formation of new protest leagues in exile.[3]

The preceding comments do not mean that there was nothing "democratic" about the movement. Clearly, there was a great deal about the protests—the calls for freedom of speech, the demands for more popular input into the way China is governed—that Westerners associate with the term "democracy." We do not wish to imply that Chinese are somehow incapable of understanding or acting upon Western concepts of democracy. Nor do we wish to imply that a Chinese movement must meet a stringent set of contemporary Western standards before it can earn the accolade "Democracy Movement." After all, as Donald Price (1989) has observed, we consider many Western states to have been "democratic" long before they reached the stage of universal suffrage. The point we do wish to stress is simply that, given the various contours of meaning the term *minzhu* had in 1989, labeling the protests a "Democracy Movement" does not take us very far in our effort to make sense of the movement. In some cases, in fact, it obfuscates more than it clarifies.

China's Spring as Political Theater

It would seem that a more productive way to understand the events of April–June, 1989, is to view them as an exercise in political theater. Scholars as diverse as E. P. Thompson (1974, 1978) and Clifford Geertz (1980), working on political systems as dissimilar as eighteenth-century England and nineteenth-century Bali, have demonstrated the value of interpreting politics in theatrical terms, i.e., as symbol-laden performances whose efficacy lies largely in their power to move specific audiences. This approach would seem ideally suited for analysis of the Chinese protests of 1989. As essentially nonviolent demonstrations that posed no direct economic or physical threat to China's rulers, the power of the protests derived almost exclusively from their potency as performances which could symbolically undermine the regime's legitimacy and move members of larger and economically more vital classes to take sympathetic action.

A number of the more insightful analysts of the Chinese protests of 1989 have already highlighted the importance of symbolism and role playing. Frank Pieke (1989, 1990) analyzes the "ritualized" quality of the protest actions and the significance of audience participation in the Chinese marches. Perry Link has compared the petitioning at Tiananmen Square to "morally charged Beijing opera" (cited in Strand 1990:30–31). In a related vein, Dru Gladney (1990) and Lucien Pye (1990) have interpreted the symbolic implications of a variety of student actions and texts, and David Strand (1990) uses theatrical metaphors to capture the mood and explain the impact of student demonstrations in Beijing since 1919. Our goal is to expand on these themes and to place the events of 1989 in a larger historical and theoretical context. In particular, it seems important to examine the relationship between political theater and ritual—a more tightly prescribed form of cultural performance which was so vital to the governance of imperial China.

What, then, was the political theater of 1989? First of all, it was street theater: untitled, improvisational, with constantly changing casts. Though fluid in form, it nevertheless followed what Charles Tilly (1978) calls a historically established "repertoire" of collective action. This means that, even when improvising, protesters worked from familiar "scripts" which gave a common sense of how to behave during a given action, where and when to march, how to express their demands, and so forth. Some of these scripts originated in the distant past, emerging out of traditions of remonstrance and petition stretching back for millennia. More were derived (consciously and unconsciously) from the steady stream of student-led mass movements that have taken place since 1919. Thus, for example, when youths paraded from school to school in 1989, carrying banners emblazoned with the name of their alma maters, and called on students at other institutions to join their fight to *jiuguo* (save the nation), they were following closely in the footsteps of the May 4th Movement's participants and other Republican-era protesters (Strand 1990; Wasserstrom 1990a).

State rituals and official ceremonies supplied other potential scripts (cf. Tilly 1986:116–17). The April 22nd funeral march in memory of Hu Yaobang was a classic example of students usurping a state ritual, improvising upon an official script to make it serve subversive ends. Chinese funerals—especially those of wealthy and/or politically important figures—have always been key moments for public ritual (Pye 1990:333–37). As newspaper accounts of early twentieth-century funeral processions show, these ceremonies were an important opportunity for elite families to display their status, with musicians and hired mourners joining family and friends carefully ordered by age, gender, and social status in a symbolic representation of the proper social order (NCH, November 19, 1902:1076–77; November 24, 1917:467–68). In the PRC, memorial services for important political leaders are a critical political moment, and the composition of funeral committees is carefully scrutinized for clues to changing political alignments (Watson and Rawski 1988). Here is political ritual with all the liminality that Victor Turner's conception requires: transition between two preferably stable political states, and thus highly dangerous (Turner 1969).

The particular danger in the case of political funerals arises from the possibility that unauthorized people will usurp the ritual and rewrite the script into political theater of their own. The most famous previous example of this was, in fact, not quite a funeral, but the Qingming remembrance that followed soon after the death of Zhou Enlai in 1976 (Yan and Gao 1986: 586–640). It produced the first "Tiananmen Incident" in which thousands of Beijing residents used the opportunity to pay their respects to Zhou and, in the process, level a variety of direct and indirect attacks on the Gang of Four. Critical to the nature of such ceremonies is the authorities' inability to prohibit them: they are politically required rituals of respect for revolutionary heroes. But when students usurp the ritual, they can turn it into political theater. Thus the funeral march becomes a demonstration. Though they march behind memorial wreaths to the deceased and carry their official school banners, they also chant slogans and hoist signs with their own political messages.

Marches of this sort inevitably lead to the central square of the city. That square normally faces the seat of government authority, which is also likely to be the venue for an official memorial service. At this point, the demonstration becomes a petition movement. The most dramatic was the petition of 1989 presented by three students kneeling on the steps of the Great Hall of the People. The symbolism of this petition was important, for it demanded an explanation of the background to Hu Yaobang's resignation as General Secretary of the Party in 1987. This demand focused on the fact that the party leaders who were orchestrating the official ceremonies inside the Great Hall were precisely the men who had removed Hu Yaobang from power. Thus the street theater unmasked the hypocrisy of the official ritual, and revealed the students on the streets to be the true heirs of the legacy of Hu Yaobang. In the end, the officially required ritual, once captured by the student actors, becomes the mechanism for attacking the authorities.[4]

Once the public stage has been captured, the street actors are all the more free to write their own script. In Beijing, they proved extraordinarily creative. They successfully upstaged two more state rituals: on the seventieth anniversary of the May 4th Movement, the party's formal commemorations paled before the students' protest marches; and in mid-May, the welcoming rally students held for Gorbachev—complete with signs bearing slogans in Russian and Chinese—stole the thunder from the official ceremonies of the summit. One reason for the success of these protests, and for the relative weakness of the official rituals they mocked, came from their respective settings.

Throughout much of May, students were in full control of Beijing's symbolic center, Tiananmen Square. The government was forced to hold its gatherings in less public and/or less powerful venues—the Great Hall of the People for May 4th, the airport to welcome Gorbachev.

The group hunger strike launched in Beijing in mid-May, which was replicated in several other cities within days, was another stroke of creative genius. Although dissident officials in imperial times occasionally refused food to show their displeasure with a ruler (Watson 1989; Pye 1990:341–42), and at least one Republican-era labor dispute involved a hunger strike (Elizabeth Perry, personal communication), this kind of group fast was not a central element in the Chinese student protest repertoire until the influential one performed in Hunan in 1980 (Yi and Thompson 1989:42–44). Its use in 1989, by students who compared their strike to those of dissidents in other nations (Yi and Thompson:172; *Newsweek,* May 29, 1989:21) showed how internationalized models for dissent had become. This hunger strike proved a potent piece of political theater and earned the protesters enormous public sympathy.

The placement of the Goddess of Democracy in Tiananmen Square— directly between two sacred symbols of the Communist regime, a giant portrait of Mao and the Monument to the People's Heroes—was another powerful piece of theater. Though Western journalists often treated this twenty-eight foot icon as a simple copy of the Statue of Liberty, and the Chinese government insisted that this was so, the goddess was in reality a more complex symbol combining Western and Chinese motifs, some employed reverently, others ironically (Yi and Thompson 1989:72; Han 1990:342–48). Some features of the goddess did resemble the Statue of Liberty—an exact replica of which *was* carried through Shanghai in mid-May (*New York Times Magazine,* June 4, 1989:28), but others called to mind traditional Bodhisattva, and even the socialist-realist sculptures of revolutionary heroes found in Tiananmen Square. It was also, as Dru Gladney (1990) notes, reminiscent of the giant statues of Mao that were carried through the square during some National Day parades of the sixties (*China Reconstructs,* December 1966, 3; *Beijing Review,* October 3, 1969, 7). A potent pastiche of imported and native symbolism, the goddess appeared in the square just as the movement was flagging, bringing new crowds of supporters and onlookers to the area.

Street theater of this sort also is dangerous because it is impossible to control the cast. As noted above, students tried at times to keep the *laobaixing* at arm's length, but this was not always possible, and in many cases organizers anxious to swell the number of protesters encouraged bystanders from all walks of life to join the crowd. Inevitably, this attracted members of the floating population of youths who had been in and out of trouble with the state apparatus. Mistreated by public security men in the past, many bore grudges they were anxious to settle. It appears that these young men were responsible for some of the violence that broke out as early as April 22nd in Xi'an and Changsha, and on June 3rd in Beijing.

Once one recognizes the movement as an instance of political theater, it becomes tempting to rate the performances. One of the best acts was put on by Wuer Kaixi in the May 18th dialogue with Li Peng. The costuming was important: he appeared in his hospital pajamas. So, too, was the timing: he upstaged the Premier by interrupting him at the very start. And props: later in the session, he dramatically pulled out a tube inserted into his nose (for oxygen?) in order to make a point. Especially for the young people in the nationwide television audience, it was an extraordinarily powerful performance.

For older viewers, perhaps the most riveting act was performed on May 20th when the CCTV news announcer Xue Fei read the official martial law announcement. Again, costuming was important: he wore all black, the suit apparently borrowed for the occasion. He read the announcement from beginning to end without lifting his eyes from the page, in a perfect imitation of the tone reserved for funeral eulogies. Xue Fei's performance was witnessed, understood, and remembered by television viewers throughout the country.

In any performance, the audience is critical. In street theater, audience participation always becomes part of the drama, and this was certainly true in Beijing and other cities in 1989 (Niming 1990; Pieke 1989). First, citizens lined the parade route to applaud the student demonstrators. Then, there were banners announcing support, and stands set up to provide food and drink. By the end, the nonstudent crowds had been fully drawn into the act, as the citizens of Beijing came out in force to block the army's entrance to the city after the declaration of martial law.

Television provided a powerful new dimension to the movement's audience appeal. Most obviously, with the world press gathered for the Gorbachev visit, the demonstrators gained a global audience. That audience certainly helped dissuade the regime from an early use of force against its critics, but the domestic television audience was at least as important. Through it, by mid-May, Chinese across the country directly witnessed the scale of the massive demonstrations in Beijing, and that knowledge emboldened young people to launch their own protest marches in cities across China. Furthermore, the Beijing demonstrators were keenly aware of the power of this new medium as they showed through their demand for a live broadcast of their dialogue with the government. As a political mode, theater is only as powerful as the audience that it can move; and this theater certainly inspired and energized hundreds of millions of people in China and across the world.

As ritual and theater, the actions of demonstrators naturally call forth certain responses from the authorities, and the efficacy of official performance is substantially dependent on how well they play these roles. The party leadership's failure to acknowledge in any way the petition of the students kneeling on the steps of the Great Hall was a major violation of ritual, and it significantly increased public anger against official arrogance.[5] This is important because ritually correct responses to earlier student petitions—such as those submitted in 1918 (the year before May 4th) and 1931 (when Japan invaded Manchuria) by youths angered by the Chinese authorities' handling of relations with Japan—had helped to defuse potentially volatile situations (NCH, June 8, 1918, 571–572; *Minguo ribao,* June 1 and 2, 1918; Israel 1966:60–61 and passim).

The refusal to acknowledge the student petition in April was but the first of a series of unskillful official performances. When Li Peng was forced to join the televised dialogue with the student leaders, he was clearly unsuited for the role and very uncomfortable in it—and, predictably, he played it very badly. Later, the visit of Li, Zhao Ziyang and other party leaders to the hospitalized hunger strikers was a ritually required act of compassion, this one performed more adroitly. The loyalist rallies the party organized in the Beijing suburbs during the week before the massacre were remarkable, but far less effective, acts of official theater: participants told Western journalists that officials had instructed them to take part, and televised coverage of the events showed a mixture of bored, unhappy, and embarrassed faces (*San Francisco Chronicle,* June 1, 1989, A21–25). Even the tanks of June 4th were a kind of theater. One does not choose tanks for their efficacy in crowd control—this was a performance designed to show irresistible power. It was a bad act, but the videotapes were skillfully edited and played over and over for the domestic television audience.

For official theater, however, nothing was more important than the ritual *biaotai* that followed the movement's suppression. These public statements of position (and here the only permissible position was one in favor of the regime) began with provincial leaders, regional military commands, and functional ministries of the national government. Rebroadcast on national television and reported in the press, they announced the speed with which the constituent parts of the state apparatus fell in behind the new party leadership. These *biaotai* of party and military elites were followed by similar performances in schools, factories, research institutes, and administrative bodies across the nation as virtually every urban citizen was required to account for his or her actions since April and publicly announce solidarity with the new hard-line policies. *Biaotai* is a special form of performance (*biaoyan*), the participants were clearly *acting*—most were not sincere—and everyone knew it. They recited memorized scripts, with key phrases lifted from articles and editorials in *People's Daily.* Because few believed the words they were uttering, most of these *biaotai* were poorly performed and bad theater. But the regime's unremittent insistence on these *biaotai* performances testifies to the importance of such theater in the Chinese political system.

It should be noted that politically sensitive members of the Chinese public recognize the practices described above as a form of theater. In their view, politics is a performance; and public political acts are often interpreted in that way. Thus, for example, a typical reaction to Li Peng's speech announcing martial law was to evaluate it as a performance, and the reviews were uniformly bad: words were mispronounced, the tone was too shrill, etc. As one Beijing intellectual put it: "He should have been wearing a patch of white above his nose"—the standard makeup of the buffoon in Beijing opera. Similarly, protesters at times represented Li as the clown or villain in propaganda skits based on traditional theatrical forms. One Beijing street performance (described for us by Henry Rosemont, Jr.) combined comic cross talk with operatic motifs to portray the attempts of a courtesan (representing Li Peng) to flatter, appease, and thereby gain the protection of an old man (representing Deng Xiaoping).

Metaphors from the world of the theater are so much a part of the language of politics in modern China (as elsewhere) that protesters and observers continually adopted theatrical turns of speech. When protesters attacked Li Peng and Deng Xiaoping, their slogans included "Li Peng *xiatai!*" (Li Peng, get off the stage) and "Xiaoping, Xiaoping, *kuaixie Xiatai!*" (Deng Xiaoping, Deng Xiaoping, hurry and get off the stage; Wu 1989:262, 267). Whenever previously little-known actors assume a major political role, there is discussion of who their *houtai* (backstage managers) might be. And after the Tiananmen incident, there was significant debate as to whether or not it should be termed a "tragedy."[6] But the sense in which the Chinese people see all this as performance was most powerfully suggested by a wise old peasant from northern Shaanxi who, when asked the difference between Mao Zedong and Deng Xiaoping, simply laughed and said, "They were just singing opposing operas (*chang duitai xi*)!" ...

Interpreting the Political Theater

As performance, the truth-value of the words and actions in this political theater is not terribly important. But that does not imply that this theater is meaningless—only that we have to pay more attention to its symbolism than to the literal meaning of its utterances. Let us consider the symbolism of 1989. The first function of political theater is quite simply to be heard, to gain attention. Initially, the audience is a dual one: the general population (both urban residents who directly witness the demonstration and those who can be reached through the media) and the authorities. But the authorities are the real audience; the value of the people is largely instrumental. The more support the demonstrators can gain from the citizenry—the larger the applauding crowds lining the demonstration route, the more concrete contributions of food and drink, the more symbolic aid in the form of banners or citizens' support groups, the greater the monetary contributions from citizens and small business—the more leverage the demonstrators will gain with the authorities.

That the authorities are the real audience is demonstrated by the petition format. But a petition also acknowledges the fundamental legitimacy of the government to which one appeals. Later, the petition is replaced by the appeal for dialogue—also a demand to be heard. But underlying this demand—even more clearly in dialogue than in petition—is a claim to entrance into the polity (cf. Tilly 1978). Groups previously excluded from the political process seek through demonstration, petition, and dialogue to be taken seriously by the authorities as participants in the political decision-making process. Even some of the violence of the demonstrations, the rock-throwing and arson, can be interpreted as efforts to gain attention, to be heard—efforts by those less skillful with and less trusting of words than intellectuals and university students.

The *public* nature of political theater is its second most important characteristic. Open to all, street theater invites all citizens to join. Once Tiananmen Square was occupied, the students often debated strategy and made decisions in public, there for all to see. They demanded a live broadcast of their dialogue with government leaders. Symbolically, such theater stands in direct contrast to the secrecy of the party-state. Significantly, the model for such demonstrations in China, the May 4th demonstration of 1919, protested against the secret diplomacy that had preceded the Versailles conference. Street theater invariably symbolizes a call to open up the political process, and the very secrecy (and lack of accountability) of the party-state naturally calls forth this sort of dialectical opposite.

Thirdly, student strikes and, even more dramatically, the hunger strike, present images of selflessness—a key value in contemporary China, with models from Norman Bethune to Lei Feng. These acts were extraordinarily effective. The most common praise of the student movement was that their motives were entirely patriotic—for love of country (*aiguo*). They sought nothing for themselves—unlike workers who might strike for higher pay. These students asked nothing, accepted not even food, and wished only the good of the nation. Their acts of self-denial stood in obvious contrast to the self-serving and corrupt leadership they attacked. No privilege of the party leadership was more visible than the enormous banquets they consumed at public expense. Now here were students refusing to eat anything at all.

Finally, the last testaments that the students wrote out, plus the hunger strike and related gestures, located the students symbolically within a rich tradition of political martyrs. These activities, as Dru Gladney (1990) has noted, linked the students to Qu Yuan, the loyal minister of the third century B.C. who showed his willingness to "die for the affairs of the nation" by committing suicide after his ruler refused to heed his advice. Such actions also recalled earlier generations of student martyrs, from Chen Dong (a Song Dynasty protester executed for his criticisms of government corruption, who served as a model for some May 4th protesters [Lee 1985:190–92; Zhongguo shehui kexueyuan 1979, 1:473]), to Yao Hongye and Chen Tianhua (two frustrated Hunanese activists who committed suicide in 1906), and the hundreds of youthful demonstrators killed by foreign and native authorities during the Republican era. When students at Tiananmen Square swore collective oaths to sacrifice their lives—the last, and most prophetic, of which was taken on June 3rd (Yi and Thompson 1989:266)—they were reenacting a scene from the May 4th Movement (*Shen Bao*, 27 May 1919, 10). Similarly, when Chai Ling bit her finger and wrote out a protest slogan with her own blood, she stepped into a role that student protesters of 1915 and 1919 had played (Shanghai Municipal Police Files, reel 65, I.D. 6691). With all this theater, the students appealed to a tradition of principled dissent and revolutionary action that the party itself had legitimized and mythologized in the attempt to claim it as its own.

If we are to understand the enormous appeal of the student demonstrations in Beijing and across China, we must begin by appreciating these symbolic meanings of their protest. The slogans—attacking the corruption of official profiteers (*guandao*), calling for a freer press, mocking China's highest leaders, advocating a never-defined "freedom" and "democracy"—were certainly important. But they gained their power because the very repertoire of the movement symbolized a demand for a voice in government, for a more open political process, and for an end to leadership by a self-serving elite.

A Comparative Perspective

The 1989 demonstrations in China were clearly part of a larger, worldwide crisis of state-socialist systems. In Eastern Europe, Communist Parties have been toppled from power, one after the other. In the Soviet Union, the Party is in the process of renouncing its monopoly on power, and various ethnic groups—led by Lithuania, but including all the Baltic states and the peoples of the Caucasus region—have been moving steadily toward some form of greater autonomy from Moscow. Increasingly, China (along with North Korea, Vietnam, and Cuba) is looking like the last refuge of socialism. As a current Chinese joke has it—playing on the official cant that "Only socialism can save China"—now "Only China can save socialism."

In each of the European transitions, street demonstrations played a critical role. This was, of course, most obvious in the dramatic events of East Germany and Czechoslovakia. There, utterly peaceful political transformations—a "velvet revolution," to use the Czech phrase—were brought about by unarmed civilians protesting in the streets. Since exactly the same sort of political theater brought forth troops and tanks and unprecedented bloodshed in China, it is necessary to try to explain the contrasting result.

Clearly, part of the answer lies in factors quite beyond the scope of this essay. The Communist Party of China (like the parties of Vietnam, Cuba, and, to a lesser degree, Korea) made its own revolution. Each of these countries thus differs from the state-socialist regimes of Eastern Europe, which were, in varying degrees, all brought into being and propped up by the Soviets' Red Army. Consequently, when Gorbachev made it clear that the Brezhnev Doctrine was dead and the Soviet Union would no longer come to the rescue of unpopular East European regimes, those regimes fell very quickly.

In addition, China and the remaining state-socialist regimes are all poor Third World countries. They have large, impoverished, and still poorly educated rural populations. At least in China, there is unquestionably substantial peasant discontent over a variety of issues—the payment for grain requisitions in IOUs and scrip instead of money, and the failure to deliver promised supplies of chemical fertilizer. But, in general, peasants displayed little sympathy for the demands of the student demonstrators. Only the attack on corruption struck a responsive chord. When the crackdown came, rural residents tended to believe the government contention that the peasant soldiers of the People's Liberation Army would not fire on unarmed civilians unless there was a genuine threat to law and order. In short, China's huge peasant population remained largely preoccupied with its own material interests, and it viewed those interests as dependent on continued political stability. Consequently, China's peasantry provided a reservoir of support for the hard-liners in Beijing that was missing in any East European regime (Zweig 1989).

More germane to our discussion, however, is the role played by the institutions of civil society in Eastern Europe (Tismaneanu 1990). These long-neglected institutions proved to have sufficient life to structure the opposition movement and sustain it to victory. The most obvious example is the Catholic Church in Poland (Machcewicz 1989). As a gathering place and refuge for dissidents in the Solidarity movement, the Catholic opposition (with a Polish Pope) was fundamental to the breakthrough in Poland—which was, after all, the first domino to fall. Hungary was the next country to make serious moves in the direction of pluralism, and here the old democratic parties played a crucial role. In Czechoslovakia, the dissident groups among the intellectuals were clearly better organized than anyone previously believed. In East Germany, the Evangelical (Lutheran) Church helped to shelter dissident intellectuals and a small independent peace movement. Bulgaria witnessed a nascent environmental movement, which played a critical role. In Lithuania, there was again the Catholic Church, plus the role of national movements and linguistic solidarity.

Virtually all of the institutions of civil society in Europe are imbued, to one degree or another, with aspects of democratic culture. We sometimes forget, as we focus on the hierarchic structures and stately rituals of the Catholic Church, that the Pope is elected and councils of bishops and other more local institutions have often operated on democratic principles. On a more mundane level, artisan guilds would, on their feast days, constitute themselves as a "republic" to manage their affairs and discipline their members (Darnton 1985:85–89). When, therefore, civil society has been allowed to prosper, it has brought with it, in the West, a discourse and a culture imbued with electoral forms and at least a minimal tolerance of dissent.

In Eastern Europe, such institutions of civil society played a critical role of translating the symbolic meaning of street theater into systematic programs for political change. When the party-states of Eastern Europe were forced to sit down to negotiate with the street protesters, there were people with organizational experience and programmatic ideas who could manage the delicate transition to democracy. The glamour-seeking media has hardly focused on this process, sometimes leaving the impression that dramatic demonstrations led to government collapse and a natural evolution to electoral forms. But that is hardly a plausible scenario, and when the full story is told we will surely find a critical role of the institutions of civil society in presiding over that perilous political process.

It is not enough, however, to focus on institutions alone. The small and vulnerable groups of dissident intellectuals and workers in Eastern Europe could certainly not match the organizational might of the party-state in these countries. But if there is one thing that the rapid collapse of communist parties in Eastern Europe and Russia has taught us, it is that social scientists have misled us into accepting an excessively reified notion of what "institutions" are. We have been led to think of the party-state almost as a physical structure, of unshakable size and weight and power. Now we are in a position to focus on the fact that such "structures" are, in fact, made up of *people* who are bound together by certain rules and habits, interests and aspirations, rituals and shared identities. The people who make up these institutions are not mindless parts of a party "machine," acting always and unfailingly in the interest of that machine. (Gorbachev and his supporters in the Soviet Union obviously cannot be understood if we identify them only as leaders and servants of the Communist Party machine.)

Once we escape an excessively institutional approach to politics in state-socialist systems, we are in a better position to appreciate the impact of the culture of civil society, the *habitus* (Bourdieu 1977:72–87) that reemerged from the collective memory to give life to the East European movements of dissent. One participant/observer of the Polish experience has noted "the explosion of national memory ... the massive turnout for anniversary celebrations" that followed the first Solidarity struggles of 1980–81 (Machcewicz 1989:19). In small rituals and mass celebrations, the *habitus* of democratic governance was revived from a culture rich in civic rituals and the theater of popular rule.

As we noted above, China's imperial state allowed minimal development of civil society. The late Qing and the Republican era witnessed a brief flowering of civil society, but its roots were not deep. In addition, as David Strand has shown (1989:98–120; 1990), this new civil society found it difficult to escape the old politics of personal networks, and the leaders of the new civic institutions tended to look for patrons within the state system. The *habitus* of autonomous association was still weakly developed. In addition, civil society in China never provided an adequate foundation for pluralist politics. To a large degree, it revealed this weakness in its rhetoric. The Chinese press (both a component and a mouthpiece of China's nascent civil society) tended to speak of the "people" as an undifferentiated whole—usually standing against an opposing symbolic category, "officials," i.e., the state (Rankin 1986:166). Thus, when Chinese began to speak of "rule by the people" (*minzhu*), the "people" were a unified mass. The separate "republics" of civil society were not sufficiently legitimized to bring, with the idea of democracy, the pluralism bred in the corporate roots of European civil society.

Under the PRC, the budding sprouts of republican civil society were cut off altogether. The rhetoric of the undifferentiated people was usurped by the state to establish a "people's democratic dictatorship." Dissidents were safely excluded as "enemies of the people." Pluralism existed neither in the organization of society nor in the rhetoric of politics. Both the party-state and its opponents appealed to the virtue of "unity." But only the party existed as a functioning political organization. The tragic result of this combination of circumstances is that the Chinese Communist Party can justly claim that there is no political force outside the party capable of ruling China. Many of the hunger-strikers conceded this point in May 1989, and they probably reflected the consensus of most protesters. In the wake of June 4th, the party's claim to legitimacy rests on little more than this fact: there is no alternative to the CCP. The *reason* there is no alternative is simple enough: the party will not permit one to exist. To preserve their fragile legitimacy, the party leaders must rigorously suppress any hint of pluralism: no autonomous student or workers' unions, no publications which might provide an alternative voice, no civil society. Then they can present the Chinese people with a bleak choice: either continued Communist rule or chaos.

Without a civil society, only street theater remains as a mode of political expression. No Chinese regime has ever been able to suppress it altogether. The smooth functioning of Chinese politics requires public rituals to celebrate the ideals of the revolution and the party-state which emerged from it. In time, students will again find an opportunity to usurp those rituals to perform their own political theater. Then the question will again arise: can they (and the state) find a mechanism to link this theater to the complex task of governing 1.1 billion Chinese?

Notes

1. Although the official rhetoric had some effect in alienating support for the students in 1986, such Cultural Revolution imagery was much less effective in 1989, in part because the students confronted the official line head on. They demanded that the leadership apologize for labeling the movement a form of *dongluan* (turmoil)—a term

that has become a code word for the Cultural Revolution (CQ Chronicle 1989:677; Yi and Thompson 1989:28). For a contrast between Red Guard uses of Mao pictures and those of 1989 students, see Orleans 1989. The Mao honored in 1989 was the selfless hero of the pre-1949 years and the early days of the PRC, not the demigod of the Cultural Revolution. As one worker from Hubei put it: "At least Mao was honest . . . He even sent his son to the Korean War. Nowadays, the leaders send their sons to America" (*San Francisco Chronicle,* May 19, 1989:A24).

2. Although his *Chinese Democracy* is replete with useful examples of the sort just cited, Nathan seems blind to this issue, and concludes with a quite unsupported discussion of "the West's—and the Chinese democrats'—identification of democracy with pluralism" (1985:227). The stress that Chinese dissidents continued to place on a noncompetitive unity in 1989 is clear from one of the students' earliest demands: that the Chinese leadership affirm the virtues of "democracy, freedom, magnanimity and *harmony*" (CQ Chronicle 1989:668 [emphasis ours]).

3. Note this May 1989 exchange between a youth, barred from boarding a bus where Wuer Kaixi was resting, and a student security guard. "'What kind of democracy is this?' [the youth] fumed. 'What kind of freedom? You are just like the country's leaders.' Responded the guard: 'You are right. But you are harming our unity. Don't say such things'" (*Newsweek,* May 29, 1989, 21; cf. Lubman 1989). Criticisms of the new exile leagues appear in Chan and Kwong 1990; and Chan and Unger 1990. Rosemont (1990) notes the influence that the "new authoritarianism" has had in Chinese dissident circles.

4. This pattern is hardly unique to China. Compare this account of a demonstration by tens of thousands of youths on November 17, 1989, in Prague. It was one of the key events leading to the fall of the Communist government in Czechoslovakia. "The memorial for Jan Opletal, the student killed by the Nazis, was sponsored by the official student organization but was transformed into a demonstration for freedom, political change and the dismissal of the Communist Party leader, Milos Jakes" (*New York Times* [national edition] November 18, 1989). Needless to say, Czechoslovakia—where the theaters were transformed into headquarters of the democratic opposition, and a playwright, Vaclav Havel, was elected President—is an excellent place to look for examples of political theater.

5. Among the students, there was significant criticism of the kneeling petitioners' servile posture. But it appears that by adopting this traditional ritual, the petitioners gained substantial sympathy from the general populace. (See Lianhebao 1989:60–61.)

6. Michel Oksenberg provoked our thinking on this point. It became clear during Nixon's November 1989 visit to China that Chinese and Western connotations of the term "tragedy" were quite different. Western notions, derived from Greek drama, link "tragedy" to unalterable fate and to some "tragic flaw" in the victim of the tragedy. Thus, from a Western perspective, calling the events of June 3–4 a "tragedy" tends to objectify them, and even to remove responsibility for the bloodshed from the hands of the Chinese leadership. In this sense, "tragedy" was an attempt to soften the implications of the term "massacre"; and it is perhaps significant that years earlier, Nixon had had no difficulty in terming the student deaths at Kent State a "tragedy" (Sale 1973:638). But Chinese "tragedy" is closer to our sense of "melodrama" and implies a clear villain—which the Chinese leadership correctly understood to be themselves.

References

Agnew, Jean-Christophe. 1986. *Worlds Apart: The Market and the Theater in Anglo-American Thought, 1550–1750.* Cambridge: Cambridge University Press.

Ahern, Emily Martin. 1981. *Chinese Ritual and Politics.* Cambridge: Cambridge University Press.

Austin, J. L. 1979. "Performative Utterances." In *Philosophical Papers,* 3rd edition. London: Oxford University Press.

Bergeron, David M. 1971. *English Civic Pageantry, 1558–1642.* Columbia: University of South Carolina Press.

Bodde, Derk, and Clarence Morris. 1973. *Law in Imperial China.* Philadelphia: University of Pennsylvania Press.

Bourdieu, Pierre. 1977. *Outline of a Theory of Practice.* Trans. Richard Nice. Cambridge: Cambridge University Press.

Brady, Thomas A., Jr. 1989. "Rites of Autonomy, Rites of Dependence: South German Civic Culture in the Age of Renaissance and Reformation." In Steven Ozment, ed., *Religion and Culture in the Renaissance and Reformation.* Kirksville, Mo.: Sixteenth-Century Journal Publishers.

Bryant, Lawrence M. 1986. *The King and the City in the Parisian Royal Entry Ceremony: Politics, Ritual, and Art in the Renaissance.* Genève: Librairie Droz S.A.

Burdick, James. 1974. *Theater.* New York: Newsweek Books.

Cavendish, Patrick. 1969. "The 'New China' of the Kuomintang." In Jack Gray, ed., *Modern China's Search for a Political Form.* London: Oxford University Press.

Cell, Charles P. 1977. *Revolution at Work: Mobilization Campaigns in China.* New York: Academic Press.

Chan, Anita, and Jonathan Unger. 1990. "China After Tiananmen: It's a Whole New Class Struggle." *The Nation,* January 22, 1990, 79–81.

Chan Wing-tsit. 1963. *A Sourcebook of Chinese Philosophy.* Princeton: Princeton University Press.

Chan, Yuen Ying, and Peter Kwong. 1990. "Trashing the Hopes of Tiananmen." *The Nation,* April 23, 1990, 545, 560–64.

Chang, Hao. 1971. *Liang Ch'i-ch'ao and the Intellectual Transition in China, 1890–1907.* Cambridge, Mass.: Harvard University Press.

Chao Hsueh-hai. 1918. "Tsing Hua New Buildings" *Tsing Hua Journal* 3.7 (June).

Cody, Jeffrey. 1990. "Architectural Fusion in the Design of Fudan University and 'Lilong' Housing." Paper presented at the annual meeting of the Association for Asian Studies, Chicago, April 7.

CO Chronicle. 1989. "Quarterly Chronicle and Documentation." *China Quarterly* 119.

Darnton, Robert. 1985. *The Great Cat Massacre and Other Episodes in French Cultural History.* New York: Vintage.

Davis, Natalie. 1975. *Society and Culture in Early Modern France.* Stanford: Stanford University Press.

Davis, Susan G. 1975. *Parades and Power: Street Theatre in Nineteenth-Century Philadelphia.* Philadelphia: Temple University Press.

Dittmer, Lowell. 1990. "China in 1989: The Crisis of Incomplete Reform." *Asian Survey* 30.1 (January): 25–41.

Du Halde, Jean Baptiste. 1736. *The General History of China.* Trans. Richard Brooks. London: J. Watts.

Durkheim, Emile. 1915. *The Elementary Forms of the Religious Life.* Trans. J. W. Swain. London: Allen and Unwin.

Eastman, Lloyd. 1974. *The Abortive Revolution.* Cambridge, Mass.: Harvard University Press.

Elman, Benjamin. 1984. *From Philosophy to Philology: Intellectual and Social Aspects of Change in Late Imperial China.* Cambridge, Mass.: Harvard University Press.

Erbaugh, Mary S. and Richard C. Kraus. 1990. "The 1989 Democracy Movement in Fujian and Its Consequences." *Australian Journal of Chinese Affairs* 23 (January): 145–160.

Esherick, Joseph W. 1977. *Reform and Revolution in China: The 1911 Revolution in Hunan and Hubei.* Berkeley: University of California Press.

———. 1987. *The Origins of the Boxer Uprising.* Berkeley: University of California Press.

———. 1990. "Xi'an Spring." *Australian Journal of Chinese Affairs* 24.

Feigon, Lee. 1990. *China Rising: The Meaning of Tiananmen.* Chicago: Ivan Dee.

Fingarette, Herbert. 1972. *Confucius—the Secular as Sacred.* New York: Harper Torchbooks.

Forster, Keith. 1990. "Impressions of the Popular Protest in Hangzhou, April/June 1989." *Australian Journal of Chinese Affairs* 23:97–120.

Fox, Josephine. 1990. "The Movement for Democracy and Its Consequences in Tianjin." *Australian Journal of Chinese Affairs* 23:133–144.

Fung You-lan. 1952. *A History of Chinese Philosophy.* Trans. Derk Bodde. Princeton: Princeton University Press.

Geertz, Clifford. 1973. *The Interpretation of Cultures.* New York: Basic Books.

———. 1980a. *Negara: The Theatre State in Nineteenth-Century Bali.* Princeton: Princeton University Press.

———. 1980b. "Blurred Genres: The Refiguration of Social Thought." *American Scholar* (Spring).

———. 1985. "Centers, Kings, and Charisma: Reflections on the Symbolics of Power." In Wilentz 1985.

Gladney, Dru. 1990. "Bodily Positions and Social Dispositions: Sexuality, Nationality and Tiananmen." Paper presented at the Institute for Advanced Study, Princeton, April 26, cited with the author's permission.

Gong, Gerrit W. 1990. "Tiananmen: Causes and Consequences." *Washington Quarterly* 13.1 (Winter): 79–95.

Gugong Bowuguan Yuan [Palace Museum], ed. 1983. *Zijincheng dihou shenghuo* [Lives of the Emperors and Empresses in the Forbidden City]. Beijing: China Travel and Tourism Press.

Guomin geming huashi. [An illustrated history of the national revolution]. 1965. Taibei.

Han Minzhu, ed. 1990. *Cries for Democracy: Writing and Speeches from the 1989 Chinese Democracy Movement.* Princeton: Princeton University Press.

Hayhoe, Ruth. 1983. "Towards the Forging of a Chinese University Ethos: Zhendan and Fudan, 1903–1919." *China Quarterly* 94:323–341.

Henriot, Christian. 1983. "Le Gouvernement Municipal de Shanghai, 1927–1937." Unpublished doctoral dissertation. Sorbonne, Paris.

Hsiao Kung-chu'üan. 1967. *Rural China: Imperial Control in the Late 19th Century.* Seattle: University of Washington Press.

Hucker, Charles. 1961. *The Traditional Chinese State in Ming Times.* Tucson: University of Arizona Press.

Hunt, Lynn. 1984. *Politics, Culture, and Class in the French Revolution.* Berkeley: University of California Press.

Israel, John. 1966. *Student Nationalism in China, 1927–1937.* Stanford: Stanford University Press.

Jarausch, Konrad. 1982. *Students, Society, and Politics in Imperial Germany.* Princeton: Princeton University Press.

Kirby, E. T. 1976. "The Shamanistic Origins of Popular Entertainments." In Schechner and Schuman 1976: 139–49.

Kraus, Richard. 1989. "The Lament of Astrophysicist Fang Lizhi." In Arif Dirlik and Maurice Meisner, eds., *Marxism and the Chinese Experience.* Armonk, N.Y.: M. E. Sharpe.

Lianhebao Editorial Department. 1989. *Tiananmen yijiubajiu* [Tiananmen 1989]. Taibei: Lianjing chuban shiye gongsi.

Lee, Thomas. 1985. *Government Education and Examinations in Sung China.* New York: St. Martin's Press.

Liu, Kwang-ching. 1990. *Orthodoxy in Late Imperial China.* Berkeley: University of California Press.

Lubman, Sarah. 1990. "The Myth of Tiananmen Square: The Students Talked Democracy but They Didn't Practice It." *Washington Post,* July 30, 1989.

Lukes, Stephen. 1975. "Political Ritual and Social Integration." *Sociology* 9.2:289–308.

Machcewicz, Pawel. 1989. "The Solidarity Revolution." *Polish Perspectives* 32.4:14–25.

Mackerras, Colin. 1975. *The Chinese Theatre in Modern Times.* Amherst: University of Massachusetts Press.

Mair, Victor. 1985. "Language and Ideology in the Written Popularizations of the Sacred Edicts." In David Johnson et al., eds., *Popular Culture in Late Imperial China.* Berkeley: University of California Press.

Mao Zedong. 1940. "Xin minzhu zhuyi lun" [On New Democracy]. In *Mao Zedong xuanji* [Collected Works of Mao Zedong]. Beijing: People's Publishing House, 1952. Vol. 2.

Martin, William. 1900. *A Cycle of Cathay.* New York: F. H. Revell.

Mirsky, Jonathan. 1990. "The Empire Strikes Back." *New York Review of Books,* February 1.

Morrison, Donald, ed. 1989. *Massacre in Beijing: China's Struggle for Democracy.* New York: Warner Books.

Muir, Edward. 1981. *Civic Ritual in Renaissance Venice.* Princeton: Princeton University Press.

Naquin, Susan. 1988. "Funerals in North China." In Watson and Rawski 1988.

Naquin, Susan, and Evelyn Rawski. 1987. *Chinese Society in the Eighteenth Century.* New Haven: Yale University Press.

Nathan, Andrew J. 1976. *Peking Politics, 1918–1923: Factionalism and the Failure of Constitutionalism.* Berkeley: University of California Press.

———. 1985. *Chinese Democracy.* New York: Knopf.

———. 1990. *China's Crisis: Dilemmas of Reform and Prospects for Democracy.* New York: Columbia University Press.

NCH. *North China Herald.* Shanghai.

Niming, Frank [pseudonym]. 1990. "Learning How to Protest." In Saich 1990: 82–104.

Orleans, Leo. 1989. "Dissidents Lack Strong New Leader." *Washington Post,* May 24, 1989.

Ozouf, Mona. 1988. *Festivals and the French Revolution.* Trans. Alan Sheridan. Cambridge, Mass.: Harvard University Press.

Perry, Elizabeth. 1985. "Tax Revolt in Late Qing China." *Late Imperial China* 6.1 (June): 83–112.

Pieke, Frank. 1989. "Observations during the People's Movement in Beijing, Spring 1989." Paper presented at the International Institute of Social History, Amsterdam, July 7, cited with author's permission.

———. 1990. "A Ritualized Rebellion: Beijing, Spring 1989." Unpublished paper cited with author's permission.

Price, Donald. 1989. Comments at a roundtable at the annual meeting of the American Historical Association, San Francisco.

Pye, Lucien W. 1990. "Tiananmen and Chinese Political Culture: The Escalation of Confrontation from Moralizing to Revenge." *Asian Survey* 30.4 (April): 331–47.

Rankin, Mary B. 1986. *Elite Activism and Political Transformation in China: Zhejiang Province, 1865–1911.* Stanford: Stanford University Press.

Rhoads, Edward J. M. 1975. *China's Republican Revolution: The Case of Kwangtung, 1895–1913.* Cambridge, Mass.: Harvard University Press.

Rogers, Nicholas. 1978. "Popular Protest in Early Hanoverian London." *Past and Present* 79: 70–100.

Rosemont, Henry, Jr. 1990. "China: The Mourning After." *Z Magazine,* March, 85–96.

Saich, Tony, ed. 1990. *The Chinese People's Movement: Perspectives on Spring 1989.* Armonk, New York: M. E. Sharpe.

Saich, Tony, and Nancy Hearst. 1990. "Bibliographic Note." In Saich 1990: 189–96.

Sale, Kirkpatrick. 1973. *SDS.* New York: Random House.

Schechner, Richard. "From Ritual to Theater and Back." In Schechner and Schuman 1976: 196–222.

Schechner, Richard, and Mady Schuman, eds. 1976. *Ritual, Play, and Performance.* New York: Seabury Press.

Schwarcz, Vera. 1986. *The Chinese Enlightenment.* Berkeley: University of California Press.

Schwartz, Benjamin. 1985. *The World of Thought in Ancient China.* Cambridge, Mass.: Harvard University Press.

Spence, Jonathan D. 1966. *Ts'ao Yin and the K'ang-hsi Emperor, Bondservant and Master.* New Haven: Yale University Press.

————. 1990. *The Search for Modern China.* New York: Norton.

Steele, John, trans. 1917. *The I-li.* London.

Strand, David. 1989. *Rickshaw Beijing.* Berkeley: University of California Press.

————. 1990. " 'Civil Society' and 'Public Sphere' in Modern China: A Perspective on Popular Movements in Beijing, 1919–1989." *Duke Working Papers in Asian/Pacific Studies.*

Strong, Roy. 1984. *Art and Power: Renaissance Festivals, 1450–1650.* Berkeley: University of California Press.

Sun Zhongshan xiansheng hauce [Dr. Sun Yat-sen: A Photo Album]. 1986. Beijing and Hong Kong.

Teng Ssu-yu and John K. Fairbank, eds. 1979. *China's Response to the West; A Documentary Survey, 1839–1923.* Cambridge, Mass.: Harvard University Press.

Thompson, E. P. 1974. "Patrician Society, Plebian Culture." *Journal of Social History* 7.4:382–405.

————. 1978. "Eighteenth-Century English Society: Class Struggle Without Class?" *Social History* 3.2:71–133.

Tilly, Charles. 1978. *From Mobilization to Revolution.* Reading, Mass.: Addison-Wesley.

————. 1986. *The Contentious French.* Cambridge, Mass.: Harvard University Press.

Tismaneanu, Vladimir. 1990. "Eastern Europe: The Story the Media Missed." *The Bulletin of the Atomic Scientists* 46.2 (March): 17–21.

Turner, Victor. 1969. *The Ritual Process: Structure and Anti-Structure.* Ithaca: Cornell University Press.

————. 1976. "Social Dramas and Ritual Metaphors." In Schechner and Schuman 1976: 97–122.

————. 1982. *From Ritual to Theatre.* New York: Performing Arts Journal Press.

Turnley, Peter, and David Turnley. 1989. *Beijing Spring.* New York: Stewart, Tabori and Chang.

Waley, Arthur, trans. n.d. *The Analects of Confucius.* New York: Vintage.

Wang Ke-wen. 1985. "The Kuomintang in Transition: Ideology and Factionalism in the 'National Revolution,' 1924–1932." Unpublished doctoral dissertation. Stanford University.

Wasserstrom, Jeffrey. 1989. "Taking It to the Streets: Shanghai Students and Political Protest, 1919–1949." Unpublished doctoral dissertation, University of California, Berkeley.

————. 1990a. "Student Protest and the Chinese Tradition." In Saich 1990.

————. 1990b. "Revolutionary Anniversaries in Guomindang and Communist China." Paper presented at the annual meeting of Asian Studies on the Pacific Coast, Stanford, California.

————. 1991. *Student Protests in Twentieth Century China: The View From Shanghai.* Stanford: Stanford University Press.

Watson, James. 1989. "The Renegotiation of Chinese Cultural Identity in the Post-Mao Era: An Anthropological Perspective." Paper presented at the

Four Anniversaries China Conference, Annapolis, Maryland, September. Cited with author's permission.

Watson, James, and Evelyn Rawski, eds. 1988. *Death Ritual in Late Imperial and Modern China.* Berkeley: University of California Press.

Wilentz, Sean, ed. 1985. *The Rites of Power.* Philadelphia: University of Pennsylvania Press.

Woodside, Alexander. 1989. "Emperors and the Chinese Political System." Paper presented at the Four Anniversaries China Conference, Annapolis, Maryland, September 10–15.

Wu Mouren et al., eds. 1989. *Bajiu Zhongguo minyun jishi* [English title: "Daily Reports on the Movement for Democracy in China"]. New York: privately published.

Yan Jiaqi and Gao Gao. 1986. *"Wenhua dageming" shinianshi* [A ten-year history of the "Cultural Revolution"]. Tianjin: Tianjin renmin chubanshe.

Yi Mu and Mark V. Thompson. 1989. *Crisis at Tiananmen: Reform and Reality in Modern China.* San Francisco: China Books.

Young, Ernest P. 1977. *The Presidency of Yuan Shih-k'ai: Liberalism and Dictatorship in Early Republican China.* Ann Arbor: University of Michigan Press.

Zhaoqiang, Gejing and Siyuan. 1989. *Xueran de fengcai* [Bloody Scenes]. Hong Kong: Haiyan.

Zhongguo Shehui Kexueyuan. 1979. *Wusi aiguo yundong* [The patriotic May 4th Movement]. Beijing.

Zhou Yuehua, ed. 1985. *Anecdotes of Old Shanghai.* Shanghai: Shanghai Cultural Publishing House.

Zito, Angela. "Grand Sacrifice as Text-Performance: Writing and Ritual in Eighteenth-Century China." Unpublished doctoral dissertation, University of Chicago.

Zweig, David. 1989. "Peasants and Politics." *World Policy Journal* (Fall): 633–45.

Germany and Japan: Legacies of World War

10

War Stories*
The Search for a Usable Past in the Federal Republic of Germany

Robert G. Moeller

In 1995, a half-century after the end of World War II, battles over its meaning still raged. In the United States, veterans' groups and the U.S. Senate roundly condemned the National Air and Space Museum's plan to use an exhibition on the *Enola Gay* mission as an occasion to discuss the broader implications of the bombing of Hiroshima and Nagasaki, triggering an extended public dispute over the political uses of history and climaxing with the decision to cancel the originally planned exhibition.[1] In Japan, the fiftieth anniversary of defeat focused new attention on the question of Japanese war responsibility, war crimes, and the compensation of victims; it also allowed victims of atomic bombs to offer a different perspective on the war's end.[2] And in Europe from London to Moscow, from the beaches of Normandy to the gates of Auschwitz, public ceremonies allowed participants to relive old memories and retell a broad range of different stories of the spring of 1945. Heads of state and historians discussed endlessly how best to commemorate May 8, and the debates made extraordinarily explicit the fact that history, public memory, politics, and national identity are intertwined.

Public controversy over the meaning of May 1945 in Germany was thus not exceptional, but it is not surprising that in the nation whose history

From *American Historical Review* 101, no. 4 (October 1996): 1008–1048. Reprinted with the permission of the American Historical Association.

*Research for this article was supported by grants from the National Endowment for the Humanities, the Woodrow Wilson International Center for Scholars, the Global Peace and Conflict Studies program of the University of California, Irvine, and the Center for German and European Studies at the University of California, Berkeley. My thanks go also to Lily Gardner Feldman, Renate Bridenthal, Josef Mooser, Robert Weinberg, Temma Kaplan, Michael Hughes, David Crew, Elizabeth Heineman, Volker Berghahn, James Diehl, Omer Bartov, Jane Caplan, Molly Nolan, Anne Walthall, Alice Fahs, and Lynn Mally, who commented on various incarnations of this article and helped me tremendously to clarify my ideas.

included National Socialism, reflecting on the war's end involved particularly wrenching soul-searching. The politics of commemoration in Germany also vividly revealed that disputes over the meaning of World War II necessarily reflected how memories of the war had taken shape since 1945; old soldiers were not all dead and neither were the war stories that had become part of public memory in the first postwar decade.

A high point in the extended public debate over how best to remember the destruction of the Third Reich came on April 7, 1995; in an advertisement in one of Germany's most important newspapers, the *Frankfurter Allgemeine Zeitung,* some three hundred prominent German citizens, among them politicians, journalists, and academics, called on the public to remember May 8 as a day of liberation and destruction. Quoting the first president of the Federal Republic, Theodor Heuss, the ad referred to the war's end as "the most tragic and questionable paradox for all of us." May 1945 brought an end to Nazi terror, but, the ad explained, it also marked "the beginning of the terror of the expulsion and a new oppression in the East and the origin of the division of our country." The ad exhorted readers to guard "against forgetting" (*Gegen das Vergessen*) and made it clear that they should remember more than one German past.[3]

In the spring of 1995, it was easy to dismiss such views as the expression of the resentment of a neoconservative minority still able to mention May 8 as the "beginning of terror" without explicitly naming those for whom the destruction of the Third Reich meant terror's end. Other press reports emphasized the huge number of public ceremonies and museum exhibitions in which Germans not only alluded to Nazi crimes but also took care to remember the names and faces of the victims of the Third Reich.[4] However, a public opinion poll conducted by the weekly news magazine *Der Spiegel* indicated that many Germans shared the view that the "paradox" of 1945 was effectively captured by juxtaposing forms of terror and fates of victims. When asked, "Was the expulsion of the Germans from the East just as great a crime against humanity as the Holocaust against the Jews?" 36 percent of all Germans and 40 percent of those over sixty-five answered yes.[5]

Appeals to establish the equivalence of German victims and the victims of Germans were not new; they conformed with established patterns of public memory in the Federal Republic. In this article, I argue that the competing pasts that circulated in a unified Germany in 1995 clearly echoed strains heard everywhere in West Germany in the late 1940s and early 1950s.[6] In the newly created Federal Republic, many West Germans sought to account for the horrors of what Chancellor Konrad Adenauer called the "saddest chapter" in their history; they acknowledged that crimes had been committed "in the name of the German people."[7] But they paid even more attention to crimes committed against Germans, crimes that, according to some contemporary accounts, were comparable to the crimes of Germans against the Jews. The most important representatives of German victimhood were the women, men, and children who left or were driven out of Eastern Europe by the Red Army at the war's end and others in German uniform for whom the war ended with captivity in the Soviet Union. There were some 12 million expellees, nearly two-thirds of whom resided in the Federal Republic in 1950. According to contemporary sources, over 3 million German soldiers had spent some time in Soviet hands, and of them, more than a million reportedly died before release.[8] These groups were joined by their common experience of a direct confrontation with the Red Army; they were eyewitnesses to the war on the eastern front, a front that moved steadily westward in late 1944 and early 1945.

This article takes issue with the widely held opinion that, in the 1950s, the citizens of the Federal Republic largely avoided all memories of the years of Nazi rule. In one famous formulation of this view, Alexander and Margarete Mitscherlich, writing in 1967, described the unwillingness of their fellow West Germans to confront their accountability for the National Socialist past, what they called the German "inability to mourn." Using Freudian categories to analyze the postwar German psyche, the Mitscherlichs argued that, after 1945, Germans *should* have come to an understanding of their deep identification with Hitler and the "national community" (*Volksgemeinschaft*), thus acknowledging their responsibility for crimes committed by the regime they had supported in overwhelming numbers. Leaving this difficult history behind was made possible by a massive self-investment in the "expansion and modernization of our industrial potential right down to the kitchen utensils." In the psychic economy that the Mitscherlichs described, creating for the future was a way to avoid the past.[9]

With few exceptions, variations on the Mitscherlichs' theme have become part of most accounts of the Federal Republic's first decade; West Germans are typically depicted as repressing or denying their responsibility for the triumph of National Socialism and the horrors that the Nazi regime inflicted on the rest of the world.[10] However, the apparent failure of West Germans to pay the high psychic costs demanded by the Mitscherlichs did not mean that they fled headlong from the past or suffered from collective amnesia. There were many accounts of Germany's "most recent history" that circulated in the 1950s; remembering selectively was not the same as forgetting.

An analysis of how the destruction of National Socialism was understood, described, and commemorated in the early history of the Federal Republic can illuminate how certain patterns for ordering the "paradox" of May 1945 emerged as soon as the shooting stopped. This article describes how in the first postwar decade the stories of expellees from eastern Germany and Eastern Europe and German prisoners of war imprisoned in the Soviet Union were crafted into rhetorics of victimization in the arena of public policy and in the writing of "contemporary history" (*Zeitgeschichte*). West Germans collectively mourned the suffering of these groups, and their experiences became central to one important version of the legacy of the war: their private memories structured public memory, making stories of Communist brutality and the loss of the "German East" crucial parts of the history of the Federal Republic. Focusing on German suffering also made it possible to talk about the end of the Third Reich without assessing responsibility for its origins, to tell an abbreviated story of National Socialism in which all Germans were ultimately victims of a war that Hitler started but everyone lost.

In the late 1960s and 1970s, West Germans came to a much more critical understanding of National Socialism. Memories of German victimization, dominant in the 1950s, were challenged by accounts in which Nazi crimes and the victimization of others by Germans were central. Still, this complication of public memory never meant the complete silencing or forgetting of another version of the past in which Germans had suffered as much as Jews and others, persecuted by National Socialism. Seen against the background of the history of certain forms of public memory in the 1950s, it becomes apparent that when themes of German victimization surfaced in the mid-1980s and 1990s, they represented nothing particularly novel but rather the return of the (never completely) repressed.

Competing pasts of the victims of World War II pervaded public policy debates in the early history of the Federal Republic. When Konrad Adenauer first addressed the newly elected parliament in September 1949, the chancellor expressed his concern about nascent anti-Semitic tendencies in West Germany and his sense of profound disbelief that "after all that has happened in our time, there should still be people in Germany who persecute or hate Jews because they are Jews." Just as troubling to Adenauer, however, was another past that lived on in the present, a past in which others were persecuted because they were German. Heading the list were "1.5 to 2 million German prisoners-of-war," whose whereabouts were unknown but who were most likely in the Soviet Union or elsewhere in Eastern Europe; expellees, "whose deaths number in the millions"; and other ethnic Germans still held against their will by East European Communist governments. Honoring the dead, bringing home the POWs and others unjustly held, and meeting the needs of all German victims of the war were essential parts of a just social contract in a new democratic republic.[11]

In the first electoral period of the West German parliament, the years 1949–1953, the Bundestag addressed these multiple pasts. In 1949, some critics were skeptical that Adenauer's government would adequately address the obligations of Germans to compensate those persecuted by the National Socialist regime. However, by the time the West German parliament ratified a treaty providing for the payment of reparations to Israel almost four years later, there was no question that the Christian Democratic chancellor was politically committed to reconciliation with the state that was home to many of the survivors of Nazi attempts to murder all European Jews.[12] In September 1951, Adenauer announced officially that "the Federal Government and with it the great majority of the German people are aware of the immeasurable suffering that was brought upon the Jews in Germany and the occupied territories during the time of National Socialism. . . . [U]nspeakable crimes were committed in the name of the German people, and these oblige [us] to make moral and material amends [*Wiedergutmachung*]."[13] Adenauer's passive construction "were committed" carefully differentiated between guilt and responsibility; crimes had been committed, but no criminals were named. Nonetheless, the chancellor left no doubt that West Germans must squarely confront the claims of Jewish victims.

West Germany's official overture to Israel met considerable domestic opposition from those who questioned the need for payments to persecuted Jews; Adenauer faced not only hostile public opinion but the resolute resistance of leading members of his own party, who claimed that reparations exceeded the means of an impoverished postwar Germany and that compensation for Jewish victims would spark resentment among Germans and a resurgence of anti-Semitism.[14] The chancellor's motives in overcoming these impediments to the reparations treaty, pushing through approval by the cabinet and ratification by the Bundestag in March 1953, are subject to more than one interpretation. There is much evidence that Adenauer was ultimately driven by his desire to convince the Western Allies that Germany would confront its moral obligations for the past in order to gain full acceptance as an equal partner in the postwar Western alliance. Negotiations with Israel also ran parallel to deliberations over West German integration into a West European defense alliance; they tied Germans' "moral rearmament" to the military rearmament of the West German state. In other accounts and in his memoirs, Adenauer's actions expressed firmly held convictions, not a response to Allied expectations and pressure. Ultimately, whatever the balance between sincerely held moral beliefs and political realism, it is difficult to imagine that without the chancellor's forceful intervention the West German parliament would have ratified the reparations agreement with Israel.[15]

The West German state also acknowledged the "saddest chapter" in its history by addressing the demands for compensation from others persecuted by the Nazis and still resident in the Federal Republic. In the same year that it ratified the treaty with Israel, the parliament approved legislation that built on state initiatives, particularly in the U.S. zone of occupation, and established a national framework to address individual claims for restitution from these other victims of the Nazis.

Constantin Goschler analyzes and documents in detail the West German attempts to "make good" (*Wiedergutmachung*) the harm done by National Socialism and shows the clear limits most West Germans placed on what constituted "racial, religious, or political" persecution during the Third Reich.

Victims not forgotten but explicitly excluded from these categories included gay men, subjects of forced sterilization, foreign slave-workers, violators of racist laws against sexual relations between "Aryans" and "non-Aryans," and for the most part Sinti and Roma.[16] These exclusions revealed a West German tendency to equate racial persecution exclusively with anti-Semitism and to collapse National Socialist atrocities into the mass extermination of the Jews.[17] Even with these limitations, however, the law to provide compensation to the victims of Nazi crimes encountered substantial criticism from many West German citizens and state officials,[18] and again, it was Adenauer's intervention and the solid support of opposition Social Democrats that provided the majority sufficient to override popular and official resistance to the compensation scheme.

Public discussion of restitution for victims of National Socialism and reparations for Israel revealed how divided West Germans remained over their responsibility for the atrocities of the Third Reich. However, the treaty with Israel and the establishment of an institutional framework to acknowledge the loss and suffering of other victims of "racial, religious, or political" persecution represented the explicit admission that the Nazi state had committed crimes "in the name of the German people." Particularly in the first four years of its history, the West German parliament, and Adenauer, did not entirely avoid or repress this part of the past.

Acknowledgment of Jewish victims of National Socialist crimes was directed at an international audience, but it also made it easier for the Bonn government to acknowledge German victims of the Red Army and postwar Communism. In the process, the fates of these two victim groups were frequently linked. On the agenda of the same session in which Bundestag delegates debated the final form of the treaty with Israel were initiatives to address the problems of those fleeing from the Soviet-occupied zone of Germany and those expelled from Eastern Europe.[19] The ghosts of victims, some Jewish, some German, often seemed to hover in the halls of parliament, competing for recognition. Victims were also joined by a language of "millions," a denomination associated with Jewish victims of National Socialism, prisoners of war in the Soviet Union, and expellees.[20] In debates over compensation for veterans returning from prisoner-of-war camps, Margarete Hütter, a staff member of the German Office for Peace (Deutsches Büro für Friedensfragen) could group together the prisoners of war, "the representative of the sacrifice brought by all Germans," with the "victim of the concentration camp." These groups were the "most tragic figures of the politics of the Third Reich," both victims of Hitler's Germany.[21]

The rhetoric of German victimization and Soviet barbarism could be traced back to the last years of the war.[22] Now, however, in the postwar years was the explicit equation of the suffering of German victims and victims of Germans. Jews and Germans had experienced the same forms of persecution, argued

Adenauer's minister of transportation, the German Party (Deutsche Partei) member Hans-Christoph Seebohm, because "the methods that were used by the National Socialist leaders against the Jews and that we most vehemently condemn are on a par with the methods that were used against the German expellees."[23] German expellees became another category of victims driven from their historic homelands because of their "ethnicity" (*Volkszugehörigkeit*); Jews persecuted by Germans were one group of victims among others.[24]

If compensation for Jewish victims was part of a West German strategy to gain favor with the Western Allies, measures to meet the needs of German victims were not. Indeed, the parliamentary discussions of German suffering unified all political parties in sharp criticism of the Western forces of postwar occupation, which were depicted as doing nothing to meet the needs of these groups; rather, the British and Americans were taken to task for viewing German losses through the distorted lens of theories of "collective guilt."[25] To be sure, in the early 1950s, descriptions of German suffering were more likely to portray the losses inflicted on Germans by the Red Army than cities destroyed by U.S. and British bomber pilots; it is not surprising that in the context of the Cold War, attacking the Soviet Union—past and present—was far easier than recounting the sins of former enemies who were now allies. However, in some cases, criticism of the Soviet Union was also a medium for denouncing the postwar settlement and the Western Allies who had unquestioningly accepted it. West Germans charged that by endorsing the mandatory removal of millions of Germans from areas in Eastern Europe seized by the Red Army and doing nothing to meet the needs of German victims of the war, the Allies had responded to Nazi injustice with unjust acts of no less consequence,[26] leaving Germans "to dish out the soup that the military governments had prepared."[27]

In a host of federal programs aimed at meeting the needs of "war-damaged" groups, particularly expellees and veterans, and, among them, prisoners of war, the West German state set out to "equalize the burdens" of the arbitrary consequences of the war. A host of social-welfare measures sought to mediate the differences between the woman whose husband had come back from the war and the woman whose husband had not, between veterans who were permitted to return immediately after the end of fighting and prisoners of war, between POWs in Soviet and Western Allied hands, between POWs whose former homes were now "behind the iron curtain" and those who had lived in western Germany before the war, and between "new citizens" (*Neubürger*), driven from their homes in Eastern Europe, and West Germans who had suffered no such dramatic displacement.[28] Achieving some measure of social justice among those who had suffered little or nothing and those who had lost everything emerged as a key measure of the legitimacy of the West German state.[29]

In the process of identifying the needs of war veterans and expellees, the West German state also allowed German victims to act for themselves, represent their own interests, and shape policy. After World War I, veterans and others who had suffered most from the war and the economic instability of the early postwar years had perceived themselves to be excluded from parliamentary deliberations of compensation for their losses; their resentment translated into loud attacks on the "Weimar system."[30] In the Bonn republic, mass organizations of expellees and veterans quickly emerged as important actors in negotiations over how best to meet their needs. Their interests were also represented in a cabinet-level office established to be the advocate for Expellees, Refugees and War-Damaged (Bundesministerium für Vertriebene, Flüchtlinge und Kriegsgeschädigte), and they spoke from the floor of the Bundestag as members of all major political parties.[31]

Despite the broad consensus favoring payments to German victims of the war and the expulsion, no victim group received everything it wanted. Finance Minister Fritz Schäffer constantly reminded his colleagues that Germany was a poor nation, barely able to contribute to containing Communism in the present, let alone to pay for Communism's past crimes against expellees and POWs.[32] Discontent over a glass half-empty, however, did not lead to massive political opposition to the Bonn government as it had to the Weimar Republic. In part, this was because veterans and expellees, the two most effectively organized groups claiming compensation, had been asked to participate in defining solutions for their own problems and had achieved at least something of what they were after. As James Diehl has convincingly argued in his analysis of those policies aimed specifically at veterans, the West German government also won acceptance for its initiatives to "equalize the burdens" of the war and compensate the "war-damaged" by stressing that it had crafted programs that were singularly German, grounded in the best tradition of the German social-welfare system and seen as the essential corrective to punitive polices imposed by the Allies in the years of postwar occupation.[33]

Defining the just claims and rights to entitlement of some and the moral obligations of others was part of establishing the bases for social solidarity in West Germany. The Germany that committed crimes against others was an aberration; it was succeeded by a Germany that helped to ease German suffering. All major political parties could agree on the version of the legacy of National Socialism embodied in parliamentary discussions of the victims of the expulsion and the survivors of Soviet captivity; the suffering of these groups remained outside the realm of party-political wrangling. The deep divisions between Social Democrats and Adenauer's government were at least momentarily bridged by a shared relationship to the lasting consequences of a common past.

For the West German state, acknowledging the pasts of expellees and prisoners of war not only involved assessing material need, it also included ensuring that the testimonies of these groups would become part of West Germany's public memory. In the case of those driven out of Eastern Europe, the Bonn government pledged to preserve the "cultural values" of the expellees by incorporating the history of Germans in Eastern Europe into West German school curricula and establishing a series of research institutes for the scholarly study of the Central European past and present. The state formally acknowledged that it would be essential to educate West Germans about the history of Germans in Eastern and Central Europe, who were now the "new citizens" in a democratic republic.[34]

West Germans were also constantly reminded of the soldiers for whom the war on the eastern front had been followed by the battle to survive Soviet captivity; those German POWs still in the Soviet Union were never far from public view. Newspaper stories describing "Graves and Barbed Wire: The Fate of Millions"[35] evoked images of millions of German POWs, not millions of victims of concentration camps; annual days of remembrance for POWs called attention to those Germans for whom the war was not yet over.[36] Little more than five years after the war's end, the Federal Republic was also calling on the United Nations to investigate charges of the violation of human rights, not of others by Nazis but of German POWs and deported ethnic Germans by their Soviet captors.[37]

The state's commitment to creating a detailed record of German loss and suffering was also apparent in its sponsorship of two projects that sought to collect the memories of POWs and expellees as sources for writing the "contemporary history" of the postwar period. A systematic effort to document the "expulsion of the Germans from the East" was formally initiated by the Ministry for Expellees, Refugees and War-Damaged shortly after the creation of the office in Adenauer's first government. Its editorial board was made up of eminent professional historians led by Theodor Schieder of the University of Cologne, who had lived and taught in Königsberg until the war drove him west in 1944.[38] His co-workers included Hans Rothfels, who also had worked in Königsberg until 1938, when he fled the Nazis, who cared only for his Jewish origins, not his Protestant baptism. Rothfels had returned from the United States, where he had spent the war years, to take a chair at Tübingen.[39] Working on individual volumes was a team that included Werner Conze, the major West German proponent of social history in the 1950s, and a number of youthful assistants, among them Martin Broszat, who later went on to direct the Munich Institute for Contemporary History, and Hans-Ulrich Wehler, who in the 1960s would emerge as the leading advocate of a "historical social science."[40]

In eight volumes, including three full-length diaries, the *Documentation of the Expulsion of Germans from East-Central Europe* (in German) described the experiences of Germans as they fled before the Red Army advance in 1944 and 1945 and as they left and were driven from their homelands in Czechoslovakia, Hungary, Romania, Yugoslavia, and from the parts of eastern Germany that became Poland after German surrender.[41] At the core of the project was a massive collection of some 11,000 eyewitness accounts recorded by expellees themselves, frequently assembled with the cooperation of their interest-group organizations. The editors were aware of the problems inherent in such subjective testimony, but they guaranteed that the fraction of reports ultimately published had been subjected to painstaking "authentication and verification" and constituted a completely reliable record of the "entire process of the expulsion in [its] historical accuracy."[42]

The "Documents of the Expulsion" were, as one review put it, "Documents of Horror."[43] Countless individual reports of terror, rape, plundering, the separation of families, forced deportations, starvation, slave labor, and death combined to give shape to the "mass fate" of Germans in Eastern Europe, the "German tragedy," "contemporary history in documents."[44] Even those eyewitnesses who claimed to have been skeptical of the terrifying picture of the Bolshevik painted in Nazi propaganda conceded that they confronted a reality that often exceeded Joseph Goebbels's predictions.[45]

The federal government complemented the volumes on the expulsion with an extensive collection of testimonies from prisoners of war. Although its work was not completed until the 1970s, the POW project also had its origins in the 1950s and was seen explicitly as an essential continuation of the effort to capture the eyewitness accounts of expellees. Detailed descriptions of the conditions in Soviet camps had been collected since the late 1940s by veterans' associations, the German Red Cross, and church organizations that had taken the lead in tracing the fates of German POWs. Since 1953, much of this documentation had been collected by the Bundesarchiv. Four years later, the West German state appointed a "scientific commission" to assemble these eyewitness accounts and other forms of evidence in order to provide a complete "documentation of the fate of German prisoners in the Second World War," an initiative that in the words of one newspaper account would create the opportunity for "Prisoners of War [to] Write Contemporary History."[46] The documentation should serve "for the present and future of our nation to secure the suffering of the prisoners, which has already begun to fade from public consciousness," a record that could meet the most demanding criteria of "objectivity" and "exactitude."[47]

Heading the project was Erich Maschke, a chairholder at the University of Jena under the Nazis, a prisoner of war in the Soviet Union until his release in 1953, and in the 1950s a professor of social and economic history at the University of Heidelberg.[48] Maschke and his co-workers ultimately sifted through more than 45,000 written and tape-recorded accounts. Of the twenty-two books published by the project, thirteen described the areas where German POWs had been most numerous, their treatment had been worst, and they had remained imprisoned the longest—Poland, Czechoslovakia, Yugoslavia, and particularly the Soviet Union, which alone filled eight volumes; the testimonies assembled were more evidence of Communist atrocities in Eastern

Europe.[49] This emphasis on the East corresponded to the contemporary assessment that the differences in the treatment of German POWs by Western Allies and Communists were ones of kind, not degree.[50]

For POWs, no concerns loomed larger than malnutrition and starvation, and they described the dangerous balancing act of remaining sick enough to avoid forced labor but well enough to avoid death.[51] Work rebuilding the Soviet Union was sometimes remembered as a source of pride and accomplishment, but it was more frequently equated with slave labor, as one POW remarked, a form of direct retribution that represented the "payment of reparations."[52] Particularly for the period of the late 1940s, reports were filled not only with tallies of death from malnutrition but also with accounts of mass shootings by Red Army troops and Communist partisans and the dumping of the dead into unmarked graves.[53]

The experiences of POWs in the Soviet Union diverged from those of expellees in important respects. The POW camp was a world without women, a sharp contrast with the westward "treks" of expellees, in which women outnumbered men. In addition, for at least some of the students in the "barbed-wire university," as POWs ironically called the camps, the school term ended only in the mid-1950s; while, for most expellees, the return "not to home [*Heimat*] but at least to the Fatherland" was complete by the late 1940s.[54] Despite these differences, the accounts of expellees and POWs also provided much evidence of the ways in which they had experienced the end of the same war. As the Red Army moved westward in late 1944, the line between front and home front dissolved. In the words of Margarete Schell, a German actress from Prague and the author of one of the full-length diaries published by the Schieder project, Germans in Czechoslovakia had lived "a soldier's life . . . only much worse."[55]

The history of National Socialism and the war that both expellees and POWs told began only at the moment when the Red Army appeared, reaching the outskirts of the village or capturing the soldier. In neither documentation project did the editors elicit testimony about Germany's war of aggression on the eastern front or German rule in Eastern Europe; both projects recorded and sanctioned silence and selective memory. In both cases as well, victimization by the Red Army followed victimization by benighted, fanatical Nazis who postponed evacuation in the face of the red flood or insisted on fighting to the bitter end. This was the same history that was told from the floor of the Bundestag in debates over measures to meet the material needs of expellees and returning veterans, a history peopled with innocents in which a handful of zealous Nazis had deluded good Germans. Victims of Germans were not completely absent from these accounts, but when those who testified acknowledged the suffering of Jews at the hands of Germans, it was most frequently in order to establish a measure for the horror of their own experience.[56] In some cases, POWs, expellees, and the editors of the documentation projects claimed that what Germans had suffered under Communists was comparable in its horror only to what Jews had suffered under Nazis.

History had repeated itself, once as tragedy, once as farce, concluded Maria Zatschek, an expellee from Czechoslovakia who remarked, "what a bad comedy all this is: nothing is original, a copy of the Hitler regime, again and again we have to hear: 'Just as you have treated the Jews.' "[57] It was this, reflected Wolfgang Schwarz, author of the volume on "cultural life" among German POWs in the Soviet Union, that made the POWs "brothers of the prisoners in the concentration camps."[58] In their assessment of the documentation on the expulsion from Czechoslovakia, the editors expressed similar views. They pointed out that the analogy between German and Jewish victims was unmistakable when Germans took the place of Jews in former Nazi concentration camps: "In some of these camps, particularly Theresienstadt, only the victims had changed: where Jewish prisoners had suffered from the National Socialist system of oppression, Germans were now tortured and maltreated."[59] Both POWs and expellees depicted themselves individually and collectively as victims of an ideology no less irrational than National Socialism; like the Nazis, the Soviets had reduced identity to ethnicity, singling out their victims only because they were Germans. The standard of measurement of the sufferings of Germans thus became "the horrible crimes committed against the Jews in Hitler's concentration camps,"[60] the goal of the Communists, nothing less than the "cleansing" and "de-Germanization" (*Entgermanisierung*) of Eastern Europe.[61]

In parliamentary debates over restitution for victims of the war, Germans and Jews were rhetorically lumped together. In the accounts provided in the documentation projects and in some of the editorial commentary that framed eyewitness stories, the overwhelming similarity of the treatment of all victims and the moral equivalence of their suffering were stated even more explicitly. Some German eyewitnesses could claim to know what Jews had experienced, not because they themselves were guilty of crimes but because what Jews had endured in concentration camps "could not possibly have been worse" than what Germans had suffered at the hands of Communists.[62]

There is no way to assess how many West Germans read the testimonies recorded in the documentation projects. The POW project only began publishing its findings in the 1960s, and the final installment was not released until 1974, partly delayed because, by the time all volumes were completed, the West German government had become far less intent on sustaining memories of Communist atrocities. In an age of "peaceful coexistence" between East and West, some pasts were best allowed to slumber or to circulate at most in small editions, distributed to research institutes and university libraries.[63] The expellee project completed publication by 1961, but its considerable bulk doubtless also limited its accessibility. However, for the tens of thousands of POWs and expellees—and the millions more they represented—the invitation to bear witness and the assurance that their memories would be preserved as part of an official chronicle made it easier, as Maschke expressed it, for these German victims to "overcome the destiny of painful and terrifying memories."[64] Public recognition and individual catharsis were parts of the same process.[65]

The federally sponsored publication projects that chronicled the fate of German expellees and POWs also corroborated other accounts of German suffering at the war's end that circulated in West German politics and popular culture in the 1950s. Expellees' and veterans' organizations encouraged their constituents to record their experiences and to publicize the enormity of their suffering; interest-group publications provided a forum in which it was possible to foster group identities.[66]

Memories of POWs in the Soviet Union and expellees also resounded in the arena of foreign policy. The record of German loss was cited as evidence in support of demands to revise the postwar settlement that had extended Poland's boundary westward significantly into territory once part of the German Reich.[67] The last remaining POWs in the Soviet Union also remained a national preoccupation until Adenauer negotiated their release in September 1955. When the 9,626 POWs began to leave the Soviet Union the next month, West German press accounts used the occasion not only to celebrate these survivors of Communist captivity but also to rehearse endlessly the horrors they had experienced.[68] As late as 1967, shortly after Adenauer's death, 75 percent of those questioned in a public opinion survey placed the release of the last POWs from the Soviet Union at the top of the list of the first chancellor's accomplishments.[69]

Themes of expulsion and the experiences of soldiers on the eastern front were also the stuff of novels and movies. For example, between 1951 and 1959, some 19 million viewers saw *Grün ist die Heide* (The heath is green), a movie that told the story of a Pomeranian landowner who flees westward at the end of the war, leaving everything behind. Only the generosity of new friends in the Lüneburger Heide and the natural beauty of the forest allow him to "forget what I have lost."[70] An entire genre of "expellee literature" told similar tales but focused less on the successful integration of expellees into West German society than on the terror they had experienced before reaching their new home.[71]

Numerous as well were popular novels, memoirs, and movies that described the war on the eastern front and the long march into Soviet POW camps from the perspective of the common soldier, victimized first by zealous Nazi leaders, then by the Red Army. These were epic dramas of suffering, inner strength, and quiet courage stemming not from ideology but from common decency and of adventurous schemes to resist Communism by whatever means possible.[72] Such accounts were part of the general tendency in the 1950s to see the returning German veteran as a noble survivor, unjustly branded by the victors as a militaristic criminal; they contributed to a conventional wisdom according to which the Wehrmacht had dutifully carried out orders, scrupulously following the established rules of warfare.[73] The same general themes gained credence among West Germany's Western Allies, particularly as the United States increased its pressure to see West Germans once again in uniform, essential recruits in the battles of the Cold War.[74]

The imposing bound volumes from the POW and expellee documentation projects did not circulate nearly as widely as these other accounts, but they told the same stories. They sanctioned and substantiated fictionalized tales and individual memoirs, blurring the line between fiction and fact. As one reviewer of the first volumes published by the Schieder project noted, this authorized record should dispel completely whatever skepticism had greeted other dramatic presentations of the experiences of expellees in the late 1940s and early 1950s. The documentation delivered "irrefutable proof of the accuracy of those descriptions" as well.[75]

The debates over material compensation for Jews and others persecuted by the Nazis made clear that these "racial, political, and religious" victims of National Socialism were not forgotten, but they remained faceless and without speech. In Adenauer's cabinet, there was no Ministry for Survivors of Nazi Persecution and Nazi Concentration Camps, intent on acknowledging, ordering, analyzing, and sanctioning the suffering of the victims of Germans. Although a number of memoirs of concentration camp victims were published in Germany in the first two years following the war, by the late 1940s this was increasingly a genre that West German trade publishers avoided.[76]

To be sure, documentation of the crimes of Germans against others was available, and the trials of leading Nazi war criminals by the Nuremberg Tribunal alone generated a mountain of evidence of German atrocities, a crucial source for key aspects of German "contemporary history." In the 1950s, the Institute for Contemporary History in Munich drew on this documentation and other sources to begin writing a critical history of the National Socialist regime. However, no attempts were made to supplement objective analysis with personal accounts of those persecuted by the Nazi regime. Thus, for example, the Schieder documentation offered many descriptions of the crimes committed by Poles and Soviets against Germans in Łódź, but neither the West German state nor West German scholars undertook systematic efforts to record Jewish voices that could have told other stories of Germans who, until the spring of 1945, called that city Litzmannstadt.[77] For the most part, victims of Germans remained objects, not subjects, of their own history, a history never told from their perspective.[78]

In 1955, Hans Rothfels, a co-worker on the expellee documentation project and editor of the *Vierteljahrshefte für Zeitgeschichte* (Quarterly journal of contemporary history), the most important new postwar German historical periodical, illuminated the "profound paradox" of the war's end by drawing up a balance sheet called "Ten Years After." He effectively summarized how competing pasts had become part of the history of the Federal Republic. Rothfels recalled both the "horrible things that took place in occupied areas, particularly in the East," and what was done "to real and imagined opponents in concentration camps," even as he described in far greater detail the expulsion of Germans from Eastern Europe and the last-gasp attempts of the German army and navy to hold off the Red Army. The way to remember May 1945, Rothfels concluded, was with an "hour of commemoration" for all victims, including those killed by Germans as well as those Germans "murdered after the end of hostilities, those who drowned or perished in the snow as they attempted to flee, who froze or starved, who did not survive the forced marches or forced labor camps . . . and also those women, who after the deepest humiliation took their own lives, or their husbands, who resisted this disgrace," an unambiguous reminder of the literal rapes that heralded the symbolic rape of eastern Germany and Eastern Europe by the Red Army. Mourning these German victims should not, Rothfels warned, diminish memories of the suffering of others. However, a complete tally could only be one that captured "reality in its horrifying totality."[79]

West Germans were by no means silent about the "horrifying totality" of the past in the first decade after the end of the war. However, their memories were selective; about the parts of that "totality" in which some Germans were perpetrators they had less to say than about the parts that encompassed their own experiences as victims. About this past—the past of their own loss—their ability to mourn literally filled volumes.

By the late 1950s and early 1960s, increasing numbers of West Germans insisted on providing a more complex account of the National Socialist regime and the war. The past in which Germans were victims receded, displaced by a history of the Third Reich in which Nazi atrocities took center stage. A full explanation of what accomplished this complication of public memory exceeds the scope of this article. Here, I will only suggest some of the most important signposts along this path to a different understanding of the Third Reich, but I will also point to representative reminders that other pasts never completely disappeared from view.[80]

Among historians, the rapidly growing commitment to identify National Socialism as a system deeply rooted in German history and politics, not as a "catastrophe" or the demonic projection of a small elite, was signaled by the coming of age of a group of scholars more likely to have experienced Nazism as adolescents than as young adults and largely trained after 1945. Many moved away from the focus on high politics that had long dominated German historiography and explored the possibilities of methodologies borrowed from the social sciences. Particularly important was the work of historians who turned an older, conservative emphasis on German exceptionalism—a *Sonderweg*—on its head. The *Sonderweg* explained not the triumph of Germany as a major power and a preeminent Kulturstaat in Europe but the peculiar route from an authoritarian Kaiserreich to an authoritarian Third Reich. In their accounts, May 1945 represented a "zero hour" (*Stunde Null*), a complete rupture that dramatically separated the Third Reich from the Bonn republic. By the late 1960s, a generation of radical students, children of the rubble who had little or no direct experience of National Socialism, added its critical voice. Reviving Marxist analyses of fascism, they discovered a path that had not ended in 1945; rather, the capitalist system that had brought fascism to Germany defined lines that tied Hitler's Germany to Adenauer's. What unified these diverse approaches was their commitment to a far more complete and troubling account of National Socialism.

The new version of the German past that emerged by the early 1970s analyzed the popular bases of Nazi support and the success of the state's efforts to invade and transform German society; it emphasized the virtual absence of German resistance to Nazi racialism, terrorism, and expansionist aggression and the presence of broad support for the regime, at least until the war turned sour after the German defeat at Stalingrad in 1943; and it charted the history of German anti-Semitism and the persecution of the Jews, including the participation of the Wehrmacht in the murder of Jews and other civilians. The authors of this critical history focused not on German suffering but on the crimes committed by Germans against others, and they explained World War II as a logical outgrowth of National Socialist ideology, not an aberration attributable to Hitler. This historiographical shift took place against a broad political background that included the trial of Adolf Eichmann in Jerusalem, the prosecution of major Nazi war criminals in the Federal Republic, and repeated parliamentary debates over the extension of the statute of limitations for prosecution of those who had committed atrocities during the Third Reich.[81]

By the late 1960s, after two decades of uninterrupted rule by Christian Democratic chancellors, many West German voters were also ready for a dramatic political change at the national level; they supported a chancellor who had spent the war not in "internal migration" nor in a Wehrmacht uniform but fighting Germans in the Norwegian resistance. Willy Brandt publicly held his fellow citizens collectively accountable for their past as perpetrators. The preoccupation of the 1950s with the crimes of Communists against Germans was dramatically eclipsed by Brandt's public acknowledgment of the crimes of Germans against Poles and Jews in his December 1970 trip to Warsaw. In this highly symbolic visit, Brandt concluded treaty negotiations that marked the postwar normalization of relations with Poland and the state's abandonment of expellees' claims to their former homeland. Brandt's stop at the monument to the 1943 Warsaw Ghetto uprising represented the commemoration of another past and drew international attention. His *Ostpolitik* was a foreign policy that at once expressed West Germany's ability to assert itself as an independent geo-political actor and West Germany's acknowledgement of the disastrous consequences of its independent foreign policy in the past. It was not surprising that, in this context, rhetorics of German victimization figured far less prominently.[82]

To be sure, other accounts of the war's legacy never entirely vanished. Two of the three diaries published by the expellee project were reissued periodically, and, by the mid-1960s, 235,000 copies of Hans Graf von Lehndorff's *Report from East and West Prussia* were in print in German.[83] The supply of eyewitness accounts of the expulsion was also constantly renewed, and those testifying insisted that they would not allow the voices of German suffering to be silenced, although the authors never specified precisely when silence had prevailed.[84]

The documentation of Erich Maschke's POW project continued to appear steadily as well. Although it was accessible only to a limited public, the controversies over restrictions on its release and circulation became a medium for the protests of those who clamored against what they saw as attempts to censor crucial parts of German history. Thus, for example, from March until July 1972, the mass-market weekly *Quick* ran a series of articles allegedly leaked in part from the Maschke documentation, presenting tales of arms amputated with nail files, brutal partisans, the "white hell" of POWs shipped behind the Urals, wedding rings exchanged for bread rations, and heroes behind barbed wire, horror stories all verified in the "secret documents in *Quick*," accounts that were "simple and straightforward, a piece of history."[85]

Other memories were regularly generated by institutes of East European research that had been established after the war to preserve the heritage of the "German East." At least in the 1950s and 1960s, the work of the scholars in these institutes focused primarily on the social, economic, political, and cultural contributions of German-speaking communities and the harmonious mix of ethnicities and cultures that had characterized Eastern Europe before the Versailles Treaty injected a poisonous, xenophobic nationalism into this multicultural idyll; Jews were virtually absent in the history of East-Central Europe presented in this scholarship.[86]

Told with an explicitly political inflection, a similar version of the history of Germans in Eastern Europe was repeated in the political lobbying of expellee interest groups that railed against any conciliatory gestures in West German-East European relations.[87] Political opposition to any moves toward better relations with East European countries in the 1970s could emphasize that "Germans had to suffer, too" by pointing to the authoritative documentation that the government had assembled and asserting that "Auschwitz is only half of the truth, according to the findings of the documentation of the crimes committed during the expulsion."[88]

Preserving memories of German victimization was by no means the exclusive territory of irredentist special-interest groups. The West German television broadcast of the American mini-series *Holocaust* in 1979, frequently cited as a high point in West Germans' confrontation with the individual face of mass extermination, was followed two years later by *Geflohen und vertrieben* (Flight and expulsion), a three-part series on West German television that documented other crimes.[89] A combination of historical analysis, documentary footage, and personal memories captured in interviews, it was announced as a courageous attempt to address directly a topic "as good as taboo" in the Federal Republic, a "consequence of our lack of historical consciousness."[90] Reinforcing the point, an inexpensive paperback edition of the original expellee documentation was reissued three years later. In a highly favorable review in the *Frankfurter Allgemeine Zeitung,* Gotthold Rhode recommended that in discussions of the commemoration of the fortieth anniversary of the war's end, the "voice of those be heard whose time of suffering only really began once the weapons were silenced."[91]

By the late 1970s, the "New German Cinema," the progressive artistic movement that sought to break in every possible respect with the film traditions of the "fathers," an older generation associated with National Socialism, was also offering empathetic reflections on what fathers—and mothers—had suffered during the war.[92] Three examples illustrate the New German Cinema's preoccupation with war stories that were not entirely new. In *Deutschland, bleiche Mutter* (Germany, pale mother), first shown in 1980, the feminist director Helma Sanders-Brahms told a daughter's story of her mother's odyssey from Hitler's Germany to Adenauer's. In Sanders-Brahms's account, World War II liberated German women, revealing their strength and resourcefulness in the absence of men; for women, the real war began in 1945, when rape by Allied soldiers and the return of German men brutally transformed them from self-reliant agents into victims. However, the film's powerful images of the decaying corpse of a German soldier and bombed-out cities were not only the backdrop for the heroic acts of the mother and daughter at the center of the movie, they were also forceful reminders of the devastation of Germany brought on by the Nazis' war. In one of the most extended sequences in the movie, mother and daughter find refuge in an abandoned factory, where smokestacks and ovens in the background implicitly associate the fate of different victims.[93]

In the political context of the late 1970s and anti-Americanism high on the Left's agenda, it is not surprising that the rapist in Sanders-Brahms's drama was a U.S., not a Red Army, soldier. However, if on an allegorical level, the rape is intended to suggest, as Anton Kaes argues, that "postwar Germany is the innocent victim of rape by America," the scene also evoked memories of other rapes, both literal and allegorical, recorded in memoirs and described throughout the official documentation of the expulsion. Much of the war experienced by the mother and daughter also takes place in an unspecified German East, where they escape the bombs falling on Berlin. And a homeless little boy, incorporated in the film with original documentary footage shot during the war, is a representative of the innocents who lost homes and family during the expulsion. Indeed, the same footage was used in the television series *Flight and Expulsion*.[94] The film thus evoked strong memories of the war in both West and East.

In Alexander Kluge's 1979 movie, *Die Patriotin* (The patriot), the war in the East figures not as background but as a central character, weaving in and out of the story of a West German high school teacher's search for ways to present German history to her students. Kluge makes much use of documentary film footage of the battle of Stalingrad, the beginning of the end of the war in the East and a battle that for thousands of Germans resulted not in death but a long stay in Soviet captivity.[95] In his analysis of the movie, Kaes suggests that Kluge's selective use of background music, composed for the movie *Night and Fog,* the French director Alain Resnais' 1958 account of the Holocaust, first shown in the Federal Republic twenty years later, "may hint at a consciousness that does not want to exclude Auschwitz from the patriotic *Trauerarbeit* [work of mourning]" in the film; but it may also suggest a consciousness in which all of the war's victims are equated. In Kluge's movie, however, Jews killed by Germans are present as a subtle musical allusion, while the fallen dead at Stalingrad and bombed German cities are vividly portrayed.[96]

Edgar Reitz's *Heimat,* the saga of one German town from the end of World War I until the early 1980s, aired on West German television in eleven episodes during the fall of 1984. Reitz painstakingly presented pasts not of Nazi crimes or even the banality of evil but of a German society cloaked in ignorance and innocence, caught in patterns of daily life that seemed entirely normal. At least 25 million West Germans watched at least one part of the series, and it was the subject of extensive media attention. Although set in western Germany, the title of Reitz's film evoked memories linked since the war's end with a German *Heimat* in Eastern Europe that had been lost literally, not metaphorically. The mini-series opens on May 9, 1919, as one of the central characters, Paul Simon, returns from a French prisoner-of-war camp, a "survivor of the western front."[97] Surely few West Germans could miss the reference to another war that ended in May and to other survivors of the eastern, not the western, front, of Soviet, not French, prisoner-of-war camps. When Reitz's saga moves into the 1930s and 1940s, his focus remains on what one reviewer called a "history of small people who live their lives in dignity,"[98] but there is little room in his drama for the history of other small people denied the right to life of any sort.

Sanders-Brahms, Kluge, and Reitz insisted on the necessity, validity, and in some ways superiority of a subjective perspective—the history of the war and postwar years seen through a daughter's eyes, a soldier's suffering, the daily lives of common people. They responded to what they perceived to be the erasure of individual experience and personal voices in historical accounts that focused on ideologies, structures, and institutions. Like the Schieder and Maschke projects, the actors in their historical dramas spoke German and were not Jewish; subjective stories of other victims of the war remained untold.

The *Wende,* the turn, is now a term most closely associated with the monumental changes of 1989 that led to the unification of the two Germanies. However, in the early 1980s, the *Wende* described the political shift rightward, as the Free Democratic Party dropped its alliance with Social Democrats for a coalition with the Christian Democratic Union and the chancellorship of Helmut Kohl. Under this conservative political constellation, pasts of German suffering, never entirely absent from political discourse and popular culture, took on far greater significance. In the spring of 1985, forty years after the end of World War II in Europe, competing German pasts became the topic of intense debate, particularly in the Federal Republic, the United States, and Israel.

Memories of victims were linked when the U.S. president Ronald Reagan joined the West German chancellor Kohl in a day of commemoration that began at Bergen-Belsen, the site of a Nazi concentration camp, and continued with a visit to a military cemetery in Bitburg in western Germany, where, among others, soldiers of the SS were buried. At ceremonies following the cemetery visit, Kohl called for remembrance of the "infinite suffering that the war and totalitarianism inflicted on nations," and at a press conference before leaving for the Federal Republic, Reagan asserted that the German dead at Bitburg "are victims of Nazism also . . . They were victims, just as surely as the victims in the concentration camps."[99]

Bitburg and Bergen-Belsen were not the only controversial sites of commemoration that spring. In his comments to the Bundestag on May 8, Richard von Weizsäcker, then president of the Federal Republic, remembered "the six million Jews who were murdered in German concentration camps" and reminded his fellow citizens who chose to focus on their own suffering that "the 8th of May was a day of liberation. It liberated all of us from the inhumanity and tyranny of the National Socialist regime."[100] In other venues, however, there were other interpretations of "liberation." Kohl followed Bitburg and Bergen-Belsen with a visit to Hanover for the annual rally of the national organization representing those Germans expelled from Silesia at the end of the war.[101] For them, 1985 marked the fortieth anniversary of the "expulsion," "liberation" not from National Socialism but from their homes in Eastern Europe. Breaking a promise to tone down their most outspokenly nationalist rhetoric in return for assurances of Kohl's attendance, some of those present at the Hanover meeting raised banners at the moment of the chancellor's appearance reiterating the claim that "Silesia Remains Ours" (*Schlesien bleibt unser*). Public opinion polls revealed that this was a minority view; 76 percent of all West Germans were ready to live with the postwar border. Still, nearly one in four was not.[102]

Historians had not defined the terms of this public debate over the German past, and their claims to a privileged role in "shaping identity" (*Identitätsstiftung*) in the mid-1980s sprung largely from their own narrow conception of the potential arenas in which identity takes shape. However, the "historians' controversy" (*Historikerstreit*), a scholarly controversy over the place and significance of National Socialism and the Holocaust in the narrative of modern German history, which ultimately involved a "who's who" of senior male historians in the Federal Republic and many students of Germany elsewhere, did focus discussions over the relationship between history and politics that Kohl and others had forcefully placed on the agenda.

The "historians' controversy" generated a mountain of books and articles, and by the late 1980s, a small cottage industry churned out commentaries on West German historians' tortured search for a historically grounded national identity.[103] However, like the memories of wars, memories of "historians' controversies" can fade; over a decade after the fact, it is perhaps useful briefly to review some of the key events in the dispute in order to locate it in the context of the frameworks for understanding the meanings of May 8 that existed long before historians and public intellectuals contested how best to remember the German past in 1985 and 1986.

In one of the most important interventions in the *Historikerstreit,* Andreas Hillgruber brought together expanded versions of two talks given independently in 1984 and 1985 to juxtapose *Two Sorts of Demise: The Destruction of the German Reich and the End of European Jewry* (in German).[104] Hillgruber had long been a student of Eastern Europe. His dissertation was a study of German-Romanian relations in the years from 1938 to 1944, and the book that earned him a professorship analyzed Hitler's planning for the war in the East.[105] Research into the war also meant reflecting on a chapter in his own history. Born in 1925 and raised in Königsberg, where his father, a schoolteacher, was removed from his post by the Nazis, he had been old enough to be drafted into the German army late in the war, and he had fought on the eastern front; much of his professional career was then dedicated to fighting over its meanings.[106]

In his short book, Hillgruber devoted most of his attention to the first of his "demises," the collapse of the German front in East Prussia in the winter of 1944–1945 and the "expulsion of Germans from East Central Europe," events that for Hillgruber defined "the destruction of the German Reich." The historian considering the war's end and searching for a point of empathetic identification, argued Hillgruber,

> must identify himself with the concrete fate of the German population in the
> east and with the desperate and sacrificial exertions of the German army of

the East and the German fleet in the Baltic, which sought to defend the population of the German east from the orgy of revenge of the Red Army, mass rapes, arbitrary killing, and compulsory deportations.[107]

From this perspective, the advance of the Red Army could be designated as a "liberation" for those victims of the Nazis released from concentration camps and prisons, but for the "German nation as a whole, it is inappropriate."[108]

In his contribution to the "historians' controversy," Ernst Nolte also stressed the comparability of the Nazis' extermination of the Jews and other forms of state terror in the twentieth century. The "final solution," Nolte argued, was not unique but, rather, an expression of extremism and politically motivated violence that could be traced back at least to the "reign of terror" of the French Revolution, reaching a twentieth-century high point with mass murder under Stalin. Nolte's emphasis on the atrocities of Stalinism was familiar to those who knew his work,[109] but what sparked controversy in the 1980s was the comparison of Stalin's and Hitler's crimes, a clear challenge to those who claimed the singularity of Auschwitz.

What went largely unnoticed in the paper wars surrounding the "historians' controversy" was that the battle lines drawn by Hillgruber, Nolte, and the politics of Bitburg had long histories, stretching back into the Federal Republic's first decade.[110] Saul Friedlander chastised Hillgruber for equating the Holocaust and the expulsion, thus elevating to "an element of learned discourse" an "image of the past carried by part of the West German population," and he criticized Nolte for transforming German perpetrators and bystanders into victims. But neither he nor any other commentator on the "historians' controversy" appreciated to what extent learned discourse and popular consciousness had reinforced such an "image of the past" in the public memory of the Federal Republic long before Hillgruber joined "two demises" and Nolte equated victims of Hitler and Stalin.[111] Rothfels had linked victims' fates "Ten Years After," not forty, pointing not only to a "system that had liquidated alleged class enemies just as thoroughly as National Socialism had [liquidated] alleged racial enemies" but also to the crimes perpetrated by Soviets against Germans at the end of the war.[112]

The musings of Michael Stürmer and others that, after the war, West Germans had suffered a "loss of history" completely disregarded the selective "contemporary history" that was written in the first postwar decade. Stürmer's claim that a German history capable of "shaping identity" was possible only once Germans had mourned "for the victims and the pain of what was lost" took no note of how much mourning of this variety had already taken place.[113] When Joachim Fest fretted that "the public sphere, despite all encouragement from the political side, has still not emerged from the shadow cast by Hitler and the crimes committed under him," he also seemed to have suffered a "loss of history," the history of the 1950s in which the crimes committed by Germans had received far less systematic scrutiny than the crimes committed against Germans.[114] Those calling in the 1980s for West Germans to escape the "shadow of Hitler" paid little attention to the fact that in the 1950s, Hitler's shadow hardly obscured a West German landscape filled with German suffering and accounts in which the real heroes were survivors of Communist aggression, not survivors of concentration camps.[115]

The call in the mid-1980s to link victims of Germans and German victims triggered vehement responses from many who protested Reagan's Bitburg visit, aggressively contested Hillgruber's juxtaposition of two "demises," and denounced Nolte's rejection of the singularity of Auschwitz. Jürgen Habermas questioned the motives of "whoever insists on mourning collective fates, without distinguishing between culprits and victims."[116] A minority opinion in the early postwar years, four decades after the war's end, Habermas's critique was endorsed and repeated with variations by a broad spectrum of West German historians, public intellectuals, and the president of the Federal Republic; this clearly distinguished debates over competing pasts in the 1980s from precedents in the 1950s. The past of Nazi crimes, described by Karl Jaspers, Eugen Kogon, and a handful of other critical observers in the late 1940s and early 1950s, had moved from the margins to center stage.[117] Still, it was by no means the only actor. The past of German victimization did not have to be written anew, because it was already in place.

Assessments in the late 1980s that the "historians' controversy" was over were premature. In the early 1990s, it was apparent that the issues raised in the rancorous exchanges among Hillgruber, Nolte, their allies and critics, and the politics of the Bitburg controversy were not isolated incidents but, rather, parts of a protracted debate over the relationship between history and memory in Germany, which entered into yet another stage following unification of east and west. In Germany after the *Wende* of 1989–1990, the search for a usable past remained no less pressing than it was in the immediate postwar years or the *Wende* of the 1980s.[118]

Even before May 1995, there were many indications that pasts of German victims and pasts of the victims of Germans were still vying for space and recognition in public consciousness. When Helmut Kohl addressed the first meeting of the parliament of a reunified Germany in October 1990, he began by calling for a moment's silence in honor of the victims of Nazism, moving without pause to call for the same measure of respect for the victims of Communism.[119] The controversy surrounding a memorial in Berlin that would commemorate victims of Nazi terror alongside German victims of the war provided additional evidence that Germans were still far from unified about whether they should "insist on mourning collective fates."[120]

Competing pasts also continued to face off in movie theaters. Steven Spielberg's *Schindler's List* played in Germany a year after Helke Sander's *Liberators Take Liberties* (in German, *BeFreier und Befreite*), which focused on the experience of women raped at the end of the war by Red Army soldiers. Joseph Vilsmaier's film *Stalingrad* marked another fiftieth anniversary and another form of commemoration that attracted nearly 1.5 million viewers; it was a movie that, in the words of *Die Zeit* columnist Andreas Kilb, "shows the Germans just as they most like to see themselves: as victims."[121]

The warning against forgetting in the advertisement that began this article was only one indication that the fiftieth anniversary of the end of the war was another moment for multiple commemorations, but the passing of the Cold War meant that 1995 would not be a repeat of 1985; President Bill Clinton's dilemma was not how to cram visits to Bergen-Belsen and Bitburg into a few hours but, rather, how to be at Arlington National Cemetery on the morning of one day and make it to Moscow by the next. The geopolitical politics of war and peace had shifted, and 1995 was a year for the United States to acknowledge other alliances, other pasts.

Still, the events of the spring of 1995 made it apparent that remembering the end of the war continues to define a central arena for debates over the relationship between history and political identity in a post–Cold War unified Germany. In his famous 1985 address to parliament, President Weizsäcker intoned a ritualistic call for German-German unity and maintained that "Germans are one people and one nation . . . because [we] have lived through the same past."[122] But fifty years after the war's end in a Germany now unified, the past looked no more one-dimensional than it did in 1945. A series in the liberal weekly *Die Zeit,* reflecting on "1945 and today," included installments on the Holocaust, soldiers, deserters, trials of Nazi war criminals, and crimes committed against Germans. In his contribution on the Holocaust, "The Elimination of a People," Elie Wiesel argued that the "Germans' attempt to kill the Jews of Europe remains a unique crime." Wiesel warned against attempts to "water down" the meaning of the Holocaust, a term that should be applied only to the attempts of Germans to eliminate European Jewry. Use of the term "genocide" also called for particular care. "We must be careful with words," Wiesel advised. "Language is very important, we must use it with care."[123] Contrary to Wiesel, Peter Glotz, writing on "The Sickness of Nationalism" and the expulsion of Germans from Eastern Europe, invoked a familiar comparison when he insisted that "the destruction of the Jewish people, planned by Hitler, was not the only genocide" of the twentieth century. "Genocidal" as well were all "expulsions that are carried out against the will of the population and without the possibility that it can be resettled altogether in one place."[124] As the *Spiegel* poll on the comparability of the expulsion and the Holocaust indicated, many Germans agreed with Glotz, not Wiesel. In the midst of the "historians' controversy," Nolte bemoaned the "past that will not pass." The forms of remembering the war's end ten years later revealed that there were still many pasts that would not pass.[125]

The commemorative ceremonies of May 1995 indicated that German reflections on the war's end were no longer framed by the global politics of the East-West conflict as they were when postwar West Germans bemoaned the loss of the "German East" in the 1950s and Reagan visited Bitburg thirty years later. In the context of the Cold War, crimes of Nazis in the past were easily tied to Communist crimes in the present. In his May 1985 speech, Weizsäcker insisted that it was essential for Germans to commemorate the date "amongst themselves." That internal process of introspection has become decidedly easier after the dramatic transformation of relations between East and West beginning in the late 1980s; as a front-page headline in *Die Zeit* announced in September 1994, with the withdrawal of the last Russian troops from Germany, "Only now is the war over."[126]

To be sure, how Germans and post-Communist nations in Eastern Europe remember the war that ended in 1945 will continue to shape their relations. Before 1989, Hillgruber's invocation of a history in which Germany served as a bridge—rather than a dividing line—between East and West could be called a "geopolitics of nostalgia," and in the midst of the "historians' controversy," no one would have predicted that the bridge would be reconstructed quite so rapidly.[127] Now it is in place. As Germans and their East European neighbors confront this dramatically altered reality, it will be important to see whether the legacy of Nazi occupation and the ravages of the SS and the Wehrmacht will inevitably be juxtaposed to the legacy of the expulsion.[128] As new democracies to Germany's east leave the shadow of the former Soviet Union, they will reassess their own histories of occupation by the Nazis, collaboration, and resistance. Former East Germans will also unearth their history as victims of the war and postwar Soviet occupation, erased by a Communist regime that euphemistically referred to the Soviet imprisonment of German soldiers as anti-fascist re-education and called the postwar expulsion of ethnic Germans a population transfer.[129] How Germans and East Europeans come to terms with their intersecting pasts will have an important influence on both foreign diplomacy and on the shape of new political identities domestically.

In addition, more than fifty years after the war's end, categories of complicity and responsibility do not carry the same highly personal meanings for Germans. Commenting on the "historians' controversy," the novelist and social critic Peter Schneider remarked, "When German historians address the past, they do so not only as scholars, but necessarily as participants too."[130] The commemoration in 1995 could well be the last major one of the end of World War II in which large numbers of participants will be alive to offer their perspectives. The second postwar generation participates in a national identity powerfully shaped by historical memory, but it was neither on the eastern front with Hillgruber, nor operating anti-aircraft guns on the home front at the war's end, nor in concentration camps or exile.

In the sixth decade after the war's end, however, the German search for a usable past is not at an end. It must involve not only the continued study of National Socialism, European Jewry before the Holocaust, the "final solution," World War II, the emergence of the Cold War, and the postwar settlement in

Central Europe but also a clearer understanding of how Germans came to terms with these pasts in the early history of the Federal Republic.[131] In the 1950s, most West Germans were able to interpret their experience only in absolute moral categories; a nation of victims confronted a handful of perpetrators. The forceful reemergence of this postwar history in the 1980s and 1990s indicates how vivid this image of the past remains.

Perhaps it is difficult to find new positions from which to assess the significance of the war's end and to incorporate an adequate account of this past into modern German history because of the problems inherent in the binary opposition of perpetrator and victim, categories that in turn imply guilt and innocence. Choosing between these two positions was the option Hillgruber seemed to offer Germans in his call for historical empathy. But in the Third Reich, if some Germans lived such absolute choices, most did not. An account of May 1945 that did not pit one past against another would deny no victim the ability to mourn, but it would follow Habermas in insisting that "mourning collective fates" is inappropriate. It would avoid any tendency to establish the moral equivalence of the victims of Germans and German victims, just as it would reject an analysis that explained the suffering of all Germans as the quid pro quo for the suffering inflicted on others by the National Socialist state. It would also move beyond a language in which the categories of victim and perpetrator were mutually exclusive; it would seek to capture the complexities of individual lives and "mass fates" by exploring how during the Third Reich it was possible both to suffer and to cause suffering in others.

Notes

1. Richard H. Kohn, "History and the Culture Wars: The Case of the Smithsonian Institution's *Enola Gay* Exhibition," *Journal of American History* 82 (1995): 1036–63, part of a special issue that devoted considerable space to a discussion of the controversy; also see Nicholas D. Kristof, "The Bomb: An Act That Haunts Japan and America," *New York Times,* August 6, 1995; Ian Buruma, "The War over the Bomb," *New York Review of Books* 42, no. 14 (September 21, 1995): 26–34.

2. Nicholas D. Kristof, "Japan Divided on Apology to Asians," *New York Times,* March 6, 1995; Kristof, "Japan Confronting Gruesome War Atrocity," *New York Times,* March 17, 1995; Kristof, "Why Japan Hasn't Said That Word," *New York Times,* May 7, 1995; Kristof, "Japan Expresses Regret of a Sort for the War," *New York Times,* June 7, 1995; Teresa Watanabe and Mary Williams Walsh, "Facing the Demons of War Guilt," *Los Angeles Times,* August 13, 1995; and Charles Smith, "War and Remembrance," *Far Eastern Economic Review* (August 25, 1994): 22–26. My thanks to Katherine Ragsdale for calling my attention to these references. See also John W. Dower, "Triumphal and Tragic Narratives of the War in Asia," *Journal of American History* 82 (1995): 1130–31; and Michael J. Hogan, ed., *Hiroshima in History and Memory* (Cambridge, 1996).

3. "8. Mai 1945: Gegen das Vergessen," *Frankfurter Allgemeine Zeitung,* April 7, 1995. My thanks to Thomas Schmitz, who first called my attention to the ad.

4. Stephen Kinzer, "Germans More Willing to Confront Nazi Crimes," *New York Times,* May 1, 1995; and "Lust am Erinnern," *Der Spiegel* no. 17 (April 24, 1995):

18–21. For less optimistic analyses of the "Initiative 8. Mai 1945," the group responsible for the April 7 advertisement, see Ralph Giordano, "Auch die Unfähigkeit zu
trauern ist unteilbar," *die tageszeitung,* April 18, 1995; Richard Herzigen, "Strategen
der Retourkutsche," *die tageszeitung,* April 15–16, 1995; and Mary Williams Walsh,
"V-E Day Events Present Paradox for German Psyche," *Los Angeles Times,* May 5,
1995.

5. See "Die Jungen denken anders," *Der Spiegel* no. 19 (May 8, 1995): 76–77; also
William Tuohy, "German Leader Stirs Flap as Britons Recall Beating Nazis," *Los
Angeles Times,* May 7, 1995; Roger Boyes, "What Did You Do in the War, Hans?"
The Times, May 6, 1995; Stephen Kinzer, "Allies and Former Enemies Gather to
Pledge Peace," *New York Times,* May 9, 1995.

6. This article does not address the forms of commemorating the war's end in the
former German Democratic Republic. For a comparative perspective on the late 1940s
and 1950s in the two Germanies, see Jürgen Danyel. "Die geteilte Vergangenheit:
Gesellschaftliche Ausgangslagen und politische Dispositionen für den Umgang mit
Nationalsozialismus und Widerstand in beiden deutschen Staaten nach 1949," in *His-
torische DDR-Forschung: Aufsätze und Studien,* Jürgen Kocka, ed. (Berlin, 1993),
129–47; and Werner Bergmann, Rainer Erb, and Albert Lichtblau, eds., *Schwieriges
Erbe: Der Umgang mit dem Nationalsozialismus und Antisemitismus in Österreich,
der DDR und der Bundesrepublik Deutschland* (Frankfurt am Main, 1995).

7. *Verhandlungen des deutschen Bundestages* (Bonn, 1950) (hereafter, *VDBT*) (1.)
Deutscher Bundestag, 252, Sitzung, March 4, 1953, 12092.

8. Kurt W. Böhme, *Die deutschen Kriegsgefangenen in sowjetischer Hand: Eine
Bilanz* (Munich, 1966), 151. A lower estimate of 2.3 to 2.8 million is offered by Ste-
fan Karner, "Verlorene Jahre: Deutsche Kriegsgefangene und Internierte im Archipel
GUPWI," in *Kriegsgefangene—Voennoplennye: Sowjetische Kriegsgefangene in
Deutschland, Deutsche Kriegsgefangene in der Sowjetunion,* Haus der Geschichte der
Bundesrepublik, ed. (Düsseldorf, 1995), 59; also Karner, *Im Archipel GUPVI: Kriegs-
gefangenschaft und Internierung in der Sowjetunion 1941–1956* (Munich, 1995), 9.
Recent revelations in Russian archives may call for an upward revision of the num-
ber of prisoners of war and suggest that all previous counts are estimates at best. See
Günther Wagenlehner, "Zweimal einem Wahn geopfert," *Das Parlament* nos. 18–19
(April 28–May 5, 1995): 7. In general, on expellees, see Gerhard Reichling, "Flucht
und Vertreibung der Deutschen: Statistische Grundlage und terminologische Prob-
leme," in *Flüchtlinge und Vertriebene in der westdeutschen Nachkriegsgeschichte:
Bilanzierung der Forschung und Perspektiven für die künftige Forschungsarbeit,* Rainer
Schulze, Doris von der Brelie-Lewien, and Helga Grebing, eds. (Hildesheim, 1987),
46–56.

9. Alexander Mitscherlich and Margarete Mitscherlich, *Die Unfähigkeit zu trauern:
Grundlagen kollektiven Verhaltens* (Munich, 1967), 19. I have also benefited greatly
from the lucid discussion of Eric L. Santner, *Stranded Objects: Mourning, Memory,
and Film in Postwar Germany* (Ithaca, N.Y., 1990), 1–6. See also Theodor W. Adorno,
"What Does Coming to Terms with the Past Mean?" in *Bitburg in Moral and Political Perspective,* Geoffrey Hartmann, ed. (Bloomington, Ind., 1986), 114–29.

10. See, for example, the characteristic formulation of this position in Wolfgang
Benz, "Postwar Society and National Socialism: Remembrance, Amnesia, Rejection,"
Tel Aviver Jahrbuch für deutsche Geschichte 19 (1990): 2. For critical perspectives,
see Hermann Graml, "Die verdrängte Auseinander-setzung mit dem Nationalsozialismus," in *Zäsuren nach 1945: Essays zur Periodisierung des deutschen Nachkriegsgeschichte,* Martin Broszat, ed. (Munich, 1990), 169–83; Manfred Kittel, *Die Legende
von der "zweiten Schuld": Vergangenheitsbewältigung in der Ära Adenauer* (Frankfurt am Main, 1993); Christa Hoffmann, *Stunden Null? Vergangenheitsbewältigung*

in Deutschland 1945 bis 1989 (Bonn, 1992); Udo Wengst, "Geschichtswissenschaft und 'Vergangenheitsbewältigung' in Deutschland nach 1945 und nach 1989/90," *Geschichte in Wissenschaft und Unterricht* 46 (1995): 189–205; and, focusing particularly on the ways in which women's experiences as victims became central to the definition of a West German national identity in the first postwar decade, Elizabeth Heineman, "The Hour of the Woman: Memories of Germany's 'Crisis Years' and West German National Identity," *AHR* 101 (April 1996): 354–95.

11. *VDBT* (1.) Deutscher Bundestag, 5. Sitzung, September 20, 1949, 27–29.

12. For a good account, see Lily Gardner Feldman. *The Special Relationship between West Germany and Israel* (Boston, 1984), 32–86; also Kai von Jena, "Versöhnung mit Israel? Die deutschisraelischen Verhandlungen bis zum Wiedergutmachungsabkommen von 1952," *Vierteljahrshefte für Zeitgeschichte* 34 (1986): 457–80; Yeshayahu A. Jelinek, "Political Acumen, Altruism, Foreign Pressure or Moral Debt: Konrad Adenauer and the 'Shilumim.'" *Tel Aviver Jahrbuch für deutsche Geschichte* 19 (1990): 77–102; Tom Segev, *The Seventh Million: The Israelis and the Holocaust,* Haim Watzman, trans. (New York, 1994), 189–252; and on postwar West German anti-Semitism, Frank Stern's superb study, *The Whitewashing of the Yellow Badge: Antisemitism and Philosemitism in Postwar Germany,* William Templer, trans. (Oxford, 1992).

13. Quoted in Rolf Vogel, ed., *Deutschlands Weg nach Israel: Eine Dokumentation mit einem Geleitwort von Konrad Adenauer* (Stuttgart, 1967), 36.

14. See Stern, *Whitewashing,* 372; and Michael Wolffsohn, "Das Wiedergutmachungsabkommen mit Israel: Eine Untersuchung bundesdeutscher und ausländischer Umfragen," in *Westdeutschland 1945–1955: Unterwerfung, Kontrolle, Integration,* Ludolf Herbst, ed. (Munich, 1986), 206–07.

15. The chief advocate of the position that Adenauer had little to gain from the Allies and acted out of genuine moral convictions is Michael Wolffsohn. See, for example, Wolffsohn, "Globalentschädigung für Israel und die Juden? Adenauer und die Opposition in der Bundesregierung," in *Wiedergutmachung in der Bundesrepublik Deutschland,* Ludolf Herbst and Constantin Goschler, eds. (Munich, 1989), 171–89. Most other interpretations place a far greater emphasis on the international context in general and American pressure in particular. See, for example, Jelinek, "Political Acumen."

16. See Michael Burleigh and Wolfgang Wippermann, *The Racial State: Germany, 1933–1945* (Cambridge, 1991), 125–57. In general, see Constantin Goschler, *Wiedergutmachung: Westdeutschland und die Verfolgten des Nationalsozialismus (1950–1954)* (Munich, 1992); also Christian Pross, *Wiedergutmachung: Der Kleinkrieg gegen die Opfer* (Frankfurt am Main, 1988); Herbst and Goschler, *Wiedergutmachung in der Bundesrepublik Deutschland;* Alf Lüdtke, "'Coming to Terms with the Past': Illusions of Remembering, Ways of Forgetting Nazism in West Germany," *Journal of Modern History* 65 (1993): 562–70; Robert G. Moeller, "The Homosexual Man Is a 'Man,' the Homosexual Woman is a 'Woman': Sex, Society, and the Law in Postwar West Germany," *Journal of the History of Sexuality* 4 (1994): 395–429; and Lutz Wiegand, "Kriegsfolgengesetzgebung in der Bundesrepublik Deutschland," *Archiv für Sozialgeschichte* 35 (1995): 73–77. The Sinti and Roma people are those referred to colloquially as Gypsies.

17. Anson Rabinbach, "The Jewish Question in the German Question," in *Reworking the Past: Hitler, the Holocaust, and the Historians' Debate,* Peter Baldwin, ed. (Boston, 1990), 49–51.

18. Goschler, *Wiedergutmachung,* 94, 169–70, 201.

19. *VDBT* (1.) Deutscher Bundestag, 252. Sitzung, March 4, 1953, 12084–90; *VDBT,* 254. Sitzung, March 18, 1953, 12236–51.

20. Konrad Wittmann, *VDBT* (1.) Deutscher Bundestag, 115. Sitzung, January 31, 1951, 4374. Wittmann had been expelled from the Sudetenland after the war.

21. Margarete Hütter, *VDBT* (1.) Deutscher Bundestag, 271. Sitzung, June 12, 1953, 13430.

22. Marlis G. Steinert, *Hitler's War and the Germans' Public Mood and Attitude during the Second World War,* Thomas E. J. de Witt, ed. and trans. (Athens, Ohio, 1977), 287; and Wolfram Wette, "Das Russlandbild in der NS-Propaganda: Ein Problemaufriss," in *Das Russlandbild im Dritten Reich,* Hans-Erich Volkmann, ed. (Cologne, 1994), 75.

23. Goschler, *Wiedergutmachung,* 203.

24. See, for example, Richard Reitzner, *VDBT* (1.) Deutscher Bundestag, 254. Sitzung, March 18, 1953, 12236. Reitzner had been active in the Czech Social Democratic Party until his emigration to England in 1938.

25. In general, on the ways in which opposition to Allied occupation provided a basis for unity, spanning the political spectrum, see Barbara Marshall, "German Attitudes to British Military Government 1945–1947," *Journal of Contemporary History* 15 (1980): 655–84; and Josef Foschepoth, "Zur deutschen Reaktion auf Niederlage und Besatzung," in Herbst, *Westdeutschland 1945–1955,* 151–65.

26. Representative of the ubiquitous charge that the Potsdam Agreement had created the enormous expellee problem are the comments of Eugen Gerstenmaier, *VDBT* (1.) Deutscher Bundestag, 48. Sitzung, March 17, 1950, 1657.

27. Hans Merten, *VDBT* (1.) Deutscher Bundestag, 233. Sitzung, October 9, 1952, 10680. I am much indebted to the insightful analysis of James M. Diehl, *The Thanks of the Fatherland: German Veterans after the Second World War* (Chapel Hill, N.C., 1993). See also Michael L. Hughes, "Restitution and Democracy in Germany after Two World Wars," *Contemporary European History* 4 (1994): 1–18; and Reinhold Schillinger, *Der Entscheidungsprozess beim Lastenausgleich 1945–1952* (St. Katharinen, 1985).

28. Hans Günter Hockerts, "Integration der Gesellschaft: Gründungskrise und Sozialpolitik in der frühen Bundesrepublik," *Zeitschrift für Sozialreform* 32 (1986): 25–41; and on the law to "equalize burdens," Schillinger, *Der Entscheidungsprozess.*

29. The most detailed study of the *Lastenausgleichsgesetz* is offered by Schillinger, *Der Entscheidungsprozess;* see also Wiegand, "Kriegsfolgengesetzgebung," 77–90. And on measures for veterans, see Diehl, *Thanks.*

30. On Weimar, see Michael L. Hughes, *Paying for the German Inflation* (Chapel Hill, N.C., 1988); and Hughes, "Restitution and Democracy."

31. Diehl, *Thanks,* provides an excellent account of those organizations that represented veteran interests; on expellee organizations, see also Schillinger, *Der Entscheidungsprozess,* 150–51, 183–86, 204; Marx Hildebert Boehm, "Gruppenbildung und Organisationswesen," in *Die Vertriebenen in Westdeutschland: Ihre Eingliederung und ihr Einfluss auf Gesellschaft, Wirtschaft, Politik und Geistesleben,* Eugen Lemberg and Friedrich Edding, eds., 3 vols. (Kiel, 1959), 1: 523–605; Wolf Donner, *Die sozial- und staatspolitische Tätigkeit der Kriegsopferverbände* (Berlin, 1960); and Hermann Weiss, "Die Organisation der Vertriebenen und ihre Presse," in *Die Vertreibung der Deutschen aus dem Osten: Ursache, Ereignisse, Folgen,* Wolfgang Benz, ed. (Frankfurt am Main, 1985), 193–202.

32. See, for example, Bundesministerium der Finanzen, *Flüchtlingslasten und Verteidigungsbeitrag: Zwei sich ergänzende und begrenzende Belastungen* (n.p., 1951); also Schäffer's comments, *VDBT* (1.) Deutscher Bundestag, 115. Sitzung, January 31, 1951, 4340.

33. Diehl, *Thanks,* 242; and on expellees, see Everhard Holtmann, "Flüchtlinge in den 50er Jahren: Aspekte ihrer gesellschaftlichen und politischen Integration," in

Modernisierung im Wiederaufbau: Die westdeutsche Gesellschaft der 50er Jahre, Axel Schildt and Arnold Sywottek, eds. (Bonn, 1993), 358–59.

34. See Karl Heinz Gehrmann, "Kulturpflege und Kulturpolitik," in Lemberg and Edding, *Die Vertriebenen,* 3: 183; Eugen Lemberg, "Das Bildungswesen vor neuen Aufgaben," in *ibid.,* 3: 383, 385–86, 388–89, 398–99. For good examples of the scholarly attempts to fill this mandate, see Lemberg and Edding, *Die Vertriebenen;* for an overview of the literature, Hiddo M. Jolles, *Zur Soziologie der Heimatvertriebenen und Flüchtlinge* (Cologne, 1965), 18–29.

35. "Gräber und Stacheldraht: Schicksal von Millionen," *Stuttgarter Zeitung,* October 25, 1950, copy in Bundesarchiv-Militärarchiv (Freiburg i.B.) (hereafter, BAMF), B205/1143.

36. See, for instance, government planning for a day of remembrance for POWs in 1950 in Bundesarchiv (Koblenz) (hereafter, BAK), B150/4448, Heft 2; "Zur Kriegs-gefangenen-Gedenkwoche," radio address of President Theodor Heuss, October 9, 1952, BAMF, B205/1043; on the 1953 events, BAK, B150/8076; and in general, Peter Steinbach, "Jenseits von Zeit und Raum: Kriegsgefangenschaft in der Frühgeschichte der Bundesrepublik Deutschland," *Universitas* 7 (1990): 638; and Frank Stern, "The Historic Triangle: Occupiers, Germans and Jews in Postwar Germany," *Tel Aviver Jahrbuch für deutsche Geshichte* 19 (1990): 56.

37. See "Complaint of Failure on the Part of the Union of Soviet Socialist Republics to Repatriate or Otherwise Account for Prisoners of War Retained in Soviet Territory," United Nations General Assembly, Fifth Session, Third Committee, Agenda item 67, December 7, 1950, Politisches Archiv des Auswärtigen Amtes, Abt. 2/2073; also Karner, *Archipel GUPVI,* 201–04.

38. Jörn Rüsen, "Continuity, Innovation, and Self-Reflection in Late Historicism: Theodor Schieder (1908–1984)," in *Paths of Continuity: Central European Historiography from the 1930s to the 1950s,* Hartmut Lehmann and James Van Horn Melton, eds. (Cambridge, 1994), 353–88.

39. Klemens von Klemperer, "Hans Rothfels (1891–1976)," in Lehmann and Melton, *Paths of Continuity,* 127–32.

40. For useful reviews of postwar West German historiography, see James Van Horn Melton, "Introduction: Continuities in German Historical Scholarship, 1930–1960," in Lehmann and Melton, *Paths of Continuity,* 1–88; Winfried Schulze, "German Historiography from the 1930s to the 1950s," in *Paths of Continuity,* 19–42.

41. The entire series, published under the auspices of the Bundesministerium für Vertriebene, Flüchtlinge und Kriegsgeschädigte, is entitled *Dokumentation der Vertreibung der Deutschen aus Ost-Mitteleuropa.* The individual volumes, each prepared by a different team of members of the project but all appearing under the general editorship of Theodor Schieder, include: Vol. 1, *Die Vertreibung der deutschen Bevölkerung aus den Gebieten östlich der Oder-Neisse* (Grosse-Denkte/Wolfenbüttel, 1954), hereafter, *Oder-Neisse;* Vol. 2, *Das Schicksal der Deutschen in Ungarn* (Düsseldorf, 1956); Vol. 3, *Das Schicksal der Deutschen in Rumänien* (Berlin, 1957); Vol. 4, *Die Vertreibung der deutschen Bevölkerung aus der Tschechoslowakei* (Berlin, 1957), hereafter, *Tschechoslowakei;* Vol. 5, *Das Schicksal der Deutschen in Jugoslawien* (Düsseldorf, 1961), hereafter, *Jugoslawien;* Käthe von Normann, *Ein Tagebuch aus Pommern 1945–1946* (Gross-Denkte/Wolfenbüttel, 1955), 1. Beiheft; Margarete Schell, *Ein Tagebuch aus Prag 1945–46* (Kassel-Wilh., 1957), 2. Beiheft; and Hans Graf von Lehndorff, *Ein Bericht aus Ost- und Westpreussen 1945–1947* (Düsseldorf, 1960), 3. Beiheft. On the background of the project, see Josef Henke, "Exodus aus Ostpreussen und Schlesien: Vier Erlebnisberichte," in Benz, *Die Vertreibung der Deutschen aus dem Osten,* 91. In later citations, I have indicated the authors of individual accounts, the date the account was written, and the volume in which it appears.

42. *Oder-Neisse,* 1/1: iii–iv, vi: On the geographic distribution of the testimonies, see Kulturstiftung der deutschen Vertriebenen, ed., *Vertreibung und Vertreibungsverbrechen 1945–1948* (Bonn, 1989), 101–05.

43. "Dokumente des Grauens," *Stuttgarter Zeitung,* September 2, 1954, copy in BAK, B150/5641.

44. "Die deutsche Tragödie," *Westfälische Zeitung,* October 30, 1957; and "Zeitgeschichte in Dokumenten," *Westdeutsche Allgemeine,* September 5, 1958, copies in BAK, B150/5643.

45. For example, see "Bericht des ehemaligen Bezirksbürgermeisters H. aus Breslau. Beglaubigte Abschrift (1946)," in *Oder-Neisse,* 1/2: 327–36. This was an exceptional testimony, because H. identified himself as a Jew and an "anti-fascist," and because he had been put in his position as mayor by the Russian forces. For a fuller discussion of this documentation project, see Robert G. Moeller, "Driven into 'Contemporary History': The Expulsion from the East in the Public Memory of the Federal Republic of Germany," Working Paper 5.30: Center for German and European Studies, University of California, Berkeley (May 1995).

46. Carl Schuster. "Kriegsgefangene schreiben Zeitgeschichte," *Aachner Volkszeitung,* April 19, 1961, copy in BAMF, B205/6. See "Entwurf für eine 'Dokumentation des Schicksals der deutschen Gefangenen des 2. Weltkrieges,'" prepared by the minister for Expellees, Refugees and War-Damaged, May 23, 1957, BAMF, B205/1720a.

47. See the notes on the discussion of the documentation staff in Munich, January 14, 1958, BAMF, B205/1754.

48. On Maschke's background, including his service in the educational and political work of the Nazi party and the SA, see Michael Burleigh, *Germany Turns Eastwards: A Study of "Ostforschung" in the Third Reich* (Cambridge, 1988), 137.

49. Erich Maschke, "Deutsche Kriegsgefangenengeschichte: Der Gang der Forschung," in *Die deutschen Kriegsgefangenen des zweiten Weltkrieges: Eine Zusammenfassung,* Erich Maschke, ed. (Munich, 1974), 3–37; and Maschke, "Quellen und Methoden," *ibid.,* 41–59; Steinbach, "Jenseits von Zeit und Raum," 637–49. The series title is *Zur Geschichte der deutschen Kriegsgefangenen des zweiten Weltkrieges.* On the background of the project, see Rolf Steininger, "Some Reflections on the Maschke Commission," in *Eisenhower and the German POWs: Facts against Falsehood,* Günther Bischof and Stephen E. Ambrose, eds. (Baton Rouge, La., 1992), 170–80.

50. In general, see Arthur L. Smith, *Heimkehr aus dem Zweiten Weltkrieg: Die Entlassung der deutschen Kriegsgefangenen* (Stuttgart, 1985), 151–69; and Dieter Bach and Jochen Leyendecker, eds., *"Ich habe geweint vor Hunger": Deutsche und russische Gefangene in Lagern des zweiten Weltkriegs* (Wuppertal, 1993). The analysis offered here is based only on the volumes that describe conditions in Eastern Europe and the Soviet Union.

51. See, in particular, Hedwig Fleischhacker, *Die deutschen Kriegsgefangenen in der Sowjetunion: Der Faktor Hunger* (Bielefeld, 1965).

52. Erich Maschke, "Grundzüge der sowjetischen Wirtschaftsgeschichte bis 1955: Der Rahmen der deutschen Kriegsgefangenschaft," in Werner Ratza, *Die deutschen Kriegsgefangenen in der Sowjetunion: Der Faktor Arbeit* (Bielefeld, 1973), xiii. Quotation in Diether Cartellieri, *Die deutschen Kriegsgefangenen in der Sowjetunion: Die Lagergesellschaft; Eine Untersuchung der zwischenmenschlichen Beziehungen in den Kriegsgefangenenlagern* (Bielefeld, 1967), 253, 259–60.

53. Böhme, *Die deutschen Kriegsgefangenen,* 151, 282–300.

54. Wolfgang Schwarz, *Die deutschen Kriegsgefangenen in der Sowjetunion: Aus dem kulturellen Leben* (Bielefeld, 1969), 34; and "Erlebnisbericht der Schneiderin

Anna Schwartz aus Schönberge, Kreis Karthaus i. Westpr. . . . 5. Juni 1952," in *Oder-Neisse,* 1/2: 103.

55. Schell, *Ein Tagebuch aus Prag 1945–46,* 50, 106; also see "Erlebnisbericht der Hausfrau A. F. aus Königsberg i. Ostpr. . . .25. November 1952," in *Oder-Neisse,* 1/1: 130; Diehl, *Thanks,* 231. On the intersecting fates of POWs and expellees, see Michael Reck, *Tagebuch aus sowjetischer Kriegsgefangenschaft 1945–1949: Aufzeichnungen,* Beiheft 1, *Zur Geschichte der deutschen Kriegsgefangenen des zweiten Weltkrieges,* Erich Maschke, ed. (Bielefeld, 1967), 14; and "Erlebnisbericht der Regierungsangestellten Elisabeth Erbrich aus Breslau . . . April 1946," in *Oder-Neisse,* 1/1: 444.

56. See the suggestive comments of Utz Jeggle, "Sage und Verbrechen," in Schulze, Brelie-Lewien, and Grebing, *Flüchtlinge und Vertriebene,* 201–06; also see Albrecht Lehmann, *Im Fremden ungewollt zuhaus: Flüchtlinge und Vertriebene in Westdeutschland* (Munich, 1991), 240–41; Alexander von Plato, "Fremde Heimat: Zur Integration von Flüchtlingen und Einheimischen in die neue Zeit," in *"Wir kriegen jetzt andere Zeiten": Auf der Suche nach der Erfahrung des Volkes in nachfaschistischen Ländern,* Lutz Niethammer and Alexander von Plato, eds. (Berlin, 1985), 198–99; and the parallels in women's memoirs, suggested by Heineman, "Hour of the Woman," 359–60; and Robert G. Moeller, *Protecting Motherhood: Women and the Family in the Politics of Postwar West Germany* (Berkeley, Calif., 1993), 8–14.

57. "Erlebnisbericht der Frau Maria Zatschek aus Brünn" (n.d.), in *Tschechoslowakei,* 4/2: 439; also see "Bericht des Studienrats Dr. rer. nat. Hans Enders aus Saaz . . . , 15. November 1946," in *ibid.,* 4/2: 300.

58. Schwarz, *Die deutschen Kriegsgefangenen,* 34.

59. Editor's introduction, *Tschechoslowakei,* 4/1: 81; see also editor's introduction, *Oder-Neisse,* 1/1: 111E; "Bericht des Kaufmanns E. M. aus Saaz . . . November 1945," in *Tschechoslowakei,* 4/2: 313, and note 2, *ibid.*

60. "Bericht des Kaplan Paul Pfuhl aus Filipovo . . . Original, 19. Oktober 1956," in *Jugoslawien,* 5: 261.

61. Schell, *Ein Tagebuch aus Prag 1945–46,* 34, note 1; and "Bericht des Organisationssekretärs Roman Wirkner aus Tetschen. Original, 1957," in *Tschechoslowakei,* 4/2: 527.

62. "Erlebnisbericht (Brief) des Kaufmanns und ehemaligen Stadtrats Hubert Schütz sen. aus Jägendorf. Beglaubigte Abschrift . . . 4. Januar 1947," in *Tschechoslowakei,* 4/2: 216.

63. Erich Maschke, "Deutsche Kriegsgefangenengeschichte: Der Gang der Forschung," in Maschke, *Die deutschen Kriegsgefangenen des Zweiten Weltkrieges: Eine Zusammenfassung,* 34–37; and Albrecht Lehmann, *Gefangenschaft und Heimkehr: Deutsche Kriegsgefangene in der Sowjetunion* (Munich, 1986), 168–69.

64. Erich Maschke, "Das Schicksal der deutschen Kriegsgefangenen des Zweiten Weltkrieges als Aufgabe zeitgeschichtlicher Forschung," in *Die deutschen Kriegsgefangenen in Jugoslawien 1941–1949,* Kurt W. Böhme, ed., Vol. 1, pt. 1 (Bielefeld, 1962), xi.

65. On the importance of this recognition, denied other groups of victims, see William G. Niederland, "Die verkannten Opfer: Späte Entschädigung für seelische Schäden," in Goschler and Herbst, *Wiedergutmachung,* 359; and Ulrich Herbert, "Nicht entschädigungsfähig? Die Wiedergutmachungsansprüche der Ausländer," in *ibid.,* 302.

66. Louis Ferdinand Helbig, *Der ungeheuere Verlust: Flucht und Vertreibung in der deutschsprachigen Belletristik der Nachkriegszeit* (Wiesbaden, 1988); and Karl Heinz Gehrmann, "Versuche der literarischen Bewältigung," in Lemberg and Edding, *Die Vertriebenen,* 3: 273–317. On the work of the Verband der Heimkehrer, the most important organization of returning POWs, see Verband der Heimkehrer, Kriegsgefangenen

und Vermisstenangehörigen Deutschlands, ed., *Freiheit ohne Furcht: Zehn Jahre Heimkehrerverband* (n.p. [1960]); and *idem, Wir mahnen: Kriegsgefangenschaft als Erlebnis und Aufgabe* (n.p., n.d.).

67. See Schieder, "Gutachten über eine Dokumentation," October 1, 1951, BAK B150/4171/Heft 1; and "Aufzeichunung über die Besprechung über die Fortführung der Dokumentation im Bundesministerium für Vertriebene am 13.7.51," BAK B150/4171/Heft 1.

68. See, for example, Heinz-Arndt Brüggemann, "Zwei Hände waren wie ein Symbol," *Westdeutsche Allgemeine,* October 10, 1955; Rudolf Weschinsky, "Alle Herzen sagen: Willkommen in der Heimat," *Hamburger Abendblatt,* October 10, 1955; and Dietrich Schwarzkopf, " 'Jetzt bist du ein freier deutscher Bürger,' " *Der Tagesspiegel,* October 15, 1955.

69. Hans-Peter Schwarz, *Die Ära Adenauer: Gründerjahre der Republik 1949–1957* (Stuttgart, 1981), 279; also Josef Foschepoth, "Adenauers Moskaureise 1955," *Aus Politik und Zeitgeschichte* B22 (1986): 30–46.

70. Gertrud Koch, Klaus Konz, Wolfgang Oehrle, Gundula Schmidt, and Barbara Wilzcek, "Die fünfziger Jahre: Heide und Silberwald," in *Der deutsche Heimatfilm: Bildwelten und Weltbilder,* Dieter Bahlinger, *et al.,* eds. (Tübingen, 1989), 88. Quotations are from Heide Fehrenbach, *Cinema in a Democratizing Germany: Reconstructing National Identity after Hitler* (Chapel Hill, N.C., 1995), 153; see also Gerhard Bliersbach, *So grün war die Heide: Der Nachkriegsfilm in neuer Sicht* (Weinheim, 1985), 39–41; Willi Höfig, *Der deutsche Heimatfilm 1947–1960* (Stuttgart, 1973), 279; and Anton Kaes. *From Hitler to Heimat: The Return of History as Film* (Cambridge, Mass., 1989), 14–15.

71. See the highly sympathetic treatment of Helbig, *Der ungeheuere Verlust:* also Klaus Weigelt, ed., *Flucht und Vertreibung in der Nachkriegsliteratur: Formen ostdeutscher Kulturförderung* (Melle, 1986).

72. See Jochen Pfeifer, *Der deutsche Kriegsroman 1945–1960: Ein Versuch zur Vermittlung von Literatur und Sozialgeschichte* (Königstein/Ts., 1981); Jost Hermand, "Darstellungen des Zweiten Weltkrieges," in *Literatur nach 1945,* Vol. 1: *Politische und Regionale Aspekte,* Jost Hermand, ed. (Wiesbaden, 1979), 28–39; Hans Wagener, "Soldaten zwischen Gehorsam und Gewissen: Kriegsromane und-tagebücher," in *Gegenwartsliteratur und Drittes Reich: Deutsche Autoren in der Auseinandersetzung mit der Vergangenheit,* Hans Wagener, ed. (Stuttgart, 1977), 241–61; Michael Kumpfmüller, *Die Schlacht von Stalingrad: Metamorphosen eines deutschen Mythos* (Munich, 1995), 199–237; Jens Ebert, ed., *Stalingrad: Eine deutsche Legende* (Reinbek bei Hamburg, 1992), 96–97; and Gerd Albrecht, "Fern der Wirklichkeit: Deutsche Spielfilme der Nachkriegszeit zum Thema Kriegsgefangenschaft und Heimkehr," in *Kriegsgefangene—Voennoplennye,* 101.

73. For a review of this literature, see Theo J. Schulte, *The German Army and Nazi Policies in Occupied Russia* (Oxford, 1989), 3–7; and on the postwar period, Detlef Bald, " 'Bürger in Uniform': Tradition und Neuanfang des Militärs in Westdeutschland," in Schildt and Sywottek, *Modernisierung im Wiederaufbau,* 392–402.

74. Georg Meyer, "Innenpolitische Voraussetzung der westdeutschen Wiederbewaffnung," in *Wiederbewaffnung in Deutschland nach 1945,* Alexander Fischer, ed. (Berlin, 1986), 31–44; and Roland G. Foerster, "Innenpolitische Aspekte der Sicherheit Westdeutschlands (1945–1950)," in *Anfänge westdeutscher Sicherheitspolitik,* Vol. 1: *Von der Kapitulation bis zum Pleven-Plan,* Militärgeschichtliches Forschungsamt, ed. (Munich, 1982), 430, 437, 497, 540, 552–53.

75. "Dokumente des Grauens," *Stuttgarter Zeitung,* September 2, 1954; "Katastrophen der Deutschen-Vertreibung aus dem Osten in Dokumenten," *Westdeutsche Allgemeine,* May 6, 1954, copies in BAK, B150/5641.

76. Helmut Peitsch, *"Deutschlands Gedächtnis an seine dunkelste Zeit"*: *Zur Funktion der Autobiographik in den Westzonen Deutschlands und den Westsektoren von Berlin 1945 bis 1949* (Berlin, 1990).

77. *Oder-Neisse,* 1/1: 348–50; 1/2: 54–56, 57–59, 593–606, 626–46.

78. Otto D. Kulka, "Major Trends and Tendencies in German Historiography on National Socialism and the 'Jewish Question' (1924–1984)," *Yearbook of the Leo Baeck Institute* 30 (1985): 222. See also the useful reflections of Dan Diner, "Zwischen Bundesrepublik und Deutschland: Ein Vortrag," in *Von der Gnade der geschenkten Nation,* Hajo Funke, ed. (Berlin, 1988), 194–95; and Lüdtke, "Coming to Terms with the Past," 558–60. Rare exceptions to this rule were Eugen Kogon, *Der NS-Staat: Das System der deutschen Konzentrationslager* (Munich, 1946); H. G. Adler, *Theresienstadt 1941–1945: Das Antlitz einer Zwangsgemeinschaft* (Tübingen, 1955); and Adler, *Die verheimlichte Wahrheit: Theresienstädter Dokumente* (Tübingen, 1958).

79. Hans Rothfels, "Zehn Jahre danach" [Ten years after], *Vierteljahrshefte für Zeitgeschichte* 3 (1955): 228, 232, 237.

80. For a good introduction to the historiography on National Socialism, see Ian Kershaw, *The Nazi Dictatorship: Problems and Perspectives of Interpretation,* 3d edn. (London, 1993); and Bernd Faulenbach, "Emanzipation von der deutschen Tradition? Geschichtsbewusstsein in den sechziger Jahren," in *Politische Kultur und deutsche Frage: Materialien zum Staats- und Nationalbewusstsein in der Bundesrepublik Deutschland,* Werner Weidenfeld, ed. (Cologne, 1989), 73–92. I have also benefited enormously from the superb essay by Jane Caplan, "The Historiography of National Socialism" (forthcoming).

81. In general, see Adalbert Rückerl, *NS-Verbrechen vor Gericht: Versuch einer Vergangenheitsbewältigung* (Heidelberg, 1982); and Jürgen Weber and Peter Steinbach, eds., *Vergangenheitsbewältigung durch Strafverfahren? NS-Prozesse in der Bundesrepublik Deutschland* (Munich, 1984).

82. The literature on *Ostpolitik* is vast. For an introduction, see Timothy Garton Ash, *In Europe's Name: Germany and the Divided Continent* (New York, 1993).

83. Hans Graf von Lehndorff, *Ostpreussisches Tagebuch: Aufzeichnungen eines Arztes aus den Jahren 1945–1947* (Munich, 1966). Käthe von Normann, *Tagebuch aus Pommern 1945/46,* another of the diaries published in the expellee project, also appeared in an inexpensive paperback edition, published by Deutscher Taschenbuch Verlag in Munich, 1962.

84. See, for example, Hans Edgar Jahn, *Pommersche Passion* (Preetz/Holstein, 1964); Rolf O. Becker, *Niederschlesien 1945: Die Flucht—Die Besetzung* (Bad Nauheim, 1965); and Wolfgang Schwarz, *Die Flucht und Vertreibung: Oberschlesien 1945/46* (Bad Nauheim, 1965). These volumes, though providing no specific citations, claimed to be based "on documents of the Bundesministerium für Vertriebene, Flüchtlinge und Kriegsgeschädigte" and the "documents from the Bundesarchiv in Koblenz." See also Karl Friedrich Grau, *Schlesisches Inferno: Kriegsverbrechen der Roten Armee beim Einbruch in Schlesien 1945* (Stuttgart, 1966); Egbert Kieser, *Danziger Bucht 1945: Dokumentation einer Katastrophe* (Esslingen am Neckar, 1978); Fritz Brustat-Naval, *Unternehmen Rettung* (Herford, 1970); Günter Böddeker, *Die Flüchtlinge: Die Vertreibung der Deutschen im Osten* (Munich, 1980); Donauschwäbische Kulturstiftung, ed., *Leidensweg der Deutschen im kommunistischen Jugoslawien,* 2 vols. (Munich, 1992); and, for a detailed review of novels, Helbig, *Der ungeheuere Verlust.* The American author Alfred-Maurice de Zayas also contributed to this steady stream, publishing in both English and German. See most recently *A Terrible Revenge: The Ethnic Cleansing of the East European Germans, 1944–1950* (New York, 1994).

85. "Wieder ein Geheimdokument in Quick: Diesmal geht es um den grausamen Tod von 1,5 Millionen deutschen Soldaten," *Quick* no. 11, March 2, 1972. The series continued through July 17, 1972; Lothar Labusch, " 'Noch mal satt werden und dann Schluss': Dokumentation unter Verschluss," *Kölner Stadt-Anzeiger,* March 31–April 1, 1973, copy in BAMF, B205/5; and see Maschke's account of the political reasons for the delay of release of all volumes, Maschke, "Deutsche Kriegsgefangenengeschichte," 27–37.

86. In the 1950s, these institutes were often filled with historians who were themselves expellees and whose scholarly careers under the Nazis included "scientific" justification of the Nazis' expansionist policies. See Christoph Klessmann, "Geschichtsbewusstsein nach 1945: Ein neuer Anfang?" in *Geschichtsbewusstsein der Deutschen: Materialien zur Spurensuche einer Nation,* Werner Weidenfeld, ed. (Cologne, 1987), 118–19; Burleigh, *Germany Turns Eastwards,* 306, 313–14.

87. See, for example, Dieter Bingen, "Westverschiebung Polens und Revisionsanspruch der Bundesrepublik Deutschland: Die polnische Westgrenze als Stein des Anstosses in den polnisch-deutschen Beziehungen," in *Unfertige Nachbarschaften: Die Staaten Osteuropas und die Bundesrepublik Deutschland,* Othmar Nikola Haberl and Hans Hecker, eds. (Essen, 1989), 155–76; Werner Jakobsmeier, "Das Münchner Abkommen: Unüberbrückbarer Graben zwischen Bonn und Prag?" in *ibid.,* 177–203.

88. Dieter von König, "Auch Deutsche mussten leiden," *Rhein-Neckar-Zeitung,* July 31, 1974, copy in BAMF, B205/6.

89. Ivo Frenzel and Peter Märthesheimer, eds., *Im Kreuzfeuer: Der Fernsehfilm "Holocaust"* (Frankfurt am Main, 1979); Jeffrey Herf, "The 'Holocaust' Reception in West Germany: Right, Center and Left," *New German Critique* no. 19 (1980): 30–52.

90. Rudolf Mühlfenzl, ed., *Geflohen und vertrieben: Augenzeugen berichten* (Königstein/Ts., 1981), 8; and see the enthusiastic reception in "Persönliches Leid, kollektives Schicksal," *Süddeutsche Zeitung,* January 29, 1981; also "Die alten Wunden: Zur Dokumentation der Vertreibung im Fernsehen," *Frankfurter Allgemeine Zeitung,* January 29, 1981; and "Wahrheit ist keine Rache," *Die Welt,* February 7, 1981.

91. Gotthold Rhode, "Das Leid der Vertreibung: Zum Neudruck einer Dokumentation," *Frankfurter Allgemeine Zeitung,* May 14, 1985. See also Josef Henke, "Flucht und Vertreibung der Deutschen aus ihrer Heimat im Osten und Südosten 1944–1947," *Aus Politik und Zeitgeschichte* B23/85 (June 8, 1985): 15–44.

92. My thought on these subjects is particularly influenced by Kaes, *From Hitler to Heimat.*

93. Kaes, *From Hitler to Heimat,* 150; Barbara Kosta, *Recasting Autobiography: Women's Counterfictions in Contemporary German Literature and Film* (Ithaca, N.Y., 1994), 144; Richard W. McCormick, "Confronting German History: Melodrama, Distantiation, and Women's Discourse in *Germany, Pale Mother,*" in *Gender and German Cinema: Feminist Interventions,* Vol. 2: *German Film History/German History on Film,* Sandra Frieden, *et al.,* eds. (Providence, R.I., 1993), 201; the insightful review of the film by Jane Caplan, *AHR* 96 (October 1991): 1126–28; and Helma Sanders-Brahms, *Deutschland. bleiche Mutter: Film Erzählung* (Reinbek bei Hamburg, 1980), 71–80.

94. Mühlfenzl, *Geflohen,* 159.

95. Alexander Kluge, *Die Patriotin: Texte/Bilder 1–6* (Frankfurt am Main, 1979), 59.

96. Kaes, *From Hitler to Heimat,* 133; see also Omer Bartov, *Murder in Our Midst: The Holocaust, Industrial Killing and Representation* (New York, 1996), 139–52. Kluge's fascination with the battle of Stalingrad long predated the film. See Alexander

Kluge, *The Battle,* Leila Vennewitz, trans. (New York, 1967) (orig. pub. as *Schlacht-beschreibung,* 1964).

97. Kenneth Barkin's review of the movie, *AHR* 96 (October 1991): 1124; Sant-ner, *Stranded Objects,* 60; and in general, the thoughtful treatment of Kaes, *From Hitler to Heimat,* 163–92.

98. Karsten Witte, "Of the Greatness of the Small People: The Rehabilitation of a Genre," *New German Critique* no. 36 (1985): 6; also see Gertrud Koch, "How Much Naiveté Can We Afford? The New *Heimat* Feeling," *ibid.,* 13–16; Kenneth D. Barkin, "Modern Germany: A Twisted Vision." *Dissent* 34 (1987): 252–55.

99. "Address by Chancellor Helmut Kohl to German and American Soldiers and Their Families at Bitburg, May 5, 1985," in Hartmann, *Bitburg,* 256. Hartmann's col-lection is an excellent source of key documents on the controversy surrounding Rea-gan's trip. "Remarks of President Ronald Reagan to Regional Editors, White House, April 18, 1985," in Hartmann, *Bitburg,* 240.

100. "Speech by Richard von Weizsäcker, President of the Federal Republic of Germany, in the Bundestag during the Ceremony Commemorating the 40th Anniver-sary of the End of the War in Europe and of National Socialist Tyranny, May 8, 1985," in Hartmann, *Bitburg,* 263.

101. Timothy Garton Ash, "Germany after Bitburg," *New Republic* (July 15 and 22, 1985): 15–17, rpt. in Hartmann, *Bitburg,* 199–203.

102. "Schindluder mit der Friedenspolitik," *Der Spiegel* no. 6 (February 4, 1985): 93. See also " 'Die Polen sind Teil des Abendlandes': Der Vorsitzende der CDU/CSU-Fraktion, Alfred Dregger, über Ostpolitik und Vertriebene," *ibid.,* 95.

103. Among the most important are Geoff Eley, "Nazism, Politics and Public Mem-ory: Thoughts on the West German *Historikerstreit* 1986–1987," *Past and Present* 121 (November 1988): 171–208; Charles S. Maier, *The Unmasterable Past: History, Holo-caust, and German National Identity* (Cambridge, Mass., 1988); Richard J. Evans, *In Hitler's Shadow: West German Historians and the Attempt to Escape from the Nazi Past* (New York, 1989); the essays collected in Baldwin, *Reworking the Past;* and Saul Friedlander, ed., *Probing the Limits of Representation: Nazism and the "Final Solu-tion"* (Cambridge, Mass., 1992).

104. Andreas Hillgruber, *Zweierlei Untergang: Die Zerschlagung des Deutschen Reiches und das Ende des europäischen Judentums* (Berlin, 1986).

105. See Hans-Ulrich Wehler, *Entsorgung der Vergangenheit? Ein polemischer Essay zum "Historikerstreit"* (Munich, 1988), 20–23, 47.

106. See the insightful analysis of Bartov, *Murder,* 71–89.

107. Hillgruber, *Zweierlei Untergang,* 24–25.

108. Hillgruber, *Zweierlei Untergang.* See also Andreas Hillgruber, "Jürgen Habermas, Karl-Heinz Janssen und die Aufklärung Anno 1986," in *"Historikerstreit": Die Dokumentation der Kontroverse um die Einzigartigkeit der nationalsozialistis-chen Judenvernichtung* (Munich, 1987), 339. The documents are available in Eng-lish: *Forever in the Shadow of Hitler? Original Documents of the "Historikerstreit,"* the Controversy Concerning the Singularity of the Holocaust,* James Knowlton and Truett Cates, trans. (Atlantic Highlands, N.J., 1993). See also Wehler, *Entsorgung,* 164–65.

109. Wehler, *Entsorgung,* 15–17.

110. Bartov, *Murder,* 120, also see 86–88.

111. Saul Friedlander, *A Conflict of Memories? The New German Debates about the "Final Solution"* (New York, 1988), 14.

112. Rothfels, "Zehn Jahre danach," 232.

113. Michael Stürmer, "Kein Eigentum der Deutschen: Die deutsche Frage," in *Die Identität der Deutschen,* Werner Weidenfeld, ed. (Munich, 1983), 84.

114. Joachim Fest, "Die geschuldete Erinnerung: Zur Kontroverse über die Unvergleichbarkeit der nationalsozialistischen Massenverbrechen," *"Historikerstreit,"* 100.

115. There are interesting parallels with postwar French history, described by Henry Rousso in *The Vichy Syndrome: History and Memory in France since 1944,* Arthur Goldhammer, trans. (Cambridge, Mass., 1991). However, the "repressed" that returned in the 1970s in France was the repressed history of collaboration and French anti-Semitism. Another potential point of reference is the Japanese case, where memories of Japanese aggression and terror were far more completely submerged. See Carol Gluck, "The Past in the Present," in *Postwar Japan as History,* Andrew Gordon, ed. (Berkeley, Calif., 1993), 64–95; Dower, "Triumphal and Tragic Narratives," 1130–31; the thoughtful reflections of Norma Field, *In the Realm of the Dying Emperor: Japan at Century's End* (New York, 1993); and John W. Dower, "The Bombed: Hiroshimas and Nagasakis in Japanese Memory," in Hogan, *Hiroshima,* 116–42. For a bibliographic overview of postwar historiography, see R. J. B. Bosworth, *Explaining Auschwitz and Hiroshima: History Writing and the Second World War* (London, 1993); and Ian Buruma, *The Wages of Guilt: Memories of War in Germany and Japan* (London, 1994).

116. Jürgen Habermas, "A Kind of Settlement of Damages (Apologetic Tendencies)," *New German Critique* no. 44 (1988): 26.

117. See, for example, Karl Jaspers, *Die Schuldfrage: Ein Beitrag zur deutschen Frage* (Zurich, 1946); Eugen Kogon, "Gericht und Gewissen," *Frankfurter Hefte* 1, no. 1 (April 1946): 29–31; and Kogon, "Über die Situation," *Frankfurter Hefte* 2, no. 1 (January 1947): 29, 34; see also Kogon, *Der NS-Staat.* The first edition of 35,000 copies was published in 1946, and a second edition of 100,000 copies appeared a year later. See also Hannah Arendt, "The Aftermath of Nazi Rule: Report from Germany," *Commentary* 10 (October 1950): 342–43.

118. See the suggestive comments of Claudia Koonz, "Between Memory and Oblivion: Concentration Camps in German Memory," in *Commemorations: The Politics of National Identity,* John R. Gillis, ed. (Princeton, N.J., 1994), 258–80; Koonz, "Germany's Buchenwald: Whose Shrine? Whose Memory?" in *The Art of Memory: Holocaust Memorials in History,* James E. Young, ed. (New York, 1994), 111–19; and Michael Geyer and Miriam Hansen, "German-Jewish Memory and National Consciousness," in *Holocaust Remembrance: The Shapes of Memory,* Geoffrey H. Hartmann, ed. (Cambridge, Mass., 1994), 175–90.

119. James E. Young, *The Texture of Memory: Holocaust Memorials and Meaning* (New Haven, Conn., 1993), 25.

120. Stephen Kinzer, "The War Memorial: To Embrace the Guilty, Too?" *New York Times,* November 15, 1993; and Daniela Büchten and Anja Frey, eds., *Im Irrgarten deutscher Geschichte: Die neue Wache 1818 bis 1993* (Berlin, 1993).

121. Andreas Kilb, "Warten, bis Spielberg kommt," *Die Zeit* (January 28, 1994): 1. See also Helke Sander and Barbara Johr, eds., *BeFreier und Befreite: Krieg, Vergewaltigungen, Kinder* (Munich, 1992); Atina Grossmann, "A Question of Silence: The Rape of German Women by Occupation Soldiers," *October* no. 72 (1995): 43–63, part of a special issue devoted to the film; Heineman, "Hour of the Woman," 365–74; and the superb treatment of this topic by Norman M. Naimark, *The Russians in Germany: A History of the Soviet Zone of Occupation, 1945–1949* (Cambridge, Mass., 1995), 69–140.

122. "Speech by Richard von Weizsäcker," 272.

123. Elie Wiesel, "Ein Volk auslöschen," *Die Zeit* (April 21, 1995): 16.

124. Peter Glotz, "Die Krankheit Nationalismus," *Die Zeit* (March 24, 1995): 16. The same issue carried a long account of "The Fight for East Prussia" in the spring of 1945. See Heinz Werner Hübner, "Noch siebzig Tage bis Pillau," 6–8.

125. See also Helmut Kohl, "Jedem einzelnen Schicksal schulden wir Achtung," *Frankfurter Allgemeine Zeitung,* May 6, 1995. It is also worth noting that in 1994, Welt-bild Verlag in Augsburg commenced another reprinting of the original Schieder pro-ject's documentation on the expulsion.

126. "Speech by Richard von Weizsäcker," 262; Theo Sommer, "Jetzt erst ist der Krieg zu Ende," *Die Zeit,* September 9, 1994.

127. Maier, *Unmasterable Past,* 23.

128. See, for example, "'Alles so trostlos': SPIEGEL-Redakteur Hans-Ulrich Stoldt über die Hoffnung der tschechischen Nazi-Opfer auf Entschädigung aus Bonn," *Der Spiegel* no. 19 (May 8, 1995): 24–25; Sabine Herre, "Viel Lob für Havel," *die tageszeitung,* February 20, 1995; Berthold Kohler, "Havels Heimkehr," *Frankfurter All-gemeine Zeitung,* February 20, 1995; "Europa, das bedeutet vor allem die Freiheit der Person: Auszüge aus der Rede des polnischen Aussenministers Bartoszewski vor dem Deutschen Bundestag," *Frankfurter Allgemeine Zeitung,* April 29, 1995; "Klaus bedauert Verbrechen bei der Vertreibung," *Frankfurter Allgemeine Zeitung,* May 8, 1995; and Alan Cowell, "Memories of Wartime Brutalities Revive Czech-German Animosity," *New York Times,* February 9, 1996.

129. Wolfgang Zank, *Wirtschaft und Arbeit in Ostdeutschland 1945–1949: Prob-leme des Wiederaufbaus in der sowjetischen Besatzungszone Deutschlands* (Munich, 1987), 142–52; the excellent framework offered by Naimark, *Russians in Germany;* and Koonz, "Germany's Buchenwald."

130. Peter Schneider, "Hitler's Shadow: On Being a Self-Conscious German," *Harper's Magazine* (September 1987): 50; also Bartov, *Murder,* 120; and Dower, "Tri-umphal and Tragic Narratives," 1124.

131. Ultimately, such a perspective would also include the former German Demo-cratic Republic. See Danyel, "Die geteilte Vergangenheit."

11

Photography, National Identity, and the "Cataract of Times"
Wartime Images and the Case of Japan

Julia A. Thomas

The Yokohama Museum of Art offered up an anomaly in the summer of 1995. No other museum in the Tokyo metropolitan area referred to the fiftieth anniversary of Japan's surrender through an exhibition of photographs; indeed, no other major exhibition that summer featured documentary photography from any period.[1] The Yokohama Museum, on the other hand, discreetly yet firmly constructed a vivid photographic recollection of the decade that saw the cessation of hostilities. This article examines *Photography in the 1940s,* as the Yokohama exhibition was called, against the striking absence of photographic documents of the war in other art museums and against the wider struggle in Japan over the purpose of history.[2] Through the analysis of this particular exhibition, I explore the larger interpretive problems presented by photographic art collections. As historians grapple with the expanding importance of visual images,[3] our analyses must account for what I see as the inherently unstable relationship among still photographs, national identity, and concepts of time as they come together in museums.[4] Understanding this critical triangulation of image, nation, and time is, I argue, the key not only to unpacking the ambiguities of *Photography in the 1940s* but a general theoretical grasp of the role of museums in the creation of historical consciousness.[5]

I will start by examining *Photography in the 1940s* as much as possible on its own terms, treating it as a visual rendering of history crafted by the museum staff that unpropitious summer. Taking into account statements of curatorial intent and the images absent from the gallery walls as well as those chosen for exhibition, I analyze three possible renditions of Japanese identity available to gallery viewers in Yokohama. Although this analysis begins by treating the exhibition as a "text" worthy of consideration in its own right,

From *American Historical Review* 103, no. 5 (December 1998): 1475–1501. Reprinted with the permission of the American Historical Association.

any interpretation must rest on a broader reading of Japan's current circumstances. The past few years have brought relentless troubles to Japan's economic, political, and social institutions. Even before the wider Asian economy soured, Japan's problems included the end of its own economic boom, the plunge of the stock market, the precarious state of Japanese banks, the death of the Showa emperor, political corruption and the Liberal Democratic Party's loss of virtually unrivaled power,[6] the revelation during the Kobe earthquake of woefully inadequate preparations for meeting natural disasters,[7] and the lethal activities of the Aum Shinrikyō doomsday cult. Together, these events have undermined the postwar national consensus on what it means to be Japanese.[8] Prosperity, political passivity, and social harmony no longer appear axiomatic national traits.

In these circumstances, artists and curators, the public and the government, respond anxiously to images in museums that might comment on a national identity largely understood as a cultural phenomenon.[9] Fine art photography exhibitions, as the anomalous Yokohama show suggests, have the capacity to become dangerous mirrors for a troubled nation seeking to understand itself. In this context, *Photography in the 1940s* might be seen as a courageous act of domestic political engagement, or as a disingenuous, even irresponsible, evasion of wartime memories, or as an inclusive vision of human solidarity. Both the exhibition's contents and its immediate context reveal deeply rooted tensions over national identity in contemporary Japan and suggest the importance of history—visual and otherwise—as an arena for contesting the future parameters of democratic practice.

This article, then, moves outward from an analysis of the exhibition itself, through a consideration of how tensions in Japan over the appropriate mode of national history impinge on our understanding of this exhibition, to theoretical concerns that transcend these particulars. The final section of the article will focus on how photography's malleable relationship with time—and thus with history—allows it to serve as a vector for fundamental concerns over national identity. Through these widening circles of interpretation, I try to demonstrate how historians can incorporate the analysis of photography in art museums into research on historical consciousness without treating the exhibitions or the images as mere illustration.

Yokohama, a commuter's train ride from Tokyo, is an old port city, one of the first to admit Americans and Europeans in the nineteenth century. The Yokohama Museum of Art, on the other hand, is new and not very inviting. Situated on a large concrete plaza, it is a vast structure with an eight-story watchtower and a cavernous gray atrium. The building radiates an appreciation of the gargantuan. However, *Photography in the 1940s* demonstrated none of this relish for sheer size. The exhibition was, instead, excruciatingly precise and exquisitely crafted.

With eighty-four photographs from Europe, America, and Japan, Assistant Curator Kuraishi Shino and the museum staff created a dense compendium of images engaging aesthetic, social, and political themes.[10] The exhibition brochure forthrightly justified choosing the theme of the 1940s through reference to the fiftieth anniversary of Japan's defeat.[11] When pressed to elaborate further, Kuraishi reiterated that it was the express purpose of the exhibition to juxtapose "aesthetic sophistication" with "the serious political confusion . . . of the period."[12] There can be no doubt that this exhibition confronted the past: the question becomes how and why it did so. Why choose to pierce the silence about the war that hung over Tokyo's photography world that summer?[13] What histories were articulated through this international collection of images? What idea of Japan took shape through these photographs?

Two images commanded the entrance to the exhibition: Robert Capa's "Collaborators, Chartres, August 18, 1944" and Ansel Adams's "Mount Williamson from Manzanar" (1942), Manzanar being one of the internment camps for Japanese and Japanese Americans in California.[14] In a sense, these paired scenes of moral failure from France and the United States set the tone for all that followed. The deliberately ordered exhibition then presented Sakamoto Manshichi's serene prints of *haniwa* (the archaic clay figurines renowned for their enigmatic smiles) and of medieval Buddhist statuary.[15] These Japanese works were followed by classic paeans to America's natural beauty,[16] particularly of the far West, by further celebratory scenes of traditional Japanese culture,[17] by a few stylized Japanese wartime propaganda shots of civilian workers, and then by images of Western soldiers at war. In the middle of the exhibition, the war ended in a few enigmatic photographs and the postwar period began to unfold. Tokyo springs up from its ashes in a frenzy of rebuilding, while New York revels in garish decadence and Paris displays elegant fashion.[18] Back and forth, the exhibition swung between "the West" and Japan, between nature and culture, between war and peace.

Two separate though interwoven narratives emerged from the images on the walls: one about "the West" and the other about Japan. In the first narrative, the West was made to indict itself. Capa plays the leading prosecutor with his photographs of French collaborators whose heads have been shaved, of an American soldier kicking a prisoner, and of a wounded child in Sicily.[19] Henri Cartier-Bresson's "Gestapo Informer Recognized by a Woman She Had Denounced, Deportation Camp, Dessau, Germany" (1945) reinforces the theme. The seeming predilection for personal confrontation among Westerners demonstrated by Capa's and Cartier-Bresson's work was evinced even in photographs not related to the war. For instance, in Weegee's "The Critic," an impoverished woman glowers at two grotesque, bejeweled matrons leaving a limousine. This apparent Western tendency to pervert social harmony reverberates as physical deformity in Lisette Model's portraits of a hermaphrodite and dwarf in postwar New York, which are used to close the exhibition.[20]

Collaborators, Chartres. Robert Capa, France, August 18, 1944. Copyright
Robert Capa and Magnum Photos, Inc.

Even the joys of victory, marked by Alfred Eisenstaedt's photograph of the
kissing couple titled "V-J Day, Times Square" (1945) and Capa's view of
Liberation Day in Paris (1944), seem, in this context, histrionic.

The cumulative psychological portrait of a race prone to excess was
unmistakable; yet the Nazis, Japan's allies, were hardly pictured at all, and
the Holocaust was absolutely invisible. The only German image in the entire
show, a show purportedly dedicated to dealing with the political confusion of
the 1940s, was August Sander's "Junger Soldat, Westerwald" (1945), a close-
up portrait of a soldier in whose face it is difficult to read anything more profound than sheer youth.

While the Yokohama Museum's indictment of Americans and Western
Europeans was precise and unmitigated, the brutality of these foreigners
seemed principally to endanger themselves. The exhibition pointedly avoided
being a parable about Western aggression against Japan. Indeed, when the
exhibition turned our gaze to "the East," the Allies became a remote, ambiguous presence. For instance, Hamaya Hiroshi's "Half-Breed in the Orphanage
of Harbin, China" (1940) depicts a Eurasian child standing forlornly behind
high gates with a European crest. The harm represented here seems indirect,
the fault obscure. Whose child is it? What East and what West come together
in this frail boy's body? Who made an orphan of the child? Even Hiroshima

The Critic, Weegee [Arthur Fellig], 1943. Copyright 1994, International Center of Photography, New York, Bequest of Wilma Wilcox.

was represented only by Kimura Ihee's 1946 photograph of a couple slumped in an overgrown field outside the city a year after the bombing. The couple appears tired, but any injuries are invisible, and the city becomes a presence only through the caption.[21] There were no depictions of Western soldiers in Asia, no representations of fighting on the continent nor any vignettes from island battlefields. It was as though East and West had never bled into the same soil, had never really touched.

The second narrative presented by the exhibition made Japan the central figure, a Japan divorced not only from "the West" but also from "the East" outside its home islands. In avoiding images of Asia outside Japan, the exhibition reduced the war in this second narrative to an overwhelmingly civilian undertaking. It was a war of defense against an anonymous, seldom-glimpsed enemy. Not only were there no representations of Western soldiers in the East but also virtually no Asian military men of any nationality and certainly no Asian men fighting each other. Only one member of the Japanese armed forces was pictured in the entire exhibition; this airman stands proudly in his clean uniform before a Douglas DC-4 in Yagi Osamu's 1941 portrait "Fighter of the Air." The staged photograph of the unnamed hero presents him and his aircraft against a blank sky without any context, as though the DC-4 were parked before a photographer's screen.

Since, with this one exception, the exhibition avoided representations of Japanese military men, its non-Western narrative highlights Japanese women, brave, beautiful, and clean.[22] They serve as military nurses, as volunteer steel workers, and as correspondents in orchestrated propaganda shots. In slightly less sanitized images, Hayashi Tadahiko depicts women lined up in a neighborhood association fire brigade in 1941 and women maneuvering lumber down a muddy forest road in 1943.[23] Together, these photographs present a heavily gendered rendition of wartime Japan as a woman's world. Only after the war ends do Japanese men appear in any number, smoking in the Asakusa district of Tokyo, selling books, and standing in unemployment lines.[24]

The conflagration of World War II subsides for Japan with Hamaya Hiroshi's quiet "Sun on the Day the War Ended, 1945," in which the sun alone fills the frame, and Morooka Koji's 1946 photograph of a sunlit city street with strolling couples titled "Peace Is Restored, Tokyo." We do not see any of the subject matter from which Japanese photographers made powerful images in the aftermath of the war: returning army personnel waiting to be discharged, Occupation soldiers patronizing strip joints and shoeshine boys, Japanese civilians scavenging through rubble.[25] The main focus is on the reconstruction of urban dwellings and shops, as in Nakagawa Kazuo's four-part series *Ginza Recovery,* which charts the rapid rebuilding of downtown Tokyo in 1944, 1945, 1946, and 1947.

The duality of the exhibition narrative is enhanced by the choice of "the forties" as its frame of reference. In a country where several alternative methods of calculating time exist, issues of dating are never entirely neutral. The concept of "the forties" relies on a system of dating imported from the West in the 1870s rather than on the official Japanese method of measuring years by imperial reigns, in which each enthronement resets the calendar at year 1. During the war, dates were usually written according to the reign year of the emperor, a method of dating that continues in governmental forms and other official papers today.[26] Alternatively, the Japanese Empire also took 660 BCE as its inaugural year, marking its calendar from the arrival of the first emperor of Japan, grandson of the sun goddess Amaterasu. Through this calculation, Japan celebrated the year 2600 in 1940. With these options before it, had the Yokohama Museum wished to convey a different history, it might have mounted an exhibition, for instance, on the Showa teens, covering 1935 to 1945. In choosing the temporal frame of "the forties," the curator used time as an interpretive device, ensuring that war was balanced with peace and "the West" was balanced with Japan, obscuring the empire's long engagement on the Asian continent.[27]

In sum, the images presented at Yokohama created a double story of Western aggression and Japanese innocence, Western shame and Japanese recovery, and the abiding beauty of Western (primarily American) landscapes and the immemorial loveliness of Japanese traditions. It was a tale underscored by the dichotomies of male and female and of nature and culture.[28] But definite as these presences were, they also conjured up absences. Where were the pictures of Koreans, South Asians, Okinawans, Nazis, Jews, Russians, Chinese,[29] and many others who might have complicated the neat oppositions on which this bifurcated tale rested? Where were Japan's leaders, Japan's soldiers, and the occupying Americans? These invisible images crowd the blank spaces on the museum walls; the exhibition seemed almost overwhelmed by possibilities foregone. In short, *Photography in the 1940s* remembered, but it remembered with deliberate selectivity.

Although curator Kuraishi Shino may have set out to convey the "serious political confusion" of the period, confusion seemed little in evidence in the expurgation of all images of Japanese militarism, colonialism, and occupation. Elsewhere, such absences might have occasioned comment and even public outcry. Imagine a German photography exhibition, especially one at a major public institution, claiming to represent the political situation of the 1940s with virtually no images of Nazis; imagine an American documentary on the 1960s without reference to Vietnam, political assassinations, or the civil rights movement. But the Yokohama exhibition, while well attended, elicited no major reviews, much less any protest. Accustomed as we have become in the United States to viewing museums and memorials as the battlefields of competing historical interpretations, it is perhaps the lack of controversy in response to *Photography in the 1940s* that most challenges us to understand its context.

For many Japanese, the aporia that seemed so glaring, at least to this American viewer, may have hardly registered. Especially before the death of wartime Emperor Hirohito in 1989, reluctance to remember the 1930s and 1940s was keen. The grandparents who never spoke of wartime or occupation experiences, the whitewashed textbooks read by children, the government officials who carefully expunged wartime images from the arena of public discussion and stridently resisted Asian demands for apology and recompense all conspired to make forgetting easy.[30] For many Japanese people, the past remains simply past and irrelevant to their current lives.[31] As I have already noted, Tokyo-area photography curators other than Kuraishi found it simple enough to avoid all reference to the war in the summer of 1995.[32]

On the other hand, in the 1990s, what might be termed a "memory shift" has accompanied the "regime shift" in Japan's political economy described by political scientist T. J. Pempel.[33] Willed amnesia about wartime activities is a less plausible stance than it used to be, and indeed, as Australian historian Gavan McCormack argues, "the question of responsibility for the war that ended half a century ago becomes more pressing for Japan" rather than less.[34] Some grandparents who never brought themselves to speak of the war with the younger members of their families now relate their experiences on a web site created by the "Computer Ōbāchan no Kai" (Society of Computer-Literate Grannies).[35] The Asahi newspaper and publishing company has created several forums for people who wish to write about their war experiences, most recently an open-ended newspaper series titled "The Torment of Memory," which solicits stories from former soldiers of the imperial army.[36] Television shows have explored aspects of the war as well. Controversy over how to represent Korean and other non-Japanese dead has disturbed the tranquility of Hiroshima Peace Park, and similar problems of representation have been raised at war memorials in Okinawa after decades of silence.

On the official level, each Japanese prime minister since 1993 has intoned "deep remorse" on the August 15 anniversary of the war's end. Partly due to the lawsuits initiated in Tokyo courts in the early 1990s by Asian victims pressing claims for apology and compensation, it has become less easy (though not impossible) to deny outright the most gruesome aspects of the war—the massacres at Nanking and elsewhere,[37] the use of chemical and biological weapons,[38] human experimentation in Unit 731,[39] and the system of sexual slavery. In 1996, Ministry of Education officials, once so adamant that textbooks present the Asian war in the mildest terms possible, permitted mention of the military sex slaves known as "comfort women."[40] From the perspective of Japan's fiercest critics, especially its Asian victims, this "memory shift" appears belated, prevaricating, and self-interested, but it has, nonetheless, changed the dynamic of recollection in Japan.[41]

As with any retrospective exhibition, *Photography in the 1940s* is an artifact of contemporary possibilities for historical practice as well as a repository of history. The very existence of the exhibition promoted the tentative shift toward recollection outlined above, but that still leaves the pressing question of exactly what conception of the nation's past and its current identity was projected by this particular collection of images. Why did the Yokohama Museum of Art assign itself the task of resuscitating wartime images and then refuse to show images of Japan's militarism? Why focus on the 1940s and then never hint that Japan was occupied by foreign troops for half that period? Why indict the West but not in relation to harm done to Japan? In other words, how are we to understand the history that *Photography in the 1940s* created?

The first possible answer to these questions might be a simple explanation involving the availability of photographs themselves. It could be argued that no pictures of Japanese military subjects, for instance, met Kuraishi's standard of "aesthetic sophistication." Of the more overtly topical photographs selected for the exhibition, most conform to a modernist documentary aesthetic institutionalized in American museum photography departments since the 1960s. Others, such as Domon Ken's conventionally stylized propaganda photograph, "Young Nurse, Red Cross Hospital, Azabu, Tokyo" may have been included less for reasons of aesthetic sophistication than the photograph's now canonical status.[42] However, by either criterion, there was a wealth of photographs available, taken by Japanese amateur, press, and military photographers and by non-Japanese all over Asia as Japanese forces advanced.[43] A more complex sense of how standards of aesthetic sophistication are created would admit a broader class of photographic imagery, including the poster art and magazine graphics that helped mobilize Japan's wartime population.[44]

The second possible explanation for the absent images might be that none existed in the Yokohama Museum's permanent collection, from which this exhibition was drawn. Given that the Yokohama photography collection is growing steadily, the museum could have obtained such pictures, had it wished to do so.[45] Even more to the point, a very different story was already available within the resources of the museum as of 1995. Its extensive Robert Capa collection alone could have provided images of Jews and of Nazis. Capa's photograph of a leveled Warsaw could have thrown the destruction of Tokyo into relief; home-front suffering could have appeared universal and not just a Japanese phenomenon with Capa's portrayals of Londoners during the Blitz. Had the time span been extended back to 1938, Capa's pictures of China could have conveyed a fuller story, revealing something of Japanese aggression on the continent. In short, neither aestheticism nor availability accounts for the twists in Yokohama's tale. The choice of images at Yokohama was not, I think, determined by necessity but rather by interpretations of the war and of appropriate representations of Japan's national history.

In turning to the possible interpretations guiding this exhibition, we enter a field sabotaged, almost literally, by secret dangers. I refer not to the explosive issues of intentionality and audience response or to the problems of museum-created histories that charge debates in the American and European contexts. Rather, in Japanese museums and galleries, ultranationalist activity, seemingly supported by the police, circumscribes what can be shown without controversy.[46] Those rare works that concern the war or the emperor system (*tennōsei*) draw ultranationalists' ire and their blaring sound trucks. Art is destroyed, artists threatened, museums harassed, the police visit at midnight, and exhibitions are closed.[47]

These far right-wing groups are no small handful of malcontents but number about 120,000 in 980 organizations across the nation. Their ties to particular politicians and bureaucrats are indistinct but potent. For instance, when an ultranationalist group objected to the Toyama Museum of Modern Art's acquisition of Ōura Nobuyuki's "Holding Perspectives," a print series with images of Emperor Hirohito, the Toyama regional assembly intervened by deeming the art offensive and publicly questioning the judgment of

museum officials. All planned Ōura exhibitions were canceled and the cata-
logues for the exhibition burned after a Shinto priest tore up the museum's
display copy.[48] In most cases, the impulse of the police, gallery owners,
museum officials, and even artists with avant-garde proclivities is to avoid confrontation and expunge from view the stray chrysanthemum (symbol of the
imperial family) or offending reference to Chinese and Korean comfort
women. Artist Shimada Yoshiko, quite exceptionally, fought back when the
Toyama Museum succumbed to right-wing complaints about Ōura's work by
sending the ashes of one of her own paintings in protest to museum authorities. The museum returned the ashes. Shimada reports that it is easier to live
outside Japan because her own work is critical of the emperor system and sympathetic to the plight of the comfort women.[49] Such protective self-censorship
and lack of law enforcement leaves the art world paralyzed to resist ultranationalist pressure.

Given this threatening atmosphere, the staff of the Yokohama Museum
did not, could not, operate without constraint in choosing images for an exhibition touching on the vexed subject of the war. The curator willingly entered
the fraught public sphere where incompatible senses of Japanese national
identity, some supported by vicious nationalists, compete for recognition.
Although he did not choose to engage such controversial issues as the guilt
of the emperor, the ruthlessness of the military, or the nation's dedication to
war, he also refused the safety of silence. In these circumstances, *Photography in the 1940s* might be perceived as an act of courage. On the other hand,
it proceeded very gingerly down the path of memory. A tense ambiguity, perhaps the frustrating consequence of subconscious self-censorship, connected
its juxtaposed images. Positioned against the competing senses of Japanese
nationhood and history outside the museum, the exhibition can be interpreted
as having given shape to three radically different forms of national identity:
Japan as a nation formed through a history of innocence and resistance, Japan
as a nation inviolable in its ahistorical essence, and Japan as a nation engaged
in traumatic self-discovery through engagement with the Other, a Japan that
finds itself in the mirror of the West.

The first possible mode of national identity emerges from reading the
exhibition as directly as possible and taking Kuraishi at his word: he sought
to confront the events of the 1940s and convey the experience of the Japanese people. The images he presented depicted a people swept away by the
tide of war, a war visited upon them not so much by the West as by some
unnamed natural force, although the West, arguably, was analogized to nature
obliquely through many photographs, particularly those of Ansel Adams.
Indeed, on close examination, many of the images convey the impression of
Japanese people being driven away from culture into nature: women into the
forests as recruits to take over logging operations, the couple into the field far
outside Hiroshima, the sun itself on the day the war ends. Against a natural

disaster of such magnitude, little resistance was possible, or so this collection may have suggested. For the general populace, the war was less action than stunned reaction.

In these circumstances, the only possible antiwar stance for practicing photographers may have been what historian Ienaga Saburō places under the rubric passive resistance, the refusal to participate enthusiastically in the war. The exhibition brochure briefly suggests this view when it mentions that some photographers, rather than be absorbed into the propaganda machine, "consciously became engrossed in Japanese traditions and conventions" and used their mastery of "the theory and practice of documentary photography" to record objects and events unrelated to the war. They tried to drop out, tried to find a place of refuge from contemporary Japan in the customary Japan of the rural hinterlands.[50]

Hamaya Hiroshi is a prime exemplar of this strategy.[51] Traveling to distant Niigata, far from Japanese military, industrial, and governmental centers, Hamaya focused his lens on folk customs. With a longing eye, his camera recorded an undulating line of boys carrying torches through a snowy night in a celebration designed to chase away imaginary evil birds and lift midwinter spirits.[52] The Fire Festival for the guardian deity of travel also captured Hamaya's attention.[53] But during the same year, 1940, when these photographs were taken, Hamaya left Niigata to go to Japanese-occupied Harbin, where, treading on conquered soil, he photographed the "half-breed" orphan whom we see later in the exhibition. Should the Harbin series be viewed as an act of resistance or as an act of complicity? Does the receptivity to circumstances under which documentary photographers necessarily work protect them from charges of active perpetration of the events around them or does it implicate them?[54]

The same question arises with the work of Domon Ken. His images of a Kyoto potter's wheel and a Bunraku puppet show may evoke timeless custom and suggest passive resistance to the war, but they are part of a body of work that also includes propaganda shots used to rally the nation.[55] The exhibition forthrightly included both aspects of Domon's work just as it did Hamaya's. Perhaps, recognizing the complexity of competing loyalties to state, society, family, and self, the exhibition implied that even inconsistent acts of non-engagement with the war should be lauded as heroic, considering the nation's general commitment to total war. As curator, Kuraishi may even have been intimating that the same was true for his own act of non-compliance with the consensus of silence on the war by photography museums that summer.

The problem of interpreting *Photography in the 1940s* in this way is that the images of tradition created by Hamaya and Domon could have worked in the 1940s as passive resistance only in the context of a society whose energies were utterly devoted to the imperial cause. The gestures of these photographers

Boys Singing to Drive Evil Birds Away, Hiroshi Hamaya, Niigata, Japan, 1940.
Copyright Hiroshi Hamaya and Magnum Photos, Inc.

attain the status of political opposition only if they are positioned against the
backdrop of a dedicated populace sending its middle school students to work
in bomb factories and its teenagers to die in suicide missions. In the Yokohama
exhibition, however, we saw virtually none of this dedication to military victory. Without the purposeful activity of empire in the foreground, the images
of traditional art and customs cannot appear to countermand the values of the
state. Instead, their loveliness is absorbed by the nation at war: the quiet vis-
age of a Buddhist statue melds with the quiet face of a military nurse. In not
showing or not being able to show photographs documenting Japanese militarism, *Photography in the 1940s* transformed passive resistance into mere
passivity. Without adequate context, the meaning of the images is transposed
from the discourse of resistance to one of acquiescence.

Ironically, then, the constraint on exhibiting imperial and military images
within art museums undermines the possibility of recollecting a legacy of
innocence or passive resistance. If the deeds of Japan's military masters and
enemies cannot be represented, the identity of the Japanese people cannot be
understood as having emerged through resistance to those deeds. Indeed, on
a more abstract level, the proposition that national identity emerges through
the contingencies of time is itself undermined. In creating a consciously retrospective exhibition, the Yokohama Museum may have hoped to suggest that
contemporary Japanese identity is rooted in history, that the nation is itself a
historical artifact, the result of various decisions, events, and accidents that
have impinged on its nature. The curator may have sought to present photographs that document moments of national becoming. In this effort, however,
Photography in the 1940s fails. That which can be shown—the impotent
innocence of the emperor's subjects and the timeless images of traditional arts

and festivals—suggests not a nation formed through contingency and will but one best understood through some timeless aesthetic essence.

The sense of nationhood conveyed through this collection is that, whatever the war was, whatever natural forces beat against the nation, Japan remained inviolate. Postwar rebuilding spectacularly and rapidly reconstituted the physical basis of life, but in these postwar years as well the identity of the nation remained the same. The brush with American occupiers vanishes without trace. The cumulative image is of a Japan that transcends the eventfulness of history for an abiding cultural essence.

Despite the curator's stated purpose of creating a history through photographic images, the indirect pressures of ultranationalist censorship won out on two levels. Not only have many of the images of Japan's war been excised from public view, but the general concept that history is the medium through which national identity emerges has also been checked. Before the "memory shift" of the 1990s and even after, Japan's far right wing has sought to project an image of Japan in which national, state, and popular interests are identical, best represented in high art forms that de-emphasize contingency and idiosyncratic creativity. Traditional arts such as kabuki and Nō, calligraphy and Japanese-style painting, lacquerware and ceramics garner large governmental subsidies, while those arts prizing individual expression or the role of chance are more suspect in that they hint at alternatives foregone and competing perspectives, only some of which can be identical with those of the state. Photographs, particularly when elevated within public museums, unless strictly dedicated to formalism or representative of trends in European and American art, threaten to shatter this ideal of Japan as a changeless culture.

In having the potential to suggest the nation's historicity by creating interactions between specific images from Japan's past and present-day viewers, photography exhibitions can promote what for the right wing is the subversive notion that national identity is always in a state of becoming.[56] Worse yet, from this perspective, if a viewer can interrogate the past on the museum wall, he or she might interrogate the policies of the present. The right-wing concept of national essence is not simply a conservative plea for the purity of the past but a contemporary polemic against democratic practices that foster respect for competing interests, constantly renegotiated through open political activity. It is not just a particular version of history but historicity itself, the necessary matrix of democracy, that becomes the core issue for the Yokohama exhibition and for the struggle over Japan's national identity in general.

Both of the interpretations of the Yokohama exhibition that I have presented so far—as proposing a mild national history for Japan and as resisting narrative history altogether—leave out a crucial element: the American and European photographs. My analysis of the form of Japanese nationhood represented in this exhibition has focused exclusively on the Japanese photographs, but this approach may be too simple, accepting a dichotomy that can be overcome. A third way of interpreting *Photography in the 1940s* might take its images of Western aggression and Western collaborators to stand in for obscured memories of Japanese brutality and national complicity. In this scenario, through sublimation and projection, Japan's aggressive past might be obliquely acknowledged.

Though implausible, this reading of the exhibition can be supported in several ways. For instance, one could argue that *Photography in the 1940s* chose not to portray the West as a direct enemy of Japan, thereby easing the way for Japanese viewers to identify with the perpetrators of violence. The right wing has claimed that the Fifteen Year War was justified due to European and American colonialism in Asia—so *Photography in the 1940s* chose not to represent Westerners in Asia. In the images on the walls, the brutality of Westerners is frequently directed at other Westerners, a fact that may recall the terrible treatment suffered by Japanese army recruits at the hands of their own officers. Seen in this light, the exhibition contained not two separate narratives—one of the West and another of Japan—but a single narrative in which the West becomes the subconscious past of a guilty nation. When the narrative required violence, our eyes were directed westward, and when the narrative depicted the home front, we saw Japanese women and culture, but, by this third reading, *Photography in the 1940s* was ultimately one story of war with innocence and brutality on all sides.

Construed in this way, *Photography in the 1940s* defies a new right-wing approach to history currently being urged by groups such as Jiyūshugi Shikan Kenkyūkai (Liberal View of History Study Group) and Atarashii Rekishi Kyōkasho o Tsukuru Kai (Society for Making New History Textbooks).[57] These groups, despite organizational and intellectual ties to the form of ultranationalism described above, aggressively revise history not merely to mask failures (although they seek to do that as well) but to affirm what they prefer to call the Greater East Asian War as an act of self-defense and purposeful liberation of Koreans, Chinese, and other peoples suffering under American and European colonialism.[58] Far from lamenting the defeat of Japan's noble aims, this version of history views the sacrifices of the Fifteen Year War as providing the foundation for Japan's postwar prosperity. In short, theirs is a tale of pure national triumph. Although such retrospective defenses of Japan's war aims are not entirely new,[59] the orchestrated efforts of these "study groups" and their aggressive embrace of history as the battlefield of national identity must be seen as a response to the general shift toward recollection in the 1990s and indeed as part of it.[60]

In keeping with the "memory shift" within Japan and recognizing that visual media serve wide audiences as "theaters of memory," the Jiyūshugi

Shikan Kenkyūkai and its affiliates vigorously promote their message not only through books[61] but through television,[62] cartoons,[63] and films such as *Pride: Unmei no toki* (Pride: The Fatal Moment).[64] Nor has the power of museums to shape historical consciousness been ignored by this new brand of right-wing revisionism. For instance, in the spring of 1998, critics connected with Jiyūshugi Shikan Kenkyūkai and led by University of Tokyo professor Fujioka Nobukatsu forced the panel advising the governor of Tokyo on a city war museum to redraw its plans. These critics denounced as "masochistic" the original plan's characterization of Tokyo as a city with military targets.[65] Although the new proposals for the museum continue to call for exhibitions at sites of former military facilities, all references to Tokyo as a military city have been dropped, and the space proposed for displays concerning the American bombing campaign (which killed an estimated 80,000 to 120,000 people) has been enlarged. In this proposed museum and in other media, the wartime history of Japan takes the form of righteous action in self-defense against the West and justified violence on behalf of other Asians. While the right-wing image of Japan discussed earlier deflected attention away from the past toward enduring cultural symbols and sought to remove the besmirching traces of time from the essence of national identity, the image of Japan molded by the new right is, by contrast, vibrantly historical. From its perspective, eventful narrative history can be revived as a basis of national unity, since memory bears no burden of shame or pain.

Seen against this aggressively triumphant vision, *Photography in the 1940s,* with its gentle portrayal of domestic Japan and strictly non-confrontational depiction of Allied violence, becomes a bulwark of moderation. If we further consider the exhibition as bridging the dichotomy between Japan and the West to create a single narrative, it becomes possible to read it as a plea for a new historical beginning, one that refuses to take the nation as the sole object of recollection. In keeping with this benign interpretation, *Photography in the 1940s* could be said to promote the transnational idea that a shared knowledge of terror and death forces us to recognize that no one nation stands alone: one nation's history always entails the perspective of others. German historian Michael Geyer argues compellingly for this response to the shattering experience of war. He portrays the "commemoration of death as work on the bond of human solidarity, mindful of a genocidal past," and insists that this commemoration is "a necessary element of the renewal of historical consciousness, which will then be able to look back on the epoch of world wars as a passing era."[66] By this light, Japanese national identity and representations of that identity in photographic exhibitions will necessarily engage other nations and other images from around the world. In this sense, there can only be one story.

Despite its attractions as a psychoanalytic reading and its suggestion of human solidarity, this third interpretation of the Yokohama exhibition is, finally, implausible. The gulf between self and other—*gaijin*, outsiders, foreigners—that structures Japanese national consciousness is such that it is unlikely that many Japanese visitors recognized themselves in Robert Capa's soldiers or Edward Weston's female nude with a gas mask entitled "Civilian Defense" (1942). The notable dearth of images of Germans also betrays a reluctance to draw parallels between Japan and the part of the West to which Japan was allied during wartime. The "West" *in toto* remains foreign. As sociologist Kosaku Yoshino has argued, "Japanese identity is the anti-image of foreignness and, as such, can only be affirmed by formulating the images of the Other; namely, the West."[67] Even the catalogue of the Yokohama Museum's complete photographic holdings is organized along this principle: the first section devoted to Japanese photographers, the second labeled *Gaikoku sakka no shashin* (Photographs by Foreign Photographers).[68] Given the refusal to represent, let alone claim, the impulse toward brutality and annihilation as universally human, *Photography in the 1940s* did not, I believe, commemorate that painful decade in such a way that historical consciousness could be renewed on an altered basis of human solidarity. Instead, eventfulness, activity, and specific histories mark the images created by Europeans and Americans; the images by Japanese are quiet and still. These two collectivities stand opposed to one another without serving as mirrors of a universal humanity.

Photography in the 1940s changes hue as our understanding of its background changes. Against the right-wing urge to forget, it appears to have made a stand for the value of remembering; against the new right's triumphal vision of Japan's wartime aims, it appears to have been a mild antidote, offering the heroism of survival rather than that of noble liberators. At best, the exhibition was a modest act of historical representation, compelling principally in its precise calibration of the limits of historical consensus in Japan at the moment of its production. Just as the "regime shift" in Japan's political economy remains open-ended, so too the "memory shift" has yet to consolidate opinion on the role and nature of modern history. Certainly, *Photography in the 1940s* did not challenge the public to confront the harsher images of Japan's past. It did, however, present it with a few tools to participate in a democratic form of history making, if history is, as Raphael Samuel argues, "not the prerogative of the historian, nor even, as postmodernism contends, a historian's 'invention' . . . [but], rather, a social form of knowledge; the work, in any given instance, of a thousand different hands."[69]

Much as it says about the current situation in Japan, *Photography in the 1940s* speaks to an issue that transcends the particularities of the exhibition, the fiftieth anniversary of Japan's surrender, and Japan itself. This larger issue is the problematic relationship of photography with time. As the Yokohama exhibition demonstrates, when art museums create visual histories, they necessarily mediate between whatever sense of time inheres within the images and the broader social conception of time and national history. In some circumstances, this mediation is relatively simple. Where nations understand themselves as entities that change through time, photography can seem naturally to mark history because it is assumed that the viewer, photographer, curator, and nation partake of the same quality of continuous, evolving time. In these conditions, documentary practices flourish, and photography in art museums can speak to aesthetic and political developments with ease. Where national identity has resisted temporality, as in Japan, the capacity of photography to mark time becomes subversive. Museums resist photography in general and documentary photography in particular.[70] In other words, these three elements—photography, temporality, and national identity—triangulate the space within which museum curators must work. In Japan, that space happens to be contested and relatively small. In the United States and Europe, where it is larger, the force of this triangulation is sometimes overlooked.

A brief examination of some critical perspectives on photography will reveal how variously photography's relation to time has been understood. Although the photography critics whom I will consider here, John Berger, Roland Barthes, and Siegfried Kracauer, do not directly address the question of how a nation's sense of time influences a photograph's relation to time, they represent the extraordinary range of views on photography and temporality. Berger, for instance, argues that a photograph *is,* in its very essence, a moment in time. He insists, "The true content of a photograph is invisible, for it derives from a play, not of form, but of time."[71] For Berger, a photograph is analogous to the movement of a conductor's baton, more allied with music than with painting. Its rhythms are the temporal rhythms of modernity, the rhythms of a public eventfulness that is assumed to be universal and democratically accessible. For Berger, time is all of one substance—"the continuum" as he calls it—and every photograph gestures outside itself to this whole. "A photograph," he argues, "whilst recording what has been seen, always and by its nature refers to what is not seen. It isolates, preserves and presents a moment taken from a continuum."[72] Indeed, Berger insists, "every photograph is in fact a means of testing, confirming and constructing a total view of reality."[73] But to conceive as Berger does of photography's destination or effect as a total reality, we must elide the differences among individuals and various forms of collective audience—the nation, the global art world, citizens of Yokohama, subjects of the emperor. The identification between photography and continuous time makes the place and mode of consumption of an image insignificant.

Other critics see photographs as causing spasms in the linear flow of time. Roland Barthes in particular admires photography's capacity to render a unique moment repeatable: "What the Photograph reproduces to infinity has occurred only once: the Photograph mechanically repeats what could never be repeated existentially."[74] In calling the camera "a clock for seeing," Barthes is not underscoring some universal, rhythmic sense of time nor is he interested in public time. Instead, through Barthes' clock, the individual witnesses madness, disorder, and death; the camera is a clock that allows us, paradoxically, to see the irregularities of time.[75]

In contrast to Berger, Barthes focuses on the problems of audience and place. He deliberately contrasts private delectation of the image with museum displays of photography, and finds the private experience far more compelling. Alone, Barthes sinks into an image, enjoying an intense private reverie. He tells us, "if I like a photograph, if it disturbs me, I linger over it."[76] Time stops, to be revisited again and again, becoming disordered. Because of this private intensity, Barthes claims, "society is concerned to tame the Photograph, to temper the madness which keeps threatening to explode in the face of whoever looks at it."[77] Society does so in part by making photography into art, into a public icon. In the public space of a museum, the photographic image is regularized and subordinated to public control—or so Barthes argues.

But in Japan particularly, the opposite seems true. Private imagery appears to disturb society little. Marking family, school, vacation, and business events with snapshots is a private ritual nowhere more stylized than in Japan. Photographs of the deceased are routine elements of Buddhist memorial services. Pornographic photography circulates with remarkable frankness and lack of constraint. Making photography into a public art, however, lifts it from the ephemerality of daily life and places it in the extended realm of national experience and memory. Here, the viewer is no longer the individual or small group but the larger civic collectivity. In the public art museum, collections of photographs appear to comment on Japan's cultural form of nationalism. Rather than taming the photograph, as Barthes suggests, this displacement tempts madness of a public, not a private, sort. This museum photography, curated deliberately, threatens to recall not only a particular collective history but collective historicity as well. The contrast between Barthes' experience and the Japanese evidence illustrates that the relationship of photography to time cannot be understood without reference to the viewer's various subjectivities (including his or her nationality), each of which has its own sense of temporality and history.

German film critic Siegfried Kracauer presents yet a third view when he argues that the photograph has no inherent relation to the time. In a 1927 article, he points out that, although a photograph may *seem* to be "a representation of time," "time is not part of the photograph."[78] For Kracauer, a photograph does not preserve time; rather, time stands outside the image, transforming and, ultimately, diminishing and desiccating it. "If photography is a *function of the flow of time*," he maintains, "then its substantive meaning will change depending upon whether it belongs to the domain of the present or to some phase of the past." Eventually, a photograph is "emptied of life" as time passes, unless we work to resuscitate it.[79] In effect, Kracauer is arguing that the continued connection between an image and a moment in time, far from being natural, is the result of purposeful effort.

The problem of "the flow of time" haunted Kracauer, who returned to the issue almost forty years later when he began work on *History: The Last Things before the Last* (posthumously published). Deepening and altering his previous analysis, Kracauer declares that time is not "homogenous"; it is not a continuum. "Because of the antinomy at its core," he argues, "time not only conforms to the conventional image of a flow but must also be imagined as being not such a flow. We live in a cataract of times."[80] If this is so, a photograph never represents a simple beat in the even, universal temporal flow, as Berger would have it. Instead, the practice of photography—and of history—must grapple precariously with heterogeneous forms of time. While for Berger, time is a string of notes in a public concert and for Barthes, the delicious yet disturbing moments of private intensity, for Kracauer, time, both public and private, is a towering waterfall, a jarring cataract of currents, each flowing at a different rate and a different temperature. From Kracauer's perspective, neither photography nor history can grasp the whole structure of this elusive, fractured reality. Kracauer believes neither in a "total reality" nor in the ability of the word or image to refer to that whole. Instead, Kracauer insists, both history and photography are inherently provisional, redeeming transient phenomena from oblivion and allowing us to "think *through* things, not above them when, and only when, we contend with the cataract."[81]

If, as Kracauer argues, photographers and historians both have contingent relationships to heterogeneous time, it follows that curators working with photographs to create histories also practice a contingent craft: they are tightrope walkers across the roaring waterfall. It is not just the curator's own views and the photographers' aesthetic and historical materials but also the outlook of a transient public audience that must be brought together to create that fragile compound: the meaningful exhibition. How the civic collectivity understands itself in relation to time will influence how photography exhibitions function within the public sphere. Kracauer is not interested in national identity per se nor specifically in the idea of atemporality within his cataract of times, although he does speak of " 'pockets' and voids amidst these temporal currents."[82] Nevertheless, his insistence on time's multiplicity and discontinuity provides a means of understanding the competing ideas of history in contemporary Japan and elsewhere. The idea of a "cataract of times" illuminates the way in which that nation can appear to conform simultaneously to the regular rhythms of modern development, to a sense of collectivity that transcends the flow of time, and to a unique and glorious beat of its own. Time thus becomes the matrix of the tension among various forms of modernity and postmodernity in contemporary Japan. Recent photography exhibitions convey this tension with particular force. Each curator must negotiate the multiple senses of time that are currently part of the Japanese identity.

The point I want to stress is this: neither photography, nor national identity, nor time is a stable element. Photography can chronicle public time, refer only to private memories, or suppress temporality in favor of strict formalism. Collectivities, national and otherwise, can share global chronologies and structures, or they can mark their differences in time and in form. Time can serve as the denominator of national development, or it can be excluded from accounts of national essence. Stable definitions of these elements are possible only in particular circumstances where ideology deftly masks its own assumptions. What the exhibition at Yokohama suggests is how precariously these three elements cohere in an atmosphere where fundamental questions about history are being raised. The triangulation between photography, national identity, and time is what makes photography exhibitions in Japan today so charged with possibilities. This triangulation makes curating photography a political as well as an aesthetic act, and it allows institutions such as the Yokohama Museum of Art to participate in Japan's contemporary struggle over the fundamental basis of its national identity.

The attempt made in *Photography in the 1940s* to suggest Japan's historicity through documentary photography is unusual. It denotes one of the many new avenues toward self-understanding being explored in post-postwar Japan. As Gavan McCormack argues, "For those who would see, the seeds for many different possible futures are sprouting in Japan. Which will strengthen and grow to maturity, and which will weaken and die, will be determined by the struggles that will ensue over the years that span the end of the century and the millennium."[83] This exhibition, however tentatively and inadequately, participated in that struggle for the future by trying to provide Japan with a usable past.

Notes

1. Concurrent exhibitions in major public museums specializing in photography included *Tokyo kokuritsu kindai bijutsukan to shashin 1953–1995* [Photography and the Museum of Modern Art, Tokyo, 1953–1995] at the newly opened Film Center of the National Museum of Modern Art, Tokyo, and two exhibitions at the Tokyo Metropolitan Museum of Photography: *-ism '95: The 1st Tokyo International Photo-Biennale;* and *Mono, kao, hanmonogatari—modanizumu saikō* [Objects, Faces, and Anti-Narratives—Rethinking Modernism]. Exhibitions at other venues that occasionally feature photography included the Meguro-ku Bijutsukan's photography exhibition, *Domon Ken: Koji junrei* [Domon Ken: Pilgrimages to Old Temples] and the Setagaya-ku Bijutsukan's *Sōken 1200 nen kinen Tōji kokuhō ten* [Treasures from the Tōji Temple on the 1200th Anniversary of Its Foundation]. I discuss aspects of these exhibitions in "History and Anti-History: Photography Exhibitions and Japanese National Identity," in Susan Crane, ed., *Museums and Memories* (Stanford, Calif., forthcoming); and "Raw Photographs and Cooked History: Photography's Ambiguous Place in Tokyo's Museum of Modern Art," *East Asian History* 12 (December 1996): 121–34.

2. The exhibition ran from April 18 to August 30, 1995, and was one of three photography exhibitions from the permanent collection that the museum mounts each year.

3. There is debate over whether visual images serve as additions to textual sources of historical knowledge or whether they overwhelm and transform traditional texts, thereby transforming the practice of history. For instance, Raphael Samuel argues that a new historiography "alert to memory's shadows . . . might give at least as much attention to pictures as to manuscripts or print." Samuel, *Theatres of Memory*, Vol. 1: *Past and Present in Contemporary Culture* (London, 1994), 27. Alternatively, Edith Wyschogrod takes the position that the inclusion of visual images within history's frame of reference "signal[s] not a mere expansion of the means for acquiring and distributing historical information but a fundamental epistemic transformation and cultural upheaval . . . Language itself has become volatilized into the image." Wyschogrod, *An Ethics of Remembering: History, Heterology, and the Nameless Others* (Chicago, 1998), 69.

4. I discuss what I see as the continued prominence of the "nation" and "national culture" as defining categories for understanding the arts in "Global Culture in Question: Japanese Photography in Contemporary America," in Harumi Befu and Sylvie Guichard-Anguis, eds., *Japan outside Japan* (London, forthcoming).

5. As is evident from my treatment of this fine art photography exhibition as a contribution to historical recollection, I think of history not as the exclusive enterprise of professional historians but as a shared social activity where many kinds of documentation are brought to bear. This article therefore participates in the growing conversation on collective memory and historical consciousness that revolves around the fundamental questions of where, how, and for what purpose history is recollected. Different perspectives on this issue are explored in great depth in "*AHR Forum:* History and Memory," *AHR* 102 (December 1997): 1371–1412. From this inclusive perspective, the past is recollected and reconstructed through a wide range of media (books, museums, memorials, parades, theme parks, drama, television, films, children's picture stories, toys, and costumes). However, as I hope to demonstrate, analyzing fine art photography exhibitions offers particular rewards. These exhibitions pull together social, technological, and art historical pasts, private sensibilities, and public ideals of civic propriety. In a public art museum, collections of photographic images refer simultaneously to "Beauty" and to "Truth," to "Commerce" and to "Art" under the eye of a visitor who sees both as a private individual and as a member of "the public." In bringing together these disparate elements, fine art photography exhibitions become not only particularly rich "mnemonic sites" (to use Pierre Nora's phrase) but, because of their unsettled mixture of elements, also capable of illuminating broad ideological tensions over the proper shape of the past. Given photography's uneasy status as an art medium, it readily illuminates multiple, competing approaches to the past—which in Japan include an aestheticized, dehistoricized version, a secular, empirical version, and a highly nationalistic celebration of an almost sacred heritage.

Doubts about the political and historical agency of photographs in the fine art context have been raised not only by historians committed to more traditional sources but by some art critics as well. Photography critic A. D. Coleman is reasonably typical of such skeptics when he compares museums to mortuaries and argues that documentary photographs in particular are "meant to serve purposes only marginally compatible with those of repositories and showcases for fine art . . . at least before the work has been generated and lived its life in the world." Coleman, *Critical Focus: Photography in the International Image Community* (Munich, 1996), 107–08.

6. Several perspectives on these economic and political problems of the Heisei (1989–) period are presented in "Symposium on Continuity and Change in Heisei Japan," *Journal of Japanese Studies* 23 (Summer 1997).

7. In response to the Kobe earthquake on January 17, 1995, Japanese photographer Eikoh Hosoe spearheaded a charity drive based on donations from 260 photographers

from twenty-four countries. These photographers donated 430 prints, which were auctioned by Sotheby's to raise funds for the Japan Red Cross and the earthquake victims. The combined efforts of Eikoh, other faculty members of the Tokyo Kōgei Daigaku Shashin Center (Tokyo Institute of Polytechnics, Center of Photography), and the Cultural Products Division of Asahi Shinbun (Asahi Newspaper) also resulted in a book by the Kobe Aid Fund, *Sekai no shashinka kara fukkō no machi e* [From the World's Photographers to a Restored Town] (Tokyo, 1996). This unusual effort demonstrates an awareness of both photography's commercial value and its potential for social engagement.

8. Takashi Fujitani, emphasizing the pivotal impact of the Showa emperor's death in 1989, points to a "new search for authenticity" in "Electronic Pageantry and Japan's 'Symbolic Emperor,'" *Journal of Asian Studies* 51 (November 1992): 849. Historian Nakamura Masanori argues that "the grand tale of Japan as an economic superpower and the world's most stable political system has already lost its power of persuasion over Japanese citizens." Nakamura, "The History Textbook Controversy and Nationalism," in *Bulletin of Concerned Asian Scholars: Textbook Nationalism, Citizenship, and War, Comparative Perspectives* 30 (April–June 1998): 28. Gavan McCormack considers multiple causes of Japan's malaise including corruption and environmental destruction in *The Emptiness of Japanese Affluence* (Armonk, N.Y., 1996).

9. Viewing the arts as one of the primary ways of defining Japanese national identity is not just a postwar phenomenon. See Satō Dōshin, *Nihon bijutsu: Kindai Nihon "kotoba" to senkaku* [Japanese Arts: Modern Japanese "Words" and Pioneers] (Tokyo, 1996), for a discussion of the Meiji (1868–1912) period origins of the term *bijutsu* (the arts) and how that category was used to define "Japan." For further analysis, see Stefan Tanaka, "Imagining History: Inscribing Belief in the Nation," *Journal of Japanese Studies* 53 (February 1994): 24–44.

10. All the names of Japanese people are written in the Japanese order with family names first unless they appear in quotations from sources that have reversed their normal order or the authors have used the English form of their names in an English-language publication. The name Hiroshi Hamaya in Figures 4 and 7 is given in English-language order, family name last, at the request of Magnum Photos.

11. "Shashin tenjishitsu: 1940 nendai no shashin" [Photography Exhibition Room: Photography in the 1940s], in "Yokohama Bijutsukan josetsuten" [Yokohama Museum of Art, from the Permanent Collection] (May 18 to August 30, 1995).

12. Kuraishi Shino, private communication with the author, August 11, 1995. I am indebted to Mr. Kuraishi for his thoughtful responses to the questions I put to him about the exhibition and for his kindness in helping me obtain copyright permissions and prints for some illustrations in this article.

13. Japanese museums (with the exception of those always concerned with representing aspects of the war, such as the Peace Museum in Hiroshima and the museum attached to the Yasukuni shrine) largely avoided marking the fiftieth anniversary of the war's end. In Washington, D.C., by contrast, the National Museum of American History, the National Archives, the National Air and Space Museum, and the U.S. Holocaust Memorial Museum all featured exhibitions explicitly dealing with the war. This confluence of exhibitions was not the result of consensus on how to remember World War II in the United States, as the controversy over the Smithsonian Institution's display of the *Enola Gay* demonstrates. For the text of the original Smithsonian proposal, see Philip Nobile, ed., *Judgment at the Smithsonian: The Uncensored Script of the Smithsonian's Fiftieth Anniversary Exhibit of the Enola Gay* (New York, 1995). For a retrospective account from the standpoint of a specialist in Japan, see John Whittier Treat, "The *Enola Gay* on Display: Hiroshima and American Memory," *positions: east asia cultures critique* 5 (Winter 1997): 863–78.

14. The wall label does not explicitly state that Manzanar was a Japanese internment camp. However, the story of Manzanar is known in Japan in part through photographs taken by an inmate: Miyatake Tōyō, *Miyatake Tōyō no shashin, 1923–79* (Tokyo, 1984). Titles of images are taken from the wall labels supplied by the Yokohama Museum of Art and do not exactly match the titles of the figures in all cases.

15. Sakamoto Manshichi, "Haniwa" (1945), "Hand of Vairocana, Tōshōdai-ji" (1945), and "Hand of Mahavairocana, Enjō-ji" (1945).

16. These works include Edward Weston, "Civilian Defense" (1942) and "China Cove, Point Lobos" (1940); Minor White, "Sun over the Pacific, Devil's Slide" (1947) and "Sandblaster, San Francisco" (1949); Harry Callahan, "Weed against the Sky, Detroit" (1948); and Ansel Adams, "Grand Teton and Snake River, Grand Teton National Park, Wyoming" (1942), "Teneya Creek, Dogwood, Rain: Yosemite National Park" (1948), and "Moonrise, Hernandez, New Mexico" (1944).

17. These include Domon Ken, "Potter's Wheel, Kyoto" (1940) and "Matsuo and Chiyo, Scene from a Bunraku Puppet Show" (1940–43); Hamaya Hiroshi's "Boys Singing to Drive Evil Birds Away, Niigata" (1940), "Welcome Fire for a Departed Soul, Niigata" (1945), and "Fire Festival for the Traveler's Guardian Deity, Niigata" (1940).

18. Richard Avedon, "René, the New Look of Dior, Place de la Concorde, Paris" (1949), "Dorian Leigh, Coat by Dior, Avenue Montaigne, Paris" (1949), "Carmen, Coat by Cardin, Paris" (1949), and "Dorian Leigh, Schiaparelli" (1949).

19. Robert Capa, "Chartres, August 18, 1944," "Collaborators, Chartres, August 18, 1944," "Leipzig, April 18, 1945," and "Troina, Sicily, August 6, 1943."

20. Lisette Model, "Lower East Side, New York" (1940) and "Hermaphrodite, 42nd Street Flea Circus, New York" (1940).

21. Recent discussions of the relationship between photographs and their captions (and text in general) include Mary Price, *The Photograph: A Strange, Confined Space* (Stanford, Calif., 1994); W. J. T. Mitchell, ed., *The Language of Images* (Chicago, 1980); Mitchell, *Iconology: Image, Text, Ideology* (Chicago, 1986); and, most notably, Mitchell, *Picture Theory* (Chicago, 1994).

22. It has been argued that during the war the Imperial House was presented to the Japanese public in a particularly feminine guise, one of motherly concern for the nation, in order to enhance its appeal. See Kanō Mikiyo, "'Omigokoro' to 'hahagokoro': 'Yasukuni no haha' o umidasu mono," in Kanō Mikiyo, ed., *Josei to tennōsei* (Tokyo, 1979). See also T. Fujitani's discussion of the emperor and gender during the war in *Splendid Monarchy: Power and Pageantry in Modern Japan* (Berkeley, Calif., 1996).

23. Domon Ken, "Young Nurse, Red Cross Hospital, Azabu, Tokyo" (1941); Hayashi Tadahiko, "Line Up of Members of the Neighborhood Association" (1941).

24. Kimura Ihee, "Asakusa Park, Tokyo" (1947) and "Booksellers' Shinbashi Area, Tokyo" (1948); Okumura Taikō, "Unemployed by the Bridge" (1949).

25. Depictions of these subjects can be found, for instance, in Kuwabara Kineo, *Tokyo: 1934–1993* (Tokyo, 1995); and Yoshida Jun, *Yoshida Jun shashin kan: Sengo fōkasu 293* [The Photographic Perspective of Yoshida Jun: Postwar Focus 293] (Tokyo, 1983).

26. The Shown era began in 1976 (Showa 1) and ended with the death of Hirohito in 1989. The current era, Heisei, then began.

27. To this day, issues of calculating time remain controversial both in indicating the span of the war by what it is called—the Pacific War, the Fifteen Year War, the Greater East Asian War, or World War II—and in how to date official documents. See, for instance, Ienaga Saburō, *The Pacific War, 1931–1945* (New York, 1978), xiii–xiv.

28. The link forged here and elsewhere between women and (Japanese) culture as opposed to men and nature undermines the assumption of several American scholars

that the association between women and nature is universal. See, for instance, the statements of Sherry B. Ortner, "Is Female to Male as Nature Is to Culture?" in Michelle Zimbalist Rosaldo and Louise Lamphere, eds., *Women, Culture and Society* (Stanford, Calif., 1974); and Carolyn Merchant, *The Death of Nature: Women, Ecology and the Scientific Revolution* (New York, 1979).

29. The only exception to the exclusion of Chinese is Henri Cartier-Bresson, "Shanghai" (1949), depicting refugees from the Chinese civil war.

30. The Ministry of Education banned a textbook series written by historian Ienaga Saburō in part because of the photographic illustrations he had chosen. These photographs—captioned "Air-raid on the Mainland," "Wartime Manners and Customs," "Damages of the War" (showing a one-armed veteran begging), and "The Atomic Bomb and Hiroshima"—were rejected, said the ministry, because "only dark pictures are included and on the whole the impression is too dark." See Ienaga Saburō, "The Historical Significance of the Japanese Textbook Suit," *Bulletin of Concerned Asian Scholars* 2 (Fall 1970): 9. For other discussions of the resistance to remembering the war, see Norma Field, *In the Realm of the Dying Emperor* (New York, 1991); Ian Buruma, *The Wages of Guilt: Memories of War in Germany and Japan* (New York, 1994); and Ienaga, *Pacific War.*

31. Although the benefit of remembering past wrongs (whether suffered or perpetrated) is seldom questioned outright, Timothy Garton Ash points out that, "historically, the advocates of forgetting are numerous and weighty." Ash, "The Truth about Dictatorship," *New York Review of Books* (February 19, 1998): 35. In Japan, many progressives and academics as well as ordinary citizens and government officials opted for willed amnesia and ignorance of the war and wartime atrocities as a way to move forward without recriminations. See Yoshida Yutaka, *Nihon no sensō-kan: Sengōshi no nakano henyō* [Japanese Views on the War: Changes in Postwar History] (Tokyo, 1995). Even in Japanese veteran groups, some of those who wished to discuss their military experience have been dissuaded on the basis that it "has nothing to do with us anymore," and the value of forgetfulness has been emphasized. Philip Brasor, "History Put on Back Burner But Front-line Tales Remember," *Japan Times* (August 20, 1998).

32. The atomic bombings at Hiroshima and Nagasaki escape the general amnesia on the war and are much more frequently and openly discussed and represented in the visual arts. Although photographs of the immediate aftermath of those events are rare because of the scale of the destruction and subsequent Occupation censorship, photographer Yamahata Yōsuke carried his camera around Nagasaki following the blast. American curator Christopher Beaver organized an exhibition of these images, "Nagasaki Journey: The Photography of Yōsuke Yamahata, August 10, 1945," which opened in Nagasaki in August 1995 and toured New York, San Francisco, and Washington. Other Japanese photographers who have taken the aftermath of bombings as their subject include Shomei Tōmatsu and Domon Ken.

33. T. J. Pempel, "Regime Shift: Japanese Politics in a Changing World Economy," in "Symposium on Continuity and Change in Heisei Japan," *Journal of Japanese Studies* 23 (Summer 1997): 333–62.

34. Gavan McCormack, "The Japanese Movement to 'Correct' History," *Bulletin of Concerned Asian Scholars: Textbook Nationalism, Citizenship, and War, Comparative Perspectives* 30 (April–June 1998): 16.

35. "Computer Ōbāchan no Kai" started its web site in early August 1998. Their home page (in Japanese), called "August 15, as We Remember It," contains photographs from the 1940s and can be found on the World Wide Web at www.setagaya.net/jijibaba8-15/.

36. Letters from an earlier series have been translated in Frank B. Gibney, ed., *Senso: The Japanese Remember the Pacific War; Letters to the Editor of the Asahi Shimbun,* Beth Cary, trans. (Armonk, N.Y., 1995).

37. In May 1998, members of the ruling Liberal Democratic Party (LDP) visited the memorial to the victims of the Nanking Massacre for the first time. While the leader of the group, senior deputy secretary general of the LDP Nonaka Hiromu, acknowledged the "scar" of Nanking as "an abnormal incident in an abnormal age," other members of his party criticized the trip. The Nanking Massacre is one of the most controversial issues of the war. The Japanese government has strongly condemned as inaccurate Iris Chang's book, *The Rape of Nanking: The Forgotten Holocaust of World War II* (New York, 1997).

38. In accordance with an international treaty to ban chemical weapons, the Japanese government has committed itself to disposing of the chemical weapons it left in China after the war by 2007. It estimates that 700,000 chemical shells remain; China puts the number at 2 million. "Japan's Chemical Weapons in China: Arms Disposal to Cost ¥100 Billion," *Japan Times* (August 14, 1998). For a fuller description of the wartime use of these weapons, see Sheldon H. Harris, *Factories of Death: Japanese Biological Warfare, 1932–45, and the American Cover-up* (London, 1994).

39. Morimura Seiichi, *Akuma no Hōshoku* [The Devil's Gluttony] (Tokyo, 1982); Hal Gold, *Unit 731 Testimony: Japan's Wartime Human Experimentation Program* (Tokyo, 1996).

40. As historians Laura Hein and Mark Selden point out, the permissible sentence or two referring to "comfort women" in middle school textbooks hardly fulfills the demands of "critics sympathetic to the comfort women [who] have censured these descriptions as inadequate for their failure to discuss, still less condemn, the system." Hein and Selden, "Learning Citizenship from the Past: Textbook Nationalism, Global Context, and Social Change," *Bulletin of Concerned Asian Scholars* 30 (April–June 1998): 10. See also Yoshimi Yoshiaki, *Jūgun Ianfu* [The Comfort Women] (Tokyo, 1995); and "Special Issue: The Comfort Women; Colonialism, War, and Sex," *positions: east asia cultures critique* 5 (Spring 1997).

41. Pragmatic apologies have helped strengthen relations with other Asian countries, but the overt instrumentality of some statements of remorse undermines their effectiveness. For instance, in August 1998, newly appointed Minister of Agriculture Nakagawa Shōichi retracted his statement that there was no evidence that women were forced to serve as sex slaves by the Japanese armed forces, saying that such comments might have negative effects on the ongoing fisheries talks between Japan and South Korea. "Nakagawa Retracts Sex Slave Comments," *Japan Times* (August 1, 1998): 2.

42. The exhibition includes Capa's "D-Day," a photograph whose borderline legibility (induced, famously, by a nervous darkroom technician) blurs the issue of aesthetic sophistication. This image assumed its iconic power as a relic of D-Day itself but now influences aesthetic standards precisely through its iconic power; the potency of comparable Japanese photographs will depend in part on the extent of their cultural circulation.

43. Important examples of Japanese war photography can be found in Kuwabara Kineo, ed., *Nihon shashin zenshū,* Vol. 4: *Sensō no kioku* [Memories of War] (Tokyo, 1987); and in Nihon shashinka kyōkai, *Nihon shashin shi, 1840–1945* [The History of Japanese Photography, 1840–1945] (Tokyo, 1971), trans. by John W. Dower, ed., as *A Century of Japanese Photography* (New York, 1980). See also John Taylor, *War Photography: Realism in the British Press* (London, 1991); and the Time-Life series *World War II,* esp. Arthur Zich, ed., *The Rising Sun* (Alexandria, Va., 1977); and Rafael Steinberg, ed., *Island Fighting* (Alexandria, 1978). The latter volume contains a

striking photograph of Japanese troops dressed in grass skirts and black face by Yanagida Fumio, 10–11.

44. See, for instance, the carefully composed image by Kanamaru Shigene and Yamawaki Iwao of two determined Japanese soldiers coming over the edge of a trench, one heaving a grenade, with a trampled American flag in the foreground, "Uchiteshi tomamu" [Ever Onward] (1943), or the graphics in illustrated magazines of the period such as *Nippon*, *Hōmu Raifu* [Home Life], *Manchuria Graph*, and *Front*.

45. Comparison between the exhibited photographs and the *Yokohama bijutsukan shozō hinmoku roku II: Shashin* [Catalogue of the Collection, Yokohama Museum of Art, II: Photographs] (Yokohama, 1989) shows that the museum continues to make acquisitions of this type of photography.

46. Positions along a political spectrum are, of course, always relative. The term "ultranationalism" (*chōkokkashugi*) was used by Japan's leading twentieth-century political theorist Maruyama Masao in discussing far right-wing activities, and it has become the customary term for describing such groups by those who disapprove of them. On the other hand, historian Hata Inuhiko of Nihon University used a different scale in making the following distinctions in relation to the 1937 Nanking Massacre: "conservatives" consider it an "illusion," "radicals" call it a "massacre," and moderates believe it is somewhere between the two. "Nanking Debate a Rallying Point," *Japan Times* (August 19, 1998): 3.

47. Gallery owners have been visited late at night by plainclothes policemen and advised not to open exhibitions, as happened with Kitagawa Yūji's exhibition in Gen Gallery in June 1993. Later, the police admitted the visits but denied suggesting that the exhibition be closed. E. Patricia Tsurumi, "Censored in Japan: Taboo Art," *Bulletin of Concerned Asian Scholars* 26 (1994): 66–70. Nor are the visual arts the only ones censored in this powerful way. For instance, "Sevuntiin" [Seventeen], written by Ōe Kenzaburō, concerns the October 1960 assassination of Asanuma Inejirō, chair of the Socialist Party, by Yamaguchi Otoya, a seventeen-year-old right-wing fanatic who committed suicide three weeks after his arrest. Ōe's story, published in two parts in the literary magazine *Bungakukai* (January–February 1961), earned him death threats and harassment from the extreme right, especially Dai Nippon Aikokutō's leader Akao Bin, who had been Yamaguchi's mentor. This story has never been republished in Japan after its controversial first appearance, and foreign rights to translation have never been granted even though Ōe was awarded the Nobel Prize for literature. Luk Van Haute, "Young and Politically Incorrect: Ōe Kenzaburō's Early Marginal Heros," in Bjarke Frellesvig and Roy Starrs, eds., *Japan and Korea: Contemporary Studies* (Aarhus, 1997), 104. For another instance of right-wing attacks against literary arts, this one ending in a bloody attack on a publisher's family, see John Whittier Treat, "Beheaded Emperors and the Absent Figure in Contemporary Japanese Literature," *PMLA* (January 1994): 100–15.

48. Nancy Shalala, "Censorship Silences Japanese Artists," *Asian Art News* (September–October 1994): 62–67; and Shalala, "Hidden Terrors Put Gag on Art World," *Japan Times* (July 10, 1994).

49. The Ota Gallery in Ebisu, Tokyo, continues to represent Shimada, and Mr. Ota kindly provided background information on the problems faced by artists such as Shimada and Ōura.

50. Kuraishi does not refer directly to Ienaga's thesis in the exhibition brochure, but his conception of "dropping out" is similar to Ienaga's concept. Ienaga, *Pacific War*, 204–08.

51. Okatsuka Akiko, curator at the Tokyo Metropolitan Museum of Photography, also discusses Hamaya's career and his decision to flee wartime work in *Nihon kindai shashin no seiritsu to tenkai* [The Founding and Development of Modern Photography in Japan] (Tokyo, 1995), 25–26. This exhibition ran from January 21 to March 26,

1995. I am grateful to Ms. Okatsuka for providing background information on the pressures faced by public art museums in Japan.

52. Hamaya Hiroshi, "Boys Singing to Drive Evil Birds Away, Niigata" (1940).

53. Hamaya Hiroshi, "Fire Festival for the Traveler's Guardian Deity" (1940).

54. The role of documentary photographers has been praised and attacked on these grounds. Don McCullin, an active practitioner, defends documentary work saying, "I hate carrying cameras, they disfigure me. I carry a conscience." McCullin, "Notes by a Photographer," in Emile Meijer and Joop Swart, eds., *The Photographic Memory* (London, 1987), 26. In contrast, critic Allan Sekula dismisses the efforts of documentary photographers as a cruel means by which "the oppressed are granted a bogus Subjecthood." Sekula, "On the Invention of Photographic Meaning," in Victor Burgin, ed., *Thinking Photography* (London, 1982), 109. More subtly, W. J. T. Mitchell argues that the aesthetic, ethical, and political goals of a documentary project may be ultimately irreconcilable. Mitchell, *Picture Theory*, 294–95.

55. Domon Ken's work was represented by four images: "Head of Anira, Muro-ji" (temple statuary, Anira is one of the twelve Yakushi generals) (1940); "Potter (Potter's Wheel), Kyoto" (1940); "Matsuo and Chiyo, Scene from the Bunraku Puppet Show 'Sugawara Denju Tenarai Kagami' " (part of a series, 1940–43); "Young Nurse, Red Cross Hospital, Azabu, Tokyo" (1941).

56. I have discussed the resistance to photography on this basis in "Raw Photographs and Cooked History."

57. These national organizations were formed in 1995 and 1996 respectively by University of Tokyo Professor of Education Fujioka Nobukatsu.

58. Fujioka Nobukatsu insists that the issue of the so-called comfort women is "a grand conspiracy for the destruction of Japan" and a falsehood that portrays Japan as a "lewd, foolish, and rabid race without peer in the world." See Gavan McCormack's discussion of Fujioka's views on this issue in "Japanese Movement to 'Correct' History," 18–19.

59. See, for instance, Hayashi Fusao, *Daitōa sensō kōtei ron* [Affirming the Greater East Asian War], parts 1 and 2 (Tokyo, 1965); *Nihon e no keikoku* [A Warning to Japan] (Tokyo, 1969); and *Hayashi Fusao chosaku shu* [An Anthology of the Writings of Hayashi Fusao], 3 vols. (Tokyo, 1968–69). Historian Hayashi's argument that Japan went to war to liberate Asia met with immediate rebuttals and denunciation.

60. The forces within Japan working to revive history have responded actively to this new threat. Historian Nakamura Masanori points out that articles in *Rekishi hyōron* [History Criticism], *Kyōiku* [Education], *Sekai* [The World], *Kikan: Senso sekinin kenkyū* [Quarterly War Responsibility Research], and *Shūkan kin'yōbi* [Friday Weekly] have denounced Jiyūshugi Shikan Kenkyūkai, although Nakamura also suggests that "historians, politicians, middle- and high-school teachers were slow to react." Attempts by Fujioka and his followers to have references to "comfort women" once again excised from textbooks have met with stout resistance within Japan, where over 200 petitions have been presented to city councils urging that these references be retained. Nakamura, "History Textbook Controversy and Nationalism," 28.

61. Best-selling books by Fujioka Nobukatsu have forcefully promoted this version of history. His best-known publication is the three-volume *Kyōkasho ga oshienai rekishi* [The History Not Taught in Textbooks] (Tokyo, 1996–97). His general themes are repeated in *Ojoku no kin-gendai shi: Ima, kokufuku no toki* [Disgraceful Modern History: Now, the Time of Recovery] (Tokyo, 1996). His attack on changes in the textbook coverage can be found in " 'Jūgun ianfu'o chūgaku ni oshieru na" [Don't Teach Middle School Students about the "Military Comfort Women"], in Atarashii rekishi kyōkasho o tsukuru kai, ed., *Atarashii Nihon no rekishi ga hajimaru* [A New Japanese History Is Beginning] (Tokyo, 1997). Other well-placed academics who have supported his arguments include Hata Ikuhiko and Nishio Kanji.

62. The Asahi Television program "Asamade" [Live 'til Dawn] on February 1, 1997, featured members of the study group attacking historian Yoshimi Yoshiaki as "sick" for his work on comfort women revealing the extent of the forced abductions and government complicity. See Yoshimi, *Jūgun Ianfu.*

63. Cartoonist Kobayashi Yoshinori is a member of the movement, publishing a cartoon series supportive of its stance on Japanese history in the magazine *Sapio.*

64. *Pride* (the original title was in English) depicts wartime Prime Minister General Tōjō Hideki as a hero vengefully hounded to death by the victorious Allies during the Tokyo trials that followed Japan's defeat. Tsugawa Masahiko, the actor portraying Tōjō, and the film's director, Itō Shunya, treated the film as an ideological as well as a commercial venture. The ¥1.5 billion production costs were underwritten by the president of a home construction company known for his links with right-wing groups. It was a box-office success and became the top-grossing Japanese-made film in the first six months of 1998. Among those defending it against a surge of protests from domestic and foreign groups, including an official protest from the Chinese government, was Hosokawa Ryūichirō, former managing editor of the major newspaper *Mainichi Shinbun,* who exonerated Japan from responsibility for the war with China by suggesting that this war was "started with a conspiracy engineered by Liu Shaoqi, a Chinese Communist subordinate of Mao Zedong." Hosokawa, "Japanese Need a Good Dose of *Pride,*" *Japan Times* (June 2, 1998).

65. "War Museum Plan Rephrased," *Japan Times* (April 21, 1998).

66. Michael Geyer, "The Place of the Second World War in German Memory and History," *Neo: New German Critique* 71 (Spring–Summer 1997): 40.

67. Kosaku Yoshino, *Cultural Nationalism in Contemporary Japan: A Sociological Enquiry* (London, 1992), 11.

68. As of 1989, the foreigners' section encompassed no East Asian and no South Asian photographers at all. *Yokohama bijutsukan shozō hinmoku roku II.*

69. Samuel, *Theatres of Memory,* 8.

70. For instance, according to its director, Ueki Hiroshi, the National Museum of Modern Art, Tokyo, did not hold any photography exhibitions between 1974 and 1995. Instead of deploring this neglect of the medium, Ueki emphatically justifies the museum's lack of interest in his foreword to the catalogue of the first exhibition to break this pattern. Ueki, "Foreword," *Tokyo kokuritsu kindai bijutsukan to shashin 1953–1995,* 7.

71. John Berger, "Understanding a Photograph" [1974], in Alan Trachtenberg, ed., *Classic Essays on Photography* (New Haven, Conn., 1980), 293.

72. Berger, "Understanding a Photograph," 293.

73. Berger, "Understanding a Photograph," 294.

74. Roland Barthes, *Camera Lucida: Reflections on Photography,* Richard Howard, trans. (New York, 1981), 4.

75. Barthes, *Camera Lucida,* 15.

76. Barthes, *Camera Lucida,* 99.

77. Barthes, *Camera Lucida,* 117.

78. Siegfried Kracauer, "Photography," rpt. in *Critical Inquiry* 19 (Spring 1993): 424.

79. Kracauer, "Photography," 429.

80. Siegfried Kracauer, *History: The Last Things before the Last* (1969; rpt. with new preface, Princeton, N.J., 1995), 199. Kracauer's argument against the homogeneity and continuity of time directly contradicts Berger's view.

81. Kracauer, *History,* 192.

82. Kracauer, *History,* 199.

83. McCormack, *Emptiness of Japanese Affluence,* 20.

Suggested Reading

Anderson, David C. "Painful Truth, Healing Truth: Commissions Help Wounded Societies Build a Future by Confronting the Past." *Ford Foundation Report,* Spring 2000, 16–21.

Arias, Artura, ed. *The Rigoberta Menchú Controversy.* Minneapolis: University of Minnesota Press, 2000.

Barkan, Elazar. *The Guilt of Nations: Restitution and Negotiating Historical Injustices.* New York: W. W. Norton, 2000.

Bass, Gary Jonathan. *Stay the Hand of Vengeance: The Politics of War Crimes Tribunals.* Princeton: Princeton University Press, 2000.

Blight, David W. *Race and Reunion: The Civil War in American Memory.* Cambridge, Mass.: Harvard University Press, 2000.

Boraine, Alex. *A Country Unmasked.* Oxford: Oxford University Press, 2000.

Bornman, Elirea, René van Eeden, and Marie Wentzel, eds. *Violence in South Africa: A Variety of Perspectives.* Pretoria: Human Sciences Research Council, 1998.

Chandler, David P. *The Tragedy of Cambodian History: Politics, War, and Revolution since 1945.* New Haven: Yale University Press, 1991.

———. *Voices from S-21: Terror and History in Pol Pot's Secret Prison.* Berkeley: University of California Press, 2000.

Crib, Robert, ed. *The Indonesian Killings of 1965–1966: Studies from Java and Bali.* Clayton, Australia: Monash University Center of Southeast Asian Studies, 1990.

Dassu, Marta, and Tony Saich, eds. *The Reform Decade in China: From Hope to Dismay.* London: Kegan Paul International, 1990.

Doyle, Kate. "Death Squad Diary: Looking into the Secret Archives of Guatemala's Bureaucracy of Murder." *Harpers Magazine,* June 1999, 50–53.

Feitlowitz, Marguerite. *A Lexicon of Terror: Argentina and the Legacies of Torture.* Oxford: Oxford University Press, 1998.

Fogel, Joshua A., ed. *The Nanjing Massacre in History and Historiography.* Berkeley: University of California Press, 2000.

Goodman, David. *Fault Lines: Journeys into the New South Africa.* Berkeley: University of California Press, 1999.

Hayner, Priscilla B. *Unspeakable Truths: Confronting State Terror and Atrocity.* London: Routledge, 2000.

Heder, Steve, and Judy Ledgerwood, eds. *Propaganda, Politics, and Violence in Cambodia: Democratic Transition under United Nations Peace-Keeping.* Armonk: M. E. Sharpe, 1996.

Hochschild, Adam. *King Leopold's Ghost: A Story of Greed, Terror, and Heroism in Colonial Africa.* Boston: Houghton Mifflin, 1998.

Jonas, Susanne. *The Battle for Guatemala: Rebels, Death Squads, and U.S. Power.* Boulder: Westview Press, 1991.

Kaplan, Robert D. *The Ends of The Earth: From Togo to Turkmenistan, from Iran to Cambodia—A Journey to the Frontiers of Anarchy.* New York: Vintage Books, 1996.

Kiernan, Ben. *The Pol Pot Regime: Race, Power, and Genocide in Cambodia under the Khmer Rouge, 1975–79.* New Haven: Yale University Press, 1996.

Kohn, Richard H. "History and the Culture Wars: The Case of the Smithsonian Institution's *Enola Gay* Exhibition." *Journal of American History* 82 (1995): 1036–63.

Kristof, Nicolas D., and Sheryl Wudunn. *China Wakes: The Struggle for the Soul of a Rising Power.* New York: Vintage Books, 1994.

Krog, Antjie. *Country of My Skull.* New York: Random House, 1998.

Lagos, Ricardo, and Heraldo Muñoz. "The Pinochet Dilemma." *Foreign Policy,* Spring 1999, 26–39.

Lederach, John Paul. *Building Peace: Sustainable Reconciliation in Divided Societies.* Washington, D.C.: United States Institute of Peace Press, 1997.

Marchack, Patricia. *God's Assassins: State Terrorism in Argentina in the 1970s.* London: McGill-Queen's University Press, 1999.

Minow, Martha. *Between Vengeance and Forgiveness: Facing History after Genocide and Mass Violence.* Boston: Beacon Press, 1998.

Newbury, David. "Understanding Genocide." *African Studies Review* 41:1 (April 1998): 73–97.

Novick, Peter. *The Holocaust in American Life.* New York: Houghton Mifflin, 2000.

Perera, V. *Unfinished Conquest: The Guatemalan Tragedy.* Berkeley: University of California Press, 1993.

Posada-Carbó, Eduardo. "Fiction as History: The *bananeras* and Gabriel García Márquez's *One Hundred Years of Solitude.*" *Journal of Latin American Studies* 30:2 (May 1998): 395–414.

Roniger, Luis, and Mario Sznajder. *The Legacy of Human Rights Violations in the Southern Cone.* Oxford: Oxford University Press, 1999.

Rosenberg, Tina. *The Haunted Land: Facing Europe's Ghost after Communism.* New York: Random House, 1995.

Schirmer, Jennifer. *A Violence Called Democracy: The Guatemalan Military Project, 1982–1992.* Philadelphia: University of Pennsylvania Press, 1999.

Schwartz, Vera. *Bridge across Broken Time: Chinese and Jewish Cultural Memory.* New Haven: Yale University Press, 1998.

Stoll, David. *Rigoberta Menchú and the Story of All Poor Guatemalans.* Boulder: Westview Press, 1999.

Wasserstrom, Jeffrey N., and Elizabeth J. Perry. *Popular Protest and Political Culture in Modern China.* Boulder: Westview Press, 1994.

Watson, Rubie S., ed. *Memory, History, and Opposition under State Socialism.* Santa Fe: School of American Research Press, 1994.